F.V.

THE
Women's
Game

THE
Women's
Game

EDITED BY

Dick Wimmer

BURFORD BOOKS

The following have been reprinted with permission as noted below:

"The Reign of Joyce" © 1978 by Edward Claflin, reprinted by permission of Random House, Inc.; "Swinging for Fences" © 1998 by Amy Ellis Nutt, reprinted by permission of the author; "Sophie Kurys" and "Dorothy Kemenshek" © 1993 by Barbara Gregorich, reprinted by permission of Harcourt Brace & Co.; "Helen Wills" © 1949 by Helen Jacobs, reprinted by permission of the Estate of Helen Jacobs; "Althea Gibson" © 1999 by *Time* Inc. reprinted by permission; "Chris Evert" and "Martina Navratilova" © 1990 by Jim Murray, reprinted by permission of Jim Murray; "Venus Williams" © 1997 by David Higdon, reprinted by permission of Miller Sports Group, LLC; "Babe Didrickson Zaharias" © 1975 by Arthur Daley, reprinted by permission of Quadrangle/New York Times Book Co.; "Nancy Lopez" © 1997 by Jim Burnett, reprinted by permission of Scribner; "Gertrude Ederle" © 1965 by Paul Gallico, reprinted by permission of the Estate of Paul Gallico; "Sonja Henie" and Nadia Comaneci" © 1996 by Bert Randolph Sugar, reprinted by permission of the author; "Janet Lynn and Dorothy Hamill" © 1998 by Michelle Kaufman, reprinted by permission of the author; "Michelle Kwan" © 1997 by Edward Z. Epstein, reprinted by permission of Ballantine Books; "Bobbie Rosenfeld" © 1998 by Barbara Stewart, reprinted by permission of the author; "Elizabeth Nagele" © 1964 by Red Smith, reprinted by permission of the Estate of Red Smith; "Picabo Street" © 1998 by Jean Weiss, reprinted by permission of the author; "Gail Doughty" © 1998 by Lars Anderson and Chad Millman, reprinted by permission of Verso; "Lisa Leslie" © 1990 by Jake Curtis, reprinted by permission of the *L.A. Times;* "Luisana Cruz" © 1999 by *Time* Inc. reprinted by permission; Robyn Smith" © 1974 by Red Smith, reprinted by permission of the Estate of Red Smith; "Marta Empinotti" and "Lisa Smith" © 1997 by David Ferrell, reprinted by permission of the *Los Angeles Times;* "Florence Griffith Joyner" © 1998 by Merrell Noden, reprinted by permission of *Sports Illustrated;* "Day to Embrace" © 1999 by Bill Plaschke, reprinted by permission of the *Los Angeles Times.*

Printed in the United States of America

10 9 8 7 6 5 4 3 2 1

Library of Congress Cataloging-in-Publication Data
    The women's game / edited by Dick Wimmer.
        p.   cm.
    Includes bibliographical references.
    ISBN 1-58080-079-3 (cloth)
    1. Women athletes—Biography. I. Wimmer, Dick.
GV697.A1 W65   2000
796'.082'0922—dc21
    [B]   00-040317

Contents

Introduction

O, what a female feast this is! The fairer sex? The weaker sex? Women *have* come a long way, baby! And about time, too. For how very few of these stellar athletes are even known by name or deed to fans and public alike. Though the progress continues day by day, and the future bodes even brighter. And this collection hopes to fuel that growing momentum with a wide-ranging variety of tales about such leading lights as:

Joan Joyce, softball pitcher supreme, one-on-one against Ted Williams; teenager Jackie Mitchell fanning Babe Ruth and Lou Gehrig; speedy Sophie Kurys, from the real *League of Their Own,* stealing 166 bases in a skirt and no sliding pads; tennis legends like drop-dead gorgeous Helen Wills, Althea Gibson, Chrissie, Martina, and Venus; Babe Didrikson Zaharias, that unparalleled all-around athlete; Gertrude Ederle, at eighteen becoming the first woman to swim the English Channel and breaking the men's mark by two full hours; FloJo and Lisa Leslie; Robyn Smith and Picabo Street; skaters and skiers; basketball, hockey, and football players; BASE jumpers and luge racers; and, finally, that amazing World Cup soccer team.

The Reign of Joyce

Edward Claflin

Edward Claflin is the author of The Irresistible American Softball Book, *from which this piece is taken.*

It's a bad idea to get Ted Williams mad. He's got a fiery temper, and he's been known to wave his fists in the direction of someone's jaw when he's really irritated. Considering the temperament of the man, it's remarkable how well he took it, that day he was struck out by a female softball pitcher. In fact, he was struck out about ten times.

It was a sunny day in 1962, and the Police Department in Waterbury, Connecticut, had scheduled a charity softball game. The women's team from Stratford, the Raybestos Brakettes, was playing against another fast-pitch team. Ted Williams was invited to hit a few off of the Brakettes' pitcher, Joan Joyce. Just as a stunt.

Now, Ted Williams (who played for the Boston Red Sox) won the American League batting championship six times, was the last man in the league to hit over .400, and is a member of baseball's Hall of Fame—but he didn't do so well against Joan Joyce.

Williams was at bat nearly ten minutes, in front of a crowd of 18,000. Joan Joyce threw 40 pitches. She threw knuckle balls, screwballs, fast balls, in-shoots, out-shoots, rise curves, and drop balls. Ted Williams managed to get one hit. He succeeded in banging another one into foul territory. But he couldn't touch the rest of her pitches.

"He was very upset," Joyce recalls, "and finally he threw down the bat and walked away."

It was perhaps unfortunate for Ted Williams that he had to face one of the greatest women's softball pitchers of all time. Joan Joyce is one of those creations commonly referred to as a "natural athlete." She plays volleyball and basketball, she's a championship golfer and bowler, and she can pitch. Oh, sister, can she pitch.

Joan began playing in 1955, when she was thirteen. Her father was a factory foreman and her mother a worker in a plant in Waterbury, Connecticut, and Joan used to fill in the after-school hours by pitching a ball against the wall of her house. Then she devised a "strike zone" made out of chicken wire stretched between two trees. Her father was a softball addict, and every night during the summer he'd take his three kids out to the park to watch the softball games. Joan and her older brother ended up loving the game.

As a young teenager Joan joined up with the Raybestos Brakettes, fortuitously located nearby in Stratford, Connecticut. For the first few years of her career, Joan was a strong pitcher but she lacked control. The problem was with her windmill style. It was the only windup she knew, but many of her pitches went wild.

The breakthrough, she recalls, came during a practice when she was about eighteen. One day she was warming up at Raybestos Memorial Field, where some workmen were stringing opening day banners around the telephone poles. One of the workmen climbed down the ladder, took a long look at Joan's pitching style, then asked her why she was using the windmill. When she told him it was the only windup she knew, the workman promptly put down his hammer and demonstrated the slingshot pitch for her. She tried it out, and it felt natural, so she stuck with it.

And that made all the difference. When the manager of the Brakettes saw the change in her style, he got Johnny Spring to come out and coach her. Spring was the hero of the Raybestos Cardinals, with a phenomenal record of victories. In 1958 he'd pitched the Cardinals (the men's team) to a championship in the nationals with a perfect no-hit, no-run game in the finals. Johnny showed Joanie the rise ball, the drop ball, and the change of pace. With the slingshot delivery, these pitches started to work and Joan's confidence took a sharp rise curve.

The Brakettes already had one ringer on their team—a formidable pitcher called "Blazin' Bertha" Tickey—and Joyce teamed up with her to win the national championships in 1958, '59, and '60 for the Brakettes. Blazin' Bertha was the best women's pitcher in the league. She had played first with the Orange, California, team (the Lionettes) and captured four national championships before joining the Brakettes in 1958. By the time she retired, at the age of forty-two, she had won a total of eleven national championships, been named eighteen times to the National All-Star Team, and was MVP eight times at the tournaments. Her lifetime record in twenty-three years of pitching was 757 won, 88 lost, with 162 no-hit, no-run games. When Joan joined forces with this big woman with swirling blond hair, the Brakettes team became virtually indestructible. That was before the Big Switch.

The Big Switch came in 1963, when Joyce left Stratford to go to college in California—and to play softball there. Her college residence was within commuting distance of the practice field of the Orange Lionettes. Joyce began pitching for the Lionettes, and the people of Stratford gritted their teeth. A showdown was bound to come.

Come it did. In 1964, on the opening night of the world championship, Joan Joyce hurled a no-hit, no-run game against her former teammates, and the Brakettes went down to a 2-0 defeat at the paws of the Lionettes. Dumped in the losers' bracket, the Brakettes fought their way through fifty consecutive scoreless innings, with Blazin' Bertha doing all the pitching. By the time they got to the final "if" game, the Lionettes had been knocked out, and Bertha had to face Erv Lind's Florists of Portland, Oregon. The Brakettes lost, 1-0.

In 1965, it was again the Orange Lionettes, led by Joan Joyce, against the Raybestos Brakettes, equipped with Blazin' Bertha and a brilliant new pitcher, Donna Lopiano, in the finals for the National Women's Fast-Pitch Championship. The match was held at Stratford, and the final game between the Brakettes and the Loinettes went 12 innings. When the dust cleared, Joanie and the Lionettes had won.

Donna Lopiano pitched the heartbreaker for Raybestos. She later recalled, "Half the crowd was for Stratford and half wanted Joanie to beat us. Most of the bad feelings had worn off by then, but it was still awfully tough to lose to Joan."

In 1966 someone checked up on Joan's fast ball. It crossed the plate at 118 mph.

By 1967 Joyce had finished college and returned to the Stratford fold, and Raybestos had the combined artillery of four great pitchers—Joyce, Blazin' Bertha, Donna Lopiano, and Donna Hebert. They combined to grab 67 wins with only 2 losses for the season, and the Brakettes did not give up a single run in the national tournaments.

As an amateur, Joan Joyce won more than 400 games for the Brakettes. In the first eighteen years of her career she pitched 110 no-hitters and 35 perfect games. And in 1974 she led the Brakettes to victory over the Japanese team in the world championship. In fact, there's only one thing wrong with this athlete. As Joan says: "It's boring to watch me."

But boring or not, she's the Sandy Koufax of women's softball, admired and well liked by just about every woman player who's ever met her. Still going strong at the age of thirty-six, she stands 5'9", weighs 160 pounds, and is known as a shy person with a tremendous desire to win.

A rival pitcher for the San Jose Sunbirds, Charlotte Graham, has faced Joan Joyce in dozens of games as an amateur and professional.

"She's a fantastic lady," Graham told a reporter. "She's my idol. I've watched her closely for ten years. She's truly the best player women's softball has ever had."

Considering Joan Joyce's record, that may be an understatement.

·~·

BASEBALL

Swinging for the Fences

Amy Ellis Nutt

Amy Ellis Nutt is a former writer-reporter at Sports Illustrated, *co-author with Helen Alfredsson of* A Good Swing Is Hard to Find, *and a features writer for the* Star-Ledger *in Newark, New Jersey. "Swinging for the Fences" is excerpted from* Nike Is a Goddess, *edited by Lissa Smith.*

Virne Beatrice "Jackie" Mitchell weighed less than five pounds when she was born in Chattanooga in 1915. Under her doctor-father's tutelage, she learned to play baseball at an early age and played in amateur games as a teenager, once even striking out nine men. In March of 1931, she sharpened her pitching skills at a baseball camp in Atlanta run by former major leaguer Kid Elberfield. Just a couple of weeks later Joe Engel, a former pitcher with the Washington Senators and then owner of the Double-A Chattanooga (Tennessee) Lookouts, offered Mitchell a minor league contract, which she signed, the first woman in baseball history to do so.

On a damp, cool April afternoon in 1931, the Lookouts hosted the major league New York Yankees in an exhibition game. The game had been postponed a day because of rain, so the field was still damp and the footing treacherous. It would not be a problem for the Lookouts with Jackie Mitchell on the mound. Mitchell came in for the Lookouts with two outs in the top of the first inning, a run in, and a man on first. The Yankees' greatest home run hitter, Babe Ruth,

7

walked to the plate, tipped his hat to the seventeen-year-old south-paw, and dug in. Ruth swung at the first pitch and caught nothing but air. The count went to two balls and a strike before Ruth swung at another sinker and missed again. With a full count, Ruth took the next pitch right down the middle for a called third strike. The Sultan of Swat had been struck out by a teenage girl.

Although Engel had a penchant for Barnum-like publicity stunts—he once staged an "elephant hunt" at Lookout Stadium in Chattanooga—Mitchell did not view herself in those terms. She had been playing baseball for most of her young life and had even received instruction from Brooklyn Dodger pitcher Dazzy Vance. A day before the scheduled start of the Lookout-Yankee game, the *Chattanooga News* reported that several major leaguers who had recently attended Elberfield's camp thought Mitchell was "one of the most puzzling southpaws" they had ever faced. Mitchell admitted years later that being only seventeen years old at the time probably helped her. She was simply too young to feel intimidated.

After Ruth was retired by Mitchell in that April 1931 exhibition game, he gave the batter's box dirt a kick, chewed out the umpire for a moment, then threw his bat down and returned to the visitors' bench. Meanwhile, the 130-pound teenager waited on the mound for the next batter. Two-hundred-pound clean-up hitter Lou Gehrig, who would lead the American League that year with 46 home runs and 184 runs batted in, stepped in against Mitchell: three pitches, three swings, three strikes. The sellout crowd of some four thousand stood and cheered wildly. The girl from Chattanooga had just struck out the best hitting tandem in the history of baseball.

When Gehrig walked back to the bench, he just smiled and shook his head. Tony Lazzeri, the best second baseman in baseball, was the third batter to face Mitchell. After fouling off the first pitch, Lazzeri kept his bat on his shoulder for the next four and earned a walk. Lookout manager Bert Niehoff then lifted his young south-paw, although Mitchell wanted nothing more than to keep pitching.

As it turned out, major league baseball wanted nothing more of Mitchell. The game was covered by dozens of magazines, newspapers, and wire services and also was filmed by Universal Newsreel, to be played over and over in theaters across the country. Within days of the exhibition game, baseball commissioner Kenesaw Mountain Landis voided Mitchell's contract with the Chattanooga Lookouts on the grounds that professional baseball was too strenuous a game to be played by women. Twenty-one years later, when a second woman was signed to a minor league contract, this time with the Class B Harrisburg Senators, baseball decided it needed to do more. On June 21, 1952, baseball commissioner Ford Frick banned women from that moment on from playing either minor or major league baseball.

As the legend of Mitchell's prowess against Murderer's Row took hold in the public imagination, so did controversy. Was Mitchell the real deal? Certainly, she could pitch. She'd proven that in amateur games before the Yankee exhibition—including games played against men—when she had barnstormed around the country. But the question persists: Did Ruth and Gehrig just play along with what Lookout owner Engel had clearly engineered as a promotional stunt? Over the past twenty years, a number of experts have viewed the film of the game, and most feel the answer to that question remains difficult to determine. Mitchell was a southpaw, whose main pitch, which she'd practiced for long hours, was a sinker. It is not impossible to imagine that both Ruth and Gehrig, both left-handers, were taken by surprise by the movement that Mitchell was able to put on the ball. And Lazzeri's taking four pitches after fouling off the first may have been his way of bailing out of a difficult situation and refusing to be embarrassed by the girl. Certainly, Mitchell, until her death in 1987 at the age of seventy-three, maintained that her fanning of Ruth and Gehrig was not a stunt on their part. She claimed that the only instruction given to the Yankee hitters about how to handle her pitches was not to hit the ball directly back at the young girl.

Whether or not Jackie Mitchell can be credited with one of the most sensational pitching performances in baseball history will long be questioned. What is not in question is that the professional career of the first woman to sign a minor league contract lasted only two-thirds of an inning. It was a momentous two-thirds.

Sophie Kurys

Barbara Gregorich

Barbara Gregorich is the author of Women at Play, *from which this piece is taken,* She's on First, *a novel, and sports articles for* USA Today.

When she was fourteen years old, Sophie Mary Kurys of Flint, Michigan, won the Mott Pentathlon for girls with a score of 4,693 out of a possible 5,000—a record that would stand for decades. If an athlete with the speed, aggressiveness, and savvy of Kurys were playing major league baseball today, the manager would have her bat leadoff and steal after she reached base. Johnny Gottselig, hockey-star manager of the Racine Belles, didn't comprehend how exceptional his five-foot-five, 120-pound player was. In 1943 he gave her the sign to steal just often enough to allow her to swipe forty-four bases. The next year Gottselig either got smarter or just looser with the signs. Sophie, playing in 116 games, racked up ninety-six hits, earned sixty-nine walks and was hit by a pitch seven times. Reaching first base 172 times, she stole a phenomenal 166 bases in 1944, seven of them in one game. And that was just the beginning.

Along with Joanne Winter, Margaret "Marnie" Danhauser, Edythe Perlick, Irene Hickson, Madeline English, and Eleanor Dapkus, Sophie Kurys was one of the original Racine Belles who

11

stayed with the team throughout its eight-year existence. As rookies the group played so well together that Racine won the AAGBL's first championship series. Although Sophie had played third and short-stop in Flint softball, Gottselig put her in the outfield. When the second baseman was injured after a few games, Kurys took over second and stayed there for the rest of her career.

In 1945 the Belles had a new manager. Although he had spent only part of one year in the majors with Pittsburgh, Leo Murphy had a twenty-five-year career in baseball. It was Murphy who understood that Kurys should be batting leadoff, where more at-bats would increase her chance of getting on base and (inevitably) stealing one or more bags, moving from first to scoring position. Says Kurys, "Johnny Gottselig had me all over the place. Leo Murphy got me to be the leadoff hitter."

In 1945 the "Flint Flash" played in 105 games and reached first base 157 times. Purloining 115 bases, she led the league in steals for the second consecutive year (and every subsequent year she played). "You pretend that you're not taking a big lead," she says of her technique. "I never took a big lead right away. Of course, they knew I was going."

Born May 14, 1925, Sophie turned twenty-one as the 1946 season began. If baseball time can be named by players, then 1946 was the year of Kurys. She played in 113 games, rapped out 112 hits, drew ninety-three walks, and was hit by ten pitches. Reaching base 215 times, she attempted 203 steals, succeeding a monumental 201 times. The Flint Flash was a steady flame, scoring a league-high 117 runs and batting .286, second only to Dottie Kamenshek's .316. Her ninety-three walks also set a league record. That same year she set a .973 fielding record for second base. The 201 stolen bases were not only a record for the year—they would remain a league record forever. The second-highest number of steals that year (Tiby Eisen's 128) was less than two-thirds of Sophie's total.

Because Kurys' base-stealing record is unequaled in baseball history (the closest is Rickey Henderson's 130 steals in 1982), the question arises whether her steals were equivalent to major league ones. Did the larger ball and shorter basepaths of the All-American Girls Baseball League give the runner an advantage that major-leaguers don't have? Dr. Robert K. Adair, Sterling Professor of Physics at Yale University, believes it's possible that a runner such as Henderson is at a 0.15-second disadvantage to the pitcher-catcher combination, whereas an AAGBL runner such as Kurys had a 0.04-second advantage over the battery. But Dr. Adair stresses that the microseconds involved are under perfect-play conditions: any variation in running, throwing, and sliding would change the numbers.

The theoretical 0.04-second advantage wasn't something every league player gained. Only one who could run at the speed of an Olympic athlete and possessed the baseball instincts of a Ty Cobb had this four-hundredths of a second "edge." Maybe it was Sophie Kurys' speed, her uncanny ability to judge the right moment to steal, her admirable aggressiveness in doing so time after time after time, that made her such a great base-stealer. Maybe it was the crowd at the ivy-covered, limestone-walled Horlick Field, cheering her on. Maybe it was the supply of Horlick's malted milk balls in the Belles' dugout. Whatever it was, nobody else in the All-American Girls Baseball League even came close to Kurys' base-stealing achievements: her 201 steals of 1946 and lifetime 1,114 steals in eight years were unrivaled.

The year of Kurys didn't end with Sophie breaking five AAGBL records (walks, steals, runs, fielding, and scoring five runs in one game), for the league-leading Racine Belles faced a best-of-five playoff series against the South Bend Blue Sox and, if they made that, a best-of-seven Shaughnessy Series. Though the Belles didn't know it at the time, their postseason play would start and end in extra-inning symmetry. In their first game against the Blue Sox, the Belles won, 3-2, when Maddy English socked a game-winning double in the bottom of the seventeenth. Racine went on to take the series against South Bend, three games to one.

In the Shaughnessy Series, Racine faced the Rockford Peaches. The Belles won two games at home, then dropped two of the three in Rockford. With the series 3-2 in their favor, the Belles headed home to Horlick Field and the sixth game. Until the seventh game of the 1991 World Series, perhaps no baseball final contest came close to matching the sixth game of the 1946 Shaughnessy Series for sheer drama.

First, there was the pitchers' duel, Rockford's Carolyn Morris against Racine's Joanne Winter. Having her best year ever, Winter had completed a 33-10 record for the season and pitched a consecutive sixty-three scoreless innings. But as reported by *Major League Baseball Facts and Figures,* the sixth game was a different story: "Winter was in hot water continually and the base paths were constantly clogged with Peaches as the Rockford team garnered 13 hits with never a runner denting the platter and left 19 base runners stranded. Meanwhile, Morris was pitching the masterpiece of them all and at the conclusion of nine innings, there had not been a safe blow by Racine."

In the tenth inning the Belles got to Morris and Bill Allington brought in Millie Deegan to relieve her. Deegan put out the fire in the tenth and the contest continued.

On and on it went, fourteen innings in all. (Although the players all remember it as a fourteen-inning game, *Major League Baseball Facts and Figures* reports it in words as a fourteen-inning game and in line score as a sixteen-inning one.) In the bottom of the fourteenth, Kurys, who had already stolen four bases that night, led off with a single and once again stood on first. "I have a passion for baseball," she says, perhaps explaining what happened. "I like the team concept. You're in there helping each other." So Kurys stole her fifth base. As she watched teammate Betty Trezza at the plate, Sophie found the favorable moment that only she could always find and lit out from second to steal third. At that instant Trezza slapped a short single through the infield. Glancing at the ball, Kurys touched the bag at third and headed home full speed, knowing her chances of scoring before the ball reached the catcher were questionable.

Throwing herself against the ungiving ground one last time, Kurys caught the plate with a hook slide a fraction of a second before the catcher tagged her, scoring the single run of the game and bringing the victory home to the Belles with her strength and spirit. Swarming across the field, the fans lifted the second baseman and carried her off on their shoulders. "It was such an exciting thing to see Sophie cross that plate," says her best friend and teammate Joanne Winter. "I'll never forget it." Hall-of-Famer Max Carey, president of the All-American Girls Baseball League, was equally excited. "Barring none," he said, "even in the majors, [it's] the best game I've ever seen!"

For her incredible baseball accomplishments, Sophie Kurys was elected Player of the Year. Not only was she the leading scorer for the season, she was the leading hitter and scorer for the entire postseason series. *Major League Baseball Facts and Figures* assessed her contribution in this way: "She turned more opportunities into runs than any other player in the history of the league."

Kurys went on to play AAGBL baseball for another four years and was elected to the All-Star team four straight seasons, 1946–49. In 1950 she stole 120 bases and hit a year-high seven home runs (tied by Eleanor Callow). When the Racine franchise folded, she went to Chicago to play professional softball for three years. After an additional year of softball in Arizona, she retired from the diamond at the age of thirty-three.

During the off-season, Kurys worked for a Racine manufacturer of electrical automotive and airplane parts. The owner eventually offered her a partnership and she accepted, contributing to the business in a team way by learning all parts and doing all jobs: she worked in manufacturing, quality control, as bookkeeper, a payroll clerk, and in the shipping department. In 1972 she left the business and moved to Arizona.

One thing about Kurys that made her a ballplayer's ballplayer and sets her apart from other masters of the steal such as Rickey Henderson: she never sought to call attention to herself. Even today, if she's being praised, she points out what others have done. Her attitude and personality are best summed up when she talks about her baseball heroes, Charlie Gehringer and, most of all, Hank Greenberg: "They didn't mouth off. They just did the job day in and day out without mouthing off." Sophie Kurys went out and did her job in the same spirit.

Dorothy Kamenshek

Barbara Gregorich

The streamliner which bore six young ballplayers from Cincinnati to Chicago in May 1943 was named the *James Whitcomb Riley*. En route to Wrigley Field, Dorothy Kamenshek and her five companions must have talked about many things: What was this "girls' baseball league"? Who among them would make the cut? What would it be like playing professional baseball 120 games a year?

Dottie Kamenshek had little way of knowing that she would become the best player in the history of the All-American Girls Baseball League. Like most of the young women signed to the league its first year, she grew up playing softball, not baseball. Born December 21, 1925, she was seventeen years old, falling just short of the median age range (18–22) of the first year's players. Standing five feet, six inches tall and weighing 135 pounds, she was at the upper limit of the average height and weight range.

At Wrigley Field, with the rain pouring down and tryouts taking place under the stands, Dottie was distraught to discover that somebody had stolen her only glove, an outfielder's model. Coming from a poor family (her father died when she was nine), she must have wondered how she could ever afford another. Maybe she wished she had persuaded her mother into letting her join the army as a way of making money and learning a skill. But Mrs. Kamenshek had firmly refused the army option, and had allowed her daughter to travel to Chicago only because she was convinced Dottie wouldn't be chosen for the new baseball league.

More than 250 women were invited to the Wrigley Field try-outs that first year. And then the cuts began. "They started weeding people out almost the first day. You'd be afraid to answer the phone in your hotel room," recalls Kamenshek. But two Cincinnati women made the final sixty—Betsy Jochum and Dottie Kamenshek. Assigned to the South Bend (Ind.) Blue Sox, Betsy went on a slugging spree that earned her the nickname Sockum Jochum. Dottie went to the Rockford (Ill.) Peaches, where her teammates promptly dubbed her Kammie to distinguish her from two other Dotties on the team.

Manager Edie Stumpf put Kammie in the outfield because that's where she had played in an industrial softball league, but after a dozen games he told the left-hander to play first base. Although a naturally good fielder and hitter, Kamenshek was the kind of person who wanted to learn more and do better.

The Rockford fans, possibly the most enthusiastic and supportive in the league, didn't recognize the cream of the crop that first year. When two All-Star teams of AAGBLers were chosen to play the first night game ever held in Wrigley Field on July 1, 1943, Rockford fans did not choose Dorothy Kamenshek. No matter: by the time the league got around to choosing an All-Star team in 1945, they chose Kammie for first base—that year and each succeeding year.

Singular fielding was what set Kamenshek apart from all other first sackers. Wally Pipp, former first baseman for the New York Yankees, declared she was the "fanciest-fielding first baseman I've ever seen, man or woman." Because the throws from the second baseman, the shortstop, and the third baseman don't arrive at first base in the same air lane, a first baseman has to keep her foot on the bag and stretch in every direction. Peaches teammate Rose Gacioch believes that "Kammie was ahead of her time. She used to make the split at first base the way they do in the majors now. It's like they learned from her."

By nature a fine athlete, Kamenshek made herself even better through hard work. "I practiced my footwork in winter on a pillow," she explains. "I threw it on the floor in front of a full-length mirror and pretended the pillow was first base. You try to make yourself as long as possible. I practiced shifting my feet. I stayed flexible year-round." She also studied major league first basemen, watching their footwork. When spring training rolled around, Kammie was always ready.

This fancy-fielding player was also an outstanding contact hitter, a Ty Cobb type who could put the wood on the ball and scratch out a hit when her team needed it the most. In 1945 the Peaches were engaged in a semifinal playoff series against the Grand Rapids (Mich.) Chicks to determine who would face the Fort Wayne (Ind.) Daisies in the Shaughnessy Series (the AAGBL equivalent of the World Series). As the *Rockford Register Republic* reported, "Kamenshek, who has batted .571 and played errorless ball in two playoff games to date, was the sparkplug of the Rockford attack last night. She scored twice, got two singles, a triple and a walk in four trips to the platter, and dug many a poor throw out of the dirt to bottle up the Grand Rapids offensive." Behind the pitching of Carolyn Morris, the bat and glove of Dorothy Kamenshek, and great plays by the entire team, the Rockford Peaches went on to beat Fort Wayne and claim their first Shaughnessy Series title.

The caliber of Rockford ballplaying had improved midway through the 1944 season, when Bill Allington took over as manager. From then on the Peaches couldn't hang around on the tree ripening at leisure: Allington drilled them with baseball history, baseball facts, baseball rules, and baseball plays—in the dugout, after the game, on the team bus. Although Allington worked them to the extreme, he believed that some players might want even more help. If so, he was there to give it.

And Dottie was there to take it. Every day, Allington would position a handkerchief along the third base line where a good bunt would drop. He would position another one along the first base line. Kammie would learn to drop a bunt in exactly that place. She could drive the ball to the outfield, too, pulling it or hitting to the opposite field. Jean Faut, the dominant pitcher of the league's overhand era, says of Kamenshek, "She was a great hitter. The free swingers were not too bad for me to handle, but she was a punch hitter and she gave me a lot of trouble."

Although the baseball world was awed by Kammie's fine fielding, she is proudest of her hitting, and in baseball it was the hitters she admired most. Once she took a bus from Cincinnati to Detroit just to see Ted Williams play. "It was one of my greatest thrills," she remembers. Her favorite player of all time was Stan Musial. Like her hero, she stood deep in the box in order to see the pitch the longest possible time.

In 1946, Dorothy Kamenshek won the All-American Girls Baseball League batting title with a .316 average, and in 1947 she took it again by hitting .306. In those dead-ball days, these were high averages. Of all long-time league players, she had the highest lifetime batting average, .292. In 3,736 at-bats, she struck out only eighty-one times. As the AAGBL ball became smaller and livelier, Kammie's yearly averages went up—.334 in 1950, .345 in 1951. A player who lived to hit, she must have experienced a wonderful thrill when the red-seamed 10⅜-inch ball was introduced in 1948. The first league ball that didn't have a plastic center, it emitted a loud crack as it came off the bat.

So great a player was this Rockford Peach that the minor league Fort Lauderdale club of the Florida International League tried to buy her contract. But not only would the AAGBL not give up Kammie's contract, she herself distrusted the Fort Lauderdale offer, believing it was designed only "to draw in an audience," not to get women into baseball. "I didn't want to be a guinea pig," she says, "so I turned the offer down."

Peaches fans admired their first baseman so much that in 1950 they held a "Kamenshek Night" to honor her. Personal friends, family members, teammates, and fans attended, bearing so many gifts that a truck had to haul them away. Asked to comment on the event, Manager Bill Allington told reporters that his first baseman "had a good cry and three hits." Asked if she cried in baseball, Kammie admits it. "I'm sentimental," she confesses.

Kamenshek retired in January 1952 after nine full seasons of play. The game to which Kammie had given so much gave her the courage and confidence to move on to another full-time career. While still playing for the Peaches, she began to attend the University of Cincinnati during the off-season. There she majored in physical education, although she had the feeling that it wasn't quite right for her. When she injured her back in 1949 (and wore a back brace while playing) and encountered physical therapy, she knew she had found her second calling. Switching to Marquette University, she continued her education and graduated in 1958, at the age of thirty-two.

After a few years as a physical therapist in Michigan, Kamenshek moved to California in 1961. There she became chief of the Los Angeles Crippled Children's Services Department. Her conscientiousness and hard work won her honors, as they had in baseball. "I ended up in the *Orange County Who's Who* for work in physical therapy," she says. "I'm just as proud of that as I am of my baseball. One thing about our league: it gave a lot of us the courage to go on to professional careers at a time when women didn't do things like that."

Helen Wills

Helen Jacobs

Helen Jacobs won the U.S. Open 1932–35 and Wimbledon in 1936. Her piece on Helen Wills is excerpted from her book Gallery of Champions.

My first national championship singles encounter with Helen Wills occurred in the 1927 tournament at Forest Hills. I think it may be said that she had reached the top of her form in that year. Driving with the same fury that marked her game in the Wimbledon final in July, when she won her first world's championship from Lili d'Alvarez (without the loss of a set), she seemed content to remain in the backcourt, hammering the ball relentlessly to the corners, alternating line drives with fast-dropping crosscourt shots. Seldom did she go to the net, depending largely upon lobs to offset the advantage of the net player against her. Although a recapitulation of the match showed that I earned more points than she, her errors were negligible in comparison with mine as I overhit the lines in an effort to match her length.

I had watched Helen often in practice against men in Berkeley. Most of them were able to defeat her without much trouble when they took to the net against her, played the drop shot [and] drew her to the net, where she was not naturally agile, very imaginative, or subtle with the volley. That, I knew, was the only game that I could win from her; all the women players with skillful volleys and overheads knew this to be true. The difficulty was in making the opening to get to the net, for, aware of her limitations in that position, Helen had perfected a defense against the volleyer that required on the part of her opponent a baseline game as sound as the net game.

To play Helen Wills was to play a machine. There was little if any conversation, no joviality, and to this the gallery obviously reacted, becoming almost grim in its partisanship. The press had long since confused incompatibility with the elements of a "feud" in our matches, which became less agreeable to both of us as they inevitably occurred. I remember no laughter from the crowded stands, though admiring applause was often thunderous. Thus, one had a feeling, would one watch the Derby at Churchill Downs, some hoping for the favorite to win, others hoping that the challenger would come through. Helen Wills fought on the court much as Gene Tunney fought in the ring—with implacable concentration and undeniable skill but without the color or imagination of a Dempsey or a Lenglen.

Matches against her were fun only in the sense of the satisfaction that one derives from pitting one's skill against the champion's. Most of Helen's opponents whom I knew well and played often had the same impression. Yet all had the greatest admiration for her game, and if the indomitable quality of her match play could only be sustained by concentration that must exclude every possibility of diversion, that was her business, for it is the undeniable purpose of champions to win.

Helen defeated me in my first American championship final, 6-2, 6-1, in 1928. My only consolation was that I won half as many points in the first set as she did and a little better than half as many in the second, and that I had been beaten by a player who had not lost a set in her triumphant march to the English and United States singles titles. To say that Helen Wills was pre-eminent, actually unchallenged, in the world of women's tennis would be redundant. She stood head and shoulders above the field. Though the challenger might fight to the last ditch, she was invariably exhausted by rallies that might be prolonged to prodigious lengths if necessary or, at the least evidence of her faltering, concluded in merciless style.

In the spring of 1929, the United States Lawn Tennis Association announced that a team would be sent to Europe for a series of international matches. The team was to consist of Helen Wills and a partner of her choosing. In this year I was ranked second in the American lists and fully expected to be invited to join the team for the tour that would have seasoned my game tremendously. Instead, however, Helen selected Edith Cross, thereby creating almost as much controversial discussion as that which was to follow our match in 1933. I could see no justification for the decision, nor could I understand the Tennis Association's acquiescence in it, considering the fact that it customarily chose its own teams.

Though I missed out on that trip, a group of San Francisco and East Bay tennis enthusiasts, who felt as I did on the subject, sent me to England for the Wimbledon championships, where Helen and I met in the final. Our match was a repetition of the final at Forest Hills in 1928. Everything written about one would apply to the other; the same can be said of my 1930 final against her in the French championships. I had not acquired the finesse to defeat Helen Wills at Wimbledon. Neither of us played in the American championships in 1930, and I did not have the chance to play her at Forest Hills in 1932, for she did not compete that year.

The 1933 season saw Helen extended to defend her title successfully in the Wimbledon final against Dorothy Round. She was forced to three sets for the first time since her initial victory in 1927. I played her that year in the final of the American championship. No tennis match within memory except the Lenglen-Mallory second-round match at Forest Hills in 1921 had quite such unpleasant repercussions as this one; none, I am sure, was more trying to both contestants.

There had been some doubts as to the value of my winning my first national championship in 1932, when, as I have written, Helen did not defend her title though she had won Wimbledon for the fifth time in July. With the opening of the 1933 season, it was considered almost certain that my reign as singles champion of my country would be short-lived; this, of course, in view of Helen's almost certain entry in the championships. A final match between us at Forest Hills was anticipated with much speculation—our supporters aligned vehemently against each other.

Helen was trying for her eighth championship, having, by this summer of 1933, held the title in 1923, 1924, 1925, 1927, 1928, 1929, and 1931. I was defending a title won only one year before, and perhaps the more precious for that reason.

The gallery was not a particularly large one the day we played—a midweek match, and uncertain weather, in addition to my tournament record against Helen Wills, were undoubtedly responsible. The day brought perfect tennis weather—no wind, not too hot— a day for exploiting all the shots Suzanne Lenglen had advocated: shots requiring accurate touch and little deflection by wind. It was also the ideal day for the volleyer who disliked more than anything else the drive that cannot be truly gauged or the lob that is pulled down toward the player by a sudden gust of wind.

I had determined that in this match I would go to the net at every opportunity. There was little sense standing in the backcourt swapping drives with anyone as superlative as Helen in that department. Of course, a net game was not enough of itself, but I had more confidence in my forehand than I had felt in years and was certain that it would stand up against the pounding I could anticipate from her, and also help to make the desired openings that would pave the way to the net. My backhand drive had seldom let me down.

It appeared, from the opening of the first set, that Helen was going to play me as she had done in every one of our meetings—playing chiefly to my forehand and, at the first evidence of my being off balance, using the short crosscourt drive to the opposite side. It was, at its best, a devastating placement, which I was determined to prevent. To do this I put everything I could into the force and placement of my service with the intention of drawing Helen out of court for the drive to the opposite side, then going to the net.

The first three games went with service. In the fourth I broke Helen's service, for a 3-1 lead. This lead seemed to inspire her to a stonewall driving defense in which she employed her familiar accuracy of corner placements, coupled with speed and pace. Games went to 3-3 as she broke my service. Then again service held to 6-6. For a while, during this stage of the first set, Helen also was playing for the net position, and it became a question of who would get there first. My backhand drive, particularly down the line, and my volley and overhead were serving me well enough to come within one point of the set at 5-4, but the fine variety of Helen's shots and her punishing steadiness saved the game for her. She was forcing me to hit lobs of difficult depth. Anticipating them, I had practiced smashing on an outside court for some time before the match began, and the practice was certainly justified. Helen Wills' lob can be a formidable weapon.

Breaking her service at 7-6 by the use of sliced drives to the corners and the volley, I ran out the set, 8-6. I had created a record for myself, winning my first set against Helen. It startled the press into wild activity. Typewriters and telegraphic instruments clacked furiously from the marquee. The set encouraged me, proving the wisdom of the net attack, which was certainly my chief weapon, and increasing my confidence in my forehand drive and slice as either aggressive or defensive shots on this day.

But one set was not the match. I had no illusions about the toughness of the road ahead of me. Helen was a fighter; she was a master of the drive and the lob. Her service required constant alertness and careful timing for the return. If I was to win, I must maintain my game at the same level for two more sets, if necessary, and hope that fatigue would impair neither my coordination nor my timing. I did not agree with those who claimed that a woman player could not attack at the net for three sets. In fact, I found it less tiring to go to the net, volley and smash, than to remain in the backcourt covering twice the ground in pursuit of Helen's magnificent drives.

But I had to continue to go the net, and as the second set opened, it was apparent how difficult the task might become. Winning my service in the opening game, Helen lashed out with blistering drives, varied by deftly paced soft shots that gave her a quick 3-0 lead. With desperate risk, I went to the net on anything close to her backline and was lucky to smash lobs for winners until I drew level at 3-3. Two obviously erroneous decisions against each of us in the next game caused an uproar from the gallery. Right or wrong, they were so patently miscalled at such an important stage in the match that neither of us could resist throwing a point in an attempt to even matters.

A series of drives overreaching the baseline, forced by Helen's deep and paceful drives and her sudden short crosscourt shots, gave her three games running and the set at 6-3.

I was glad of the respite that came at the end of the second set, as I am sure Helen must have been. But she remained on the court, sitting on a chair at the umpire's stand, while I went to the dressing room to refresh myself. When I returned to the court after the ten-minute intermission, Helen opened the third set with service, going to 30-15 in spite of a double fault before I won the game. On my service two unretrievable drives by Helen forced errors from me and she led 0-30. Then, in turn, she overdrove twice, evening the score. A winning volley took me to 40-30, and a netted drive by Helen brought me to 2-0. Helen won the first point of the third game on a forcing service, but forehand and backhand passing shots, successful for me, and a forehand drive beyond the line by Helen gave me the lead at 3-0.

I turned to the ball-boy for the balls, speaking to him once and then again, before I realized that his eyes were fixed on the opposite court. I repeated my request before I turned to see that Helen had walked to the umpire's stand and was reaching for her sweater. It was a confusing moment. I hurried to the stand as Ben Dwight, the venerable umpire, announced that I had won by default. As Helen put on her sweater I went to her.

"My leg is bothering me. I can't go on," she said.

"Would you like to rest for a while?" I asked.

"No, I can't go on," she answered.

Officials, press, photographers rushed onto the court. It seemed unnecessary to subject her to this post-match ordeal. "If you're in pain there's no sense in continuing," I told her. "Why don't you leave before the photographers descend on us," I suggested. Helen left then, escorted from the court by one of the tournament officials.

I went back to the dressing room, where Molla Mallory was waiting for me. A radio commentator had asked her immediately after the match to broadcast a statement on the default in view of her experience with Suzanne Lenglen. She did, in biting terms, and was still full of it when we met.

There is no doubt that Helen, for her own sake, would have been wiser if she had remained on the court for the twelve points necessary for me to end the match in the third set. But what one does under the stress of emotion and pain cannot be calculated in the cold-blooded terms of the spectator. Helen's temperament had always been her most valuable asset. On this day it was her greatest liability.

Before I had finished dressing, Elizabeth Ryan came into the locker room in a state of wild excitement. Helen, her partner in the ladies' doubles, had announced that she would play the doubles final. Knowing the probable reaction of the gallery if she did, Elizabeth was determined to default. Fortunately, one of the officials, who had long been a friend of Helen's, persuaded her that she simply couldn't return to the court after the default.

As far as I was concerned, Forest Hills was real bedlam that day. A stream of reporters was in and out of my apartment until late in the evening; the phone never seemed to stop ringing. "Would I make a statement?" was a question that fell on my ears like a phonograph record stuck in a groove. There was nothing I could say. Of course, I was disappointed that the match had ended as it did—who wouldn't have been? But that was water over the dam. I had retained my championship and was happy about that. But how could I, how could anyone for that matter, dispute with Helen her statement that she felt on the verge of fainting when she defaulted? The fact that she walked back to her apartment in the Forest Hills Inn and later wanted to play the doubles final did not make her lot any easier with the reporters who knew of it, but I still did not feel that anything except the winning of my match concerned me.

There were repercussions of the match for months to come. The story of its ending was greatly distorted by many reporters, in most instances by those who obviously had not seen it. What I said to Helen was garbled by journalists whose hearing couldn't have extended to the umpire's chair. Some had it that I begged her to go on, the last request it would have occurred to me to make. Some wrote that she refused to shake hands and others that we shook hands, were photographed, and that she was then helped from the court. The truth of the matter is that, although we did not shake hands, Helen did not refuse to do so, nor was she assisted from the court. She left it, as soon as she had donned her sweater, under her own power.

She appeared next in major championship tennis in 1935 at Wimbledon. Beaten by Kay Stammers at the Beckenham tournament while she was again getting her "tournament legs," Helen had, with one exception (a three-set match against Fräulein Cepkova in the fourth round), a fairly easy time to the final of the Wimbledon meeting.

We met again, this time on an intensely hot afternoon with a slight breeze blowing. Both of us were playing well, but Helen went to a 3-0 lead in the first set before I could make much of an impression on the match. I believe she has always liked the fast Center Court turf, and she was hitting with wonderful length and great speed. The next three games to me evened the score, then Helen took the set, 6-3.

Up to this stage the match had not been as scintillating as our Forest Hills final of 1933. To defeat Helen once was to draw forth from her a more wary game; and having defeated her was to emphasize to the opponent the importance of taking chances at every opportunity, of playing boldly from backcourt and net, and yet of maintaining a sound defense and steadiness to match hers—a considerable challenge.

I think there was, in the beginning of the third set (which started without the ten-minute intermission that is customary in this country), some restraint in our hitting. But with the advantage of service, I was able to go to 4-2 and then, as Helen missed an easy smash, to 5-2. Helen won my service for 5-3. It was in that game that I held match point. At 30-15 in my favor, on Helen's service, a questionable sideline decision caused some delay before we could resume play. I hit a drive along Helen's forehand sideline that appeared to be in. Evidently the umpire thought it was in, but the linesman called it out. The umpire questioned the linesman, who repeated his call, and the game went on. With the score at 30-30, I won the next point to move to within one point of the match. After one of the longest rallies I can remember ever having survived, Helen, out of court on her backhand side, put up a shallow lob. The lob appeared to be headed for midcourt. I moved in to hit it, but a gust of wind caught it, pulling it in toward the net. By the time I was able to judge where it could best be hit, it was a short lob, very close to the net. I was almost on my knees for the smash, the ball hit the edge of my racket frame and rolled along the net cord before it fell onto my court.

That was really the end of the match. Though we were at 30-30 and deuce in the eleventh and twelfth games, Helen won the set at 7-5. She had made a magnificent comeback to win her seventh Wimbledon championship. Unfortunately, some widely read members of the press reported what had been an exciting sporting test in such a manner that the so-called feud between us was the highlight of the reports. I, the loser, was represented as accepting defeat with tears in my eyes. Helen was represented as a far more jubilant victor than good taste would have dictated. These reports were so contrary to the facts as to make one wonder if it is not better not to report at all than to report inaccurately. Far from having tears in my eyes after this match with Helen Moody, I had enjoyed the match, for it had been a real test of skill and staying power, of tactics and strategy and nerve. Naturally, one regrets losing any big championship final, but it seems to me an unfair commentary on the behavior of women in competitive sport that it should be necessary, in order to create reader interest, to report the loser in tears and the winner gloating.

It has been my experience during eighteen years of tournament tennis that women are no more given to tears in defeat than men, nor is their enthusiasm in victory more excessive. To claim, even facetiously, that it is, is to lessen public regard for the important place that women have achieved, against immeasurable disadvantages, in all the games that Americans, Europeans and Asiatics love to play.

Althea Gibson

Michael Bamberger

Michael Bamberger writes for Sports Illustrated *and* Time, *from which this piece is taken.*

A white man took a black woman's hand, two tennis champions at a summer dance. Few witnessed the event, and nobody wrote about it. All the champs did was perform a two-step and improve the world—or at least one timeless and beautiful spot in it. This was at Wimbledon, in the summer of '57, two months before nine black kids tried to enter Central High in Little Rock only to find a group of Arkansas National Guardsmen blocking the door, on the orders of the Arkansas governor, Orval E. Faubus. All the newsmen were camped out there in Little Rock. I'd have taken the dance instead. The Wimbledon men's champ in 1957 was Lew Hoad, a dashing Australian. The ladies' champ was Althea Gibson. Althea, the groundbreaker.

The 29-year-old Gibson knew the customs of the All England Club. She knew about the strawberries, the white-only tennis outfits, the proper protocol upon meeting the queen. For the fortnight of the tournament she was staying in the West End flat of a friend, Angela Buxton, a Jewess, as they said in London in those days.

A year earlier, in '56, Buxton and Gibson had won the doubles title at Wimbledon. The Jewess and the colored girl, they were a curiosity, but most Britons were too polite to fuss over them much more than that. At the '57 tournament, though, Buxton was injured and unable to play. Instead, she designed Gibson's tennis outfits, all white, of course, which suited Gibson just fine, since white showed off her smooth, dark skin and her torch-singer good looks. The outfits were mostly shorts or divided skirts; she needed clothes in which she could move.

Gibson was one of the favorites at Wimbledon in 1957. The previous year she had won the French Open, her first major title. One is tempted to say that, at 29, she was at the peak of her powers, but it is hard to know. It wasn't until 1950, when she was 23, that the United States Lawn Tennis Association allowed Gibson to become the first black player to participate in the U.S. Championships at Forest Hills. She had spent her Harlem youth often riding the subways all night to avoid her drunken father's beatings and playing paddle tennis during the day on 143rd Street. She came to "proper" tennis late. A group of Harlem businessmen had paid Gibson's way to London.

It was a sound investment. Gibson made the net her personal property, overheads were automatic points, and she didn't lose a set. She played with an athleticism never before seen in women's tennis. She was Venus and Serena a generation before Papa Williams had his first tennis vision for his yet unborn daughters. In the semifinal Gibson trounced a popular English schoolgirl named Christine Truman 6-1, 6-1. The bursting Center Court crowd cheered lustily for the loser, because she was English and because she was the underdog. In the evenings after her matches Gibson returned with Buxton to the flat, where Gibson relaxed with a string of cigarettes and whiskeys and slept practically until match time.

In the final, in 90° heat, Gibson defeated a Californian, Darlene Hard, 6-3, 6-2 in 50 minutes. Gibson "was the first representative of the Negro race ever to win a Wimbledon [singles] title," but, as *Sports Illustrated* reported at the time, the fans at Center Court "raised only an apathetic cheer when the Queen presented her with a big gold salver and Darlene hugged her with sisterly enthusiasm." Gibson played a masculine game, and the English didn't know how to respond to it. For Americans, of course, winning is the thing, and she returned as a public icon, to a ticker-tape parade down Broadway. (Today, though, Gibson rarely talks publicly about her Wimbledon victory, or anything else.)

Only a couple of months after Gibson's Wimbledon victory, the forced integration of Central High in Arkansas turned into a violent, ugly spectacle. At the All England Club that summer, integration had come about naturally and cordially. During the Wimbledon Ball, after the two champions danced and before the final toast was raised, Gibson took the bandleader's microphone and sang, in her deep and sultry voice, *I Can't Give You Anything but Love.* She was now a member of the All England Club: An honorary membership comes with the singles title. She was, as far as anybody knows, the first black woman to be a member. Nobody cared. Or if people did, they pretended not to.

It is naïve to think that you could write a story about two club members—both tennis champions, one black, the other white—sharing a dance and that such a story could influence the thinking of the likes of Orval E. Faubus. But I would love to have tried.

In the summer of '58 Gibson came back and won Wimbledon again, and in time the black kids in Little Rock walked through the front door at Central High, just like everybody else. Talent had won out again, and so, finally, had reason. In some immeasurable way, Miss Gibson must have helped us get there.

Chris Evert

Jim Murray

Jim Murray was honored by the National Sportscasters and Sportswriters Association as Sportswriter of the Year a record 14 times. This selection was taken from his book The Great Ones.

They called her "the Ice Maiden." Penguins could live on her, they said. She had the mean average annual temperature of an iceberg.

She was so shining white, it hurt to look at her. She was like a ski slope in the sun.

She played tennis as if she were pouring tea. No one ever saw her perspire.

She was a throwback to the days when women played in hobble skirts and flowered bonnets.

She never left the baseline. She knocked everybody out at long range like the USS *Missouri*. She played tennis the way an orchestra played Beethoven, deftly, lovingly but with intense concentration on the notes. Other players might be rock 'n' roll or bombast. Chris Evert was a Moonlight Sonata.

It irritated some people. They wanted more dash and fire. They wanted Chris to come to the net, to slash more, serve and volley, lose her temper, come apart. Be human.

She wouldn't. She was as cold as a marble statue. She never dived for a ball, skidded into a net. She looked as easy to beat as a pair of treys.

You couldn't get a ball by her in a tank. She had the patience of a schoolmarm. She made Job seem impetuous. She would hit balls back at your feet till you wanted to scream.

The crowd wanted Dempsey and they got Willie Pep. Sugar Ray. Chris jabbed you to death.

She was at pains not to look like it, but she was a tremendous athlete. She made the two-handed backhand popular, which made the Establishment need smelling salts. Chris just smiled sweetly. She didn't run on court, she'd glide. She'd remind you of a great center fielder. DiMaggio in his prime. When the ball came down, she was there. And when she hit it back, it had hair on it.

But she elevated defense to a high art. No linebacker ever had a surer instinct for the ball than Chris Evert. She once won 125 consecutive matches on clay. She won seven French Opens. She was unbeatable where the ball bounced true.

She walked with the graceful little mincing steps of a belle at a cotillion. You half expected her to have a parasol. She didn't appear to have a nerve in her body. I once wrote that she played with the bored detachment of a pro giving a lesson to an old dowager. It was true to the end.

She played a heady game. She had to. "My serve was not a weapon," she laughs. "I put it in there to start a point, not to ace anybody off the court."

She resisted temptations to turn into a serve-and-volleyer. She stuck to what brought her. Not even when Martina Navratilova came along with a game modeled after marines storming the beaches did Chris leave the baseline.

She won nine of every 10 matches she played. She won 157 singles titles, 1,309 matches in all, more than any female player. She won 18 Grand Slam titles, which, as it happens, is one more than Martina.

Whatever she was doing must have been right.

But I always thought Chris Evert's enduring contribution to the game was not tenacity, it was femininity. Not since Helen Wills and Moody Roark had the game seen anyone with the aloof, dedicated perfection of Evert. They used to call Wills "Little Miss Poker Face." Chris Evert presented the same unruffled, confident exterior. You could never tell from looking at her whether she was down four-love or up two sets to none.

Chris Evert never managed to look as if she just got off a tugboat or just put out a cigar. She wore ponytails and earrings and hair ribbons. Even necklaces. She played in bracelets till they got in the way. Louisa May Alcott would have loved her.

Chris Evert has left the baseline. She put away the rackets and 19 years of cross-court volleys, drop shots and two-handed backhands last fall at the U.S. Open when she lost in the quarterfinals to Zina Garrison, a player who stood in line for an hour to get Chris' autograph only nine years before.

It was only the second time in her career that Evert failed to make at least the semifinals there. She played in 113 U.S. Open matches. She won five Opens and was a finalist three times and a semifinalist eight.

There is no senior tour as such for tennis. Will Chris Evert now retire with her clippings, her trophies, her ski-slope husband, Andy Mill, to a condo in Aspen?

Hardly. As a matter of fact, she's going to the net. "Don't make me out to be a dynamo," she pleads. But she will do tennis commentary for NBC Sports, her Evert Enterprises is active in the sports fashion business, and on March 3–4 at the Hyatt Grand Champions Resort in Indian Wells, she will head the pro-celebrity phase of the Virginia Slims of Indian Wells tournament to benefit the Women's Sports Foundation.

She spanned the era from Billie Jean King to Steffi Graf with grace and taste. She kept Martina from swallowing the game whole.

King and Graf were/are great players. But could they have won wearing an evening gown and a diamond tiara?

Chris Evert could. All but did.

Martina Navratilova

Jim Murray

If I were to tell you one of the greatest athletes of the 20th century—and maybe the greatest of our times—would be appearing in Manhattan Beach this week, would you go there expecting to see: (a) Jose Canseco, (b) the ghost of Jim Thorpe, (c) Nick Faldo, (d) Pete Rose, (e) Joe Montana or (f) any Detroit Piston?

What you would find there is none of the above. What you would find is an athlete who is pound for pound, inch for inch the greatest of the era, an athlete who weeps in victory, smiles in defeat, wears designer clothes and actually looks good in earrings.

No one is sure whether God is a woman, but it just may be that the greatest tennis player in history is.

Listen, when you talk of all-time sports feats, hitting in 56 consecutive baseball games, pitching six no-hitters, scoring 100 points in an NBA game or winning three Super Bowls stands out.

But wining nine Wimbledons?! That makes the list with any of them at any time.

It is the tennis feat of all time. It makes Martina Navratilova the best ever to play that game. Big Bill Tilden? He won three

Wimbledons, thank you. Don Budge? Two Wimbledons. Rod Laver? Four Wimbledons. Bjorn Borg? Five Wimbledons. Ivan Lendl? None.

You have to dip into antiquity to find a matchup for Navratilova. Only the elegant Helen Wills Moody, who won eight Wimbledons, is in her class.

That's what you have to do with the truly marvelous—measure them not against their contemporaries, but against their ancestors, against history. Helen Wills was to tennis what Babe Ruth was to baseball. Henry Aaron breaking Babe's all-time record was no greater an accomplishment than breaking the great Queen Helen's. People thought neither of them would ever be matched.

Martina won more than a tournament. She won her way into legend. She now plays for the ages. She escapes the fine print. To be in the same paragraph with Helen Wills is an achievement. To reduce her to a footnote is to take over tennis.

Helen Wills used to play with the fixed expression of someone trying to win a pot with two treys. Martina plays with the intensity of a deer fleeing a forest fire, but she turns as coldly efficient as a serial killer when the Queen's cup is on the line.

She is in a business where the average age seems to be somewhere between 14 and 19 but, at 33 nearing 34, she manages to dispatch these younger, fiery schoolgirls with the steady competence of someone plucking chickens.

Martina never seems to come to a game in emotional disarray. She is as tough and focused as Mike Tyson with his man on the ropes or Nolan Ryan with a guy looking for the curve.

She dispatched a schoolgirl (Debbie Graham, Stanford) in a little over 45 minutes Tuesday with almost bored nonchalance. It was like watching someone pull wings off a butterfly—except that Martina treats every match as if it is a Wimbledon final. She confided afterward that she was fearful after a five-week layoff that she might have forgotten how to play.

How could Martina forget how to play tennis? What does it take to win nine Wimbledons in the first place? What does it take to be and remain Martina Navratilova?

Plenty. It calls for the tenacity of purpose of a bulldog on a rope. In Helen Wills' time, tennis was not exactly a profession. It was more of a pastime for the not-so-idle rich. Tournaments were spaced, outdoors and relentlessly amateur. Silver cups were at stake, not silver Rolls-Royces.

The competition was genteel. Tennis was largely something to do before the cotillion started.

Today, it's Wall Street with rackets. Big bucks, high pressure. It's a jungle out there.

You need your own masseuse. You need your own osteopath. You travel in an entourage. You're on an airplane, in a limo—or on the court.

You have to watch what you eat. "Your body is like a vintage Rolls-Royce," Martina says. "You have to be careful what fuel you put in."

You have oatmeal and carrot juice for breakfast. Doughnuts are out. Even orange juice. "Sugar is a drug," Martina insists. "A mind-altering drug. It is the most abused drug in America. It gives you a high and then it does what all drugs do—brings you down and in despair. Robs you of precious energy."

Red meat is OK. Once a month. "I love hamburgers," Martina admits. "But if I ate them every time I wanted them, I wouldn't make the quarterfinals."

The body is treated as deferentially as a sovereign. Some women check the mirror for their beauty. Martina checks it for her health. It is her belief that only her mind is 33 years old. The rest of her is still in her teens.

"It's a narcissistic life," she says. "But it's necessary."

Most people wear glasses so they can see 20/20. Or even 20/30. Martina can already see 20/20 with the naked eye. She wears glasses because they correct her vision to 20/10. Martina takes every edge into the match she can muster.

She lifts weights not to build up her muscles, but to build up her endurance. Martina's body is not a set of muscular knots. It's chorus-line round.

She ices her knees after every match. She's a late sleeper. The body is pampered, but Martina shows little patience with the athlete in it. She is an expert skier, defiant of the possibility of a fracture.

If tennis were a morality play, Martina would be the villain. She has a nice smile but in the early years of her career, she used it sparingly. She had come into the game out of the gloom of Kafka's Czechoslovakia, where smiles were rationed like sausages. She learned to play tennis hitting a ball against a barn door. "It's hard to learn the game when your competition is a wall." When she began to beat the golden Chris Evert and everybody's darling of the center court, Evonne Goolagong, Martina was treated like a truck driver at a royal lawn party.

Not anymore. Martina is the royalty on the court now. The crowds come to see her in the Virginia Slims tournament at Manhattan Country Club this week. She is an American heirloom.

She is, typically, hardening her body and toughening her mind for the U.S. Open. After all, she has only won four of those. (Borg never won any.)

But her ambition is not a 10th Wimbledon or a fifth U.S. Open, it's to win a gold medal for the United States in the Barcelona Olympics in '92.

It's an interesting ambition. Even curious. Until you remember that Helen Wills won one in 1924.

Venus Williams

David Higdon

David Higdon contributes to Tennis *magazine, from which this piece is taken.*

Here sits Miss Venus Williams, bored out of her beads. We're face-to-face on a canopied cement deck adjacent to a red hard court that has "Williams" emblazoned in huge white letters across its green backdrop. Behind Venus, two lefties are blasting forehand after forehand at each other on one of the two clay courts. The rest of the Williams family compound—a modest-sized white home, several garages, two lakes, one shattered Yonex racquet, a huge inoperable rusty satellite dish, a half-dozen riding lawnmowers and twice that number of cars, including a blue Impala and white Rolls-Royce—is scattered over 10.6 acres here in Palm Beach Gardens, Fla.

Williams, seventeen, sports the retro cool look—a pink, yellow, purple and mint-green sweater-and-slacks get-up—popular with so many other sixteen-year-olds today. Thanks to her combination of size (6 feet, 1½ inches, last anyone checked), color (black) and sweet sassiness ("That question does not compute"), she reminds me more of the lead character played by Teresa Graves on the '70s TV staple *Get Christie Love*—minus the Afro, of course—than anyone out of *Clueless*. It will be ixnay on this interview, however, if I can't stop Miss Williams from yawning.

Suddenly, we hear a distant shriek. Williams vaults out of her chair and my heart stops beating. I turn around, expecting to find Venus's free-spirited fifteen-year-old sister Serena caught—helpless, mangled—under one of those ubiquitous lawnmowers. Instead, I see her wrestling with two dogs. Venus beams now, her braces brightening up her face. She hops up and down like a kid trying to peer over the candy store counter.

"I haven't seen my dogs in two days," says Williams, restraining herself from dashing off because she would consider it rude. "I'm so glad they're back. They go into the woods." Suddenly her mood shifts from solace to ire. "That's their last chance. They don't need to worry me like that. Queen—not the Dalmatian the other one—taught Chase how to run away. They're not going to teach Star, though, because I'm going to keep them away from Star."

Star, I discovered earlier in my visit, is a floppy-eared brown puppy the girls acquired a few weeks ago. The dog seems permanently attached to Serena's lap even as she tools around the property at full speed on a beat-up golf cart filled with grass clippings, a baseball mitt, garden tools and a roll of blue tennis strings. It's Serena who later explains why she and her big sis get so worried whenever Chase and Queen disappear.

"This is Lake Inferior," she says during a tour of the Williams's property, pointing to the smaller of the two lakes. "If it was up to me, I'd cover this lake up. This lake took my dog's life. Her name was Princess. I would always throw her in the water, and she would always swim back. She was a homebody; she never went anywhere. She loved us. She loved everybody. One day, we were looking everywhere for her, and my dad saw her here, floating in the water."

Fledgling tennis pros Venus Williams, hailed as a "ghetto Cinderella" by her father, Richard, when she first rose out of the gang-ridden Los Angeles suburb of Compton at age ten, and Serena

Williams, who some believe will be as good a player, if not better, than her older sister, are home. It's where they cried when their dog died and where they giggle when discussing their father's fear of snakes. It's where they have bike-dived into "Lake Superior." It's where they crank up alternative rockers such as Rage Against the Machine, Rancid and The Foo Fighters and turn down countless requests from IMG, Advantage and ProServ agents drooling over representing them. It's where skateboarders are cool but in-line skaters are posers. Explains Serena: "We don't like in-line skaters, we don't like people who like in-line skaters and we don't talk about in-line skating."

"Thank you, Serena," says Miss Williams.

"You're welcome, Venus," answers Miss Williams.

Silence, for effect, then guffaws. The Williams sisters are home. Here is where they are when they're not on tour, where they haven't been much of the time.

Though Venus has flirted with the WTA Tour since turning pro in 1994, this season will serve as her true coming-out party. "I think this year will probably be the most fun I'll ever have on the tour," she says, "watching my ranking progressively get better." Venus played three tournaments this past winter, registering her first win over a top-ten player (Iva Majoli) at Indian Wells before falling to eventual champion Lindsay Davenport in a quarter-final match decided by a third-set tiebreak. Later at the Lipton Championships, she again produced an upset (Jennifer Capriati) and lost to the eventual champion (Martina Hingis). This month Williams is expected to make her Grand Slam debut at Wimbledon, though the French Open was still a consideration at press time.

Until she travels overseas for the first time in her life, though, Williams will remain at home. It's here where the mysterious Williams sisters transform into two gifted, spirited, bright, goofy, athletic, gutsy, charming kids. They couldn't care less that I believe they're two of the most captivating athletes to surface in women's tennis—no, make that women's sports—this past decade. Big deal that their critics—mostly petrified peers on the WTA Tour—feel they should be competing more often for silver trophies and gold plates than for Gatorade and Snickers bars. Role models? Of course. Child prodigies? Ob. Future burnout victims? Nuh-uh. These girls just wanna be No. 1.

"[Venus] puts a lot of pressure on you," says Pam Shriver, who has trained with the sisters. "When we played, she didn't know tactically how to play points yet, but she had weapons and has this natural way of intimidating. If I missed a first serve, I immediately thought: 'Criminy!'" Adds Davenport, about her Indian Wells match: "She was getting some balls back that I guarantee you most girls never get back against me."

"No one is ever going to back [Venus] up," says Rick Macci, the Florida pro who jump-started Capriati's career and has worked on and off with the Williams sisters over the last three years. "She'll have the game to play through Hingis on certain occasions. She's lost more matches in practices than any junior I've coached in my life, but she's going to be a champion."

Not everyone seems convinced. "I didn't think she was that great," said Majoli after her loss to Williams. Sixteen-year-old Anna Kournikova agrees: "I have watched both Serena and Venus play, and they're not that good. They don't know how to play points or how to win." Macci has repeatedly heard juniors with whom he works and their parents dismiss Venus's abilities after watching her play. "All they see is Venus spraying balls everywhere and looking gangly," he says. "Meanwhile, every week, her stock is going up in my eyes."

There stands Mr. Richard Williams, surrounded by a cluster of men. He smokes a cigarette, then another, then another. I am sitting high in the bleachers behind the baseline at the 1995 Acura Classic in Manhattan Beach, Calif. I spot Williams outside the stadium where his daughter Venus is getting thrashed by a nondescript

Swede named Asa Carlsson. Daddy ain't watching. "A psychiatrist told me if I want my daughter to be successful, try your best not to be there when she plays," Richard tells me later. Venus agrees with such sentiment. "I would prefer to think for myself," she says.

Richard Williams has been called a "liar" and "genius" and everything in between. Most of the "in between" is not printable in this family publication. Here is one, however: "Irascible." Here's another: "Insane."

"He says things people don't like to hear," says his lawyer, Keven Davis. "He makes people uncomfortable."

Not me. I think he's hilarious, unpredictable and delightfully eccentric, the best thing to hit our sport since the days when Pete Fischer, Pete Sampras's mentor, spewed venom at the tennis establishment. That's one reason why I invited Fischer to join me for Williams's match against Carlsson. I also knew that Fischer was coaching a girl, Alexandra Stevenson, who is six months younger than Williams and competed against her in girls' twelve-and-under tournaments in Southern California.

"[Venus] is a great athlete who just happens to be a tennis player," Fischer said. "She's tall, muscular and fast. Plus, she's totally coachable. She listens. I've watched her work with coaches and Richard, and she's got terrific concentration." Fischer claims to have spotted future greatness in Williams back in the days when she would trash his current protégé in tournaments and then skip off with Stevenson to go swing on monkey bars. "I said back then," Fischer claims, "that these two would be playing in the final of the U.S. Open in seven years."

That would be 1998, a highly unlikely scenario, considering their limited professional experience, but you never know. Williams stopped playing junior tennis at age eleven, an oft-criticized decision made by the man who says he's been trying to get his daughter to quit playing tennis ever since she was eight years old. "She's a track runner," he boasts. Whether or not Williams is serious or simply yanking my chain is unclear, but one thing is obvious: Here is a man who loves to rattle the cage.

"Everyone I've ever met who plays professional tennis is a nut," he says. "They're all crazy. And when I say all of them, that includes my daughter Venus. Anyone who picks up a racquet and heads out there and thinks they have a career is a fool. Venus is going to be out of tennis by age twenty-four, twenty-five. And if she lives to be fifty, she has twenty-five more years to be a fool, and I don't want that. I might be doing it the wrong way, but in the end, she will benefit from it."

Here is the Williams Way: He interrupts carefully scripted workouts to make Venus and Serena study French with practice partner Gerard Gdebey. He seeks counsel from a Seattle-based attorney because, as Davis says with a chuckle, the man "likes his lawyers as far away as possible." On the eve of Venus's professional debut, he whisked his family off to Disney World for a few days of roller-coaster rides and Mickey Mouse sightings. Venus told me she hates it when people ask her to describe a typical day in her atypical life. "It's like the wind blowing," she explains with a shrug. "It can change direction." Richard likes it that way.

Richard Williams grew up in Louisiana, the oldest of five children, the only son of a single mother who picked cotton for a living. He and wife Oracene, whom he met at church, have raised five daughters. He's been surrounded by women his whole life. When Venus was born in June 1980 and Serena fifteen months later, the Williams family lived in Compton. It's a city where, Richard says, "AK-47s, drugs, PCP, ice and welfare checks are more prevalent than anywhere else in the world." That's an exaggeration, but you get the drift.

The athletic Williams eventually discovered the joy of tennis. A veterinarian who sat behind me in Manhattan Beach and graciously gave me a tour of the Williams's old stomping grounds the following day said Richard Williams was a "crafty" player who could hit with both power and finesse. "He was an expert at all the angles," said Dr. Edward Pygatt, describing Williams's game exactly the same way many people today describe his handling of Venus's tennis career. Williams taught tennis to all his daughters—Yetunde, Isha and Lyndrea as well as Venus and Serena—but Venus showed the most promise.

It wasn't long before Venus Williams, the little girl from the ghetto playing tennis as gang-fire rattled the spray-painted wind screens, started making headlines. Jack Kramer saw her play and proclaimed her a future Grand Slam champion. *Tennis* magazine ran its first article about her in 1991. That year, Richard asked Macci to visit Compton to consider coaching his daughters.

"I hear it all the time: 'I've got the next Jennifer,'" says Macci. "Richard said he'd like to meet me but the only thing he could promise me was that I wouldn't get shot. All I could think of was: 'Who is this guy?'" It was Macci's first lesson in what WTA Tour CEO Anne Person Worcester admiringly calls "The Richard Williams School of Publicity." Sure enough, Macci soon was footing the bill for a flight to L.A.

"Richard picks me up in this Volkswagen bus that has dents all over it," Macci recalls. "There were tennis balls, clothes, McDonald's wrappers, Coke cans, everything scattered throughout this wobbly bus. It was 7:30 in the morning when we arrived at East Rancho Dominguez Park, and there must have been thirty guys there already playing basketball and another twenty lying in the grass passed out.

"We started working out, doing some drills, and after about an hour, I thought I was wasting my time. Then Venus asks to go to the bathroom and as she walks out the gate, she walks at least ten yards on her hands. I was stunned. Then she went into these backward cartwheels for another ten yards. I'm watching this and the first thing I thought was: 'I've got a female Michael Jordan on my hands.'"

Here crouches Miss Serena Williams, wiping her hands on the front of a Green Day "Insomnia" T-shirt. Her heavily muscled arms and legs bulge as she reaches for one of two surfboards lying on the floor of a shed that houses "all our stuff we don't want to clean." That includes a drum set both ladies admit to having no clue how to play. "We were going to have jam sessions in there," says Serena, pointing to a Nirvana poster hanging by one thumbtack on the wall. "We even bought guitars. But we got preoccupied."

Surf happens. A hobby one day, clutter the next. There are jet skis near the lake that haven't been used in ages, a basketball court that serves as parking space for another one of those damn lawnmowers. But Serena remains obsessed with riding waves. "I was at the beach and there was this program going on for little kids," Serena explains after we hop back into the golf cart. "They all had surfboards and I had a rotten, ugly, horrible, nasty, funky boogie board. I got a short board, which allows me to rip and shred, but Venus went crazy and got a ten-footer."

If Mike and Carol Brady had been black, these two could have been Marcia and Jan. (Repeat after me: "Venus, Venus, Veeenus!") The two sisters always are trying to one-up each other, but if there's ever animosity between the two, it doesn't surface in public. Venus claims baby sis used to steal things from her when they were little, but they've always been doubles partners. "I'm a good sister," Venus says. "I let her sleep while I'm driving." On tour, the two always seem to be sharing some kind of inside joke, whispering and then giggling uncontrollably. They never appear more than six feet from each other unless Venus is playing singles matches or seducing the media in interviews.

During those moments, Serena always has seemed a little out of place. She's been described as a pit bull, and at 5-foot-9, she's got the chiseled and somewhat intimidating physique of a sprinter (think Gail Devers with a gap between her two front teeth). "With Venus, everything comes so easy, whether it's athletic or academic," Oracene says. "With Serena, it comes a little harder, but that makes her work harder, too. She's more of a stick-to-it person."

Unlike Venus, who grasps things quickly yet tires at the same speedy pace, Serena needs time, whether it's learning how to hit a forehand passing shot, adjusting to a move ("I didn't mind the area," she says about their Palm Beach Garden digs, "I just didn't like the land and the house") or warming up to strangers. It explains why Serena volunteered to take me for a leisurely spin around their property while Venus darted off into the house to see what was planned for dinner. Venus says Serena is "kind of a perfectionist, though not neurotic or psychotic."

Richard Williams likes to boast that Serena "will be better than Venus." When you watch her attack the net with the fearlessness and foot speed of Pat Cash, you have to at least consider the possibility. Aggressive, offensive-oriented players always evolve slower than your standard baseliners; Serena's middle name, Billie Jean King once joked, is "Forward."

Serena devours pro tennis on TV, though she claims not to be too fond of the senior tour. "All I ever see is [Jimmy] Connors playing [Andres] Gomez," she complains, "or Gomez playing someone else." She would prefer to see more of John McEnroe, a player whose on-court style she always has admired. And, of course, more surfing. Turning the tables near the end of my visit, she asked: "Don't you want to ask me about my surfing career?" When I acquiesced, she responded: "I could really be good if I had the time." Then she challenged me to a game of tetherball and kicked my butt.

Here sits Mrs. Oracene Williams, complaining about the decor of her house. "It's not really me," she says. A lone blue bead lies on the kitchen floor by her feet. A stack of mail sits precariously on the edge of the table. She wears brown beads in her braided hair, which Serena tugs at during a brief foray into the kitchen.

"That's me, though," she then says, pointing to some ceramic and wood figurines on the nearby bookshelf. "I see the collection as old black figures showing how they communicate with their kids. There's a religious one over there, one with a mother spanking her kid . . ." Venus, who also has joined us temporarily, interrupts. "They come alive," she says, cringing as she gingerly lifts one figurine off the shelf.

Oracene laughs, then shoos her daughters out of the kitchen. If you think it must be tough for Serena to carve out her own niche with Venus around, imagine what it must be like for Oracene in the overwhelming presence of Richard Williams. Like her husband, Oracene (a.k.a. Brandy) was the oldest child in a large family, though she had seven siblings to Richard's four. She's been nurturing children her entire life. "Since both Richard and I were the oldest, we're both used to being in control," she says. "So that's where we would get a little conflict. I had to learn to back off."

That doesn't mean she doesn't share her opinion with him. Or put her foot down when necessary. She's even gotten more involved recently in coaching her daughters, shouting out comments during practices and offering advice during water breaks. Like any mother, she worries about her children as they embark on their chosen careers.

"When I first went to a tournament," she said, "all the players looked so sad. They look like they hate to be out there, that they're scared. Even the top ones, with the exception of Hingis. They're scared of the competition when they should be inviting it. Venus doesn't worry about winning, because she knows she isn't going to lose."

Over the last several years, Venus and Serena practice only with each other or hard-hitting male tennis partners. They learned tae kwon do, worked out with a professional boxer, practiced gymnastic moves, threw a football around. They even did the hula hoop to work on lower-body coordination. But why skip junior tennis?

Richard and Oracene believed early competition would hamper their ability to learn and experiment on the court—and figured it would distract them from their education away from it. Venus played Oakland in 1994—when she beat 59th-ranked Shaun Stafford and was up a set and a break on Arantxa Sanchez Vicario before crashing—solely to avoid falling under the tour's pending age restrictions. Then she played a restricted schedule anyway.

"I think the family should be credited with sticking to their word that they weren't going to push Venus out there and force her to play maximum numbers of tournaments," Worcester says. "That had everything to do with family and going to school and learning Chinese and lots of other hobbies and interests, which we feel is healthy and try to promote with all our players."

Oracene Williams expresses no fear that her daughters' limited competition and isolated environment will stifle their professional growth. "When we moved to Florida from California, it was to make sure we were doing the right things and teaching the right ways," Oracene says. "Richard has always supervised their workouts and more or less given them instructions on what he wanted to work on. The only thing I worried about was Venus losing her ability to be natural." When Venus starts playing tennis full-time, Oracene adds, "you'll see a new wave of tennis."

Here come Venus and Serena Williams, eyes blinking in the spotlight. The beads in their braids clatter as they walk. Friends and family follow in their wake. Venus has just lost a professional tennis match. She and her sister are stopped by a stunningly beautiful and familiar black woman. It's Angela Bassett, the Oscar-nominated actress from nearby Tinseltown. "Oooh Venus, baby," she coos. "Give me a hug." The statuesque Williams, resplendent in a silky Reebok outfit, bends awkwardly to embrace the lithe Bassett. Venus and her sister smile for a photo taken by one of Bassett's entourage. Moving on, Venus rises to her press conference perch above a sea of white faces. "She doesn't see anything after she loses," Oracene says, explaining Venus's nonchalant reaction to celebrity. Here is what Richard said: "Everyone in tennis is a fool."

Babe Didrikson Zaharias

Arthur Daley

Arthur Daley wrote sports for the New York Times *for forty-seven years and won a Pulitzer prize. This selection is from his book* Sports of the Times: The Arthur Daley Years.

The team championship at the National Amateur Athletic Union track and field meet in 1932 was won by the Employers Casualty Company of Dallas. Its points were achieved through the winning of five individual championships and the tying for a sixth. The entire "team" consisted of one 18-year-old girl, Babe Didrikson.

Implausible is the adjective which best befits the Babe. As far as sports is concerned she had the golden touch of a Midas. When she was only 16 she was named to the All-America women's basketball team. She once hit thirteen home runs in a softball double-header. Her top bowling score was 237. In the 1932 Olympics she won two events, setting world records in each, and placed second in the third test although again breaking the world record.

But it was as a golfer in her later years that she gained most renown, dominating the distaff side of the divot-digging pastime with awesome efficiency. Best remembered is the rueful flippancy Bob Hope tossed over his shoulder after pairing with her in a charity match.

"I hit the ball like a girl and she hits it like a man," he said. Hope was at least half-correct. The Babe hit the ball like a man.

But behind that steel-sinewed, square-jawed facade was feminine softness and gushy sentimentality. The first time the Babe ever had any extra money she took her mother to a department store in her native Beaumont, Texas.

"Momma, pick you out a dress," drawled the Babe pridefully. Momma did.

"Pick you out another one," urged the Babe, glowing with satisfaction at the astonished look on her mother's face. The Babe kept urging until eight dresses were selected.

"Momma," said the Babe triumphantly, "now you got a dress for every day in the week and two for Sunday." Her devotion to her beloved Momma and Poppa was heartwarming.

There was a tender awkwardness to her romance with George Zaharias, the massive wrestler. They were mutually attracted the moment they met and their love story was a rich and rewarding one through courtship, matrimony and beyond.

Babe Didrikson Zaharias made a strange confession in her autobiography *This Life I've Led,* a wonderfully human character exposition that she wrote with the aid of Harry Paxton.

"Before I was even in my teens," she declared, "I knew exactly what I wanted to be when I grew up. My goal was to be the greatest athlete that ever lived."

This was an odd ambition because the best woman athlete in almost any sport is about on a par with a schoolboy champion. Yet the Babe became the greatest of her sex beyond question and her golf frequently attained unbelievable proficiency. It was no accident, no reliance on natural ability alone. She worked at it with the same indomitable ability with which she fought against the cancer that was to take her life.

Before she started out in the first golf tournament of her career, a reporter asked how well she expected to score.

"I think I'll shoot a 77," she said nonchalantly. This was a bit of bombast which she airily characterized as "Texas talk."

So the gal from Texas shot a 77. It was a freak, of course, and she did not linger long in the match play rounds which followed. But this experience impressed on her the need for giving polish to her game. She did it in typical fashion.

The Babe practiced sixteen hours a day each weekend. On weekdays she was on the course at 5:30 A.M. for a three-hour session. Then she went to her regular job. Most of her lunch hour was spent chipping balls onto a leather chair in her boss' office. After work she took lessons for an hour and practiced until dark.

"I'd hit golf balls until my hands were bloody and sore," she once grimly explained. "Then I'd have tape all over my hands and blood all over the tape."

The price for perfection was high but she paid it willingly. The rewards were high, too. Yet there never were any shortcuts for the Babe in anything, either in getting to the top or staying there. Once she was leading a tournament when she discovered that she played the wrong ball out of the rough. She alone knew it.

"That's it," she said resignedly to the officials. "I've been playing the wrong ball and I have to disqualify myself."

"But no one would have known the difference," remarked some unthinking spectator.

"I'd have known the difference," said the Babe sharply, "and I wouldn't have felt right in my mind. You have to play by the rules of golf just as you have to live by the rules of life. There's no other way."

This was no mere muscle girl who died the other day. The greatness of her athletic achievements permeated the entire character of Babe Didrikson Zaharias until the strength and splendor shone through. She was a remarkable personality.

Nancy Lopez

Jim Burnett

Jim Burnett is a regular contributor to Golf *magazine and the author of* Tee Times, *from which this piece is taken.*

Nancy Lopez can't putt.

Ten years ago that would have been like saying Sugar Ray Leonard couldn't box or Chris Evert couldn't volley from the baseline. In her prime Lopez was the queen of the greens.

But that was then and this is now. Yesterday, in the first round of the Sara Lee, Lopez hit the ball decently and still shot 78. In frustration she even changed her putting grip during the round, switching from an interlock to something close to a baseball grip. She birdied two of the final four holes to avoid a dreaded snowman. (Scores of 80 or above are called snowmen, because of the shape of the 8 and, perhaps, because they leave the player out in the cold.) Caddie Thorpe says the grip adjustment "keeps her stroke from breaking down as much. It's a little more solid, not as wristy. She just needs to practice. She took three weeks off and played about three times."

About 150 people are following Lopez on a lovely spring Saturday with just a hint of a breeze, after near gale-force winds the last few days. She is paired with tall, slender Susie Redman, 30, also a mother of three, and Page Dunlap, a dark-haired 30-year-old touted for possible stardom a couple years ago but struggling to keep up with the pack lately.

Lopez has virtually no chance of making the cut. She's playing for pride today. In Lopez's book, that means she's playing for the most important thing of all. In fact, the word *pride* pops up repeatedly in Lopez's two books and almost all her press conferences. Example: "Competitors take bad breaks and use them to drive themselves just that much harder. Quitters take bad breaks and use them as reasons to give up. It's all a matter of pride."

Several years ago Lopez said, "I think my problem is that I want too much. I want to be great golfer. I want to be a great mother. I want to be a great wife. I don't know if I'm good enough to be all three."

She's close.

Lopez has juggled her roles quite adroitly since marrying baseball star Ray Knight in 1982, and giving birth to Ashley Marie in 1983, Erinn Shea in 1986, and Torri Heather in 1991. (Torri's middle name honors Heather Farr. When a three-month-pregnant Lopez won the Sara Lee in 1991, she dedicated the victory to Farr, who was undergoing chemotherapy treatment.)

In many respects Lopez revels in her role as a traditional mom, cooking and shopping and raising the kids at home in the sleepy town of Albany, Georgia, and hunting and fishing with Ray on their woodsy 600-acre farm.

Yet she and Ray are enmeshed in jet-setting careers—Knight recently took the reins as manager of the Cincinnati Reds—that would tax the constitution of the highest-flying businessperson. Lopez plans to take weeks off when the Reds play at home in the summer; when Knight hits the road, Lopez will pack up the kids, the nanny, 15 pieces of luggage, and rejoin the Tour. ("I'm a professional packer," says Lopez. "I know how to pack any truck that exists. I give airport employees tips.")

Can Lopez play world-class golf with such a schedule? Obviously. She placed 14th, 25th, and 28th on the money list in 1993, 1994, and 1995, despite a limited schedule of fewer than 20 tournaments per year.

But that's not nearly good enough to suit her, especially since Lopez hasn't hit the winner's circle since 1993. "Forget accepting a slump," Lopez wrote in *The Complete Golfer*. "No golfer worth his or her salt will do that."

In an attempt to regain her top form, Lopez has lost 30 pounds since January. She looks and feels marvelous. She also talks fat grams with the zeal of a missionary.

In March during Dinah Shore week, after Lopez finished a practice round and a two-hour workout in the LPGA fitness van, a large trailer that travels with the Tour, she talked about her transformation.

Still dressed in her workout clothes—pink T-shirt and white shorts over black tights—Lopez walked into the Mission Hills clubhouse with a white towel draped around her neck and a plate of honeydew melon in her hand. She ordered ice water with lemon.

"I got tired of not feeling really good or healthy," said Lopez. "I'm going to be forty this year—and that really bothers me!" she added with a laugh. "I'm feeling real strong, real confident, and I haven't felt that way for a long time. My endurance is so much better. Last year I worked hard on my game, but I was kind of sluggish, kind of tired—no get up and go."

Lopez always has had a sweet tooth—when she left Nabisco and signed an endorsement deal with Sara Lee, it may have been partly for the desserts. ("The pound cake is really good. It doesn't *feel* like you're eating a lot of calories. And you can just throw it in your bag.") In 1993, after huffing and puffing her way up and down the hills of the Stratton Mountain course in Vermont, Lopez said bluntly, "I'm fat. I admit it. I know I need to lose weight."

Diets and exercise regimes followed, but not for long, and Lopez yo-yoed up and down the scale. Finally in January, her pride overcame her fondness for McDonald's quarter-pound cheeseburgers and the five-pound restaurant-style cheesecakes Sara Lee sent her. ("Eat one of those and you *gain* five pounds.") Lopez hired an Albany aerobics teacher as a private fitness instructor; she gave Lopez the drill:

1. Two-hour workouts six days per week, including an hour on the StairMaster, treadmill, or bike, 200 sit-ups, and lots of stretching
2. A stringent limit of 20 to 25 fat grams per day

Nibbling on the lemon slices from her ice water, Lopez explained what foods were okay: bagels with jelly, cereal with fruit, no-fat waffles and syrup, an occasional egg, pasta, vegetables, pizza without cheese, sandwiches with mustard but not mayonnaise. Her addiction to cheeseburgers slowly has been replaced by a craving for fruit.

Lopez also was feeling better about her putting. Gardner Dickinson, a fine PGA player and instructor who is married to LPGA player Judy Dickinson, told Lopez her tempo had speeded up. "You could almost count out my putting tempo," said Lopez, as she finished chewing the lemon slices down to the rinds. "It was one . . . two going back and one . . . two forward. Gardner said I was putting like everyone else—a fast stroke."

Husband Knight helped too. Bothered by kidney stones, Knight has trouble sleeping, and when he does, he often pulls out golf videotapes of LPGA tournaments. "He'll wake me up at three in the morning and say, 'Nancy, you've got to look at this!' So I get out of bed and go watch my putting stroke."

In her first book, *Education of a Golfer,* written after her rookie season in 1978, Lopez stated that she could make any five-foot putt "99 times out of 100."

When asked if she meant that literally, she nodded. "Even standing over the ten-footers. I knew I was going to make it. I wasn't afraid to ram it by, because I knew I would make the one coming back—and a ball that's rolling hot has a much better chance of going in than a ball rolling soft and being so much more affected by the line." You might get an argument about that theory from Ben Crenshaw or any other great die-them-at-the-cup putters. But the critical point is that Lopez believed it and it worked.

No longer. Lopez is wrestling with the same bugaboo as Tom Watson, the other great, boldly aggressive putter of the 1980s. It's easy to blast putts at the cup when the comebackers seem as easy as tap-ins. But when you stand up to the three-, four-, and five-foot comebackers and jangling nerves make you feel like you're putting on the rolling deck of an ocean liner, the game begins to cramp your mind like a vise.

"I've got my tempo back," said Lopez as she carefully fished a few pretzels from a glass bottle containing nuts and other bar snacks. "Now it's a matter of practicing and practicing and practicing to build confidence to make the five- and six-footers, the ones you have to make."

Lopez was a natural talent of extraordinary dimensions as a child, the equivalent of a one-in-a-generation chess prodigy or math whiz. The first time she set foot on a golf course, the 4-year-old tot astounded her parents by hitting the ball square on the nose and lofting it over their heads and down the fairway. She won a 27-hole junior tournament by 110 strokes.

But her genius was honed through blindingly hard work. "I used to putt for hours," said Lopez. "Sometimes I putted so long I couldn't stand up straight when I left the course."

Lopez looks marvelous. The gallery comments on her sleek, healthy appearance. But all those sit-ups haven't reduced her putting woes, and Lopez misses birdie putts of four and five feet on the first few holes. Rarely do you see steam coming out of Lopez's ears—too much pride—but you can often sense it percolating below the surface. Finally she rolls in a nice five-foot birdie putt on the 147-yard 5th hole, and her fans have a chance to cheer.

They don't need much encouragement. Consider Jennifer McCormack, 30, who works as a mortgage lender for the Bank of Mississippi in Tupelo. McCormack endured "the roughest flight of my life," bouncing around the sky in the fierce winds earlier this week, in order to see Lopez in person for the first time.

Yesterday McCormack, a 10 to 12 handicapper who plays nine holes almost every night after work, and local tournaments on the weekends, got an autograph from her idol, whom she admired even as a child. "It's just a pleasure to watch her play. To me she makes golf what it is. She did the same thing for the women that Arnold Palmer did for the men."

Lopez finishes with a mediocre 73. When she emerges from the scorer's tent two reporters collar her for quick interviews. Then she's surrounded by a crowd of about 100 autograph seekers. Lopez signs everything from caps to lounge chairs. The fans say, "Thank you." Lopez says, "Thank you." When Lopez was 15, she stood in line for an autograph from one of the biggest stars on the PGA Tour (Lopez has never revealed his name). But when she got almost to the front of the line, the pro said, "I don't have time for this. I have to go."

"I felt like a piece of trash," says Lopez. "It really bothered me and hurt me." When Lopez began signing autographs herself, she vowed never to stiff anyone, especially a child.

Ellen Hunter, 13, an eighth-grader from Memphis, excitedly tells Lopez, "I did a book report on you for English class!"

"What grade did you get?" asks Lopez.

"A hundred!" says Hunter.

Hunter happily brings her signed poster over to her parents, watching from the outskirts of the crowd.

When Lopez took the Tour by storm in 1978, the response from her colleagues was a frosty jealousy and resentment. "The first and second year I was winning so much I was never in the locker room," says Lopez. "I'd play, do interviews, practice. When I got back to the locker room, everyone was gone. People never saw me, so they'd say, 'Nancy's a snob.' It was a tough time for me."

A snob? Don't tell that to Jennifer McCormack or Ellen Hunter or any of the thousands of fans who have met her. "Nancy Lopez has the patience of a saint," LPGA communications director Elaine Scott once said. "She never says no to anyone."

One story that exemplifies Lopez came earlier this year in the first round at Tucson. The event was simply a warm-up exercise, a chance to try out a new set of Tommy Armour 855 irons, featuring a wider flange at the bottom, and tune up her game before the Dinah Shore.

Lopez played miserably. "Lots of skulled shots," caddie Thorpe said later. Lots of lousy chips and putts too. An embarrassing performance, regardless of the circumstances. Then, on the last hole, Lopez hit a sensational iron to within a foot of the cup. A small gallery along the ropes near Lopez cheered. Lopez turned toward the fans. A beaming smile, a smile that rivals Magic Johnson's as the best in sports, a smile as warm as the sun, lit up her face. Her eyes danced with pleasure. Lopez has loved the game since she was captivated by the crunching sounds of spikes on cement when she was a toddler. She still does. As casually as one weekend golfer would remark to another, she said, "That one shot always keeps us coming back, doesn't it."

Lopez takes a step and signs an autograph, takes another step and signs, takes another step and poses for a picture with a fan, doing the Superstar Shuffle.

The crowd finally satiated, Lopez walks toward the clubhouse where Torri is waiting with her nanny. When Torri sees Mom, she runs over and buries her head against Lopez's waist. "Hey, baby," says Nancy, kissing her daughter and hoisting her in her arms.

Gertrude Ederle

Paul Gallico

Paul Gallico wrote frequently on sports and was the author of such books as The Poseidon Adventure, The Snow Goose, *and* The Golden People, *from which this selection is taken.*

If you will look today into a modern almanac or record book, you will find under the heading of Channel Swimmers some two columns of names of men and women who have conquered this treacherous body of water under their own steam. Why they bothered to do so, and still do, is anybody's guess. Even recently that much abused strait has been trampled and threshed by individuals determinedly trying to eke out firsts from its cross-currents, heavy tides, and choppy waters, including children and graybeards looking to be the youngest or the oldest or the fastest. Others have been attempting to swim it both ways in one gulp.

But up to the year 1926 there were only five who had made it: Matthew Webb of Britain, 1875; Thomas Burgess of Britain, who crossed in 1911; Henry F. Sullivan of the United States who, along with Enrique Tiraboschi of Argentina and Charles Toth, another American, swam it in 1923. Of these five the fastest time recorded was that of the Argentine, who swam from France to England in sixteen hours and thirty-three minutes. Many more had tried and failed, and those who succeeded were well-larded giants.

Women had attempted it in vain. The test of that particular body of water was thought to be too severe for the so-called weaker sex. This situation was corrected on August 6, 1926, when another name was added to this brief list. It was that of an eighteen-year-old girl, an American. She hustled from Cap Gris Nez to Dover in fourteen hours and thirty-one minutes, not only breaking the time record of the fastest man by two whole hours, but achieving the only first that really mattered from then on. Her name was Gertrude Ederle and she was the pioneer of her sex to succeed in this arduous passage.

Females have been making the crossing ever since but the trips are meaningless. Everest had been climbed, so to speak. It was Gertrude Ederle who once and for all had softened the English Channel for women and showed that it could be done.

That was thirty-nine years ago and nothing remains today but that single line in the record books and the memory of the great din unloosed in New York Harbor the day of her return from abroad, when the whistle-cord of every steamship within range was tied down. Sirens brayed and hooted as airplanes buzzed and thundered overhead, pelting her with flowers as she stood upon the deck of the city tug *Macom,* surrounded by municipal dignitaries in plug hats and frock coats, who were escorting her up the Bay.

In my ears still rings that great rolling roar which followed her triumphant motorcade up Lower Broadway, swelling from block to block as the crowd, packed from sidewalk to sidewalk, caught its first glimpse of the young, brown-haired girl standing in the back of an open car, her arms extended as though to embrace them all. In my mind's eye I can see this mass, so dense that motorcycle police had to thrust open a lane for her passage as the wildly enthusiastic welcomers rushed and fought for the privilege of touching the car in which she rode. She progressed through the canyons of the skyscrapers beneath the bizarre August snowfall of ticker tape, torn-up telephone books, shredded newspapers, broker's sheets and toilet rolls descending upon her from every window.

For this paper blizzard was something new in the line of welcomes to returning heroes, which had developed since the war, along with the incumbency as official City Greeter of the late Grover Whalen, appointed to that stately office by New York's Broadway playboy mayor, Jimmy Walker. Mr. Whalen was a gorgeous piece of man, born to the top hat, striped trousers, frock coat, and gardenia in the buttonhole which was his uniform when he went down the Bay to receive an incoming celebrity. With his pink face and black, toothbrush mustache, he was as much a part of the municipal scene as Battery Park, the Aquarium, and the downtown skyscrapers.

A routine had evolved in which the *Macom* chuffed down to Quarantine, the arriving V.I.P. was received officially by Mr. Whalen, transferred from the liner to the tug, and decanted at the Battery, where a cavalcade of open motorcars awaited. Then followed the ride up from Lower Broadway to City Hall, where his Honor the Mayor was enthroned to climax the reception.

Office workers in the tall buildings lining both sides of America's most famous street, having been alerted, waited like excited children with their homemade storm. When the motorcade came past, they unloaded from the heights and the paper, fluttering down, was one of the prettiest sights you ever saw and strangely moving as well.

Spectators usually lined the sidewalks to watch the procession go by, but for Ederle the largest crowd ever turned out, spilling from the curbs and jamming the thoroughfare. Never before in the history of the city had there been such a demonstration for a sports hero; never before had the Department of Sanitation been called upon to sweep up so many tons of Broadway confetti. Not until the following year, when Lindbergh came back from France, were the decibels of cheers, tonnage of shredded paper, and hysterical warmth of welcome equaled or surpassed.

And all this for a simple, unassuming girl, the daughter of a German-American family who owned a small delicatessen store on upper Amsterdam Avenue in New York City.

This was the kind of welcome one would expect to be reserved for conquering admirals and generals, or crowned heads. But it was in this era that America produced a new royalty, the kings and queens of sport, as a vivid and thrilling demonstration of the workings of this unique democracy, where the poorest and the humblest could instantly become national heroes and heroines.

Gertrude Ederle, or Trudy as she was universally known both from affection as well as compact headlining, was one of these, and a shining example of the sudden magic that could envelop ordinary persons and overnight elevate them to fame and fortune.

One moment, as it were, she was an unknown, one of the faceless millions inhabiting our teeming cities, a young girl who enjoyed the exercise of swimming competitions and the companionship of her clubmates, and the next she was a world celebrity.

And had she but understood the nature of the excitement, love, and admiration she had touched off, had she been less modest, simple, and unambitious, she too might have become a millionairess, a Queen Midas, turning everything she fingered to gold.

As it was, the day after the news of her courageous triumph over self and one of the world's most treacherous bodies of water had been broadcast, merchants, promoters, manufacturers, and motion picture and theatrical producers were lined up in the offices of her "managers." They were trying to thrust large sums of money upon them for endorsements of articles, personal appearances, engagements, and services of every kind connected with the gilded name of Ederle, which could be expected to bring an equally gilded return from the almost hysterical Ederle-loving American public. The child had, so to speak, done nothing that was either useful, good, or serviceable to humanity, and yet as far as we of that era were concerned, she had done everything and we were prepared to drown her, who had survived the Channel, in a flood of dollar bills.

The fact that most of these offers were fended off with some arrogance by a group of "managers" that suddenly mushroomed around this celebrity, was part of a personal tragedy that dogged Gertrude Ederle, but did not alter the fact that here was an attempt for the first time in the memory of man to bestow riches upon a swimmer.

The art itself had barely become a sport. Up to that time, practically, swimming was something one did at the beach in the summer, or when one fell into the water or capsized when sailing, to keep from drowning. What, then, was there suddenly about this, and particularly women's swimming, which saw it in this decade elevated to the very pinnacle of publicity?

For the answer one looks again at our times.

Still heavy-handed, hypocritical, censorious prudes, we had but recently emerged from the age of the long-stockinged, full-skirted, bosom-swaddling bathing costume, the most ridiculous collection of woolen garments ever to conceal the female form divine. Men looked silly enough in their long drawers and half-sleeved, candy-striped, jersey tops, but it was the women dressed, apparently, more for going down into a mine than entering the sea, who really took the cake. One reason that swimming had failed to develop as a sport was simply that no one could move in the damn things. All they were good for was holding on to a rope and bobbing up and down in the Sea Bright, Sheepshead Bay, or Coney Island breakers. Any attempt at forward progress was soon brought to a halt by the drag of some twenty pounds of waterlogged clothing.

The revolutionary heroine who put an end to this nonsense and freed women from this form of bondage was an Australian girl by the name of Annette Kellerman, a polio victim who took up swimming at the turn of the century as therapy for her crippled legs. It was Miss Kellerman who claimed that no woman had the brute strength to swim the English Channel, for she had made several attempts to do so herself and once had gotten three-quarters across before being forced to give up.

But it was not for this that her name became world-famous, but the fact that she introduced the first one-piece bathing suit for women. A spectacular exhibition swimmer, she went into vaudeville and motion pictures clad, or rather unclad, in this daring garment and girls, forever thereafter freed from the drag of shoes, stockings, bloomers, blouse, and hat, bought themselves "Annette Kellermans" and began to swim.

When I was a boy Annette Kellerman was a household word and I remember her, smooth and glistening as a seal, performing in a tank on the stage of the old Colonial Theater on Broadway and 62nd Street, a house devoted to high-class vaudeville. The S.R.O. sign was out at the theater, and the balcony spotlights were reflected from many a bald pate. The sellout attendance had come ostensibly to see her doing the crawl, the backstroke, the jackknife, and the swan dives, but nobody at the box office was being kidded. The original Annette Kellerman bathing suit was still a slightly bulky affair of jersey wool, even though skirtless and sleeveless. Nevertheless, it made the question of how ladies were put together no longer a matter of vague speculation.

The tight-fitting, black silk racing suit was only a few years away, and women's swimming and diving competitions became a major attraction. Newspaper publishers discovered that whereas reproductions of nightclub cuties in leotards or tights might bar them from the mails, due to the Nice-Nellies in the post office censorship in Washington, photographs of an octet of naiads lined up at the end of the pool in their wet, clinging, one-piece garments were legit, even though far more revealing.

An appreciable part of the great Florida real estate boom was built upon photographs of girl swimmers used in advertising, and certainly no newspaper ever suffered a drop in circulation when it was able to publish this kind of cheesecake. Even as late as 1932 the publisher of the *News,* Captain Joseph M. Patterson, one of the canniest newspapermen ever to give the public what it wanted, commanded me to instigate and organize a great swimming meet to be held in the public parks, and which I staged first in Central Park and later at Jones Beach, filling our pages for days with girls, girls, girls. And what girls!

Back in 1917, a scattering of young secretaries and career women had formed an organization known as the Women's Swimming Association around a nucleus of a small pool on the Lower East Side under the chaperonage of a remarkable woman, the late Charlotte Epstein, and coached by L. B. de Handley.

From this nucleus there exploded like fireworks the most astonishing and breathtaking collection of scintillating stars who were not only record-breaking championship swimmers and divers, but exquisitely lovely girls who became beauty queens and celebrities equal in fame almost to the reigning royalty of Hollywood. These included such unquestionable pippins as Aileen Riggin, Sybil Bauer, Martha Norelius, Helen Wainwright, Helen Meany, two sensational blondes named Georgia Coleman and Dorothy Poynton, Esther Williams, Josephine McKim and, of course, the one and only Eleanor Holm, the backstroke champion and one of the most beautiful nymphs ever seen in a bathing costume.

Gertrude Ederle, the daughter of the Amsterdam Avenue liverwurst purveyor, joined the Women's Swimming Association when she was thirteen and received all of her early teaching, coaching and training there.

While Trudy was never a member of the W.S.A. beauty chorus, she was far from plain, and her somewhat Teutonic chubbiness, round, dimpled face, and fair-brown bobbed hair were offset by agreeable features and an extraordinarily sweet expression.

She was of average height and not heavily muscled. Seeing her, you would have said there was just not enough girl there to pit against the thrust and slap of angry waves and relentless pressure of the winds prevailing across this tricky, punishing stretch of water. Perhaps her lack of beauty had something to do with her choice of ordeals. Certainly her decision to try to become the first woman to swim the English Channel was one of the most unselfish ones in the annals of sport. She wanted to accomplish this solely to bring a mod-icum of fame to the club she felt had done so much for her. She had not so much as the faintest foreshadowing of the celebrity it would make her personally, or the chance at fortune. And by that decision she touched off one of the supreme fairy tales of our times.

Trudy's specialty had always been long-distance swimming; at the age of fourteen she had already made headlines by beating more than fifty opponents, including Britain's foremost girl swim-mer, in a three-mile international race in New York Bay. A year or so later she swam from the Battery to Sandy Hook in record-breaking time. In 1925 the W.S.A. tapped its meager savings and Charlotte Epstein took Trudy Ederle abroad for her chance at the Channel.

No fanfare attended the attempt and even less its unhappy result. She failed. A turn in the tide accompanied by a sudden squall raised mountainous waves. Little more than half-conscious from nausea, waterlogged from the seas she had swallowed but still fight-ing, her limbs moving with indomitable automatism, she was pulled weeping and struggling from the Channel.

The naming of women as the weaker sex is a cliché which becomes even more frayed around the edges when such an example as that of Gertrude Ederle appears. In the failure this slight girl showed enough courage for a regiment, and displayed a fiber one never would have suspected in such a shy and otherwise ordinary person. Yet, as far as the American press and the rest of the world was concerned there was no story in defeat, and Miss Ederle was just another one of the many who had not swum the Channel.

There were two people, however, who were not convinced by this fiasco. One was Gertrude Ederle herself, and the other Captain Patterson of the *News*.

What brought these widely separated characters together was the fact that Channel swimming was an expensive business. There was transportation abroad and return, a long training period on the spot to become familiar with temperatures, eddies, rip tides, in short the nature of the enemy, the engaging of coaches and the hiring of accompanying craft. The resources of the Women's Swimming Association were insufficient to stand the cost of a second attempt. It was suggested to Captain Patterson that the *News* and the Chicago *Tribune* syndicate step in to back another try in exchange for the exclusive story should she succeed. With the prescience that made him the outstanding publisher he was, Captain Patterson agreed, gambling that if she made it, it would be the event of the year. But I doubt whether even he was aware of how big a story it would turn out to be.

A contract was prepared backing her with expenses, plus salary and a bonus. It called for a big decision on the part of an eighteen-year-old girl, for it meant giving up her amateur standing. Thereafter she would be a professional and denied all further amateur competition. It meant winner take all; loser forfeit everything. The iron determination and stubborn ambition concealed beneath that disarmingly gentle exterior left her no choice. She had challenged the Channel and she was unwaveringly resolved to defeat it. She signed.

We packed her off to Cap Gris Nez in France to train for her final effort. With her went her older sister, Margaret, herself a talented W.S.A. swimmer, Westbrook Pegler, then Chicago *Tribune* columnist and his wife, the late Julie Harpman, crack cityside reporter of the *News*. The coach who joined the party abroad was none other than that Thomas Burgess who, fifteen years before, had been the second to make the Channel crossing; his time, twenty-two hours and thirty-five minutes.

But in 1926 we were still innocents, not disillusioned. We had not yet had our noses rubbed into the fact that the dead of the 1914–18 war had indeed died in vain; that nothing whatsoever had been settled and that the democracies of the world were less safe than ever they had been before. To us virtue had scored a victory over evil in this war; white had beaten black, and we were established more firmly than ever in our belief in the favorite American fairy tale, the triumph of the artless good over the scheming iniquitous.

Such a story almost immediately began to build up at Cap Gris Nez, where the *News*–Chicago *Tribune*–Ederle party set up training quarters and Julie Harpman, covering, began to send home reports of cabals, disloyalties, and downright sabotage. We learned that our tender, guileless Trudy, the first All-American girl to arouse the nation to a frenzy of hysteria, had become enmeshed in a web of intrigue and hostility. In addition to having to contend with the furies of the Channel, it seemed there were those most necessary adjuncts of the bona fide *conte des fées,* ogres galore, and to the palpitating Americano, the best of all villains—furriners.

Neither the French nor the British wanted the girl to succeed in her attempt. As the *News* published Miss Harpman's stories with their unveiled hints of what was going on, the rest of the town and the country as well began to sit up and take notice, aware that being enacted daily before their eyes, as it were, and approaching its climax were all the elements of our most cherished type of dream. That climax failed no one.

The swim began the morning of August 6, the sea fairly calm, the forecast favorable. But weather prediction then was not what it is today. Evening and change of tide brought on a line squall, whipping the Channel into a hell of tide race and battering waves. With the chalk cliffs a few miles off Trudy would gain one yard and then lose two to the elements. Already the captain of the French escort tugboat had tried to break up the swim by bearing across her course until he was forcibly restrained by members of Trudy's party.

At twilight when she had been in the water for twelve hours, fighting fatigue, nausea, and all the devils of the deep against her, Thomas Burgess shouted from the tug that was lurching and wallowing in the heavy seas, "She must come out! But I will not take the responsibility of waiting for a sign from her indicating that she wishes to come out."

Whatever Burgess' motive might have been—perhaps sheer humanity rather than obstruction—it was the voice of authority and experience and once more the success of the adventure hung in the balance.

Someone leaned over the side and yelled into the teeth of the wind, "Trudy, you must come out!"

The girl raised her head out of the water and looked up from the deep trough of black waves, against which her legs were still threshing their six-beat trudgeon as regularly as the thumping of the engines from the accompanying vessel, and asked, "What for?"

With those two words, innocence and pluck triumphed. She battled onward. Two hours or so later Trudy walked out of the sea, up onto the sands of Dover to be met, I am afraid, if my memory is not tricking me, by a British immigration officer who solemnly kept her standing at the water's edge, demanding her passport, an idiocy which I note was repeated only this last summer in the case of another young girl swimmer who had just crossed for the exercise.

During her remarkable effort the story drove all other news off the front pages, and her feat was recorded in millions of words in thousands of columns of newspaper space. There had never been anything like it before.

In order to be the first to present the pictorial record of her accomplishment the *News,* as a picture paper, organized the swiftest and most expensive relay in the history of journalism up to that time. Sets of photographs were placed aboard four express liners departing from Southampton the same day. All of these were scheduled to arrive in New York simultaneously and practically at the same hour, which meant that our competition would have them as soon as we.

One of these ships, however, was a Canadian Pacific liner, an empress steamer, whose destination was Montreal and thus, traveling the great circle route, reached the rim of the North American continent a day before the others. Employing two aircraft, one a sea and the other a land plane, a racing car with a famous driver, a railroad locomotive and an ambulance for the last leg, the photographs in waterproof wrapping were snatched from the ocean by the seaplane, where they were thrown overboard at the mouth of the St. Lawrence River, and then speeded on their relay through fog and dirty weather, to land in the *News* office twelve hours in advance of any others, a clean scoop. When we appeared on the street at eight o'clock that night with the picture of Gertrude Ederle greased, goggled, emerging from the sea near Dover, there was not another such picture in the whole of the United States. However, just as a wry epilogue to the journalism of those times, our competition, the rival *Mirror,* simply photographed our front and back pages and reproduced these in their next edition.

And thereafter all of America lay at her feet. The cornucopia of plenty, beyond the most fantastic dreams, awaited her, ready to be tipped and pour forth gold in an unending shower. She was at that moment the most famous girl in the world and promoters were queuing up, checkbook in hand.

To handle her affairs and sift these offers the family had engaged the services of a smooth and canny lawyer, the late Dudley Field Malone. But alas for Trudy, Mr. Malone was wise and smoothly practiced mainly in the matter of securing Paris divorces for American dollar princesses anxious to shed dull husbands. As an international lawyer this was his specialty; he was tops. But he was far from experienced in the handling of a new kind of celebrity, and particularly one of the caliber of Gertrude Ederle. So dazzled was he by the offers that came pouring in, that instead of confirming the best and bona fide ones accompanied by cash deposits immediately and thus assuring his client a lifetime competency, he held out for more. If so much was being offered while Trudy was still wiping the protective layer of grease from her body and shaking herself dry, how much more would one not be able to glean when she returned to the reception that was building up for her?

One can fault Mr. Malone for greed and inexperience, but it must be remembered that the greed was on behalf of his client. How was he to guess that the very sweetness, innocence, and guilelessness that characterized Gertrude Ederle was to prove his and her undoing and hand us our first jolt as to the inevitability of the happy ending?

For in spite of the furor that attended her achievement and the urging of our reportorial staff that she return immediately to the United States, Trudy remained unconvinced either of her celebrity or the importance of cashing in at once. She was a stubborn girl, too, in her simplicity, and instead of catching the first packet Sandy Hook–bound, she went off to some little village in the Black Forest of Germany to pay a visit to *Grossmutterchen,* her dear old grandmother, whom she had never seen. There she spent some three idyllic and fatal weeks, during which time a second woman swam the English Channel.

Her name was Mrs. Mille Gade Corson, and she was the mother of two children, the first mother, then, to swim the Channel. In those days the word "mother" was still sacred in the U.S., still a tear-jerker *par excellence.* Only a scant ten years before, vaudevillians had been warbling a lyric that went something like: "M-o-t-h-e-r spells mother, the sweetest word in the world to me," leaving not a dry eye in the house.

It took Mother Corson an hour longer to negotiate the twenty-one miles between Gris Nez and the white cliffs of Dover, but it rubbed the edge off Trudy's feat and knocked the bottom out of her market. She was no longer the only woman to have swum the Channel and thereby a salable freak for public exhibition. One by one the would-be entrepreneurs, who had been sitting hat in hand in Mr. Malone's antechamber, slipped away. The gold and silver that would have made her comfortable and independent for the rest of her life, turned to ashes.

Her welcome, when she finally did return, was unstinted, for American hearts then were not fickle, nor were they commercially involved. Her journey through the canyons of downtown Broadway brought forth a most tremendous outpouring of love from the people of New York, and the thunder of her name as they cheered the girl with exalted, tear-stained face, rolled and echoed from side to side of the tall buildings.

And here the fairy tale should have ended with, "And she grew rich, married a prince and lived happily ever after." But that wasn't how it went.

Once, she had named as her heart's desire a red Buick Roadster. As a bonus for her courage, determination and success, Captain Patterson bought her one and it was waiting at the Battery for her when she disembarked from the *Macom*. Her "managers," who were engaged in keeping everyone away from her, would not even allow it to be presented by us, and she only received it late that night before the delicatessen shop on upper Amsterdam Avenue. And in effect it was all she ever got for her pains, beyond some chick-enfeed for one or two endorsements and personal appearances, much of which she used to reimburse the Women's Swimming Association for their original outlay on her behalf.

The cruel buffeting she had taken on the sides of her head during that grueling crawl permanently affected her hearing. Later, during an aquatic performance she hurt her back and spent eight months in a plaster cast. A professional henceforth and forced to earn a living, she took a job as swimming instructress to teach the young and quietly disappeared into the limbo of the forgotten—forgotten, that is, by all but her own friends.

She never complained about those who had mishandled and failed her. She remained wholly unspoiled by the great outpouring of adulation and publicity. She was never bitter, rude, or snobbish, nor wavered in that buoyancy and essential innocence which marked her character. The golden decade reached its end and America entered the crucible of change. Gertrude Ederle, for one, emerged from it a greater human being and one of the true Golden ones of the era.

FIGURE SKATING

Sonja Henie

Bert Randolf Sugar

Bert Randolf Sugar has written fifty-four books, been the editor of The Ring *and* Boxing Illustrated, *and serves as a TV commentator. This selection is taken from* The Sports 100.

The Winter Olympics, conceived by the International Olympic Committee to give competitors from the habitually slighted smaller nations an opportunity to achieve glory on ice and snow, first came of age in 1924 at Chamonix, France. One of the stars of that first Winter Olympics was a little, underage blond doll from Norway with toothsome Viking features who would soon change the face of figure skating.

In a sport then known for its mechanical perfection and scrupulous plainness, eleven-year-old Sonja Henie, unencumbered by reputation or expectation, looked like a little schoolgirl out on a romp as she took the ice. Wearing skates as white as the proverbial piece of linen and a fur-lined skirt as short and serviceable as modern fashion and modesty would allow, the 75-pound wunderkind, knee-high to a herring at five feet, made everyone sit up and take notice. And although she was to finish eighth and last in the field, one of the judges gave her the highest scores in the free-skating portion of the program.

The press also sat up and took notice of this child prodigy, one scribe writing, "Future aspirants for the world title will have to reckon with Sonja Henie of Norway, already a great performer who has every gift—personality, form, strength, speed, and nerve."

Young Sonja went home to Oslo to devote herself to fulfilling that promise. Working everlastingly at improving her style, she grafted on new skills and lyrical movements until, like a panther, she positively purred as she moved about the ice. One of those stylistic improvements included the adoption of innovative short skirts that swirled above her knees in eye-catching colors, all the better to catch the eyes of the fans and the judges as she executed her breathtaking spins.

The alchemy began to pay dividends in the 1926 World Championships, as Sonja, alternately flashing her brown eyes, blond hair, and variety of colors as she whirled around the ice, finished second. The young skater vowed never to finish anywhere but first from that point on. It was a promise she would keep, but not without another addition to her repertoire.

Before the 1927 World Championships, the still-impressionable young Sonja chanced to see the immortal Anna Pavlova perform. Calling the performance "the greatest influence in my life," Sonja incorporated the ballerina's movements into her figure skating, along with choreographic design. With the "Dying Swan" sequence from *Swan Lake* now part of her repertoire, along with balletlike movements and gravity-defying spins, Sonja won the first of her ten straight World Championships.

By the time the Winter Olympics got around to its second change of scenery—this time St. Mortiz—Sonja, by now fifteen years old, had become the darling of the multitudes. Reacting to her girlish charms and veritable smorgasbord of moves—which included difficult double Axel Paulsens, jumps ending in graceful splits, and brilliantly executed spins, twirls, and jumps, as many as nineteen of them—they rent the air with cheers for her every move. The judges, too, reacted to her artistry on ice and, with six of the seven awarding her their first-place votes, she won the first of her gold medals.

Sonja Henie's star had taken on such a stellar brightness by the time the Olympics traveled across the pond to Lake Placid in 1932 that even though the United States was in the throes of the Depression, scalpers were able to ask for, and receive, $50 in hard-earned Roosevelt dollars for a ticket to see the phenomenon with the winning smile. Reporters, too, were overwhelmed by the beautiful five-foot-two, 109-pound youngster they quickly labeled, fittingly, the Pavlova of the Ice. Smitten by her little-girl dimpled good looks and beautiful blond locks, they made her the focal point of story after story. And even though she had difficulty breaking through the language barrier, she still was able to convey the thought that "most always, I win."

And win she did, capturing all seven judges' votes—and her second gold medal.

The young girl-woman—who had been skating for eighteen years and harbored ambitions that included "winning three Olympics and ten World Championships . . . and then the movies"—now postponed, at least until after the 1936 Winter Olympics and the World Championships, her plans for retirement.

Arriving in the little Bavarian resort of Garmisch-Partenkirchen to defend her gold medal for the last time, Sonja felt the pressure—both from within and without, as the police had to be called out to control the crowds demanding to catch a glimpse of the superstar. Those who did get in to watch her in her practice sessions were astounded to see a possessed whirling dervish going through her practice routines, her skates ablur as she spun around as many as eighty times at speeds that frightened the timid of heart.

Her frayed nerves continued on exhibit as well. And when the first day's compulsory figures, showing Sonja only 3.6 points ahead of her heiress apparent, fifteen-year-old Cecelia Colledge of Great Britain, were posted, she did something unknown to the porcelain world of figure skating: she lost her temper. Doing a slow burn, she ripped the offending notice off the board and tore it to shreds.

The girl who was called "the Iron Butterfly," steel-willed and wily, steeled herself not only to do better, but to win. And win she did, her third Olympic gold.

One week later, as per invoice, she won her tenth consecutive World Championship and hung up her skates—at least her amateur ones—to begin her film career. But not before this picture-perfect skater had won three gold medals, ten consecutive World Championships, and a total of 1,473 medals, cups, and trophies and changed the shape—or the "figure"—of her sport.

FIGURE SKATING

Janet Lynn and Dorothy Hamill

Michelle Kaufman

Michelle Kaufman is a sportswriter for the Miami Herald *and has won numerous writing awards for the Associated Press Sports Editors Association. This piece was included in* Nike Is a Goddess, *edited by Lissa Smith.*

In 1971, a blond pixie with a radiant smile spurred a dramatic change in the way figure skating was judged. Janet Lynn, an Illinois schoolgirl, would go down in history as the most memorable skater never to win an Olympic medal. Lynn could never master compulsory school figures, a tedious portion of the competition that accounted for 50 percent of the final score and required skaters to etch six of forty-one possible figures on a patch of ice in an empty rink. Judges would then crouch down and measure the figures with rulers, giving points for precision of carvings, which the television viewing audience never saw.

Lynn won five consecutive national championships from 1969 to 1973. Her powerful and creative free-skating programs mesmerized audiences, but her mediocre school figures always dragged down her marks. Before the 1972 Olympics in Sapporo, Japan, Lynn graced the cover of *Newsweek* magazine, and inside was the following prediction: "Lynn is a virtual cinch to enchant the Sapporo audiences with her dazzling free skating—and almost equally certain to fall short of the points accumulated by Austria's Beatrix Schuba in the dull compulsory competition."

Lynn floated across the ice, danced into her jumps, fell into a flying sit spin, spun around on the ice in a sitting position, smiling through it all, and the Japanese crowd was silent—its greatest display of honor. But the gangly, clumsy Trixie Schuba of Austria had built up a huge lead with near-flawless compulsory figures, and she won the gold medal despite a seventh-place finish in the free-skating event. Even the generally polite Japanese fans jeered at the decision.

A year later, responding to public outcry about Lynn's bronze and the scoring system, the International Skating Union introduced the short program and reduced the importance of school figures. Skaters would be required to complete seven elements during a short program (two minutes), and that would count for 20 percent of the total score. Figures would drop to 40 percent, and the long program would be worth 40 percent. School figures decreased in value as the years went on and were finally abolished in 1991.

Lynn stayed in the sport that 1973 season and signed a $1.45 million deal with the Ice Follies, making her the world's highest-paid female athlete at the time.

By 1976 the tumult of the sixties had subsided; Americans were celebrating the bicentennial and seemed ready again to embrace traditional values and clean-cut entertainment. Television and the emphasis on free skating over compulsory figures made figure skating more exciting for fans.

Enter Dorothy Hamill, an insecure, nearsighted nineteen-year-old who was born in Chicago, Illinois, and grew up in Riverside, Connecticut, near Greenwich. Her father, Chalmers Hamill, was an executive at Pitney Bowes. Hamill received her first pair of skates as a Christmas present when she was eight years old. She tried them out on a neighborhood frozen pond and was jealous of the kids who could skate backward. She begged her mother, Carol, for group lessons and before long was receiving high praise from her instructors.

She hired a personal coach, and in 1976 she was ready to show the world what she had learned. Wearing thick glasses, she conquered compulsory figures at the Olympics in Innsbruck, Austria, and then ditched the glasses for uncomfortable contact lenses to perform a near-flawless free skate to win the gold medal. Unlike Henie, Hamill had neither the money nor the personality for flashy dresses, so she wore a simple $75 pink knit dress sewn by a friend's mother—a far cry from the $13,000 designer dress Nancy Kerrigan would wear eighteen years later.

A television audience of millions fell in love with Hamill, the girl with the perky wedge haircut. Skating fans were further endeared to her when she had to squint to see her scores (eight 5.8s and a 5.9 in technical merit and all 5.9s in artistic impression). In the months following the Olympics, women and girls everywhere asked their hairdressers for Dorothy Hamill wedge cuts, and the hairdo became as popular as she was.

The public adulation overwhelmed Hamill; she was never comfortable with her celebrity status. From the time she began skating in second grade, she was shy and unsure of herself. She frequently burst into tears before competitions and suffered long battles with stage fright and loss of confidence. "She is critical of herself to the point of being negative," said her coach, Carlo Fassi. "I keep telling her if you want to convince the judges that you're the best, you must first convince yourself."

Hamill's fragile psyche was evident during a world competition in Munich in 1975. Unhappy with scores awarded a West German skater before her, the fans booed. Hamill, about to start her free skate, thought the boos were for her; tears streamed down her face, and she left the ice. When she realized her mistake, she smiled shyly and went back to center ice to begin her routine.

Despite her insecurities, Hamill always appeared confident once the music began. A 1974 *Sports Illustrated* article describing her U.S. title–winning performance said: "Her assurance and speed made the competitors who preceded her appear to have skated in slow motion. Her high, clean double lutz came not after but out of a dazzling display of footwork so neatly accomplished that the judges might have missed it."

Hamill's most famous move was a delayed axel jump in which she seemed to hang in the air before completing the one-and-a-half revolutions. She also prided herself on high-speed spins. At the time, her moves looked impressive—but the world had no idea how much more athletic female skaters would become. Hamill was the last Olympic champion to win without a triple jump. (Two decades later, teenagers Michelle Kwan and Tara Lipinski each included seven triple jumps in their long programs.) Hamill's Olympic gold-medal routine probably would not even earn a U.S. junior title in 1998.

Upon her return from the Olympics, Hamill's hometown of Riverside held a parade in her honor and renamed the town's ice rink after her. Neighbors remembered her as one of dozens of young girls who took up skating as a hobby. More than 100,000 children take group skating lessons in the United States, and hundreds of those develop such a passion that they begin taking private lessons. From those hundreds, the best twenty-five or so in each category (novice, junior, senior) advance to the regional championships. The best four from each region make it to sectionals, and then a field of about twenty make it to the national championship.

Hamill had been through all the ranks and finally reached the pinnacle of her sport—that glorious, spine-tingling moment listening to the national anthem from atop the Olympic medal podium. She was asked to give speeches and pose for thousands of photos, and she immediately signed with an agent. A female figure skating champion, especially one with a squeaky-clean image, stood to become a millionaire. The Ideal Toy Company manufactured Barbie-like Dorothy Hamill dolls, and little girls all over the United States rushed to toy stores to get them.

One of those little girls was Kristi Yamaguchi, who would mention the doll when she won the 1992 Olympic gold medal sixteen years later. Yamaguchi was born with deformed feet that required braces and corrective shoes, and when doctors suggested she take up a sport, she remembered Hamill and chose figure skating. Though Yamaguchi was one of the most athletic and artistic skaters of all time and a fan favorite on post-Olympic skating tours, she was not swarmed with endorsement deals. Some marketing experts surmised that corporate America was not ready for a Japanese-American to endorse their products. But over the next few years, Yamaguchi would reap benefits from her gold medal. She made several hundred thousand dollars performing for professional ice shows, coauthored the book *Figure Skating for Dummies,* and was named spokesperson for the 2002 Winter Olympics in Salt Lake City.

Hamill signed a $1-million-a-year contract with the Ice Capades in 1976. She would do thirteen shows a week, eighteen to twenty-three weeks per year. She moved to Hollywood, California, and married Dean Paul Martin, the son of Dean Martin, at a lavish wedding attended by many of the biggest film and TV stars. Tabloids chronicled her every move, and the mercurial Hamill didn't respond well. Her marriage to Martin ended in divorce after two years, and in 1987 she married Ken Forsythe, a sports physician and former member of the Canadian Olympic ski team. They purchased the Ice Capades but sold it a few years later. In 1995 Hamill and Forsythe divorced, and in 1996, Hamill filed for bankruptcy.

Michelle Kwan

Edward Z. Epstein

Edward Z. Epstein has written biographies of Mia Farrow, Paul Newman and Joanne Woodward, and Lucille Ball. He is a dedicated figure skater and former Middle Atlantic States Novice Champion. These selections were taken from his book Born to Skate: The Michelle Kwan Story.

This was the moment.

Eyes closed, she lowered her head and clasped her hands tightly as though in prayer. She was deeply focused—this, after all, was the fulfillment of a dream, an incredible adventure.

Here she was, fifteen-years-old, at the highest level of figure-skating competition. All the discipline and training, dedication and sacrifice had been leading up to this.

Her skates were laced properly, with just the right amount of tension. She knew she must *concentrate, concentrate, concentrate*—focus on one element at a time, must not permit herself to be overwhelmed by everything that has to be done. . . .

And she mustn't forget to *breathe!*

Poised to skate her long program in the 1996 World Championships, Michelle was on the ice, standing at the barrier of the rink with her coach, Frank Carroll. They were waiting for the announcer to call her name.

China's nineteen-year-old Chen-Lu, the previous year's world champion, had just delivered a stunning performance, and the judges rewarded her accordingly, including two perfect 6.0s for artistic merit. *Was there still a chance for Michelle to win?*

True, two nights earlier Michelle had won the short program (Chen-Lu was second), but the "short" required less energy, less skating time. It was the strongest short Michelle had ever skated; she had worked "really hard on artistry, every finger, every movement," she later recalled.

And it had paid off—she received first place from seven of the nine judges. Tonight's long program, however, would count for two-thirds of the final score. In addition to Chen-Lu, Michelle had seventeen-year-old European champion Irina Slutskaya breathing down her neck. In third place, the Russian was a strong favorite with the crowd and judges.

To Kwan's surprise and dismay, one of her childhood idols, Japanese champion Midori Ito, plagued by health problems and the pressure of competition, had been having a disastrous competition. She fell on her triple axel in the short, and wasn't able to complete a much-simpler jump combination. The former (1989) World Champion was in sixth place coming into the long.

Kwan's fellow U.S. teammates, Tara Lipinski and Tonia Kwiatkowski, weren't doing well either. Lipinski, thirteen-years-old, fell twice and was in twenty-third place after the short. Kwiatkowski, at twenty-five, one of the oldest competitiors in the vent, was in ninth place despite a very good performance. ("Tonia is the crime of the competition. Everyone is appalled," exclaimed former Canadian champion and 1976 Olympic Bronze Medalist, Toller Cranston.)

Figure-skating competition—could anyone really figure it out?

Everyone knew that winning the short merely put a skater in position to win the vent. Many a competitor has won the short and lost the Gold Medal.

That night, Michelle was all too aware that a figure skater could never take anything for granted—quite the contrary. Every time one stepped onto the ice to compete, one was vulnerable.

Kwan was as finely trained as a fighter pilot, a vibrant young athlete in tune with her body. She felt confident. ("Confidence is a fleeting thing—treasure it when you have it," observed former World Champion, Kurt Browning.)

Michelle had proven herself to be a skater with that some-thing extra that could thrill a crowd—provided that tension and nerves didn't sabotage the performance.

"Ladies and gentlemen, representing the United States of America, Michelle Kwan!"

Over the applause, Michelle listened intently to the final few words of instruction and encouragement from Frank Carroll. She'd practiced her program countless times. Performed all the elements successfully. Today was no different—simply a repeat of what she had done so many times before. Carroll told her that she had to believe in herself, that she could do it. She was one of the best skaters in the world; he knew she could do it. She knew she could, too, and she would!

She nodded in acknowledgment of the applause, relaxed her shoulders, skated to center ice, and assumed her opening stance, in itself a moment of grace and beauty. Her striking costume provided just the right touch of drama and color. The crowd grew silent—expectant.

For Michelle, *this was the moment.* Would she seize it and make it her own? The seductive opening strains of Miklos Roska's, *Salome,* filled the arena as she launched into her program.

A year earlier, Michelle had been preceived in the skating world's corridor of power as too young—"cute" but "still a girl"—to merit seroius consideration for world-championship status. So her coach had devised a bold, controversial plan to offset this dilemma: he would present the skater as the biblical femme fatale who performed the *Dance of the Seven Veils* for King Herod in exchange for the decapitated head of John the Baptist!

Kwan's father, Danny, hadn't been comfortable with this idea—was it seemly for his strictly reared youngest daughter to wear obvious make-up and reveal her midriff? He didn't like to see her put any make-up on at all; in his view, skating was a sport, and he wanted "a sport to be a sport."

But he also wanted his daughter to become World Champion, and reasoned that "she has to become a young lady sometime." However she appeared, Michelle was "still a good citizen and a good student, and that's all I'm concerned about."

Besides, her father knew that Michelle was an intelligent young woman, one who kept things in perspective. She was ripe for the challenge of an image change, and Carroll's plan appealed to her sense of drama.

"When I was little, I always wanted to tell a story with my performance," she recalled. Still, she had found the tale of seductress Salome somewhat shocking.

Beyond the makeup, the metamorphosis included sophisticated costuming and coiffure. Michelle's signature ponytail, an emblem of many perky teenagers, had disappeared, her hair swept up into a new sleek head-hugging hairdo.

"It's good to have another look. It's very different for me to play something unusual and exotic," she reasoned. Plus, it enabled her to break through her natural reserve, to allow her imagination to ignite, her inner feelings to be expressed through her art.

For this performance, Michelle didn't skate the role of Salome; she *lived* it. It was there inside her, stored up and waiting to be turned loose. Skating is an art when it is made an art . . . and that is what Kwan accomplished on this evening.

She paced herself perfectly, letting "air" in at certain moments to enable the audience to savor key movements. At one point she had to do some fast thinking, because when her triple-triple-toe-loop combination (the only one in the competition) came up, she did a triple-double combination instead.

Immediately the contingency plan clicked into gear: instead of a double axel at the end, she'd have to put in a triple toe, always a difficult move but even more so at such a moment, since she'd be exhausted.

It was very hard for me, after all those great skaters . . . I was near the end . . . I had to put it all on the line . . .

The moment came. Not only was the jump performed, it was completed *powerfully,* with spring, height, and perfect form in the air and on the landing. A blockbuster last impression to leave with the judges.

A roar of approval boomed from the audience; Michelle seemed in a daze. She'd been mentally prepared for her performance, but nothing could have prepared her for the excitement she felt when it was over.

"I'm speechless," she finally said.

Could she have skated any better? She didn't think so.

Michelle had once been asked if she thought of herself as fire or ice. Her reply: "*The wind*—I'm just gliding over the ice, watching everyone skating, seeing the crowd. I'm just flying everywhere. . . ."

Bobbie Rosenfeld

Barbara Stewart

Barbara Stewart is the author of She Shoots . . . She Scores: A Complete Guide to Women's Hockey *and a regular contributor to* Hockey Illustrated. *This piece was included in* Nike Is a Goddess, *edited by Lissa Smith.*

The 1920s were the golden age for women's hockey in North America. By now, there were hundreds of senior amateur, college, and junior-level teams and leagues—there was even a national championship, reminiscent of the Stanley Cup—and female players were earning public attention for the first time. However, because women's hockey lacked the same kind of media profile as the men's game, those women who wanted to carve themselves a niche in the world of sport had to turn elsewhere to get noticed. Canada's Bobbie Rosenfeld best exemplifies the era. As a standout athlete, weaned on a diet of hockey, she had to turn to track and field to make her mark in the public imagination.

Born in Russia in 1905, Fanny "Bobbie" Rosenfeld arrived in Canada one year later. Her parents settled in, fittingly, Barrie, Ontario, a port city at the westernmost point of Lake Simcoe. Early on, Bobbie proved herself to be a gifted athlete, excelling at half a dozen sports: hockey, softball, tennis, golf, basketball, and track. It's been said that the best way to sum up her sports accomplishments is to say that she wasn't good at swimming. She was a born athlete. Although not tall, no bigger than five feet five inches, nor particularly heavy, she was wiry and muscular. She had a curious look to her; her head was slightly too large for her body, and she wore her hair in a close-cropped, flapper style, even years after it had been fashionable. But perhaps her most striking feature was her eyes: dark, focused, burning with intensity. She was famous for her competitive flair, not that she was physically aggressive with her opponents—she was always gracious, on and off the playing field—but because of the way she gave her all. While other athletes gained a popular following through their colorful personalities, Bobbie remained earnest and relatively low-key. But it was this intensity that appealed to the public.

Bobbie first caught the public eye in 1920 when she was barely fifteen. She was playing in a softball tournament with her team when someone convinced her to enter an exhibition hundred-yard dash. She won the race, unaware that she had beaten out Rosa Grosse, then Canadian champion in the event and an eventual world-record holder. Grosse was furious—and the two athletes remained rivals throughout their careers—but Bobbie's win caught the eye of many of the country's sporting elite. From that race, her fame spread, and soon after, she moved to Toronto—Canada's economic and social heart—to take a job in a chocolate factory and compete at the highest levels possible in track, hockey, softball, and tennis.

By 1922 she had a national reputation. She was considered by many to be the finest sprinter in Canada and was well on her way to being a world-class runner. Before she hit her twentieth birthday, she set the world record in the 220-yard event: twenty-six seconds flat. But that honor was taken away a short time later when officials discovered that the track was exactly one yard short of the international standard. But Bobbie persevered. A few months later she helped her company-sponsored track team, the Patterson Athletic Cub, win the Ontario Ladies Track and Field Championships, the most prestigious women-only sporting event in the province. In a single afternoon, the club came in first in the 220-yard race, discus, long jump, and 120-yard hurdles and had second-place finishes in the javelin and the 100-yard dash. Not bad, considering Bobbie was the only entrant on the Patterson team. The papers heralded her accomplishment, but she was only warming up.

Fittingly, the highlight of this tremendous athlete's career came at the 1928 Olympics in Amsterdam. These were the first Olympic Games in which women were allowed to compete in track-and-field events, and the change did not go unnoticed. Pope Pius XI himself denounced the move, believing women unsuited for this sort of intense athletic competition, while the founder of the modern Olympics, Baron de Coubertin, personally protested women infringing on the "solemn periodic manifestation of male sports." But Bobbie Rosenfeld didn't seem to care one way or the other what anybody thought. This was her chance to shine on the world stage, and she wasn't going to let the opportunity slip through her fingers. She made her own way to the Olympic trials in Halifax, on Canada's eastern coast, competing in shorts and a YMCA T-shirt she'd borrowed from her brother, and her father's socks for good luck. The socks must have worked: She set Canadian records in the 200, the discus, and the broad jump. Successful at the trials, she moved on to the real thing, the Amsterdam Olympics. Her first event was the 100 meters. It was a close race, with four of the six runners only a few inches apart at the finish line. Bobbie finished neck-and-neck with the American sprinter Betty Robinson, but the judges awarded the gold medal to Robinson, and, under the protests of the Canadian coach, Bobbie Rosenfeld took second. Her next event was the 400-meter relay, which Bobbie and her teammates Ethel Smith, Myrtle Cook and Florence Bell won handily, in 48.4 seconds, a record that was to last until the 1950s. Bobbie might have been content going home with a gold and a silver medal, but she saved her greatest triumph for the end. Though she was known primarily as a short-distance runner, Bobbie's coach inserted her into the 800-meter event at the last minute. He didn't expect her to win; he just wanted her to offer some encouragement to Jean Thompson, the seventeen-year-old runner who'd been trained for the event. Running ninth in the final stretch, Bobbie pushed until she was right on Thompson's tail. The younger runner was starting to falter, but Bobbie paced her on to finish a respectable fourth. Bobbie Rosenfeld was fifth, although it was obvious to anyone who watched the race that she could have passed her teammate at any time. The race was in controversy. Some of the runners reportedly collapsed at the finish line, overcome with exhaustion, although other reports observe that the women were no more tired than the men at the end of the event. In any case, many critics pointed to the race's aftermath as proof that it was unsafe for women to compete in track and field; the "weaker sex" simply couldn't take the strain, they said. Bobbie disagreed. "Any girl who satisfactorily passes a medical examination and who accepts and practices the correct methods of training is capable of running the 800 meters," she told a reporter from the Canadian news magazine *Maclean's*. Then she added with characteristic understatement, "Even though I did not train specifically for it, there was no undue effort required to enable me to finish." The detractors won the day, however, and the women's 800-meter race was banned from the Olympics until the 1960 Games in Rome.

While Bobbie Rosenfeld could claim ownership of Olympic medals, world records and the mastery of half a dozen sports, she never stopped playing her favorite sport, hockey. She'd learned the game on the outdoor rinks and frozen ponds back home in Barrie, honing her skills—as did most of the best female players in the sport—by playing alongside the boys on the rinks and ponds in unorganized games. Throughout the 1920 and into the early 1930s, before arthritis ended her career, Bobbie was the driving force behind the Toronto Patterson Pats, one of the first dominant forces in women's senior amateur hockey. By the 1920s women's hockey was well established in Canada and even in parts of the United States: the

University of Minnesota had as many as three women's hockey teams at one time. In 1924 the Ladies' Ontario Hockey Association (LOHA) was formed by a group of senior amateur women hockey players, including Rosenfeld, and that league became the model for the dozens of women's teams that competed for local, regional, and, eventually, national championships. But despite the widespread acceptance of the sport, a sense of novelty persisted. There was a pervasive notion that athletic competition was somehow masculine, and commentators bent over backward to stress that these female hockey players were just "regular" girls. The result was a kind of coy irony that undermined the sport. "The Ottawa lassies who crossed sticks with the Patterson's Pats looked more like a school girls' team," wrote Alexandrine Gibb, a former athlete herself who was female sports reporter for the *Toronto Star,* in her coverage of the 1929 Ladies' Ontario Hockey Association finals. "They must have picked all the beauties from in and around Ottawa and taught them how to play hockey. From the tiny Olive Barr in goal, with her fair hair and innocent, child-like face, to the tallest defense girl, they were all easy to look at," she continued. This kind of patronization persisted, despite the fact that the best women players at the time, and this certainly includes Bobbie Rosenfeld, could have easily earned a place on top-level men's teams. The men simply wouldn't allow it. Ability or not, when it came to hockey, the sexes were segregated.

During the 1920s and 1930s several female sportswriters, most of whom were former athletes themselves, had weekly and even daily columns in Canada. Phyllis Griffiths wrote for the *Toronto Telegram,* Bobbie Rosenfeld had a daily in the *Globe,* Alexandrine Gibb wrote for the *Toronto Star* and Myrtle Cook wrote for the *Montreal Star.* And they all wrote about the most popular women's sport: hockey. Today the lack of publicity, media coverage, and recognition of female hockey players by sports editors is striking; the sports section regularly reports on the NHL and every minor league going, but never carries regular summaries of the Central Collegiate

Women's Ice Hockey Association in the United States or Canadian senior leagues like the modern-day Ontario Women's Hockey Association.

Why has women's hockey consistently been overshadowed by the men's game? There are undoubtedly a lot of complicated answers to that question, but perhaps Rosenfeld personified many of the issues. Her very presence in the game was something of a novelty. Certainly her name brought people in to watch hockey games, but her fame had come not through her prowess on the ice but through her achievements on the track, particularly at the 1928 Olympics. The fact that her reputation transcended the sport, and that her fame as an athlete eclipsed that of virtually any amateur male athlete in Canada at the time, probably left some people with a sour taste in their mouth. And it didn't help that she was rather openly, for the time, a lesbian; in the eyes of some, this did not "set a very good example" for young hockey players. Worst of all was that Bobbie played the game like a man; she was physically and mentally aggressive—not one to break the rules but the kind of player who didn't slow down when someone got in her way. In short, she understood the nature of the sport completely. In terms of strategy, hockey is a team sport like no other. In some sports—baseball, and even football to a certain extent—individual players have their personal territory clearly defined: the pitcher has the mound; the quarterback has a place secure behind the offensive line. But hockey is an entirely fluid game, a team sport that relies on individual players to constantly adjust, restore, and maintain their proper position. The aggressive player has a competitive edge; she can get in position for a shot on net, and she can play an effective defensive role by pushing, bumping, and outpowering her opponent. The result is that while other sports could easily be modified to fit the more socially accepted image of the passive female athlete, it's impossible to change or to "tone down" hockey without changing its very nature. Rosenfeld understood that and used her own competitive intensity to its full advantage.

Bobbie Rosenfeld's domination of the sport of women's hockey was to be short-lived. She led the Toronto Patterson Pats to numerous LOHA and national championships, but within a year of her triumphs at the Amsterdam Olympics, she was stricken with crippling arthritis. She spent eight months in bed and another full year on crutches. To some, it was further proof that women simply weren't built for the athletic life. But, always the competitor, Bobbie fought back. By 1932 she was back playing the sports she loved, earning the hitting title in her softball league and winning honors as the top player in the LOHA. Her illness had taken its toll, though. She was noticeably weaker and played under constant pain. When questioned about her medical problems, she would just shrug her shoulders. In 1933 the arthritis flared up again and Bobbie Rosenfeld was forced to retire from sports once and for all. She took a job on the other side of the fence, as a sports reporter for the *Toronto Globe,* and kept her hand in the game she loved by becoming a prominent hockey coach—helping her beloved Patterson Pats to maintain their place as a dominant force in women's hockey—and league organizer. Her achievements were not forgotten. In 1949, sixteen years from the last time she shot a puck or nailed a home run, sportswriters named her Canada's Woman Athlete of the Half Century. It was her proudest moment, capping a career that paved the way for Canadian women athletes to come.

Elisabeth Nagele

Red Smith

Red Smith wrote for the Herald Tribune *and the* New York Times *and is considered by this editor as the finest sports stylist of the 20th century. He died in 1982. This selection is taken from his column in the* New York Herald Tribune.

Innsbruck, 1964.

No doubt about it, said a guy in the Winter Olympics press center, a story had to go with this. He had heard that on the Swiss *luge* team there was a forty-two-year-old mother of five whose maternal duties did not deter her from swooshing down Alps in mile-a-minute lunges through a twisting trough of sheer ice while stretched supine on a toy sled.

The guy had been told that her fifth child was born only four months after she won the world championship three years ago. So apparently she'd had a stowaway aboard, although there is no doubles event for gals in *luge* racing.

If this was true and if there was anything to that theory about prenatal influence, then the chances were that by now Mom's littlest darling would be faster on a sled than Kris Kringle with all his bloody reindeer.

Obviously this called for investigation, not in a prying spirit but only to advance the science of eugenics. After all, in the Kentucky bluegrass horsemen breed for speed.

Well, sir, it was a pity. The story had everything except the virtue of truth.

Run to earth in Olympic Village, Elisabeth Nagele turned out to be a hausfrau, all right, but a hausfrau of thirty, not forty-two, a dewy and tasty thirty. She is a compact Swiss bonbon only five-feet-two with green eyes, rose-petal skin, a shy, sweet smile and long auburn hair clasped at the back and just allowed to ripple.

Wrapped from throat to shapely ankle in a snowsuit of fire-engine red, she looked like something under the tree on Christmas morning.

With one of the girl guides they have around here interpreting, the question about junior's prenatal competition was put as discreetly as possible.

Nein, said Frau Nagele, sweetly but firmly. She won the world championship in February 1961. The baby wasn't born until December.

Ah, well. The conversation continued on less clinical grounds.

Frau Nagele's husband, Robert, is coach of the Swiss *luge* team, or *rodelbund*. Growing up in the village of Schiers, Elisabeth went belly-flopping on these devilish contraptions as all Alpine kids do, but she didn't see competition until 1955 when she married and moved to the winter sports resort of Davos.

She dug the racket, which proves there is no accounting for a lady's tastes.

The *luge* racer, new to the Olympics this year, stretches himself spine down and feet foremost on his tiny steel-shod sled. Zooming and clattering down the chute, he steers by dropping a shoulder to shift his weight.

The sled leaps and bucks and plunges, bashing his crash helmet against the ice. He wears thickly padded gloves. If he should graze the wall without this protection it would be look, Ma, no fingers.

It was on one of these infernal things that a member of the British team was killed before the Games started.

Still, little Mrs. Nagele loves it. Six years after her first ride down a racing course she was champion of the world. Her eldest daughter—there are three girls and two boys, aged two to eight—is already first-rate.

Four times Frau Nagele went tearing through the hairpin turns on the lower slopes of Patscherkofel to finish twelfth in the first Olympic competition.

"Nicht gut," she said.

She rolled up her right sleeve to show technicolor bruises along the inner side of the elbow. A few days ago, she said, the muscles were swollen clear out to here. She had mashed the arm on a practice run and the pain handicapped her. Made her, she was afraid, a mite too cautious in competition.

"What did the coach say about your twelfth place?"

"He is not satisfied," Frau Nagele said. She made a wifely little snoot.

Picabo Street

Jean Weiss

Jean Weiss is the former editor of Women's Sports & Fitness *magazine. This selection was excerpted from her piece, "Rhapsody in White," in* Nike Is a Goddess, *edited by Lissa Smith.*

During the 1990s, skiing's future began to take shape with the rise of superstar Picabo Street. Street wasn't just a skier. She was a personality who became women's skiing's poster girl. To Street, her unprecedented wins were all part of some larger plan. "There are times when I'm really shocked and times when I'm like, 'This is what was meant for me; this is my destiny,'" she told *Skiing* magazine in 1995.

Street was born on April 3, 1971, in Triumph, Idaho, to Stubby and Dee Street. Classic 1960s holdovers, they named her Baby Girl Street, but since the government wasn't enthralled about generic names on passports, Stubby and Dee picked the name Picabo, which to the Native American Sho-Ban tribe located nearby is supposed to mean "shining waters." Street lived an unconventional childhood. She traveled through Central America with her family, took long domestic cross-country road trips, grew her own food, chopped wood, and was raised in a house with no television. The one convention was this: Like most children growing up outside of Sun Valley, she began skiing at an early age. She didn't start racing until her high school formed a varsity team, but the five-foot-seven-inch Street, who weighs in at 158 pounds, was aggressive and fast. When she made the U.S. ski team a year later, she was relying primarily on natural talent, winning the national junior downhill and Super G titles in 1988 at the age of sixteen.

Natural talent and nothing else began to look like laziness. In 1990 she was kicked off the U.S. ski team when she showed up for training unprepared and out of shape. She got her act together, rejoined the team, and in four years, between 1991 and 1995, rose from sixty-fifth to eighteenth to eighth to first rank in world downhill. Then she won her silver medal in downhill at the Winter Olympics in Lillehammer. Her Olympic medal was followed by a string of victories at the World Cup during the 1994–95 season. After winning six out of nine downhill races, she became the first American woman to win the World Cup title.

Following a successful 1996 World Cup season, Street began training for the 1998 Games in Nagano, Japan. Then tragedy struck. In 1997, during a training run at Vail, Colorado, she spun out of control and tore the anterior cruciate ligament in her left knee. It's rare for an athlete to compete again at top level following such an injury. Yet with the help of the doctors at Vail's famous Stedman Clinic, as well as her trainers, Street believed that with aggressive rehabilitation she could regain her position and make it to the Nagano games one year away. It was a crapshoot, which she undertook with characteristic gusto. Just months before the Games, her comeback was on course. Then she knocked herself unconscious during a crash in Are, Sweden. Things looked bleak to everyone, but not to Street. Considering the complications, her hairbreadth 1998 Olympic victory was all the sweeter.

At the 1998 Olympics held in Nagano, Japan, Picabo Street ripped through the course of the Super G to win a gold medal by $\frac{1}{100}$ of a second, a margin as thin as the hot-melon-colored suit she was wearing. The victory was stunning: not just because of Street's celebrity, or because the Super G is usually her weakest event, or because it's rare for an athlete to remain a top-level competitor after destroying a knee as Street had done only a year earlier. The victory was important because it showed how far American women's skiing had come. As Street stood on the podium to collect her medal, radiating all the fresh-scrubbed confidence you'd expect from a young woman who believes in past lives and auras and her inalienable right to excel, she earmarked the progress from a time when American women were competitors but not competitive to now, when they are first-place contenders. From the original American Olympic women's ski squad in 1936, when the well-bred Elizabeth Woolsey bested her teammates to place only fourteenth among the international lineup, to this: sixties love child Street gathering up her gold medallion. It was clear that in the United States, women's skiing had come a long way.

Gail Doughty

Lars Anderson and Chad Millman

Lars Anderson works for Sports Illustrated. *Chad Millman is an associate editor at* ESPN Magazine. *This piece was taken from their book* Pickup Artists.

Gail Doughty walks onto the basketball court at 11th and Lombard in South Philly. Soft leather Reeboks, bought that morning, cushion her feet. She wears flame-red nylon pants that billow when the wind blows, exposing a neon yellow beeper hanging from her pocket. Rings adorn three fingers on each hand, and gold hoop earrings dangle from her ears. She looks more like a showcase for everything you can buy at the mall than a basketball player looking for a game.

At one end of the concrete court stands Don Levon, a North Philly guy who has apparently lost his way, shooting by himself with an underinflated ball. His shirt is off. His shoes are untied. Slim blue jeans cling to his thighs. His long, striated muscles have the look of someone who has spent years hustling games on the asphalt. Gail, however, appears undaunted. As she approaches, he flashes her a look that says, "You don't belong here." But she just smiles, her sweet round face hinting devilishly that she knows how to handle a bonehead like Don. She has played here before, with Philly's best: Mo

117

Cheeks, formerly of the 76ers, ex-Villanova star Jason Lawson, former LaSalle All-American and NBA player Lionel Simmons. Gail has always held her own, and skinny Don Levon with the shaved head will not be a problem.

"Can I shoot wichya?" Gail asks.

"What?" he answers incredulously.

"You mind if I join you?" she repeats, with less softness in her voice this time—more a declarative statement than a question.

As Gail says this, she grabs a rebound just outside the lane and, in a fluid motion, dribbles through her legs, takes one step, and lays the ball back in the hoop, tapping her fingers on the bottom of the backboard on her way back down.

You can always tell a basketball player by the first touch of the ball. The first shot means nothing. Any fool can sink a 10-footer. It's the way a player corrals a pass, grabs a rebound or just picks a ball up off the ground like it's the most natural thing in the world. That is the telling thing. These are the most minute of first impressions, unnoticed by those who aren't players themselves but impossible to ignore by those who are. The player controls the ball with grace, spinning it in the palms, leisurely hoisting shots or dribbling with nonchalance. Such moves say, I've done this before and I've done it well. Those who haven't just look clumsy. With her one layup and without uttering another word, Gail has let Don know that she is a player. Confused, all he can do is shake his head and say, "Yeah, you can shoot."

Of course she can shoot. And she can dribble and pass and rebound and, occasionally, she can play defense. Thirty-three years old, and Gail can do just about everything she did at twenty-three. Gail is a product of the playground, running on the courts at 11th and Lombard or 23rd and Reed or the rec center at 34th and Haverford since she could tie her shoes. If she wasn't going to the court, her grandma wouldn't let her out of the house. It was too dangerous in Philly—South Philly, West Philly, North Philly—to let little Gail walk the streets with nothing to do. She would play ball with the girls, although she'd rather play with the boys. That's how you got better. Take an elbow to the kidney—that's how you made a name for yourself around the city. No respect comes from earning a spot on the girls' All-Public League first team.

"Even the simple games, horse or whatever, if you win against the guy it builds confidence," says Doughty. "Besides, when you win, that's just one more guy who believes there are some girls who can compete."

So when Don Levon tires of the monotony of passing the ball back to Gail after she sinks yet another twenty-footer, he innocently asks, "You wanna play 21?" Gail can't help but smile. Another convert coming up.

The Philly rules for 21 are simple: Sink a shot from the top of the key for 2 points, make a rebounded shot for 1 point and then back up to the top of the key. For a few minutes neither player seems to have the range to consistently sink a shot from the top of the key. Their legs seem tired, the wind is swirling, and a bunch of kids playing hooky on another court keep letting their ball interfere. Then Don breaks the seal on the basket: 2 points. He grabs his rebound off the make and sinks the layup: 1 point. He goes through this routine three times. Before Gail has the ball again, she is losing 9-0 and Don is holding a bony hand up to his mouth to hide his snickering.

They begin trading three-point plays. Don 12, Gail 3; Don 15, Gail 6; Don 18, Gail 9. Then Gail gets hot. She reels off six in a row. Don then nails a two-pointer but chokes on his layup. He is ahead 20-15. Both players are screaming with each miss, contorting their bodies to direct the ball through the hoop. A small crowd has formed around the fence along 11th Street as Gail lines up for a chance to win. Trailing 20-18, she lets fly from the top of the key. If the net had been hanging by more than a shred of twine Gail's jumper would have made a beautiful sound as it went through the hoop. But the soft wisp of the dangling net says enough: game over. After Gail casually sinks her layup, Don grabs the ball and leaves. As Don Levon walks away, he mutters, "Nice game."

When Gail reaches the exit to the court, a man with a nappy beard yells out, "There she is, Miss Gail, still conquering the court." Gail laughs and mutters, mostly to herself, "Around South Philly, everyone knows me. I just can't seem to get known anywhere else."

Loneliness and frustration are the reward for a legendary player destined to be considered among the greatest who never made it. That status has long been the exclusive domain of men. Guys like Earl Manigault, "Helicopter" Knowings and Lamar Mundane have yearned for a shot at the big time, at the million-dollar contracts, the crowds, the women, the cars and—most alluring—the fame. Instead, they were condemned to obscurity while their legends continue to grow years after their last airwalk or thirty-foot jumper.

Now the kings of the court will have to make room for its queens. Before now, the greatest women players in the world disappeared to Europe after college. Now that the women's game has hit it big on American soil, there's more at stake, more to gain—and thus more to lose. At the playground level are the female versions of the wouldas, shouldas and couldas. Count Gail Doughty as one of the first.

"Gail Doughty has all the skills to play at the next level," says Philadelphia native Dawn Staley, a 1996 Olympic gold medalist and an all-star guard with the ABL's Philadelphia Rage. "She's explosive, like Charles Barkley, and she could intimidate people the same way. She is as good as anyone I've played with. No question, she's capable of playing in the pros. But who knows why some people don't get the opportunity and others do."

It's a little bit timing and little bit luck. "Five years ago I know I would have been one of the first people getting a tryout for a pro league," says Doughty. "Now I can't even find out where or when one is."

"So much of it comes down to having a name," says Linda Page, a four-time All-American at Philly's Dobbins High School in the late 1970s and a two-time All-American at North Carolina State in 1982 and 1983. "Gail's a playground player. Even though she could play with anyone, no one outside of Philly knows her."

When Gail was growing up, wandering from court to court looking for a game, she was always the first girl picked, the one everyone wanted to be like. She studied the game as a coach would, videotaping the Sixers and watching them over and over late at night with the sound low and her face inches from the screen. She wanted to see the rotation of the ball when Julius Erving shot his free throw. She needed to know how Mo Cheeks planted his foot on the entry pass. Every night she crammed, because every day on the court was a final exam. "She's from the old school," says Staley who, at twenty-six, is a decade younger than some of the women still haunting the Philly playgrounds. "If someone were to describe me as a player, I would want them to say I could play with Linda or Gail. They're smarter than players today. They have the sweet skill, but they also have great basketball knowledge."

For women, conferring upon someone a professorship of the playground is the highest compliment. The standard is different for men. What matters in the male game are get-backs, facials, hard-core retaliation and Globetrotter-like exhibitions. Can you pick a quarter off the top of the backboard from a standing jump? Do you make the guy guarding you wobbly at the knees when you snap a fresh move that proves you've got the juice? That is how men are measured on the playground. Style over substance is the rule, and the flashier a player is, the bigger the legend. Put Dick McGuire and Earl Manigault on the same playground today and, unless Dick's brother Al is watching, every spectator would pick the Goat as the NBA great—yet Dick is the one in the Basketball Hall of Fame. Somewhere along the way, the team game became lost out on the boys' playgrounds. For women, though, the team game is the only option. Move the ball, find the open player, set the pick at the top of the key. That's how women players survive among the men in the street game.

"When I went to the playground I would have to set picks for my teammates if I ever wanted someone to consider letting me play," says Carol Blazejowski, who finished her career at Montclair State in 1978 as the leading scorer in the history of women's college basketball, was elected to the Hall of Fame in 1994 and is general manager of the WNBA's New York Liberty. "And I would have to develop a great outside shot because no one would let me drive. I'd be smart and let the guys worry about showing off."

Doughty was indoctrinated into the game early. She was playing ball with two of her older brothers, Meechie and Sandy, when most other girls were playing with dolls. When recess came during grammar school, Gail headed to the playground inside the fence while the other girls stayed outside the iron gates playing hopscotch. Every time she got into a game, if only for one play, she gained confidence and made believers of her male classmates. In one game, she recalls, she was pushed from behind, fell face-first onto the concrete, and chipped her tooth. But she came back again the next day. If she was the first one outside, she'd hold the ball until the boys had no choice but to let her into the game.

"I stayed out there on the basketball court so when they got out there and wanted to play full court, they couldn't get rid of me," says Doughty. "Every now and then someone would Bogart [hit] me, and when they did that I would just push them out of the way. Some guys don't want to see a woman beat them, and they will do whatever it takes to beat 'em. But I'm not gonna let a female take advantage of me, and I am not gonna let a male take advantage, either."

By the time Gail was in the eighth grade at Pierce Elementary, only a handful of boys could outplay her. When the girls' season ended that year, the boys' coach invited her to play on his team for the last two weeks of the season. She said yes, knowing her biggest challenge would come not on the court but off. Her team-mates whined that she was getting more playing time than they were. Then she had to deal with the nasty looks from opposing players and fans when she was the sole figure trotting out of the girls' locker room to join the guys' layup line. "Gail was always strong," says her oldest sister, Diane, "mostly because of who raised her."

Grandma Francis was the best rib-cooking ordained minister south of Market Street. The woman could preach fire and brimstone during her sermons, but none of the listeners could ever envision an apocalypse with her around. Grandma Francis was strong enough, and loved enough, to shield her flock from all things evil. And Gail was her chosen one.

Gail's mother and father had fourteen children, two of whom died in infancy. Gail was third from the youngest. By the time she was born, neither her mother nor her father could quite handle the idea of raising another child. They sent Gail off to live with Grandma Francis down the block. "I guess my mom needed a break when I was born," Gail says. "I knew my mom because she was always around, but I was closer with my grandmother. She was my pride and joy. She made sure I did everything right. Besides, I knew I would get more spoiled living with her than with all my brothers and sisters."

The deal Grandma offered was straightforward: Do right, which meant going to school, and Gail would never have to worry about having spending money, new shoes or anything else a kid wants but doesn't always get. Besides, considering Gail's other leisure-time options, a bribe or two to keep her in line made sense. The gangs were always out there, ready to grab a malcontented young kid wandering the street. Though she was strong, Gail was impressionable, and if it took a bidding war with the gangs to keep her safe, so be it. But Grandma Francis had an ace in the hole. If Gail ever faltered, if she didn't live up to her end of the bargain, if she didn't go to school, she knew there would be no basketball. The gangs never had a prayer: Gail went to school. And afterward, she went to the Mantua Rec Center.

The corner of 34th and Haverford, where the Mantua is located, is called "the Bottom." The way Philly's West Side is laid out, that section of the city happens to be at the bottom of a hill. "But," Gail adds, "it also happens that a lot of the people living here have nowhere to go but up." Tacked up to a bulletin board just inside the Mantua's doors is another reminder of the grip basketball has on the area. A flyer advertises the first annual alumni basketball classic: legends of the 1970s, 1980s and 1990s. One team is called "Evens" and the other "Odds," and the players are a collection of guys who made their mark at the Bottom but never made it to the top.

Every day after school, Grandma Francis gave Gail two options: come straight home or go to the rec center. Either way, there was no stopping in between. "She kind of adopted me as her friend," says James Wright, the director at the Mantua. "That way she could stay as late as she wanted, and she knew I would take her home." Wright became Gail's personal basketball coach. The lessons extended beyond the confines of Mantua. On the drive home from the rec center, the two would stop for cheesesteaks, Wright diagramming pick-and-rolls on greasy napkins. "The difference between ballplayers and people who think they are ballplayers is attitude," says Wright. "The ballplayers know what the game is about. They understand the moves and the rhythms of the game and how to work those into the team. Those who think they are good because they make an individual play—well, they might be talented, but they aren't ballplayers. Trust me: Gail was and is a ballplayer."

That much was obvious once Gail entered University City High in 1978. Along with William Penn, University City boasted the top girls' basketball program in Philly. When Gail arrived her sophomore year, the school was the defending public league champs and featured Yolonda Laney, the best player in the city. Yolonda and Gail had been playing with one another for years on the playground. With them together, there was little doubt that University City would repeat. "There was something special about their chemistry from the first practice," says Lurline Jones, who has coached University City since 1974. "They knew each other inside and out. But they were also fierce competitors with each other. If one made a great play the other one had to make a better play. Usually, though, Gail was the consummate playmaker."

University City rolled through the regular season undefeated, and Gail and Yolonda were both named to the All-Public League first team. The girls were so sure of their talent that Yolonda, who also was editor of the school yearbook, which had a deadline in February, dedicated a full page to the girls' back-to-back championships, even though the yearbook closed a full month before the finals. "I called up Yolonda the night before the championship game after I heard about this from one of the other teachers," says Jones. "I was freaking out. But when Yolonda was on the phone, I heard Gail in the background singing the song 'Ain't No Stopping Us Now.'"

No one did. University City beat William Penn 73-58 to win the Public League title. Yolonda, a senior at the time, went on to become an All-American at Cheyney State in Cheyney, Pennsylvania. Gail dominated the Public League for the next two years. Every school along the eastern seaboard clamored for her services. "What she could do with a basketball for someone her size was unnatural," says LaRue Fields, who was the coach at Morgan State in Baltimore at the time. "Everyone said she played just like a guy, whatever that meant. I just thought, 'What a talent.'"

Gail was equally impressed with Fields, and she chose Morgan State without visiting another school. "It's not like I had to worry about going to a big school and impressing some NBA scouts," says Gail. "They offered me a free ride, and it was close to home. I didn't want to be too far from my grandma in case I wanted to come home."

Almost immediately, though, Fields and Doughty clashed. "Gail was a street-ball player, probably the best around, but usually those players don't have the discipline to stay within a structured game plan," says Fields. "She didn't like me much, I got angry at her a lot, and she just wanted to go home from the first week." Even at eighteen, Gail was still a grandma's girl. Although she was a starter and averaged 12.5 points and 7.3 rebounds in 1982–83, Gail was miserable. She'd call home every night, crying because she missed the city, the neighborhood, her grandma's barbecued ribs. She hated the school. She didn't get along with the coaching staff. The team was full of first-year players, and they never won. Grandma Francis would listen and quietly issue the same response every time, "You know you can't come home, Gail."

"Me and my grandma, we talked about everything," says Gail. "We were more like mother and daughter than my mother and I. That's why I looked up to her so much. She didn't have to raise me but she did. I love my momma to death; I just love my grandmother more."

When she needed her support the most, however, Grandma Francis wasn't there. Gail could handle being way from home and playing on a bad team as long as her grandma was around for a reality check. She would remind Gail about the education she needed if she wanted to move on. Basketball was nice, but school made it happen. It turns out, however, that Gail didn't so much learn the lessons her grandmother taught her as simply follow along. Gail thought she was a strong woman who struggled her way out of the ghetto, but she was actually pushed out against her will. The shell she thought was so hard turned out to be delicate as a robin's egg—apply even the slightest pressure, and she would crack. Unfortunately for Gail, she didn't learn this until Grandma Francis died.

Toward the end of the first semester of her sophomore year a call came into her dorm room one evening shortly after practice: the cancer that for the past few years had slowly been attacking Grandma Francis had run its course. Until that point, Gail's motivation for staying in school had been her grandmother's constant prodding. "You went there for a reason," she would tell Gail. When

Grandma Francis died, Gail realized that the biggest reason she stayed in school was to make her grandmother proud. With her gone, what point was there in staying? Gail left school that day and she never went back. "When my grandmother died, I lost interest in everything," says Gail. "Nothing mattered. All my focus was on her. It's hard when you're around someone your whole life, and then you don't really know how to deal with them not being there the next day."

"Basically, she was gone once her grandma died," says Fields. "I don't mean from the team, which was obvious, but from a mental standpoint. Her grandma was the thin thread keeping her in school. When she died, that snapped."

For thirteen years since then, Gail has floundered. She lived with cousins in Pittsburgh for five years, playing ball in women's night leagues there. She came back to Philadelphia and worked for UPS until she threw out her back. A cycle of self-pity that begat bad luck that begat more self-pity left her occupying the third floor of her younger sister Tanya's house in South Philly, living off money her brothers gave her. She never started a family of her own because she didn't want to miss time on the court by getting pregnant. Then the new women's professional leagues started popping up, and Gail thought maybe they'd be her shot. "I haven't had anything to hold on to for a long time," she says. "This is something to shoot for."

Though still in its infancy, the women's pro game in the U.S. is morphing to match the NBA's penchants for showmanship and poor fundamentals. Lost in the bustle of becoming famous is the team concept that made women's hoops such a welcome departure from the gotta-get-my-shot attitude permeating the NBA. As Dawn Staley says, the "throwbacks" like Page, Doughty, Lytle and Laney play a style of ball that produces wins anytime, anyplace.

"Here is the biggest problem with today's women's game," says Staley. "We are getting too much hype. The game used to be about the team working as one. That's why people started watching us. They found it refreshing compared to all the individual play in the NBA. We weren't superstars, just good ballplayers working together, playing the game as it was meant to be played. Now, with all the publicity, some girls are coming into the league and changing that. Some of these girls think they're Michael Jordan and want to get famous. Both leagues are going to suffer because of it."

"I used to be a ballgirl for the pro team in Philly when the first women's league was around," says Linda Page of the Women's Basketball League, which ran from the late 1970s through the early 1980s. "It broke my heart to see that first league fold. I dreamed about it. When I didn't have the opportunity to play in the States it hurt."

Gail adds, "You see Lisa Leslie and players like that—they're good, and I give them their props, but I see some of them who aren't good, and how they got the opportunity I just don't know. I'm not knocking nothing from nobody. But if we get a fair chance, we can go out there and prove ourselves. I can take five players from Philly who can go out there and beat anybody."

"I honestly feel I can still compete," says Page. "A lot of the 1990s ballplayers—except for the Olympians—are hotdogs. They don't have the discipline, the fundamentals, that we old-fashioned players have."

Page was a high school All-American for four straight years at Dobbins Tech in North Philly. She had a sweet jumper with a quick release spawned from years of playing against bigger, stronger boys. After high school, she went on to become a three-time All-American at North Carolina State before playing two years professionally in Spain and Denmark. She is thirty-four years old, hasn't played organized ball in ten years, and, like Gail, wants her shot.

"I see this as a dream I never got to fulfill," says Page. "If you want it you can motivate yourself to get it. I feel like a new woman because of it."

Page has been Gail's backbone in Gail's quest to stretch beyond the playground. She makes Gail work out. She tells Gail she can make a team if she has some discipline, gets in shape, commits herself to it. No one has offered her such guidance since Grandma Francis died. "Gail is the perfect playground player," says Page. "She knows where all the games are, and she knows she'll get on a court there. It's comfortable for her. She wants to be recognized, but she may not want to work for it."

Adds Fields, "All she has to do is get conditioned, and she'd be playing for money in a pro league in the United States right now. But she doesn't understand that working hard is not a seasonal thing but a yearly thing. She has all the talent. But what about the drive? Maybe she's just paying lip service to the idea of playing pro."

Fields may be right. Even with something, literally, to shoot for, Gail still seems directionless. Laney had a tryout in the pros. Page had one set up for late 1998. Gail talks to both of them almost daily, yet somehow she says she can't figure out how to get a tryout herself. She is a walking contrast, contending that she'd like to play, then in the next breath emphasizing that she doesn't need vindication. Gail once said, "I walk around here and get compliments for my play all the time. I don't worry about the WNBA or ABL because I know I could have been there. If only someone gave me a shot."

As different as the men's game is from the women's, a common thread binds every player who shines brightest and burns out on the playground: All are certain sure they could have made it at the next level if they hadn't somehow been slighted. It's never their fault. Gail has the excuse. She wouldn't be a legend if she didn't.

BASKETBALL

Lisa Leslie

Jake Curtis

Jake Curtis wrote for the Los Angeles Times, *from which this piece was taken.*

USC freshman phenom Lisa Leslie already has produced two historic performances—one to satisfy the basketball purist and one to astonish the everyday fan.

Let's start with the mundane. Her 30-point, 20-rebound performance against then seventh-ranked Texas in her collegiate debut provided the first evidence for the theory that she may become the best women's basketball player ever.

That's the stuff that makes All-Americans, and that's what people will see when the 6-foot-5 Leslie and the Women of Troy play at USF tonight.

To capture the imagination of people who don't know a basketball from a basket case, though, Leslie has another, more fascinating performance in her résumé.

Last February, when she was a senior at Morningside High School in Englewood, Leslie scored 101 points in a game against

South Torrance, a remarkable feat that left her five points short of the women's high-school record set by Cheryl Miller in 1981.

The kicker, though, is that she scored her 101 points in—and this has been verified—*one half.*

Suddenly, she was a star. "I went to eat after the game," she said, "and when I got home, everybody was looking for me. Every TV channel from 2 to 13, every newspaper. Everybody wanted a tape of the game. I didn't know it was that big."

It was that big. With the team trying for an individual record, Leslie made 37 field goals and 27 foul shots in the span of 16 minutes—two eight-minute quarters.

"It was beyond my wildest dreams," said Frank Scott, then Morningside's coach and now a part-time assistant at USC. "It was like the twilight zone."

Morningside, which was talented without Leslie, pressed its smaller opponents the entire game, and Leslie was at the point of the press.

"And once we got the ball over half court," said Scott, "we just kept feeding her. The other team knew it (which led to some quadruple teaming), but she was making jump shots, hook shots, everything."

Once she stayed under the Morningside basket while teammates played defense, but Scott halted that and told her to defend anything. "We don't want to taint it."

She had all of her team's first-period points.

"She was like in a daze," said Scott.

"I thought it was halftime," said Leslie. "I didn't know what was going on."

When she scored 52 more in the second period—a teammate scored one point—the opponents had had enough. South Torrance, with two players already fouled out and another out with an injury, had only four healthy players left and forfeited.

Leslie had taken 91 shots: 56 from the field, 35 from the line, an average of one every 10.6 seconds.

It's a breathtaking bit of history which makes for great headlines. Now, however, she's establishing herself as being as good as suspected.

She is exactly what the women's game needs, a spectacular talent who can dunk—she did it all the time in high school but has yet to do it in college—and already has autograph seekers for her after the game.

"With the dunking and stuff, I want to elevate the game to a higher level," she said. "I think I play a big part in that now, because it's the people who decide those things, and that's what people have told me."

She can probably handle it. A three-time class president who carried a 3.5 grade-point average in high school, Leslie is the product of a single-parent home. Her mother spent stretches of time away from home as a truck driver to support her three children.

Ready or not, Lisa Leslie is women's basketball's present and future.

Editor's note: Lisa, who now plays for the L.A. Sparks, was the MVP of the first WNBA All-Star game in 1999.

Luisana Cruz

Steve Lopez

Steve Lopez writes for Time *magazine, from which this selection was taken.*

So we're at the Lincoln High School varsity football practice two days before the big homecoming game, and the fullback,
during a break in the pop and crunch of colliding pads, says to the
halfback, "I still have to go pick up a dress for the dance."

This can't be just any dress either. Luisana Cruz, a 17-year-
old senior, is a finalist for homecoming queen at her mostly Hispanic
school in the Lincoln Heights section of Los Angeles. She hopes to
wear both a football helmet and a crown before the day is done on
Friday. "I want it bad," says Cruz, who is also student-body president
and is listed on the football program at 5 ft. 6 in., 151 lbs. "But that's
with the pads," she says defensively of her weight. She doesn't have a
date for the dance yet, so there's some sensitivity there.

Ordinarily, a football huddle would be the last place a girl
would go for advice on making the decision between a strapless gown
and a halter dress. But on this team, Cruz can talk fashion with the
halfback, Diocelina Macias (5 ft. 6 in., 137 lbs.), as she's doing now. Or
she can try defensive tackle Patricia Mora (5 ft. 7 in., 170 lbs.). Imelda

Chaparro (5 ft. 8 in., 226 lbs.), another lineman, would be another option, but she's on the sidelines after suffering a concussion in last week's game.

Yes, the world as we knew it has changed forever. There are four girls on the Lincoln High varsity, all of them 16-year-old juniors except for Cruz. And it's not as if they're just bench warmers. Although none of them start, they all play on special teams and as backups, and coach Leo Castro doesn't hesitate to send them out there. "They're not afraid to take the hits," says Castro, which is a good thing, because Lincoln is 0-8 going into the game against 8-0 Franklin. "I'll put them in before a lot of the other players, because their work ethic and attitude are so good."

Although 708 girls played high school football in 1998, according to the National Federation of State High School Associations, it's not clear if there have ever been four on a varsity team. And it wasn't as if the four Lincoln girls got together to make a statement. Mora and Chaparro went into it together, curious to see if they could hack it. But Cruz and Macias decided independently to do the unexpected. "It's my senior year," Cruz says. "I wanted to try as many things as I could, because it's my last chance."

"The cheerleaders don't like us," Chaparro says. "They thought we were doing this to get dates." The boys on the team weren't wild about it initially either. "We thought they were trying to make us look silly," says middle linebacker Roger Sepulveda, 16. But Sepulveda, who hits like a truck, once knocked Macias out of her shoes. "And she just popped right up," he says admiringly. "I see the girls as a little better than some of the guys on the team."

"The hitting is a rush," says Chaparro, who was angling to get back out there less than a week after having her bell rung, passing out on the sidelines and being rushed to the hospital. A lot of guys don't realize they're lined up across from a girl, she says, but they don't pull back when they find out. "I've got bruises all over my body," says Macias, who ran for 16 yards on three carries in one game and could be a starter next year, according to coach Castro.

On Thursday another fullback, Eulices Sierra, asked Cruz to the dance. That night she found a sassy little purple number with a sheer top. And then at halftime of the game on Friday, the princess in shoulder pads traded her helmet for a crown and climbed into a white Mazda Miata convertible for the parade of queen candidates. She looked stunning, if a little sweaty.

It would be nice to report that Lincoln upset Franklin with a last-minute touchdown by Cruz and that at the dance afterward, she was crowned homecoming queen. But Hollywood is located several miles west of here. Lincoln went down, 34-0, and another girl got the crown.

But what would a fullback want with that silly thing anyway? Belmont High is up next week, Cruz says. "And I just know we can win that game."

Robyn Smith

Red Smith

This piece was taken from Red Smith's book Strawberries in the Wintertime.

Now is the winter of their discontent, the melancholy days without a thoroughbred running this side of Philadelphia, the cruel times when New York horseplayers are thrown upon the mercy of Howard J. Samuels and his off-track gambling hells.

Beaming through charcoal-gray darkness, yellow lights on the tote board at Aqueduct gave the time as 4:29 P.M. when the winner reached the finish of the 2,187th race of the season. Moments later the reedy voice of Fred Capossela came over the public-address system for the last time: "The result of the ninth race is official. The winner, No. 4, Canning, a chestnut horse by Datour. . . . Thank you, and good afternoon." On laggard feet, 25,380 immortal souls took their leave.

Reluctantly, they would go home. They would note with interest how the children had grown since March. Somehow they would get through 76 dark days squandering their earnings on rent and beer and shoes until the sun would shine again, however bleakly, and the bugle would call the horses to the post on March 1.

In the catacombs below the stands, a man rapped on a door marked "Lady Jockeys."

"Are your eyes gray or blue?" he asked Robyn Smith. "Green," she said, "but right now they're red and green."

She was wiping away mud kicked into her comely face by Canning and Sip Sip Sip, who had burst out of the fog and rain and gloom in the last few yards to finish one-two in the final race and move her back to third aboard Advance Warning.

Robyn had five mounts on getaway day. She won smartly with Princely Margin at 50.40 for $2, was third with Advance Warning and third with Schnappy, an 18-to-1 shot, finishing sixth and seventh with the others. Princely Margin was her 15th winner of the Aqueduct fall meeting. In 51 days she had 124 mounts and finished third or better with 37. Only nine males had a higher winning percentage.

"You've made it in the toughest league in the world," a visitor told her. "You are one girl who has done what the others talked about."

She agreed with a matter-of-fact nod. But she said, "I feel that when I lose my bug I'll be starting all over again."

The "bug" is the five-pound weight allowance an apprentice jockey loses one year after riding his fifth winner, provided he has had 35 winners by that time. Robyn's year expired Nov. 30 but was extended to mid-January to make up for six weeks lost because of a broken hand. Some riders can't win without the weight advantage.

"I notice you like the rail," her visitor said. "That's one mark of a good, unmarried jockey." (In threadbare racing slang, the longer but safer outside route is known as the "Married Man's Highway.")

"I like to save ground when I can," Robyn said, "but I can go outside if that's where the trainer says the horse does best."

"Does it get a little scary on the inside at times?"

"Not for me." Her tone was conversational without a trace of bravado. "What upsets me, though, is to get locked inside with a horse that wants to run. It happened the other day. My horse was full of run and I had no place to go. When I lose by a head or a nose, I always feel I could have done something else."

"Has there been one ride that gave you special satisfaction?"

"The day at Saratoga when I rode Beaukins to a track record for Allen Jerkens. Kennedy Road was in the race, a good horse, and some other good ones that I forget. The boy on Kennedy Road lodged a claim of foul for interference leaving the gate, but I knew exactly what I was doing. I left just enough room inside for Kennedy to go through, but it was tight enough to make the boy wonder. It made him hesitate a little. Then he went through—I knew he'd want to be on the lead—and he really used his horse. I waited, then came around him and won by a length."

Brenda Felicetti, the pretty little trainer of Schnappy, appeared in the doorway. "You rode him beautifully," she told Robyn.

"He was coming strong at the end," Robyn said. "I didn't want to go to the rail, but I had no choice."

"I could see that."

"I think he was a little green going to the turn," Robyn said, "like, 'where am I?' So I snugged him down a little. Then he finished full of run."

"He's young," Miss Felicetti said, "and I think he might prefer a firmer track. I'm taking him to Gulfstream, but I'll probably race him once at Tropical."

"He'll run good at Tropical," Robyn said. "I'll be at Gulfstream for the opening. I'd like to ride him again down there."

Marta Empinotti

David Ferrell

David Ferrell is a staff writer for the Los Angeles Times, *from which this piece was taken.*

D e Land, Fla.—Usually she begins at night or dawn hopping barbed-wire fences, creeping where she can up stairwells, climbing high ladders and girders.

Her goal is elevation, the height she can reach by sneaking onto the roof of a skyscraper or the top of a radio tower. The practice is known as "stealing altitude": risking arrest to reach a precipice. For a moment she is still, and then she leaps off, free falling through space and parachuting down—a kind of Russian roulette played with shadows and distance and time.

The plunge often approaches 100 mph, creating a dose of terror far more intense than she can get by skydiving. The earth is not distant and abstract; it is right there—cars, fences, trees, all flying toward her. Her margin for error shrinks to two or three seconds. In that hyper-reality, she receives a jolt of adrenaline so intoxicating that she must have it over and over again.

"I couldn't live without it. I would die inside," Marta Empinotti says, the words streaming out in rapid Portuguese cadences. "In a way it's not a choice . . . like you don't choose to eat. I need it for my soul, to keep me balanced, to keep happy. . . . Everything is so alive when you jump. Every single hair of my body is alive."

Adrenaline junkies heavily populate the world of alternative sports; they include extreme skiers and white-water rafters, downhill mountain bikers and street-luge racers, aerial surfers who dance with the clouds, and ocean surfers who skim the faces of 60-foot waves. Marta is a member of an especially hard-core breed: BASE jumpers, a narrow underground subculture as elusive as moonshiners.

BASE jumpers are the fringe of the fringe. In the 17 years since the sport was invented by four friends in a Texas living room, only 480 men and women have been awarded an official BASE number, signifying a leap from all four types of objects that constitute the acronym: Buildings, Antennas, Spans (bridges) and Earth (cliffs). That the jumps are often illegal has kept the society clandestine and elite.

Marta is BASE No. 206, a 32-year-old Brazilian with quick brown eyes and a penchant for one-liners. For more than a decade the rush has been the dominant force in her life—a singing electrical charge that has spun her halfway across the globe to high-rises in Los Angeles, Miami and Chicago, bridges in West Virginia and Northern California, cliffs in Norway, radio antennas across the South.

Three mornings a week she rises at 5 A.M. to satisfy her craving. Most of the time she jumps with friends from a 1,400-foot FM radio tower well outside this quaint college town near Daytona Beach. On nights of the full moon, she pursues the obsession to even greater extremes, driving for hours to reach a 1,250-foot antenna that affords the luxury of an elevator. Freed from the rigors of climbing, she can jump from dusk to daybreak.

Within the thinly scattered network of BASE jumpers, Marta is known worldwide, and her status is important to her. She loves the camaraderie. Most of her friends are jumpers. Her small company, Vertigo, manufactures the specialized, fast-opening rigs that BASE jumpers use. Marta spends most of her days in a narrow cinder-block room lined with sewing machines, where she works irregular hours, taking orders, stitching harnesses.

There is an easy-going charm about her. Her hair is long and honey blond, tied back in a pony-tail. She wears faded jeans or combat fatigues. Her eyes crinkle with laughter as she tells stories about her jumps: the day she went topless and her canopy malfunctioned. "We call it the 'topless malfunction.'"

Being a Sagittarius, she says, she enjoys the outdoors at odd hours: the foggy dawns when the landing area is blanketed in white. The dewdrops bejeweling the spider webs. The nights when the sky is a glittery black slate.

Although Marta admits that the subterfuge of the sport can be exciting—her eyes light up as she recalls a night she was chased by a police helicopter—she has been busted three times. The fine for jumping cliffs at Zion National Park was more than $1,000. She would love the chance to leap from the 1,454-foot Sears Tower in Chicago—so far an unconquered object—or the 1,483-foot Petronas Towers in Kuala Lumpur, Malaysia, the world's tallest buildings, but the chances of going to jail, or being roughed up by foreign police, are just too daunting. "It's not worth it," she says. "I'm just having fun. Now you're going to put me in jail, mistreat me? I'm not a terrorist. I'm not used to roughness with people being impolite."

She is gracious, sensitive, but also a woman of contradictions. Her breeziness masks an acute mind that knows the velocity of a falling body at any designated second and the heights of buildings, antennas and bridges all over the nation.

She loves her sport, though close friends have died doing it. She shrugs and downplays the dangers—"We know we're going to live"—but before every BASE jumping trip she phones her parents in Porto Alegre, Brazil, in case final words from her might be a comfort.

She climbs antenna girders at 1,000 feet, despite recurring bouts of dizziness. Years ago she passed out during a climb; two other jumpers had to pin her to a ladder several hundred feet up, supporting her weight until she regained consciousness.

Harsh sun wakens her. Every two hours she must eat. Requiring eight hours of sleep, she is often too busy working, traveling and jumping, and settles for six or seven.

Marta talks about slowing down—"just a little bit"—but has difficulty doing that. Not feeling quite right, she will affix a carabiner—a metal ring—to her vest and create a tether to secure herself while climbing, rather than miss the action.

If she started out with nine lives, surely she has expended a few. How many might she have left?

Marta laughs. "I owe a couple."

Rising in the Florida dusk, the 1,250-foot antenna is a ladder to the stars: a skinny, three-sided spike of crisscrossing girders nearly as tall as the Empire State Building. Steel guy wires hold it upright: at various elevations strobe lights flash a warning to aircraft—a slow arterial pulse.

Marta and her friends roll along a weedy dirt road and hide their van deep in a tangle of shrubs and trees. With her are Mario Richard, 31, who came down from Quebec to find and jump this tower, and Kiddi Palsson, 30, a jumper from Iceland.

Like a guerrilla soldier, white-haired Bob Neely emerges from the shrubs to greet them. By far the oldest, at 48, he is a local who often jumps here alone, gaining access through the antenna's protective fence by knowing the combination to the padlock. An affable, cocksure professional skydiver, he made his first BASE jump in Louisiana from a 1,800-foot microwave tower, one of the most perilous types of antennas. On a microwave tower, your dental fillings may heat up like kernels of popcorn.

Radio engineers warn against climbing on any type of TV or radio antenna. An AM tower is so charged from top to bottom with electrical current that it can sear the flesh if you touch it while standing on the ground. Even an FM antenna like this one packs a heavy punch of non-ionizing radiation whose health effects are uncertain—thus a posted sign: "Caution! High Level Radio Frequency Energy Area. Keep Out."

Marta passes the sign without a glance, wearing military-style camouflage pants she has owned 11 years. Arc lights affixed to a low equipment building throw harsh shadows across her face. The setting is surreal: boxy machinery of indistinguishable purpose thrashing and booming like an old washing machine, hundreds of spiders overrunning the steep metal stairs and high catwalk that lead to the base of the tower. The tower itself, perhaps a dozen feet in diameter, unimaginably tall and forbidding, nothing but forged steel.

The elevator is a perforated metal box no larger than a phone booth. The contraption is slow—12 minutes one way—so everyone will ride at once: Marta and Bob inside, Mario and Kiddi on the roof, up in the cables and passing girders. A jarring metal screech and it begins to climb, the ground receding outside the collapsible metal door.

At 500 or 600 feet up, something goes wrong—the overloaded elevator starts slipping: rising a few feet, dropping back, rising, slowing, dropping. The lurching progress is accompanied by grating and grinding noises, bringing a dark look to Marta's face.

"Bob, shouldn't we stop?"

He shakes his head. "As long as it's going . . ."

The elevator continues to lurch, speeding up, slipping, rising again. They fret over the likelihood of a free fall, or the motor burning out. Near 700 feet Marta suggests that maybe they should stop and get out and climb. Bob watches the girders moving by. "Come oonnnn, little choo-choo."

Jean and Carl Boenish, two skydiving photographers from Hawthorne, were half of the foursome who sat in Phil Mayfield's living room in Houston in the fall of 1980 and devised a name for their sport. Jean, BASE No. 3, a dark-haired, bespectacled woman who admits she looks like a librarian, still maintains The Book—the blue three-ring ledger that records the sport's milestones. Its pages are filled with the names of all 480 jumpers who have completed the BASE jumping cycle, as well as the 39 who have died in accidents. Jean's husband Carl, BASE No. 4, appears in both columns: he was killed jumping a cliff in Norway in 1984.

Long before the sport was given a name, people were parachuting from tall objects. Someone had leaped from the Statue of Liberty around 1920. Yosemite's El Capitan had been jumped from a number of times in the 1960s and 1970s. New York's World Trade Center had been leaped from in 1975.

What the founders did was create a framework for an underground society that was waiting to emerge. Phil Smith, BASE No. 1, planned the first jumps from radio antennas. He devoted weeks to spying on security guards and doing trials with weights and parachutes. Phil liked to experiment, conceiving challenges befitting a high school physics book; in 1983, he hurled himself from a train as it rolled across a 300-foot-high bridge above the Pecos River.

"We had to figure out how fast we were going on the bridge, how far we had to jump to clear the bridge and where to exit to clear the rocks down below," Phil says. Now 45, with two teen daughters and retired from BASE jumping, he is proud of having been a pioneer. "There wasn't reference material. There wasn't someone to call."

Slowly the network fanned out, a loose, far-flung affiliation of daredevils and mavericks. Marta's friends are scattered to Hell and back—Hell being the name of a small town in the Cayman Islands where Lee Marcoux claims to be the only BASE jumper in the West Indies. One of Marta's favorite jumping partners is John Vincent, 29, of New Orleans, the fourth and most recent person to have leaped from the World Trade Center. That stunt, in 1991, was followed a year later by an even more audacious feat: John, wearing suction cups, scaled the 630-foot face of the St. Louis arch, a two-hour climb that ended in a short, breathtaking leap, several moments of TV air time and three months in federal prison.

Such spectacles have created tension within the world of BASE jumping. In another well-known incident, years ago, John was caught leaping during the day from an unfinished high-rise in Atlanta, a blunder that ruined the object for the local jumpers. They were so infuriated they tracked him down in New Orleans; three men burst into his room, bound his wrists and ankles in duct tape, and administered that age-old ignominy: a tarring and feathering.

Times change—the principal assailant is now one of John's best friends—but John is again at odds with the purists, joining a faction of BASE jumpers intent on making legal jumps for financial gain. He has appeared in TV commercials and magazine ads. He and Marta were scheduled to perform this year at the Super Bowl in New Orleans, until a bungee jumper was killed during rehearsals for a different act and their gig was canceled.

By obtaining permits and working with local authorities, BASE jumpers have organized a growing number of legal competitions. West Virginia is the site of one of the oldest: "Bridge Day," the third Saturday in October, the one day of the year that jumps are allowed from the new River Gorge Bridge. Hundreds leap from the 876-foot-high span and land in the river rapids or on the rocky shoreline.

The attention appalls many purists. They fear more publicity will mean more jumpers and more security at prime objects that will never be legal no matter what. Silence and chicanery are the only way to protect their domain, they believe.

Jumpers have been known to finagle keys, to pick locks, to scam their way past lobby guards by wearing sports jackets and ties, carrying their parachute rigs in gift-wrapped boxes. Often they perch on rooftops like gargoyles, waiting hours for nightfall so they can take wing. As with illicit sex, the secrecy heightens the thrill, at least for some. "It brings out the James Bond in you," as one jumper put it. "It has to stay hush-hush."

Word of exceptional jumping spots filters through the network. Buildings under construction are often ideal; usually they have stairwells but no windows, multiple points of entry and minimal security. A new high-rise going up in, say, San Francisco, is likely to come to Marta's attention in Florida.

Although she may or may not travel there, her circle of friends offers entrée where she chooses. Local knowledge is important, especially around buildings, where landing areas are notoriously small and winds can play havoc. Even aside from the sport's illegalities, many professional skydivers refuse to attempt a BASE jump because it is so much more dangerous.

"I would say it's 10 times as risky," says James Hayhurt, 44, a board member of the United States Parachuting Association and a veteran of more than 4,000 skydives. "I personally would never do it. I always open [the parachute] at 2,500 feet; that gives me 15 seconds of time to deal with an emergency."

The parachuting group's guidelines say a skydiver can be barred from drop zones if he opens below 2,000 feet. In BASE jumping, there are no rules; canopies pop between 1,000 and 200 feet, sometimes even lower. If this suggests that jumpers have a death wish, most deny it. "I've got 9,000 skydives," one jumper says. "If I had a death wish, I would have failed one of them."

Still, the need for an adrenaline hit causes some jumpers to keep raising the stakes, balancing their own skills and past successes against the perceived likelihood of death. Mike Muscat, 45, of Van Nuys nearly killed himself trying to earn his BASE number in Oakland, jumping at night from a 30-story building. His chute malfunctioned, opening in a direction that carried him straight backward. He sailed through an open window and crash-landed, breaking his ankle and lying semiconscious for hours before being discovered by a construction crew.

Bill Legg, best known for unscrewing window mounts and leaping from the top of Houston's 570-foot San Jacinto Monument in

1989, figures he's broken 30 bones during his 42 years on earth. To heighten his own flow of adrenaline, he ignores the advice of friends who urge him to wear a reserve chute.

At Bridge Day in 1987, Bill stood at the river's edge and watched two accidents in a row. The first was relatively minor: Phil Smith's lines became twisted, plunging him into a boulder that shattered his left foot and right kneecap.

Medics were loading him into an ambulance when a blond, Nordic-looking jumper named Steve Gyrsting, only 25, pulled the cord on a chute that failed to deploy, then yanked on a reserve that was too slow to open. He smashed into the river at more than 100 mph.

"You could tell he was fixin' to die," Bill remembers.

Marta was watching the same jump from up on the bridge. Steve was her boyfriend. They had been going together for two years.

From the exit point, 1,150 feet up the antenna, the flat Florida landscape stretches in all directions—rowed fields, dark clumps of trees, an inky depression that gives this object its nickname, the "Black Hole." A stiff breeze shoves broken clouds across the moon.

The balky elevator has delivered the jumpers to a tiny platform contained within the tower. From there they will climb through the girders—any false step could mean a fall of several hundred feet—and fling themselves out into the night.

The direction of the breeze is critical. Mario sets adrift a scrap of tissue paper. It disappears into the darkness between the guy wires, a good sign; when the wind blows it directly toward the wires, the risk of the chutes getting caught there is too great to leap. Conditions now are ideal save for one last-minute problem: a single headlight suddenly visible far below, a one-eyed car creeping along a farm road. The jumpers must wait. Ten minutes go by before the car disappears and they edge into position, gloved hands gripping the tower.

Bob leaps first, then Marta. Fit and sinewy, she moves with sureness; the years have made her comfortable on a tower. Her hiking boots find balance on a girder and she springs out, her body disappearing into the blackness.

At 400 feet, a metal deck encircles the tower. This is the point where Marta pulls, dropping at nearly 100 mph after a six-second free fall. The canopy emerges with a sound like a crumpling paper cup, black and rectangular, a set of raven wings invisible against the sky. Gliding in long arcs, she swings below the moon and the guy wires before landing in the grass.

The jumpers stumble forward as they hit, grinning and laughing. Marta gives Kiddi a high-five as he swoops to the ground near her. The rigs are carried back to the tower and repacked under the arc lights.

The gear Marta manufactures—considered among the best in the sport—is reinforced to withstand the jolt of quick openings. The speed with which they deploy is regulated by the size of the pilot chute—a small round one that emerges first, dragging the larger canopy into the air—and by a mesh device called a "slider" that controls the separation of the chute lines. The canopies themselves are larger than those used in skydiving and are designed for a slower forward movement.

Repacking, the jumpers discuss the one-eyed car. Marta recalls a night when a tower worker showed up unexpectedly, forcing them to shut down the elevator and run. They left, grabbed a bite and came back, lurking out of sight until the worker finally left at 1:30 A.M., when they reclaimed the antenna.

"And this other jumper goes, 'We're like cockroaches,'" Marta says, her laugher filling the night. "That's exactly how I felt, because as soon as he turned his back, man, we were in, and we jumped until sunrise."

The sky became her escape. This was long ago, a young woman eager to see the world, a young man wanting her to stay and get married. Marta was just 20, one of four sisters from an upper-class family in Porto Alegre, contemplating a career as a psychiatrist. Her wanderings—to Europe, the United States—led to a split.

"He got tired of me always taking off, so he broke up with me," she recalls. "I was very devastated. . . . And a friend of mine called me and said, 'Guess what I did this weekend—I went skydiving.'"

She wanted to try it. Loved it. Putting off medical school for one long, last tour of the world, she ended up settling in Florida. At a drop zone there she met Steve, a tall, outgoing mechanical engineer who built jet engines. On weekends they jumped from planes. Steve admired her joyous spirit; he'd tell her, "I hope life is always pink for you."

It was Marta's idea to attempt a BASE jump—Bridge Day, October 1986. There were 15 mph winds, and Steve tried to discourage her. She did it anyway, deploying her chute so late that the jolt made her see stars. Two months later, she made her first jumping trip, a two-week sojourn to Los Angeles, forming quick friendships with those in the underground. She was hooked. Steve finally tried a jump in early 1987. That October, at Bridge Day, he died.

"I had this distorted idea that . . . life was very pretty. If you worked hard, you could get what you wanted. *Bang,* he disappeared, and every breath I took I was further away from him. When that happened, it hit me: It's not like that. You can get a lot of things, but certain things you just can't."

She couldn't jump for six months. She would climb a tower, look down and cry. Marta was confused, aching, almost ready to give up the sport. She finally made her return by jumping the 760-foot Auburn Bridge near Sacramento. In a bad frame of mind, she planned a three-second free fall and instead took five.

"I didn't want to let go of my pilot chute. I shouldn't have been jumping. It was like a fight with myself. I wanted to die. I wanted to be with Steve."

Landing safely on the rocky river shore, she endured a reprimand from a friend. The enthusiasm began to return soon afterward during the frenzied nocturnal "campaigns" of L.A., when hundreds of covert jumps were carried out from the unfinished skeletons of office towers on Bunker Hill. She was drawn to a man from Redondo Beach named Mark Hewitt, BASE No. 46, a pioneer she much admired. Mark, Marta found out, was "naked BASE No. 1," the first to jump all four types of objects in the nude. "And I go, 'Who is naked BASE No. 2?'" Nobody, she was told. She couldn't believe it. "It's the coolest number. I'm not into numbers, but this number, this is a cool one. And I go, 'I want to be naked BASE No. 2.'"

She accomplished that mission, wearing only a helmet, kneepads, shoes and her parachute, looking "like a character in a Monty Python movie." Naked BASE Nos. 1 and 2 were married in 1989, a turbulent union that lasted four years. Jumping was what held them together. "Whenever we had problems," Marta says, "we would plan a BASE jumping trip."

Mark ended up in Hawaii, a professional skydiver with 720 BASE jumps now. Marta kept Vertigo, the firm they launched together. A modest operation—there are only two employees—it is the primary source of her income. Looking ahead, she has begun to study for her pilot's license, hoping someday to fly commercial aircraft.

Over a beer she can talk for hours about jumps that fill her logbook: her lines getting twisted in a leap off Half Dome, crashing into a narrow ledge that saved her. Seeing herself plunge down the side of a mirrored office building in Caracas, Venezuela, in a jump for a Ruffles potato chip commercial. Landing in the trees below 3,200-foot Angel Falls in Venezuela. Being hit by lightning in South Africa, just enough to cause a day of soreness. Cliff-jumping at dawn, the suspended rock climbers winking their flashlights at her, like so many wonderful fireflies.

"It's a good life. I like my life a lot," Marta says, beaming. Had she gone down a different road, become that psychiatrist she once planned to be, she would assess herself this way: "I think I'm more balanced than most people. I think I'm fortunate to know what my inner being and soul really loves."

No regrets, no guilt—not even over Steve's death. "It's still very sad for me," she says. "I'll never get over it in a way. But I never feel guilty. Even when I take a student jumping, I always make sure the person knows the risks. Steve made his own decision."

Her canopy, packed for a leap from 800 feet, opens too quickly for her when she jumps again from 1,150. Marta walks away with an aching neck. But by now it is time to rest for a while, and she naps in a sleeping bag in the high weeds. Mario and Kiddi lie in the van, Bob on the unprotected outdoor deck of the antenna, 400 feet up. "No mosquitoes," he explains, "and you always wake up a half-hour before dawn." Just don't roll off the bed.

At dawn there is time for one last trip up the elevator. It will be a special jump—No. 500 for Marta and Bob both, a milestone they have decided to reach together. High over Florida, the two friends kiss, and then all four jumpers edge out onto the girders. In unison they leap, a rare four-way, the chutes popping open one by one on the way down. In the field they laugh, taking snapshots, relishing the glory of the rising Florida sun.

"That was primo!" Marta exults. By the look on her face, life has never been more pink.

Ultra-Marathon

Lisa Smith

David Ferrell

Badwater is a madman's march, a footrace through the summer heat of the hottest spot in America. It extends 135 miles from a stinking water hole on the floor of Death Valley to a piney oasis 8,300 feet up the side of Mt. Whitney. The course is nothing but asphalt and road gravel. Feet and knees and shins ache like they are being whacked with tire irons. Faces turn into shrink-wrap.

Lisa Smith is 102 miles into it. She has been running, and now walking, for almost 27 hours, through yesterday's 118-degree heat, up 6,000 feet of mountain passes into a 40 mph head wind. The night brought her 40 minutes of sleep, if that—two catnaps.

Her feet are blistered and taped up, and she is wearing shoes with the toes cut out, to relieve the pressure. Her right ankle, sprained twice since February, is so swollen she can no longer wear the air cast that was supporting it. She is also cramping with diarrhea.

"It's bad," she says, gasping. "My stomach is killing me."

Grimacing, spitting, bending over at times to fight the nausea, she trudges on, pushing down the undulating highway toward

Keeler, a ramshackle mining outpost. Visible ahead is the serrated peak of Whitney, as distant as Oz. If she can hang on, it will take most of the day—and a 4,000-foot ascent over the final 13 miles—to get there.

Every year, two or three dozen elite ultra-marathoners come to Badwater, and every year Badwater beats them down. About a third fail to finish; after 50 miles or 70 miles or 110 miles the torture exceeds their desire to go on, and they end up rolling away in their cars and minivans, faces covered with wet towels, their bodies stretched out like corpses.

For a thin slice of society—zealots who live to train, who measure themselves by their mental toughness—the ultra-marathon is the consummate test of human character. No other event in sport, except possibly a prizefight, is as punishing, as demanding of the mind and body. No other athlete is more revered than the distance runner. Indefatigable, heroic, celebrated in poetry and myth, the Greek soldier Pheidippides ran 26 miles from Marathon to Athens to herald victory over the Persians in 40 B.C., then collapsed and died. It was the first marathon. To fill the unforgiving minute, to persevere, is one of the highest ideals of man—who, after all, was born to hardship, cast from Eden.

The explosion of extreme sports in recent years has produced an unprecedented number of ultra-endurance races. Several thousand men and women travel the country—and abroad—competing in events from 30 miles to more than 300 miles. There are weeklong "adventure races" by foot, bike and kayak across Patagonia, South Africa, Australia.

In Morocco, there is the Marathon des Sables—"the Marathon of the Sands"—a six-day trek, in stages, across 150 miles of the Sahara. Colorado has the Hardrock 100, snaking 100 miles through the 11,000-foot peaks of the San Juan Mountains. In Alaska it's the Coldfoot, a 100-miler in October with the wind roaring and the temperatures plunging to 40 below.

Death Valley has Badwater: "probably the most physically taxing competitive event in the world," according to the runners' handbook, which warns that you could die out here—though no one yet has. "Heat illness or heat stroke . . . can cause death, kidney failure and brain damage. It is important that runners and crews be aware of the symptoms . . . vomiting, headache, dizziness, faintness, irritability, lassitude, weakness and rapid heart rate. . . . Heat stroke may progress from minimal symptoms to complete collapse in a very short period of time."

Twenty-seven runners have entered this year's 10th anniversary race, a field drawn from North America and Europe. Lisa, 36, is the only woman, a fitness trainer from Bernardsville, N.J., who has run 60 marathons—her fastest in 2 hours and 48 minutes—and four ultras. Bjarte Furnes, 23, a molecular biology student from Norway, is out to become the youngest ever to finish. Beacham Toler, 69, a retired boilermaker from Amarillo, Texas, is already the oldest; he aims to better a personal best by breaking 50 hours.

The course record, set five years ago, is 26 hours and 18 minutes, but few concern themselves with that or the first-place prize money—$500. The main goal is to go the distance, because Badwater, like every extreme race, is less a competition among runners—whose training and talents vary widely—than it is a struggle between each runner and the miles. To conquer the course, you must get through it in less than 60 hours. Those who make it in under 48—two days and two nights—are awarded a special memento, a belt buckle, a modest hunk of bronze featuring a bas-relief of the desert.

"If I don't make it, I'll be back every year until I do," vows U.S. Marine Corps Major W. C. Maples, 33, a second-time entrant from Camp Pendleton who stands now at the starting line, shortly before dawn. Three years back, during Utah's Wasatch 100, he got off the floor of an aid station despite hypothermia and winced through the last 50 miles with a stress fracture in his right leg.

But Badwater got him a year ago. The Major, as other runners call him, quit after vomiting up a bunch of pink, fleshy tissue that turned out to be part of his stomach lining. It was the only endurance race he failed to complete.

"I have fumed over that," he says. "One way I define a challenge is something that does not have a guaranteed outcome. I know that on my worst day I can strap on a pair of shoes and run 26 miles. But here, no matter what kind of shape you're in, there's no guarantee you're going to finish. I can relate to that. I train for combat. Combat does not have a guaranteed outcome."

The race begins in the dawn glow of a clear, breezy morning, below a craggy cliff of the Amargosa Mountains on the valley's east rim. From a casino-hotel on the Nevada-California border, where the runners spent the night, it has taken more than 40 minutes to reach Badwater, so named for an acrid, amoeba-shaped pool of salt and brimstone just off the road. Its brittle white edges look like crusts of ice, but that is a desert illusion because the temperature at 5:30 A.M. is 92 degrees.

A weather-chipped placard notes that the earth here sinks to the lowest point in the Western Hemisphere—282 feet below sea level. Minivans and cars fill a narrow parking lot. The support crews tend to number one to four people—wives, coaches, in-laws, friends, gurus, anyone willing to dispense water, food and exhortations. The vans are packed high with provisions—gallons of water, sandwiches, fruit, candy bars, protein bars, Gatorade, pretzels, crackers, salt tablets, sea salt, socks, shorts, blister pads, tape, towels, ankle braces, sunglasses, sunscreen, five or six pairs of shoes, and a bathroom scale.

Sahara hats are popular—white, Lawrence of Arabia headgear that shades the neck and cheeks. A few runners, like the Norwegian, wear them tailored to hold clumps of crushed ice, a cold skullcap. Dr. Dale Sutton, 57, a San Diego dentist, carries ice atop his head and in hanging pouches near his cheeks as well as in the pockets of his running togs: pinstriped blue pajamas sliced with ventilation holes. He is known as the Pajama Man.

Runners stretch, mingle and pose for pictures—all in eerie quiet, because it is so early, or because they are about to wage combat, or because the open desert sky swallows up most of the sound. At 6 A.M., they assemble on the road. No speeches, no fanfare. They are told to go. They take off to the whoops and claps of the support crews.

In all the miles to follow, these will be the only spectators; no one else will appreciate their toil, except perhaps the whizzing motorists and the occasional bystanders who have stopped for a Coke or radiator coolant in towns hardly larger than a gas station.

At first the road climbs gradually north along the valley floor, away from hills and escarpments named Funeral Peak, Coffin Canyon and Dante's View. The ruddy desert loam tilts toward ridges to the east and falls to the yellow-white valley bowl to the west. For long stretches there is almost no vegetation, just rocky fields divided by the winding asphalt.

They move at a fast, easy gait. For superbly fit athletes, who train by doing 10 or 20 miles a day, the early stages of a long race often produce the euphoric sensation that they could go forever. Runners like to savor it, aware of their own breathing, the length and balance of their strides.

"I focus on what I'm doing, how I'm feeling," says the man who takes the early lead, Eric Clifton, one of America's great ultra-marathoners. "I'm constantly monitoring myself, keeping my legs relaxed, running smoothly, keeping my arms relaxed. Is my face tensed up? I'm trying to be as efficient as possible."

The 39-year-old movie buff, a theater projectionist from Crownsville, Md., has won more than half of the 68 ultra-marathons he has completed; he set an unofficial record last year by running a 100-miler in 13 hours and 16 minutes. Like most who venture into such extreme races, Eric began more modestly, running the two-mile in high school, later dabbling in five- and 10-kilometer road races. Once he realized his own exceptional stamina, he advanced to marathons and triathlons, then ultra-marathon cycling races.

With his long, pendular strides and short, pink socks, Eric moves well in front, followed by a pack that incudes Lisa and the Major, steady at 9 minutes per mile.

At 7 A.M., the sun emerges above the Amargosas; it is 105 degrees—in the shade. At 7:15, it is 106. At 7:25, it is 110. A hot, dry wind pushes the competitors along. Dragonflies blow around in it. Tinder-dry weeds quiver in the canyon washes. At Furnace Creek, 17 miles out, the runners veer northwest on California 190, passing a borax museum and descending again into the yawning desolation of a dry lake bed where the thermometer reads 114. The asphalt is at least 20 degrees hotter.

Faces and shirts are sweat-soaked. Support vans play leapfrog with the runners, moving ahead a mile or so at a time. Runners stop briefly to drink, many alternating water and electrolyte supplements. How much they drink, eat, weigh, how hot they are, how fast they are going—every detail is logged by crew members, who take on the mien of anxious scientists, recording the vitals of subjects in some grotesque lab experiment.

The body is already under enormous assault; the success of the hours ahead will hinge largely on the fickle alchemy of supplying it proper nutrition. Sweat loss alone in this heat can exceed a gallon an hour. Dehydration is a constant danger. Usually, it is accompanied by the depletion of blood sugar and electrolytes—sodium, potassium and other ions that are vital to cells and muscles.

Cells die, muscles cramp. In extreme cases, the heart may go into fibrillation, which can be fatal. More often, the body channels extra blood to the heart and brain, robbing it from other places—the skin, kidneys and bowels. A runner gets the chills. Kidneys clog with protein from damaged muscles, damming up toxins in the blood. The walls of the empty bladder sometimes rub at the pubic bone, causing internal bleeding and producing an intense urge to urinate. Pieces of the bowel or stomach wall may slough off in diarrhea.

Rarely, the body temperature climbs high enough, 104 degrees, to affect the brain. The runner may slip into convulsions or a coma.

Drinking is a safeguard, but huge amounts of water may overwhelm the gastrointestinal tract, causing cramps, bloating, nausea. Even sports drinks may not contain enough electrolytes—or the body may not absorb them well enough—to prevent problems. It is often a matter of luck, experience or genetics that enables one runner to endure while the man behind him folds up like a scarecrow.

Badwater delivers its earliest savagery to those from cooler climes. A Swiss runner with stomach cramps is the first to drop out. Bjarte, the Norwegian, vomits after 18 miles—the beginnings of an agonizing downward spiral that would end with his surrender, 10 hours later, at Mile 53, by which point he had thrown up, in the estimation of one crew member, at least 60 more times.

A 33-year-old Canadian, Paul Bredon, once ran a Colorado 100-miler in which his blisters got so bad he had to cut off his shoes with scissors, drain the wounds and go the last 15 miles with sandals taped to his feet. But that was not as agonizing as the cramps and nausea he now suffers as he nears Devil's Cornfield, a grave of clumpy arrowwood bushes 36 miles out.

With the wind raking across the road, with the temperature reaching 118 degrees, Paul drops a red flag—a legal means of temporarily leaving the course—and accepts a car ride to Stovepipe Wells, a burg at 41 miles consisting of a motel, a saloon and a convenience store. There, officials from Hi-Tec, the athletic gear company that sponsors the race, help him into the back of a refrigerated bottled-water truck. His legs keep cramping and he is screaming so loud that a few tourists wander over, trying to see what is going on.

A white-haired race official administers a carbonated electrolyte beverage whose effect is immediate: Paul vomits all over the truck bed. The theory is that his balky digestion—gummed up by too much fruit—will now return to normal. Looking queasy, Paul is driven back to his flag. He resumes, suffers more cramps, ends up resting, falling asleep and finally dragging himself back onto the road in the evening, when the worst of the heat is over.

Finishing the race is the rite of passage of the distance runner. The sport culls out the weak and rewards the dogged. The runner learns that pain is temporary, but the gulf between those who drop out and those who finish is vast and enduring. With every step, an investment is made. It is either lost on the roadside or it becomes a jackpot that you reap at the end.

Having completed Badwater three times, Barbara Warren, a San Diego sports psychologist, has found that "the deep satisfaction in life comes from this enormous achievement. You feel like a giant."

Often, athletes spend months training and planning for Badwater, which raises the emotional stake in how it turns out. Paul tried to prepare himself for Death Valley by traveling to Amarillo, Texas, a month beforehand, running 10 to 15 miles a day in 100-degree heat.

The Major began training for Badwater in January, expanding his regimen to include twice-monthly workouts in the desert near Borrego Springs. Every trip he ran 25 to 30 miles, alone, bored, baking in the sun. "By the end of June, I had put in almost 1,600 miles just for this one race," he says. There are other forces. All the Marines at Camp Pendleton who know he is representing the Corps—what will they think if he quits? The lessons he learned from his mother, who has spent 27 years battling a degenerative stomach disorder, and his grandfather, who survived the same malady until he was 87, still mowing his lawn at 86.

If you get through a thing like Badwater, a lot of life's other problems seem far more manageable, the Major says. But the moment you let yourself quit, you step onto a slippery slope. One day you quit at 90 miles and the next you quit at 60. Before long you are getting by with the minimum, rationalizing mediocrity.

"Quitting is a disease," he says. "I can't bear the idea of looking in a mirror and seeing a quitter."

The Major is now bearing down on the 50-mile mark, nine miles beyond Stovepipe. It is well into afternoon. The road climbs; it will reach 6,000 feet at the end of the 18-mile stretch to Towne's Pass in the Panamint Mountains. The wind is coming downhill, and it is directly in the runners' faces—a steady blast that seems to come from some humongous hair dryer. No one runs; they walk, tilting into the wind at comical angles, like a bunch of Charlie Chaplins.

The Marine Corps flag snaps wildly from the rear of the Major's support van. His face, faintly freckled, is rigid, his eyes fixed on the road. All of his elaborate philosophy has been bludgeoned down into a tight-lipped, 10-word mantra: "Mind over matter: If you don't mind, it doesn't matter."

Much of the first half of the field is scattered along the 18-mile climb. Eric is still well in front—he's already through the pass—trailed by a runner from Tennessee and then Lisa, in third place, but well back and struggling. Her 10- and 12-minute miles have disintegrated to this: a mile logged at a woeful 25 minutes.

Nauseated, wakened by diarrhea that began the night before the race—a result of nerves, her crew thinks—she is limping too, with an air cast supporting her bad right ankle. It is still hot—107 at 4:30 P.M.—and she has at least 24 hours to go.

She tries not to think about the punishment ahead. Long-haired and purposeful, a former springboard diver at the University of Wisconsin, she is a staunch believer in mental strength, spiritualism, holistic healing. Like the Major, she is inspired by the courage of others: her younger sister, Julie, a member of her support crew, who overcame life-threatening surgery to repair three small holes in her heart; her cousin, Joe, who was Lisa's age when he died last year of AIDS.

"He got a tattoo in New Orleans," she says. "Seven guys all used the same needle. All seven of them are dead."

Music from a movie they enjoyed together, *The Last of the Mohicans,* plays on her headphones.

All the runners are adrift out here, sorting through their thoughts, weighing the reasons to push on. A few miles behind Lisa is the 69-year-old Texan, Beacham, who slumps into a folding chair to gulp water from a plastic bottle.

"This right here is pretty agonizing," he says, but nothing of the ordeal shows on his face, thin as a hawk's. Beacham looks as if everything soft in him has boiled away on the hard roads—and maybe it has. He runs 3,000 miles a year, seven or eight ultra-marathons.

Despite a poor spell at 35 miles, where he had to lie down and take some chicken noodle soup, he is keeping up a formidable pace. The drive seems to come from a fear of growing old, says crew member Jim Davis, who is 58. Ultras are especially important to Beacham because without them, without all the training, he would figure to start withering away.

"I think he wants to get in as many of them as he can," Jim says, "before he gets to where he can't."

Evening is falling. The corrugated mountains near Towne's Pass glow warm orange and black, painted by slanting sunlight and shadows. Bruised clouds blow over the ridges. At 7:30, the sun sinks into the clouds rimming 6,585-foot Panamint Butte, gone until morning, and a soft violet haze settles over Death Valley. The plum-colored Amargosas, where the day began, are a ruffled curtain across the other side of the world.

The heat subsides—it is 86 degrees at 8:10, when the first automobile headlights fill the shadows. Eric, the race leader, descends into the Panamint Valley, where indolent followers of Charles Manson are still said to inhabit the brushy foothills near the Barker Ranch.

Eric is now feeling it. Downhills are murder on the thighs; after the intense early pace, his are aching like "somebody was beating them with baseball bats." At Mile 68, near a motel stop called Panamint Springs, he is passed by a 45-year-old investor named David Jones, who has yet to take a rest. Even when he had to vomit, up at the pass, he turned his head, retched and pressed on.

David opens a substantial lead. With the light fading in a landscape of rolling hills and ridges, Eric and Lisa contend for second place. A quick glance up to a stream of purple-orange clouds and Lisa sees a face—her cousin Joe's face, a vision that lasts an instant and is gone. It inspires her, but also saddens her. She cries. She tells her crew about it. Soon, the sky deepens, and even those tangled clouds disappear, leaving her there on the road toiling.

The darkness takes over. She sees a shooting star and is heartened by whatever hope it might portend, but before long she is crying again.

Night is hard. Night is for demons. Night is when rationality shrinks away, slipping down a rabbit hole, and nothing remains but the black asphalt and black sky and the questions that flicker through shorting mental circuits, like: Where is the horizon, what creatures are out here, why does it matter, really, to keep on going?

Hallucinations are not uncommon. Two years ago, when she got through Badwater in less than 42 hours, her first ultra-marathon, Lisa had a conversation with her dead grandmother. She heard babies crying, Indians chanting. "I saw things flying through the air," she remembers. "All the trees on Whitney, I thought they were people climbing."

Others have seen dogs, herds of cows, miniature people pushing tiny sleds, women showering, cactuses magically transformed into rocket launchers, highway skid marks shooting away like harpoons, flying off to infinity. One runner remembers an elaborate bridge under construction, spanning the highway, with an office building next door. Only the next day, when he was driving back over the course and looking for it, did he learn from his crew that all of it was pixie dust.

The runners are illuminated for periods of time by headlights, until the support vans pull ahead, leaving them to catch up again. At the west rim of Panamint Valley is another climb, through a 4,000-foot pass called Father Crowley's. It is cool enough there for long sleeves and sweatpants; the runners change during the stops. Here and there, they nap—half an hour, an hour, rarely longer.

Two more drop out, one because of a long, purple thigh bruise, the result of a pinched nerve and tendinitis. Eric goes lame on the downside of Crowley's; he dawdles through 10 miles in six hours and quits at dawn at Mile 94. Having won so many times, he places no stigma on stepping away, regrouping, aiming for another race. That is not the case for the less accomplished. For most who quit, the failure is a trauma almost equal to the pounding of the miles.

A runner who stops ceases to be a runner. It is a death of that identity, marked by an ignominious epitaph: "Did not finish." The phrase is abbreviated on the printouts that list the winners, and the slang verb, "DNF-ing," has an obscene sound, foul with shame. The runner who succumbs often goes to extraordinary lengths for resurrection, training for months and traveling back to the same race, the same course, a year or two later, to try again.

Twenty-four hours have gone by. Fatigue seeps like ice water into bones and joints. Walking is the rule now. Rest stops lengthen. Closing their eyes, they get leg massages. They take time to patch blisters, tape their feet, change shoes. They go up half a size when the swelling is bad. They drink hot soup and get up with the painful slowness of old men.

Gossip travels up and down the course in irregular pulses, moving from race officials to support crews, then to the runners. They crave information about the whereabouts of others, how they are doing. Eric's withdrawal is surprising news. It is rare now that one runner sees another, except on arduous grades or during long stops when someone is passed.

Lisa slips into third place. Beacham drops back into 10th, an hour ahead of the Major. Only twice during the night has Beacham slept, once for 15 minutes, another time for 20. He maintains a steady pace through Crowley's despite a blister on the ball of each foot, wounds that have been growing for almost 60 miles.

"It was pretty painful until I got them lanced," he says, his breath as sharp as piston strokes. "They hurt now, but I can stand it."

Beyond the pass the road levels out near 4,000 feet, angling northwest along the Saline Valley and the dry Owens Lake bed; contoured terrain that grows nothing but rust-colored scrub. A wall of white mountains fills the far horizon. This is another of Badwater's psychological slams. One of those distant, chiseled peaks is Whitney.

"You can see the finish," says a runner, "but it's 51 miles away."

The sun climbs into the blue vastness of space and they pass one by one down the long, rippled road, a line of asphalt that runs forever.

"The sun's coming up, and pretty soon the sun will go down, and that's what you have to think about," says Dale, the Pajama Man, who at 7 A.M. is distracting himself, playing mental word games, his gangly limbs swinging as if they are loose in their sockets. "You have to dissociate your body from the pain."

At a drink stop, he sips slowly, to avoid spitting it up, and tries to gauge his progress.

"I have, what? Thirty-five miles to go?"

"No," a crew member tells him. "Forty-seven."

In spite of the distance remaining, race officials are able to make a reasonably accurate projection of the finishers. They can see who is going well, the ones who will probably hang on.

David Jones, victorious only once in 57 prior marathons and ultra-marathons, is far ahead in first, already nearing Lone Pine, the tree-lined town at the base of Whitney. He is on his way to clocking 29 hours and 10 minutes, more than five hours ahead of the man in second.

Most of the top 10 runners will earn a buckle. Beacham's blisters will continue to plague him, but he is on his way to finishing in 43 hours and 53 minutes, well under his goal of 50 hours. The Major limps on a swollen right knee and is chafing so badly in the crotch that a streak of blood runs to the knee of his white sweatpants. His crew has dubbed him "Mad Mood Maples"; he is headed for a time of 45:15.

At least 18 others are also on the way to finishing. Seven have quit. That number might reach eight. Lisa is the one in doubt—the only remaining runner in serious trouble who has not yet withdrawn.

At 102 miles, she clings to third, reeling from her bad ankle and diarrhea and sleep loss. To go the next six miles to Keeler takes her four hours. Lone Pine is 16 miles beyond Keeler. Morning turns to afternoon. The sun beats down; temperatures soar into the 90s. The highway veers right into Lone Pine, past an airport, motels, diners, then left at a traffic light onto the two-lane road up Whitney.

This final stretch, a 4,000-foot ascent over 13 winding miles, is by far the most daunting. It begins gradually—the road flanked by a sagebrush and boulders and tall rock formations that look like brown crispy cereal all glued together. Soon it rises to impossible steepness.

Lisa is still on the lower slopes at 3 o'clock, taking ice treatments on her ankles. They are both so badly swollen they barely move. Coming out of the motor home, she is staggering. Turning uphill, her mirrored glasses catching the hot sun, she looks ready to cry. Two crew members walk alongside, ready in case she should collapse.

"Never, Never Quit," says a spray-painted slogan across the back of the motor home, but sometimes such lofty ideals must give way to reason. Her crew huddles in the road, discussing whether to make her stop. Her mother, Dot, squints up the mountain.

"It's scary," she says. "She doesn't want to give up. I think we're trying to make the decision for her. My theory is, live to reach another day."

Arguing for surrender is that in two weeks she is a scheduled to compete in a 300-mile adventure race, a team event for which she and her friends have paid hefty entrance fees. It is unthinkable to miss it, but the recovery from an ultra-marathon can take weeks. Most runners are fortunate to begin training again in six or seven days; stamina may not return for a month or two.

Lisa, though, doesn't always make the rational decision. Crew member Tony Di Zinno remembers an earlier adventure race, when she suffered a sprained ankle and a hairline fracture of her right leg on the second day out. She strapped on an air cast and kept going, six more days, 250 more miles.

Her hope had been to break the women's record for Badwater—36 hours and 19 minutes, set during a race that began at night. That goal is now out of reach. With eight miles to go, Lisa disappears into the motor home. Sister Julie stands outside, helpless, wondering if this is where Lisa will yield.

"She says she's never felt this bad," Julie says. "She can't bend her ankles, they're so swollen. There's no blood in her urine yet, but she thinks she lost her stomach lining."

For almost half an hour, there is only this still-life picture: the motor home under a cloudless sky, the rugged mountainside rising above it. Now and then a breeze stirs, but all the air seems to move at once, muffling sounds, preserving a strange hush. Insects clicking softly in the sagebrush. Inside, Lisa lies on her ravaged stomach. She will explain later that it is unwise at this point to sleep. The body begins to shut down. Instead, she meditates. In her mind she makes a list of all those reasons she should quit, the complaints of 127 horrific miles, every negative thought. When the list is as long as she can make it, she lights a tiny imaginary fire—and she burns it.

The door opens. She is helped down to the pavement, and she turns to confront the mountain.

"I'm going to get to the top."

Upward, then, with the road growing steeper. Her ankles cannot handle the slope, and so she turns around, walking backward, tiny three-inch steps. Up, up, up, staring into the sky. Whitney rising behind her. At 5:45, she is well up the mountain, the road at last curving into the afternoon shadows.

Pine trees begin to appear. Her legs look puffed up, rubbery, but they keep moving. Where the road levels out she turns around, walking forward until it rises again. At 6 o'clock, she has less than four miles to go. Every step is precarious, but her mood soars—"it's beyond exhilarating"—and she talks in strained breaths about a book, *The Power Within,* by Chuck Norris, and how its lessons helped her through the hard moments.

Less than a mile to go and the road rounds a steep turn. Lisa goes through it backward, her arms out, as if dizzy. Immediately, four Marines—the advance guard from the Major's group—jump out of a van and join her, like jet fighters forming an escort, but they drop away after the final curve, letting Lisa take the last hill alone.

Whitney Portals, where the race ends, is tucked within a nook of chalky granite, a clear pool fed by a plunging waterfall, hillsides thick with tall evergreens. A yellow tape is stretched across the road and Lisa hits it, finishing in 37 hours and 1 minute. It is not the record she wanted, but it is the fastest a woman has gone from a daytime start, when the racers cross the floor of Death Valley in the heat.

Officials, crew members and five or six bystanders surround her, applauding. She is weeping, relieved, overjoyed, falling into the embrace of her sister, her mom, her friends. She looks up at the sky and says thank you. A huge bouquet of red roses is placed in her arms, spilling over them in a glorious scene of triumph—a portrait somehow perfect, but also fleeting, because Lisa quickly hands the roses away.

"Can't hold them," she whispers. "They're too heavy."

Nadia Comaneci

Bert Randolf Sugar

In the eighth decade of the twentieth century, all that the sports world knew about gymnastics could be written on a postcard already crowded with a description of a small foreign village.

And then, at the 1972 Munich Olympics, an elfin, four-foot-ten, 84-pound munchkin from one of those small foreign villages—Grodno, Byelorussia, to be exact—named Olga Korbut changed all that.

Known only by her first name, Olga was not the best woman gymnast in the Olympics, nor even in her native Soviet Union. That honor belonged to teammate Lyudmila Tourisheva, who captured the all-around championship. But Lyudmila's style was one of a surgical nature, while Olga's was one that saw her ride her horse vaults and her own particular hobbyhorse to her own delight—and that of her audience, both present in Munich and in front of their TV sets around the world.

ABC Sports served as the witting middleman in the making of the legend, as their cameras fell in love with the impish seventeen-year-old with the infectious smile and little-girl pigtails. Ironically, however, it was not her success in becoming the first gymnast ever to perform backward somersaults on the balance beam and uneven parallel bars that made her a media darling, but her failure. Leading after six of the eight events in the team competition, Olga slipped and fell off the uneven bars. As the cameras zoomed in to reveal the youngster's face hidden behind a veil of tears in an up-close-and-personal look, millions of devotees of the life nonstrenuous took her to their hearts.

That little one-act drama merged Marshall McLuhan's so-called global village and the Olympic Village into one, as Olga Korbut became the darling of the games. By the time the Olympics had come to a close, Olga had captured not only gold medals in the balance beam and floor exercises, but the imagination of a worldwide television audience. "Through television," wrote Paul Attner of the *Washington Post,* "the American public saw a fascinating, delicate creature, the little girl down the street who seemed as removed as possible from the unemotional, cold Communist stereotype perpetuated by her teammates. Here was a Russian who actually smiled and laughed and cried and waved to the crowd."

But even though this Russian Barbie doll was flattered, boosted, and covered in the media like the Burning of Rome, Part II, she was, as teammate Nellie Kim said, "not gymnast; Korbut artist." It remained for another gymnast to combine artistry and athleticism. And for another Olympics to put her talents on display.

Four years later, at the 1976 Montreal Olympic Games, a little five-foot-nothing fourteen-year-old Romanian with the melodious Italian-sounding name of Nadia Comaneci—pronounced Coh-man-NEECH by the Forum crowds, in a strangulated rapture—saw the artistry of Olga Korbut and raised it to a higher level. To a perfect 10.

Young Nadia had been discovered by Bela Karolyi, who had seen her as a small girl doing gymnastic exercises during recess in another of those small foreign villages that constantly show up on postcards, this one Gheorghi Gheorghin-Dej. With Karolyi's help, and painstaking effort, Nadia entered the world of gymnastics. In her first meet, at the age of six, she fished thirteenth. Karolyi gave her a doll and told her "it was for good luck. I told her, 'You must never finish thirteenth again.'"

She never would. In fact, over the next seven years she never finished anywhere but first. By 1976 her doll collection had grown to several hundred, and her skills had grown proportionately. In late March, competing in the American Cup, Nadia had done the ungraspable and astonished the gymnastics world by scoring the first perfect 10 in international gymnastics history. Cathy Rigby, the ABC commentator, could only marvel, "In my twenty years in gymnastics, I have never seen such technical perfection and confidence."

Four months later Nadia arrived in Montreal for the XXI Olympiad, and immediately announced her intentions: "I don't come here to smile. I come here to do a job. I leave the smiling to Olga."

But this time around Olga didn't have much to smile about, as that Aladdin's lamp known as TV quickly adopted Nadia as its new darling and left its ex-sweetheart to stand around, like a fly in coffee, attracting attention and comment but hardly enjoying it. For not only did Nadia have Olga's number, she had her own: the number 10.

On the very first night of the team competition, Nadia made Olympic history by receiving a score of 10 on the uneven bars, the first perfect score ever awarded in Olympic gymnastics history. Even the scoreboard wasn't prepared for the phenomenon, as it was unable to record the historic number. But those programming the scoreboard would have several more opportunities to correct their shortsightedness, as Nadia continued to create new standards of excellence, racking up more 10s than could be seen at a Bo Derek film festival.

The following night, sixteen thousand people crammed into the Forum to see the young lady with astonishing gravity-transcending abilities turn in two more flawless performances, on the balance beam and the uneven bars. Before the Olympics were over, Nadia had been awarded seven perfect 10s, winning the gold in the all-around, the balance beam, and the uneven bars, and taking a bronze in the floor exercise.

Her sheer technical prowess and effortless execution had captured the imagination of the world, even its critics. Jim McKay had likened her to "a woman swimming in an ocean of air." And another critic, answering those who thought Nadia's perfect scores had been given away too freely, said, "When Nadia can flawlessly exceed the most hazardous degree of difficulty in the point book, the judges have no choice but to give her a 10."

Asked by one reporter after the Olympics if she planned to retire, the young Nadia answered, "I'm only fourteen." She was to come back to participate in the 1980 Olympics, winning the beam and floor exercise events, to give her a total of five golds, three silvers, and one bronze in Olympic competition.

Nadia Comaneci not only won, she was perfect, as proven by the thirty-one perfect scores of 10 she rang up over her brilliant twelve-year career. And while the glory for putting gymnastics on the map might belong to Olga Korbut, the spoils belonged to an incredible athlete named Nadia Comaneci, who proved that practice makes perfect indeed.

Florence Griffith Joyner

Merrell Noden

Merrell Noden is a Sports Illustrated *correspondent who covered Griffith Joyner's memorable 1988 Olympics for SI. This eulogy appeared September 22, 1998, the day after FloJo's death, on the CNN/SI.com Web site.*

All those numbers we use to measure an athlete's worth—the number of home runs in a season, the precise time it takes to run 100 meters down a track—seem small and insignificant when set against the awful, incontrovertible fact of death, especially an early death like that of Olympic sprint champion Florence Griffith Joyner, who was only 38.

Griffith Joyner, who died in her sleep on Monday of an apparent heart attack, was an astonishing athlete, and also a controversial one. Competing at a time when the sport's profile was sinking, Griffith Joyner was like a gaudy comet flashing across the sky. In mid-1988, in the short spun of 75 days, she transformed herself into FloJo, a flesh-and-blood action hero who dazzled the world with her six-inch-long fingernails and sexy running attire, scorching tracks and retinas with her line of skin-tight negligées, some of which she dubbed "one-leggers."

The 100-meter record (10.49) she set at the 1988 U.S. Olympic Trials in Indianapolis stands unchallenged to this day, and it will surprise no one if it remains in the books for another 20 years. Indeed, the time was so fast it immediately ignited rumors of drug use that even she was unable to outrun. After all, as Kenny Moore pointed out in a story for SI's 1988 Olympic Preview Issue, 10.49 was the equivalent of a hand-timed 9.4 100 yards—equal to O. J. Simpson's best time, and he had been part of a world-record relay team.

The running was actually the simple part. What was tougher was explaining how Griffith Joyner went from world-class to something previously unseen on this planet. When she added the world record for the 200 (21.34) in Seoul and then abruptly retired just months later, before she could reap all the financial rewards which no doubt would have been showered on her, she could not escape the suspicion that she was fleeing the sport while she could. Despite the persistent rumors, Griffith Joyner passed 11 drug tests in 1988 and always denied she had done anything unethical.

In contrast to her husband, 1984 Olympic triple jump champion Al Joyner, who was unfailingly sweet and happy-go-lucky, Griffith Joyner could seem distant at times. Her exotic beauty made her appear remote and unapproachable. What she possessed in enormous quantities was an astonishing determination to succeed.

Growing up poor in the Watts section of Los Angeles, the seventh of 11 children, she decided very early on to make something of herself. As a student at Cal State—Northridge, she rode L.A. city buses for hours each way to attend classes. In the end, unable it seemed to settle on any one career, Griffith Joyner chose them all. She was the author of a series of children's books featuring a character named Barry Bam Bam, and she was also a poet, fashion designer, actress and model. In 1989 she even helped design new uniforms for the Indiana Pacers.

At the time of her death she was serving as co-chair of the President's Council on Physical Fitness and Sports. President Clinton eulogized her as a champion of children. "We were dazzled by her speed, humbled by her talent, and captivated by her style," he said. "Though she rose to the pinnacle of the world of sports, she never forgot where she came from, devoting time and resources to helping children—especially those growing up in our most devastated neighborhoods—make the most of their own talents."

As she made the most of hers.

Day to Embrace

Bill Pleschke

Bill Pleschke has a regular sports column in the Los Angeles Times, *from which this piece was taken.*

Once again, they gave us the shirts off their backs.

And what a marvelous and fitting gesture it was. Brandi Chastain ripping off her white jersey, throwing it into the air, then dancing into the arms of the largest crowd ever to watch a women's sports event.

Once again, the U.S. women's soccer team stripped athletics down to its barest passion.

And once again, we cheered like we never thought we could cheer, for ponytailed and earringed wonders we never dreamed would be giants, in a world that is changing with every kick.

The U.S. women won soccer's World Cup championship at the Rose Bowl with a 5-4 shootout victory over China after penalty kicks were required to settle what 120 minutes of scoreless soccer could not.

They won it when Chastain, after goalkeeper Briana Scurry blocked a shot from China's Liu Ying, belted her penalty kick into the upper right-hand corner of the net past a diving Gao Hong.

Chastain stripped down to her shorts and sports bra before running into the arms of teammates. The roars from 90,185 fans seemed to shake the San Gabriel mountains. Glitter fell from the hot and muggy sky.

"I temporarily lost my mind," Chastain said.

Didn't we all?

It was a triumph of character from a group of women who spent the last month carrying the hopes of all women's athletics on their thin shoulders, delightfully skipping under the weight.

It was also a triumph of a nation that may be finally starting to understand that courage and strength have nothing to do with gender, that heroes can come in all shapes and sizes and shades of lipstick.

"This was about more than the game, more than the day," said Kristine Lilly, whose overtime head save of a shot by Fan Yunjie earned her the game's most valuable player award. "It's about female athletes. It's about sports. It's about everything."

It was about thousands of moms showing up at the Rose Bowl with thousands of little girls proudly lacking in sugar and spice. Their hair was pulled back, their T-shirts were rolled up at the sleeves, their game faces were on as they swaggered the concourses of an event that unquestionably belonged to them.

"I hope every young kid left the stadium today saying, 'I want to be there,'" U.S. star Mia Hamm said.

It was about thousands of dads showing up at the Rose Bowl with, believe it or not, thousands of young boys.

Who wore, believe it or not, Mia Hamm jerseys.

On Saturday, nobody accused anybody of throwing like a girl.

"They play hard, they're like . . . guys," said Sean Giroux, a 13-year-old Orange boy wrapped in an American flag and shouting for the USA as if he were shouting for the Angels.

"Mia Hamm, she's awesome," he said. "And Michelle Akers, she's my-thug."

THE
CHURCH
IN THE
BARRIO

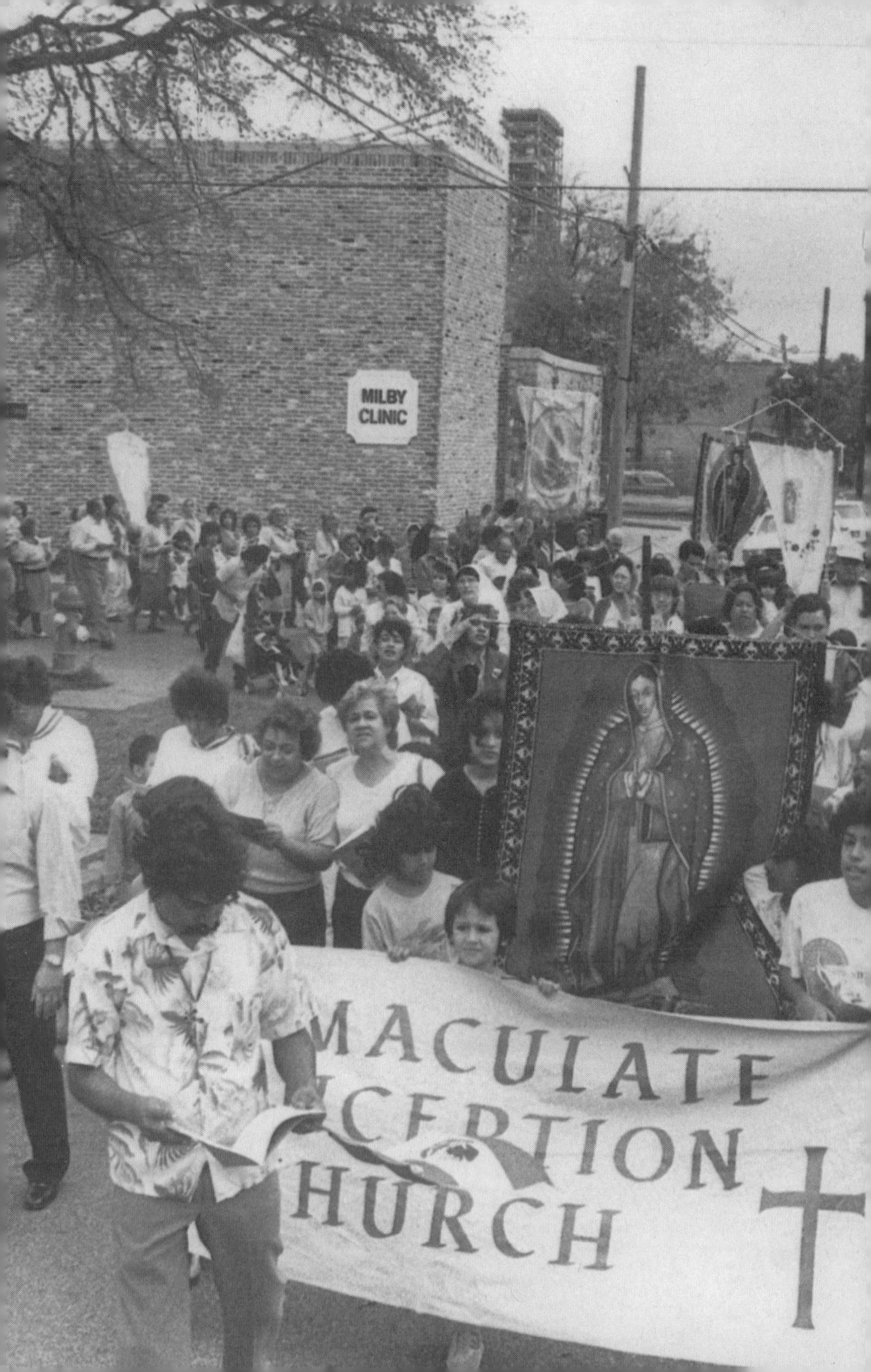
MILBY
CLINIC
MACULIATE
NCERTION
HURCH

The Church in the Barrio

Mexican American
Ethno-Catholicism
in Houston

Roberto R. Treviño

The University of
North Carolina Press
Chapel Hill

Designed by Rebecca M. Giménez
Set in Monotype Dante
by Keystone Typesetting, Inc.

The paper in this book meets the guidelines for permanence and
durability of the Committee on Production Guidelines for Book
Longevity of the Council on Library Resources.

Library of Congress Cataloging-in-Publication Data
Treviño, Roberto R.
The church in the barrio : Mexican American ethno-Catholicism
in Houston / Roberto R. Treviño.
p. cm.
Includes bibliographical references and index.
ISBN-13: 978-0-8078-2996-7 (cloth: alk. paper)
ISBN-10: 0-8078-2996-x (cloth: alk. paper)
ISBN-13: 978-0-8078-5667-3 (pbk.: alk. paper)
ISBN-10: 0-8078-5667-3 (pbk.: alk. paper)
1. Church work with Mexican Americans—Texas—Houston.
2. Catholic Church—Texas—Houston—History. 3. Houston (Tex.)—
Church history. I. Title.
BV4468.2.M48T74   2006
282'.7641411'08968—dc22   2005022338

cloth   10 09 08 07 06   5 4 3 2 1
paper   10 09 08 07 06   5 4 3 2 1

Portions of this work have appeared, in somewhat different form,
in Roberto R. Treviño, "Facing Jim Crow: Catholic Sisters and the
'Mexican Problem' in Texas," *Western Historical Quarterly* 34, no. 2
(Summer 2003): 139–64 (© Western History Association; reprinted by
permission); and "In Their Own Way: Parish Funding and Mexican-
American Ethnicity in Catholic Houston, 1911–1972," *Latino Studies
Journal* 5 (September 1994): 87–107 (reprinted by permission).

Para mis padres,

GERÓNIMO R. TREVIÑO (1920–1995)

and

HILARIA R. TREVIÑO,

mis primeros y mejores maestros

CONTENTS

Illustrations

PREFACE

I grew up in a very Catholic culture, even though I am not Catholic. I spent my early childhood in Mathis, a speck on the rural landscape of the South Texas Gulf Coast, where almost everyone was Mexican and Catholic. My Presbyterian parents' home was next door to my Catholic grandparents, within walking distance of several aunts, uncles, and cousins—all Catholic—and almost literally surrounded by Mexican American Catholic friends and acquaintances. Six days of every week I lived and played in a largely Catholic world; alongside my brothers, my Catholic cousins were my best friends and constant companions, my Catholic grandparents, aunts, and uncles a source of knowledge, emotional succor, delicious food, and entertainment. But on Sundays we went our separate ways. They went to Mass (however infrequently, I noted jealously) and we unfailingly attended services either at the local Menonite Church or at our *Iglesia Presbiteriana Mexicana* in what seemed to be faraway Beeville, some thirty miles down the highway. Later, in Houston, Mexican American Catholicism would also permeate much of my social and professional life. Indeed it still does.

Growing up as a minority within a minority, I compared myself and my mother's Protestant side of our family to my father's Catholic side, and wondered about that familiar yet foreign world that enveloped me. As a child I never entered a Catholic church but I distinctly recall wondering what it would be like to go inside. My Catholic family's religious world remained mysterious to me despite the familiarity it came to have for me through all I experienced of it as a child—the flickering votive candles casting a warm glow on pictures of relatives and saints; the ever-present *Guadalupana* gracing calendars year after year; and the occasional gentle teasing that reminded us we were the *aleluyas* (Protestants) of the Treviño clan. None of this difference and mystery mattered much to me as a child—we were all family and friends, all simply *mexicanos*. But as an adult I became increasingly intrigued by Catholicism's pervasiveness and potency in my people's history and culture. I sensed that this religiosity that had always been everywhere around and so close to me was at the core of the Mexican American experience; I wanted to know how this could be. This book is the result of those long-gestating ruminations. Reflecting on how I have tried to understand my family and my people through their religious history, I realize that I have been working on this book for a very long time.

Many people helped me write this book. The project began as a doctoral dissertation at Stanford University, where a Mellon Fellowship in the Humanities, a Ford Dissertation Fellowship, and the Department of History's Fellows Program generously funded six years of graduate study. I also benefited greatly from two postdoctoral opportunities, the Pew Program in Religion and American History at Yale University and the Young Scholars in American Religion Program at Indiana University–Purdue University at Indianapolis. I am grateful to these organizations for helping me become a historian.

The professionalism and patience of many archivists, librarians, and women and men of the Catholic Church greatly facilitated my research. At the Archives of the Oblate Fathers of Mary Immaculate in San Antonio, the late Father William Watson and his assistants, Gladys Novak and Gloria Pantoja, led me to a wealth of information. Sister Mary Paul Valdez and the late Sister Theresa Joseph Powers provided many useful documents and oral history leads at the Archives of the Congregation of the Sisters of Divine Providence, San Antonio. Brother Michael Grace likewise made useful suggestions and pointed me to important materials during my visit to the Archives of Loyola University of Chicago. I am grateful to Bishop Joseph A. Fiorenza for access to the Archives of the Diocese of Galveston-Houston, to Monsignor Daniel Scheel, who facilitated my research at the Galveston-Houston Chancery and in various parishes in Houston, and to Mary Acosta, Marion Zientek, Bob Giles, and Lisa May, who made my research in Houston very fruitful. I greatly appreciate Bishop John McCarthy's graciousness during my research at the Catholic Archives of Texas in Austin, his contagious enthusiasm for church history and politics, and his interest in my research. In Austin, archivists Michael Zilligen and the late Kinga Perzynska gave me invaluable help. The staff at the Stanford University libraries gave me crucial support, and I am particularly indebted to Sonia Moss. In Houston, Louis Marchiafava and his staff at the Houston Metropolitan Research Center were ever forthcoming and helpful, and I am especially grateful to my friend and respected colleague Dr. Thomas H. Kreneck, who opened many doors for me in the Bayou City and beyond and gave me generous and expert guidance. I am also greatly indebted to the parishioners who graciously opened their homes and hearts to me and taught me much about the Mexican American Catholic experience in Houston; without them this book would be much poorer.

Additionally, I have been blessed with the friendship and tutelage of outstanding individuals who have shaped my intellectual development and the writing of this book. My fellow Tejanos, Tatcho Mindiola, Arnoldo De León, and Tom Kreneck, have long been sources of encouragement and good counsel. Similarly, I was also helped along the way by such exemplars as Anne Butler, Clyde Milner, Neil Foley, Ramón Gutiérrez, James Kirby Martin, George Fredrickson, Renato Rosaldo, Jon Butler, Harry Stout, Philip Gleason, and my former colleagues in the Department of History at the University of Colorado at Colorado Springs, particularly Harlow Sheidley. At the University of Texas at Arlington my history department colleagues have been ever supportive, as have my colleagues at the Center for Mexican American Studies. I am especially thankful for those individuals who took time from their busy lives to comment on all or parts of the manuscript. Timothy M. Matovina's close and repeated readings of the entire manuscript provided challenging questions that significantly improved my work. Others, including Rudy Busto, John McGreevy, Arnoldo De León, Gilberto Hinojosa, Jay P. Dolan, and Christian Zlolniski, also generously shared their time and wisdom to help me strengthen this book. For his steadying influence early in my career and unfailing support over the years I am grateful to my friend and mentor, Professor Albert M. Camarillo. My sincere thanks also go to senior editor Charles Grench and his fine staff. I will be ever grateful for Chuck's crucial encouragement and guidance, and for the skill and professionalism shown by the individuals at UNC Press who helped bring this work to fruition.

Most of all it is my anchor in life, *mi familia*, that deserves much of the credit for this book. I thank my brothers and sisters for their encouragement, and my sons, Robert André and Samuel Benjamin, for their special inspiration. My wife, Barbara, sustained me throughout the peaks and valleys of this work with constant good humor and enthusiasm; her role in writing this book was immensurable. My most profound thanks, of course, are reserved for my first and most important teachers, *mis padres*, Hilaria and Gerónimo Treviño, for a lifetime of unconditional love.

THE
CHURCH
IN THE
BARRIO

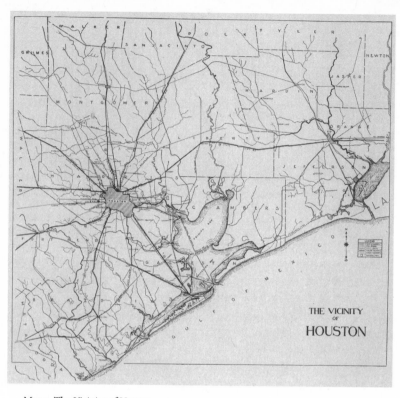

Map 1. The Vicinity of Houston, 1929

INTRODUCTION

With nervous anticipation, nineteen-year-old Angie García and two friends drove toward the city of Harlingen in the Rio Grande Valley of South Texas. They were on their way to enroll in a technical training course, betting it would bring exciting new adventures into their young lives. Yet even as important as it was to arrive on time at their appointment, the threesome just *had* to make one stop along the way—at the town of San Juan, Texas. San Juan is home to the famous Shrine of the Virgin of San Juan del Valle, a popular pilgrimage site for Mexican American Catholics modeled after the seventeenth-century shrine of the Virgen de San Juan de los Lagos located in Jalisco, Mexico. "As surely as they must breathe air to live," a newspaper reported, "they must first pray and ask the help of the Virgin Mary as they take a new step in their lives."[1]

On the same page of that newspaper, another article described a common scene at the older shrine in Jalisco, Mexico. There "thousands—sometimes tens of thousands of people—crawl, pray, weep and hold infants aloft . . . in the suffocating heat," as they "work their way inch-by-inch up the aisles and, at long last, kneel reverently before the image of the Virgin Mary." Marveling at the sight of the faithful in Jalisco, a cleric remarked, "Everyone who sees this can, at the very least, begin to understand faith."[2]

UNDERSTANDING MEXICAN AMERICAN ETHNO-CATHOLICISM

But how are we to understand this faith? How can we begin to appreciate its importance to Mexican Americans today—people like Angie

García and her friends in South Texas, for example? How do we fathom its meaning among the legions of Mexican faithful who, year after year, trek to the seventeenth-century shrine in Jalisco? And how can we understand the mystical bond that connects Mexican and Mexican American Catholics in different places and times? In short, how can we understand the role of Catholicism in Mexican American history? These are timely questions when we consider that today Latinos comprise more than one-third of that faith tradition and very soon roughly half of all U.S. Catholics will be Latinos. "The U.S. Catholic Church is being inexorably transformed into a Latino church," a prominent cleric recently observed. "That presents an interesting challenge to the historically Anglo-dominated church in the United States, which does not respond to another style of Catholicism that is more graphic and expressive."[3] For many Americans, Mexicans evoke images of fervent Catholicism. Indeed, many people automatically associate "Mexican American" with "Catholic" and would readily agree that Catholicism has played an important role in Mexican American history, as the conventional wisdom has long assumed. But precisely *how* has that importance revealed itself in the Mexican American experience? That is the driving question behind this book. *The Church in the Barrio* offers some answers to that question. Based on the history of Mexican American Catholics in Houston, it examines some of the ways this faith has shaped Chicano history.[4]

Throughout this book I use the term "ethno-Catholicism" to refer to the Mexican American way of being Catholic. As a result of Spain's encounter with the New World, pre-Reformation Spanish Christianity blended with Mexican Indian worldviews to produce a unique Mexican Catholic identity and way of life. Mexican Americans in Texas and the Southwest carried on this ethnoreligion that, in the spirit of its medieval and Indian roots, made room for faith healing and other practices deemed superstitious by clergy; favored saint veneration, home altar worship, and community-centered religious celebration that blurred the line between the sacred and the secular; and tended simultaneously to selectively participate in the institutional Catholic

Church yet hold it at arm's length. Ethno-Catholicism was essentially countercultural, as it represented an "organic, holistic worldview . . . at odds with post-Enlightenment notions of time and space, of the material and the spiritual, and of the person's place within time and space, within the material and spiritual dimensions of reality."[5]

The Church in the Barrio refutes the notion that this so-called popular Catholicism was (is) an inferior expression of spirituality. Despite the fact that I show how clergy often denigrated Mexicans' way of being Catholic and how Mexicans doggedly clung to it, I do not rigidly juxtapose the institution's religion against the people's. Framing religious experience as dichotomies—"elite versus popular" or "folk versus formal" religion—may indeed reveal struggles between the powerful and the less powerful in a society, but it also distorts historical reality.[6] Such neat categories simply do not convey the complexities of the *interaction* that has characterized the relationship between the faithful and religious institutions. While tensions have certainly existed between Mexicans and the U.S. Catholic Church, historical evidence also suggests that this social distance has not been totally unbridgeable nor completely antagonistic; ethno-Catholicism is not the polar opposite of institutional Catholicism.[7] Rather, Mexicans in the United States have had an *interactive* relationship with the institutional church, one that at different historical moments has been characterized by varying degrees of resistance and accommodation.

I found a sensible framework for understanding the role of Catholicism in Mexican American history in cultural resistance theory and historical studies that explore the centrality of religion among African Americans and other "outsiders." Those familiar with the works of James C. Scott, Lawrence W. Levine, Eugene D. Genovese, Albert J. Raboteau, and R. Laurence Moore will see their influence in this book. In different ways, each of these scholars has cogently shown how people have relied on their faith traditions to resist oppression, define themselves, build communities, and thrive in hostile environments. The ideas of two anthropologists, Deborah Reed-Danahay's notion of French subalterns "making do" and Margaret A. Gibson's portrayal of "accommodation without assimilation" among Sikh immigrant students, also helped me understand how Mexican Catholics coped with pressures of social and religious assimilation in Houston.[8] As Reed-Danahay and Gibson have shown, it is important to distinguish between resistance and accommodation. Marginalized peoples who face pressures to assimilate choose from a range of responses when they confront threats to their identity and way of life. Some of their responses clearly are forms of outright resistance. However, ethno-religious minorities historically have also adopted other strategies, including cultural change or compromise, a mix of resistance and compromise, or various degrees of compliance. In other words, they have found ways of "making do" and have chosen "accommodation without assimilation" in addition to clear-cut resistance.[9]

Houston's Mexican and Mexican American Catholics, like other folks in history, responded in a variety of ways to the assimilation pressures exerted by U.S. society and the Catholic Church—and their faith was central to those responses. Catholic theologians are increasingly recognizing the importance of this aspect of Latino Catholicism. Historian and theologian Timothy Matovina observes that in the "continuing struggle with prejudice and cultural rejection, ethno-religious celebrations . . . reinforce group identity, engender a sense of belonging, and express a collective protest and resistance against the assimilatory demands of the dominant culture."[10] As Matovina's work has capably shown for the nineteenth century and as my book illustrates for the twentieth, Catholicism has long been a shaping force in the spiritual and material lives of Mexican Americans.

It is important to read this book as a social history. I did not set out to write a theological treatise on Mexican American Catholicism or to advance new theoretical frameworks with which to reconceptualize the study of Chicano history. Rather, the book is intended to show how a particular faith tradition, Mexican American ethno-Catholicism, historically has played an important role in the social arena. The Mexican American way of being Catholic is layered with historical meaning. Understanding this faith tradition not only allows us to appreciate those things usually associated with religion—devotional practices, attitudes toward the sacraments, patterns of church attendance, and so on—but, equally important, it also gives us insight into other aspects of Mexican American history. That is the main purpose of the book. I hope to show that by understanding ethno-Catholicism we can more fully understand the construction of ethnic identity, the formation of communities, the sources and processes of social change, the ways people find their place in a society, and some of the implications of gender relations—subjects that too often are studied without much attention given to the role of religion. Scholars in other disciplines may find *The Church in the Barrio* useful for their own purposes, but those seeking new models with which to understand Mexican American Catholicism per se should consult the writings of Virgilio Elizondo, Orlando Espín, Roberto Goizueta, and other such insightful theologians for epistemologically and methodologically distinct interpretations.[11]

But why study Houston? Part of the answer, of course, is that I wanted to know more about the place where I came of age and spent much of my life. Beyond that, though, I have long been struck by the inattention historians have shown to "new" Chicano communities, communities that are rooted in the twentieth century, not in the Spanish colonial and Mexican eras. Of course, we can never know enough about communities that were planted during the Spanish/Mexican past, and historians should continue to study them. But years ago when a friend asked with exasperation, "Do we really need another study of Chicanos in Los Angeles?" he was making an important point. For some time now a number of cities—Houston, Dallas, Denver, Phoenix, and others—have had numerically significant and culturally vibrant Mexican communities that developed during the twentieth century, but their history remains largely unknown to us. In particular, places like Houston and Dallas—situated as they are in the East Texas borderlands between South and West—invite comparison between the two, as well as with the more familiar communities located deeper in the Southwest from which we derive much of our current understanding about Mexican American history.

Houston's early Mexican immigrants truly encountered *terra incognita* upon arriving in the Bayou City. Very little looked or sounded familiar to them. Unlike San Antonio, Los Angeles, or Albuquerque, Houston had no Spanish or Mexican past—no missions, no familiar place names or village padres, no gentle reminders of home that could help ease the new residents' transition into a bewildering new environment. Established Mexican American communities offered advantages that life in Houston lacked, such as the comfort and security of fellow Mexicans in large numbers and the social and religious networks and institutions that came with them. For Mexicans who immigrated to Houston in the early twentieth century, life was complicated by the absence of an established Mexican presence that required them to transplant and develop anew—not simply reconnect with—the cultural underpinnings of their lives. Surely this would have been more difficult to do in Houston than in the more familiar and supportive surroundings of long-established Mexican communities. In these circumstances, some aspects of religious life took on added significance, especially the kinds of customs I examine in this book that were equally social and religious and promoted a sense of community and security. In a place like Houston, the lived religion of the people of necessity cemented faith, family, identity, and community in ways that were more conscious than in the familiar atmosphere of a deeply rooted Mexican community. This is not to devalue Catholicism in older places. We know, for example, that in San Antonio, home of the Alamo, Tejanos countered inequality partly by claiming legitimacy in the region on religious grounds.[12] Rather, it is simply to remind us that the Chicano experience has not been monolithic, either in terms of region or religion, and that we should be alert to the nuances the interaction of these two factors may produce. How the relative importance of ethno-Catholicism in older versus newer Mexican American communities will be borne out awaits the findings of historians willing to use religion as a vantage point from which to examine Chicano history. For certainly our vision of the past will remain skewed without studying those new Chicano communities and their religious history.

The Church in the Barrio unfolds during the years 1911–72. I focus on this time frame because it forms a discrete part of the history of Houston's Mexican American community in at least two ways. In the social and political history of the community, these years encompass its immigrant beginnings to its maturation as a predominately native-born population at the height of the Chicano movement. That era would then be followed by a new phase as the liberal politics of the civil rights era gave way to conservatism, and immigration from other parts of Latin America raised the profile of non-Mexican Latinos in the city beginning in the early 1970s. The years 1911–72 also bracket a distinct phase of the *religious* history of Mexican Americans in Houston. The year 1911 marks the beginning of a Roman Catholic institutional presence in Houston's barrios with the arrival of the Oblates of Mary Immaculate, the missionary priests brought to the city by the Galveston Diocese (renamed the Galveston-Houston Diocese in 1959) to minister specifically to the growing Mexican population. At the other end of this time frame, the year 1972 signals the participation of lay and church leaders from Houston in the Encuentro Hispano de Pastoral (Pastoral Congress for the Spanish-speaking). That national event stands as a watershed in the religious history of Mexican American Catholics in Houston and the United States and is a logical ending point for the story of *The Church in the Barrio*.

In trying to understand some of the ways Catholicism molded the Mexican American experience in Houston, I was guided by two interrelated questions: What has been the nature of the relationship between Mexican Americans and the Catholic Church in the United States? And what role did Catholicism play in Mexican Americans' everyday lives? These broad questions raised others. How did representatives of the Catholic Church view Mexican people, and what effects did their perceptions and attitudes have on the spiritual and material life of Mexican Catholics? Part of this study analyzes how priests' and nuns' attitudes toward Mexicans affected the church's relationship with the Mexican American community. I also explore how Mexicans themselves viewed institutional requirements and the women and men who represented the Roman Catholic Church. In this regard, I show how generation, class, culture, and gender differences influenced the parishioners' religious expression and their association with the church. I was also interested in shedding light on how Catholicism was (is) related to the formation of Mexican American ethnicity, to community-building, and to notions of social justice. To reveal some of those relationships I examine, for example, *altarcitos* (home altars), *quinceañeras* (fifteen-year-olds' rite of passage), and other traditions that were both religious and social, customs that helped to mold identity and propagate strong communities. I also show how Mexicans pressed the church not only to minister to their spiritual lives but also to support their struggles for equality and a better material life.

I use both chronological and topical chapters to tell the story of *The Church in the Barrio*. Chapter 1 sketches the evolution of Mexican Catholicism from Spanish colonial times to the early twentieth century. Given their isolation and the weak institutional presence of the Roman Catholic Church in the Southwest, Spanish and Mexican Catholics in Texas developed an ethnoreligious identity rooted in home- and community-based religious practices. That ethno-Catholic way of life kept the faith alive while it celebrated their cultural heritage and helped them endure a harsh frontier existence and the social and political changes that buffeted their lives. This brand of Catholicism defined itself against (and often found itself in conflict with) the Euro-American Catholicism that accompanied the American takeover of Mexican Texas in the nineteenth century. The rest of this chapter completes the historical backdrop for the book by tracing the development of Houston's Mexican *colonias* (communities) from the nineteenth century to the early 1970s. In a city predicated on a Southern Protestant ethos, Mexican Catholics competed for cultural space not only with the Anglo majority, which included various groups of white Catholics, but also with a large black population and a Mexican Protestant presence as well.

Chapter 2 dissects the concept of ethno-Catholicism in order to illustrate its central place in this Catholic community history. A blend of the religious worldviews and practices of Old World Spanish Christians and New World Indians, Mexican ethno-Catholicism combined selective participation in formal church activities with a vibrant lived religion that prized family- and community-centered traditions. A religious style that blurred the line between the sacred and the secular and gave singular expression to the people's identity, this ethnoreligion reflected and sustained the cultural independence of Mexican American Catholics and their resistance to social inequality. Within the institutional framework, they participated in the sacraments of the Roman Catholic Church and in its organizations, but they often did so on their own terms. Similarly, keeping alive popular traditions frowned upon by church representatives allowed Mexican Catholics to assert their personal worth, confront inequality, and maintain viable families and communities.

Chapter 3 examines church representatives' perceptions of Texas Mexicans, how and why these changed over time, and the implications these shifting attitudes had for Mexican American communities. Relations between Mexicans and the church in Houston during most of the twentieth century were distant, reflecting both deeply rooted negative views held by many Catholic officials about Texas Mexicans and the parishioners' traditional ambivalence toward the institution. Nonetheless, the relationship improved over time partly because of positive attitudinal changes that developed among Catholic officials but more so because of pressures exerted by Mexicans and Mexican Americans. Their burgeoning presence and increasing political activity captured the church's attention. From the 1910s to the early 1970s, representatives of the Galveston-Houston Diocese gradually but unevenly gained a deeper understanding of Mexican-origin people and their style of Catholicism, thus paving the way for a more effective pastoral and social ministry.

Chapter 4 examines religious institutional development in two ways. First, I document the spread of parishes in Houston's barrios, arguing that while the church provided more Spanish-speaking personnel and financial support to Mexican communities over time, it was the parishioners' own initiatives that laid the groundwork for actually establishing, maintaining, and expanding Catholic churches and schools in the barrios. The rest of this chapter discusses two types of parishes, territorial and national (the former bases membership on residence within defined boundaries, the latter on a common language or ethnicity).[13] Membership in one type of parish or the other revealed social distinctions among parishioners that reflected their varying notions about ethnic identity and found expression particularly in the degree of Spanish, English, or bilingual church services used and in the names given to the parishes themselves. Houston's inner-city parishes tended to be home to people who earned less money and had closer ties generationally to Mexico, while native-born Mexican Americans who could afford to move out of the barrios often formed their own parishes in predominately white or mixed neighborhoods, or integrated themselves into existing ones.

In a different way, Chapter 5 also deals with religious institutional growth. Here I focus on parish fund-raising in order to show its links to faith, identity, and community among Mexican American Catholics. Essentially, I argue that fund-raising was both a product and a process of ethno-Catholicism. In other words, the strategies used to generate money for the parishes not only drove institutional development but also promoted a sense of ethnic and religious identity and solidarity that preserved the Mexican American way of being Catholic. In order to illustrate the strong connection between fund-raising and ethno-Catholic identity, I present a case study I call the St. Joseph–St. Stephen controversy. Reacting to the forced merger of their *iglesia mexicana* (Mexican church) with an Anglo church as a threat to their identity and way of life, parishioners at St. Stephen Parish resisted the diocesan leadership until it restored their former status as an independent Mexican national parish.

Chapter 6 traces the changing nature of the church's social ministry among Mexican parishioners between the years 1911 and 1965, emphasizing both the Mexican community's traditional self-reliance and the church's shift from ad hoc relief to more systematic material aid for its parishioners. This chapter shows how individuals within the Catholic Church had concerned themselves early on with the material needs of Mexican parishioners while, at the same time, the Mexican community had its own self-help tradition to alleviate crises and combat persistent poverty in the barrios. Over the course of the twentieth century, however, the church's social ministry gradually expanded beyond ad hoc charity. Beginning in the 1940s, Catholic social ministry slowly became more systematic even as the charitable works by nuns, priests, and other compassionate individuals continued.

Chapter 7 carries the story of social ministry from the mid-1960s to the early 1970s by focusing on the role of the Catholic Church in the Chicano movement in Houston. I argue that the church's involvement in the Chicano movement, however tentative and cautious, was significant nonetheless and that it resulted from the convergence of changing clerical attitudes and internal and external pressures exerted by Chicanas and Chicanos. The Galveston-Houston Diocese responded to the Chicano movement on two levels, individual and institutional, and with various strategies, some of which were traditional and others new. While individual Chicana nuns and Chicano priests led struggles for social equality, the church as an institution avoided fully joining in the fray of secular politics directly, trying instead to nurture rather than initiate solutions to social problems through lay rather than clerical leadership. Eventually the pressures for change culminated in 1972 in an institutional response called the *encuentros*, a series of forums to air the grievances of Latino Catholics throughout the nation.

The Church in the Barrio argues that ethno-Catholicism was a nurturing way of life for Mexican Americans in Houston, one that sustained their sense of ethnic identity and provided ways of coping with their marginality in the Catholic Church and American society. Long considered second-class Americans and often treated as social pariahs, Texas Mexicans found in ethno-Catholicism the wherewithal to overcome the stigma associated with their ethnic and religious outsider status. Their faith helped mold and preserve the people's identity; it structured their family and community relationships and institutions; it provided them both spiritual and material sustenance; and it girded them in their long quest for social justice. Ethno-Catholicism played a central role in the ongoing Mexican American pilgrimage toward greater inclusion in the religious and civic life of the Bayou City.

THE BIG PICTURE: LATINOS AND U.S. CATHOLIC HISTORY

In 1970 a group of scholars decried the scarcity of literature about Chicanos and religion, claiming that "*no* literature exists on the role of the church among the Mexican American population."[14] That claim was somewhat overstated, but not by much. More puzzling, however, is the fact that more than three decades later the religious history of Mexican Americans remains understudied despite their long association with Catholicism and their growing importance in the American Catholic Church today. The recent flourishing of U.S. religious history and the growth of Chicano history notwithstanding, scholars remind us that we know relatively little about religion as a historical force in the Mexican American experience. There have been numerous important studies about Euro-American religion in recent years, but similar attention has yet to be given to Mexicans in the United States, even by historians of the Chicano experience.[15] Fortunately, in the mid-1990s two publications, *Mexican Americans and the Catholic Church, 1900–1965* and *Tejano Religion and Ethnicity: San Antonio, 1821–1860*, began to address the lack of in-depth historical studies about Mexican Americans and religion.[16] My study resonates with both of these pioneering works, particularly with Timothy Matovina's focus on the links between Catholicism and ethnic identity and community-building in *Tejano Religion and Ethnicity*. More recently some important studies, mostly in essay form, have added to the developing historical literature on Mexican American Catholicism.[17] *The Church in the Barrio*, however, is the first book-length treatment of the role of Catholicism in the history of a twentieth-century urban Mexican American community.

Scattered observations about Mexican American Catholicism reveal that the experiences of Latino Catholics outside of Texas have both mirrored and contrasted with those of Mexican Houstonians. The style of Mexican Catholicism that evolved in Texas developed in much the same way in Mexican communities throughout the American Southwest and Midwest, its main traits evidenced in its home- and community-centeredness, its mix of institutional marginality and fervent "popular" expression, and in the faith's centrality to the people's identity.[18] Puerto Rican and Cuban Catholics in the United States also shared commonalities with Mexican Americans as they, too, followed essentially a medieval Christianity modified by New World conditions.[19] However, alongside these similarities there were some differences, the most obvious and important of which was the African influence in Puerto Rican and Cuban society. *Mulataje*, the racial and cultural mixing of African and Iberian peoples, was much more pronounced in the Caribbean than in Mexico and the Southwest, where *mestizaje*, or Spanish and Indian mixing, predominated. This basic difference explains the historical presence of the African-derived religion, *Santería*, among Cuban Americans rather than Mexican Americans, as well as Puerto Rican devotion to Our Lady of Monserrate, the Black Madonna, in contrast to Mexican American fealty to Our Lady of Guadalupe, *la morenita*, or the brown (Indian) Virgin.[20] *Mulataje* figured prominently in the history of Puerto Ricans and Cubans within the American Church, as did *mestizaje* in the Mexican American experience. While Mexican-origin Catholics were saddled with a "pagan" Indian image, the largely negative perception of Puerto Ricans in the Northeast reflected the racism and color-consciousness that infected both the American church and society in general.

Racial prejudice was also an important, though not the only, reason behind the intensive Americanization efforts aimed at Latino Catholics.[21] Of course, Latinos held no special claim in this regard; the U.S. Church subjected numerous other Catholic groups—Germans, Poles, French-Canadians, and many others—to its Americanizing zeal before Latinos had their turn. Then, too, some aspects of Americanization had a positive side, particularly nationality parishes that were meant to be way stations to Americanization. Many European immigrants preferred their own segregated and relatively underfunded national parishes where they and "their kind" worshipped in Old World familiarity. Having successfully transplanted not only their beliefs but also important tangibles such as clergy, schools, and other resources to these ethnic islands, European newcomers to America made their national parishes havens of cultural continuity, sources of emotional strength, and, equally important, training grounds and springboards for upward social mobility.[22]

But here lies a fundamental difference between the European and Latino immigrant experiences. Mexican and Puerto Rican immigration was *not* accompanied by a large-scale transplantation of their own clergy and religious structures and resources. They thus lacked the kinds of support that most European immigrants used to soften incorporation into a new society.[23] In contrast, Cuban immigrants brought with them many clergy, and they transplanted a number of important religious schools and other organizations to Miami in their post-1959 migrations, much like European immigrants had done. Like Puerto Ricans, however, Cubans continued to see themselves as temporary sojourners in the United States, and they also clung to their religious identity and Cuban roots.[24]

Aside from the more obvious differences between Latino and Euro-American immigration experiences—that is, the nearness of Latin America and its ongoing immigration versus the distance of Europe and its subsiding immigration—two factors clearly set Latinos apart from most Euro-American Catholics: their mix of pre-Reformation Christianity and indigenous African and Indian religions, and their status as people of color in a race-sensitive society. Here, too, there is one important exception to note. As we shall see, Mexican ethno-Catholicism offers striking parallels with the Catholicism of southern Italian immigrants who arrived in the late nineteenth and early twentieth centuries. U.S. Church leaders generally saw and treated southern Italians much the same way they did Mexican Americans, ridiculing and chastising their infrequent church attendance, their devotional practices that centered on shrines, pilgrimages, holy cards, and other sacramentals, and their "deficient" understanding of doctrine. But this is an exception that proves the rule: southern Italian Catholics received treatment similar to Mexicans because both groups shared an ambiguous racial status and a style of Catholicism considered suspect.

Ironically, the significant differences between most Euro-American and Latino Catholics made the latter's historical trajectory in some ways more akin to that of African American Protestants. As historian Jay P. Dolan aptly recognized, Latinos "have fashioned a Church within a Church" and recent developments in Latino Catholicism are "very similar to what has happened in the African-American Protestant Church over the course of the twentieth century."[25] Over time, both groups have created a distinct style and character within the larger frameworks of their U.S. churches, complete with unique liturgies and theologies. However, with regard to a social ministry, the black Protestant experience has differed significantly from that of Latinos. As Albert Raboteau and others have shown, African American Protestantism historically has significantly nourished not only its people's spiritual needs but also their social, economic, and political aspirations. Obviously, that has not been the case with Latinos and the Catholic Church, although the twentieth century saw some movement in that direction. The basic difference has been that African Americans historically have owned their churches and Latinos have not. Since the 1960s, Latinos have become an ever-larger part of the lay membership of the U.S. Catholic Church, but they remain a tiny portion of the clergy and episcopacy that controls it.[26]

Although the Mexican American Catholic experience in Houston has much in common with other peoples' struggles to find a place in the United States, it is more than just another chapter of American church history or simply another piece of the American cultural mosaic. By probing this religion-as-a-way-of-life, *The Church in the Barrio* goes beyond what traditional denominational history can teach us, allowing us to better understand the complicated relationship between the U.S. Catholic Church and Mexican Americans, as well as how religion permeated and influenced many other aspects of their lives. Moreover, by illuminating some of the ways Catholicism and culture interact, this book helps explain Mexican American cultural perseverance in the United States, and it challenges us to resist easy generalizations about the complex roles religions play in shaping the broader national experience.

In 1964 historian Henry May noted that a "recovery" of American religious history was under way. Subsequent decades saw the emergence of a "new religious history" as historians and other scholars rejuvenated the study of religion and its impact in the American experience.[27] This book is offered as part of that ongoing work and in the hope of enlisting others in a task too long ignored and still in its infancy—the recovery of Chicano religious history.

ONE

They started gathering at four in the morning at the rail depot where the nuns were supposed to depart. There were about 300 of them by nine o'clock, 300 angry Mexicans. They were furious at their bishop for not letting some refugee Sisters of Charity from Mexico stay and minister to their community in Brownsville. The nuns were badly needed, and the parishioners, though impoverished, were willing to help feed and house them. But the bishop refused, and he ordered the nuns to move along quickly. Incensed, the protesters' numbers and passions quickly swelled. Three thousand strong, they made fiery speeches and unhitched and pulled away the rail car the sisters were going to board. *¡Que se vaya el obispo!* yelled the crowd— Make the bishop go! *¡Fuera el obispo!* they cried—Out with the bishop! The police were unable to control them. Desperate, the mayor appealed to the bishop to calm the crowd, but the bishop refused. He declined to face his parishioners—the "half-civilized Mexican greasers," as he was wont to call them.[1]

This telling incident in Brownsville, Texas, in 1875 reveals important elements that helped shape the lives of Mexican Catholics in Texas and the Southwest. In the nineteenth century and well into the twentieth, most Mexican Americans were both socially and religiously marginalized; they were, in the eyes of many Americans, a pariah community. The same was true in early twentieth-century Houston. There, parishioners considered themselves *muy católicos*, very Catholic, yet churchmen and Anglo society often held them in contempt. Over time, however, Mexican and Mexican American Catholics in the Bayou City shed much of their status as social outcasts and made strides toward greater participation in the city's religious and civic life. How can we explain this? The answer to that question is the central story of this book, and to begin to answer it we must first understand the historical context in which that gradual transformation took place.

This chapter traces the history of Tejano Catholicism and the development of Houston's Mexican community. It introduces the concept of Mexican American ethno-Catholicism: a home- and community-based faith that melded Spanish medieval Christianity and New World indigenous religion into a style of Roman Catholicism ambivalently tied to the formal church but inextricably fused with the people's ethnic identity. This chapter, then, forms the backdrop for the remainder of the book, mapping the religious and historical landscape across which Mexican Catholics journeyed to forge a place for themselves in the Bayou City.

CATÓLICOS IN A CHANGING SOCIETY

The antecedents of Tejano Catholicism and Houston's Mexican community reach back to 1519, when Spanish explorers claimed the territory that later became Texas as part of Spain's empire in the Americas. Spain never paid much attention to Texas because it lacked the glitter of the Aztec empire in central Mexico. Consequently, the scattered outposts of hardy soldiers, priests, and colonists who represented Spain's tenuous claim to frontier Texas remained isolated from Spanish culture and institutions, separated by vast distances from the hub of colonial society in Mexico City and imbued with a spirit of independence.[2] By the time Mexico broke from Spain in 1821, the Gulf Coast winds had long since swept away any trace of El Orcoquísac, a fort and mission complex that once stood some thirty-five miles east of present-day Houston. Spain lost Texas to Mexico but laid the foundation of Mexican and Mexican American Catholicism.[3] In turn, Mexico lost Texas when a flood of illegal immigrants from the United States set the stage for the war of Texas independence, a revolution that the Texans won at the battle of San Jacinto in April 1836—in the swampy land that eventually developed into suburbs of the soon-to-be city of Houston.[4]

Seeking to protect its flock in the predominately Protestant Republic of Texas, the Vatican began paying more attention to this region by transferring administrative control of it from the northern Mexican Diocese of Linares to the Diocese of New Orleans in 1840. In 1847 Rome established the Diocese of Galveston, and in 1849 Bishop John M. Odin imported a small group of French missionaries, the Oblate Fathers of Mary Immaculate, to work among the Mexican population in Texas. The Oblates faced huge difficulties, given the enormity of the Galveston Diocese (which then comprised all of present-day Texas and some neighboring territories), their widely scattered parishioners, and a perennial shortage of clergy.[5] Class differences, cultural animosities, and racism compounded these problems. Clerics steeped in European values and traditions directed the church's work well into the twentieth century. Mostly French initially, some of these churchmen denigrated Mexicans and their brand of Catholicism. In deep South Texas, for instance, two highly placed clerics, Father Florent Vandenberghe and Father Dominic Manucy, dreaded having to work with destitute Mexican parishioners, preferring instead "civilized" people, that is, Americans and European immigrants—their racial and cultural cousins who gave them greater financial support.[6] Clearly, the Catholic Church in Texas mirrored the racial hierarchies and social relations of the time, and, consequently, some of its policies helped propagate the social inequality that marked the lives of Mexicans and other people of color.

In the face of prejudice and neglect, Texas Mexicans developed an ambivalent relationship with the institutional church, alternately accepting and rejecting its requirements and ultimately interpreting and practicing their faith in ways that met their own needs. They had an unbounded reverence for Our Lady of Guadalupe and other saints and often expressed great respect for the priesthood. Mexicans followed the basic tenets of Roman Catholicism and faithfully observed traditional holy days, but they also ignored some requirements, such as marrying within the church. And they clung to unsanctioned traditions such as home altar worship, a custom that bypassed the institutional church by personally invoking the intercession of saints. In the eyes of most churchmen, Mexicans were not good mass-and-sacraments Catholics; clergymen often criticized their sporadic church attendance and chafed at their "indifference" toward the sacraments. On the other hand, priests noted how scrupulously Mexicans attended to *particular* rituals, especially baptism and confirmation. Tejanas and Tejanos were ignorant about doctrine, reports claimed, but they displayed great reverence for certain aspects of the faith; they saw themselves as "good" Catholics, while church leaders often viewed them as "bad" ones.[7]

Ethnic animosity and class and cultural barriers partly explain these polar views, but they also stemmed from the distinct histories of Latin American and U.S. Catholicism. The Catholicism Spain brought to the Americas in 1492 was actually medieval Christianity, the religion shared by western Europeans before Martin Luther's Reformation split them into warring factions of Protestants and Catholics in 1517. In what is now central Mexico, conquered indigenous peoples syncretized the old Spanish medieval Christianity with their own religions, giving rise to a distinct "Mexican" Catholicism. Somewhat later in Europe—after the Columbian voyages and the Protestant Reformation—a new form of Catholicism began to develop as a result of the Council of Trent (1545–63). Often called the Counter-Reformation, the Catholic reform and revitalization movement that began at Trent led to the rise of "Tridentine" Catholicism (derived from *Tridentum*, Latin for the city of Trent, Italy). This new style of Roman Catholicism—a modernized and intellectualized version of the old medieval Christianity—spread throughout northern and western Europe. Later it came with the British to

North America, where eventually it would confront the old medieval Christianity—or "pre-Tridentine" Catholicism—the Spanish had brought earlier.

These two Catholic traditions differed in important ways. Tridentine Catholicism emphasized doctrinal knowledge and decorum over emotional display; required strict church attendance and adherence to church-approved practices; and tended to separate the sacred from the secular and "real" religion from superstition or other popular religious customs that the church hierarchy regarded as inferior "folk" Catholicism. In contrast, Catholicism in New Spain (Mexico) remained essentially pre-Tridentine, flavored by the Mesoamerican religious worldview with which it blended during the initial Spanish conquest and evangelization. This way of being Catholic embraced the permeability of the spiritual and material realms—religion, superstition, and magic all overlapped in daily life. Pre-Tridentine Catholics worried little about the nuances of theology or the issue of decorum in worship, finding in pilgrimages, saint veneration, and feasts ample outlets for their fervent religious expression and celebration. This outlook typified fifteenth- and sixteenth-century European Christians, most of whom "were still viewing life through a Medieval prism, possessing a worldview that knew no separation between religion and society. . . . The two realms were interwoven in such a way that it was unthinkable to distinguish the sacred from the secular, to separate religion from the activities of daily life."[8]

Over time this pre-Tridentine way of being Catholic spread northward from central Mexico to the Spanish northern provinces (present-day Texas and the Southwest). There, during centuries of frontier isolation, it became the Spanish / Mexican cultural core, permeating and integrating all aspects of Tejano life and becoming intimately tied to the people's very identity—it became Tejano ethno-Catholicism. This was the religious and cultural world of Texas Mexicans when, after the Mexican-American War of 1846–48, they suddenly found themselves under the critical eye of a more modernized Roman Catholic Church of the United States.

Anxious to find its niche in a Protestant nation, the Catholic Church supported the U.S. takeover of the Southwest and portrayed the Mexican Catholicism it encountered there as an embarrassing anachronism. All of this did not augur well for Texas Mexicans, a mestizo (mixed-race) people who followed a religious tradition loathed by their conquerors.[9] Nonetheless, nineteenth-century Mexican American Catholics made sense of their lives through their ethnoreligion:

> By taking those beliefs and practices from Catholicism that fit into their life as poor and oppressed folk, Tejanos continued syncretizing old religious world views. While seemingly backward and superstitious at times, their religion rejected the lessons of passivity and resignation historically inculcated into dependent classes by institutional Catholicism. . . . Instead, their religion . . . gave them a vital insight into life, one which . . . played a crucial role in perpetuating the conditions of normalcy in Tejano homes. It was what permitted them to go on searching for an improved economic, social, and political life.[10]

Texas Mexicans held tenaciously to their own brand of Catholicism because it suited their particular spiritual needs and helped them deal with their social subordination. "By taking refuge in this religious world . . . [Mexican Catholics] were also preserving one of the most important roots of their cultural identity." Catholic lay societies also reinforced a sense of peoplehood. By creating and controlling these institutions themselves, Mexicans expressed their independence from the clergy and strengthened their communities.[11] A form of cultural resistance, ethno-Catholicism gave Tejanos the self-respect and confidence with which to cope with material deprivation and social marginality; it served them well despite the disdain with which much of the modern Catholic leadership and society viewed it in the nineteenth century.

As the twentieth century dawned, Spanish priests increasingly replaced the French missionaries who had predominated in the work among Texas Mexicans.[12] But, although they could at least communicate with their parishioners, Spaniards often proved to be as condescending toward Mexicans as their predecessors, and an icy gap separated them from their charges.[13] Nuns and priests fleeing the dislocations of the Mexican Revolution of 1910 augmented the work of the Spanish clergy in Texas during the early twentieth century. The church set up "Mexican" churches, clinics, and other facilities so as not to offend Anglos accustomed to separation of the races.[14] Thus both immigrant and native-born Mexicans had long been social and religious outsiders in the eyes of many Americans when Houston's *colonia* (community) began to form.

MEXICANS IN THE BAYOU CITY: BEGINNINGS, 1836–1930

In August 1836, John and Augustus Allen mapped and began selling land in a speculative town they named Houston, in honor of the hero of Texas independence, General Sam Houston. The creation of the Allen brothers' masterful boosterism, the new town began inauspiciously on the mosquito- and snake-infested banks of Buffalo Bayou, only twenty miles from the site where Texas independence had been won scarcely four months before.[15] There was a Mexican presence in Houston from the city's very beginning, albeit involuntary. Alongside slaves, Mexican prisoners of war cleared and drained the swampy land on which Houston was built, and local officials parceled out some 100 prisoners as servants in the city between 1836 and 1839.[16]

Apparently, few Mexicans lived in Houston during most of the nineteenth century. Mexican immigrants were not drawn as much to the East Texas region around Houston as they were to El Paso, San Antonio, and the Rio Grande Valley, places with large and long-established Mexican populations. East Texas Anglo communities steeped in Deep South traditions preferred white and Negro share-croppers; they made it clear that Mexicans were not welcome.[17] Consequently, Mexicans were almost invisible in Houston during most of the nineteenth century. Census counts listed only six to eighteen individuals in the city at various times between 1850 and 1880.[18]

Meanwhile, in the last three decades of the nineteenth century, far-reaching changes unfolded in Mexico and the American Southwest that would steadily draw more Mexicans and Mexican Americans into Houston. The 1870s saw the beginning of intensive industrialization in Texas and the Southwest, as well as in Mexico under the dictatorship of President Porfirio Díaz, in ways that complemented both regions. In the headlong rush to modernization, the expansion of railroads throughout the Southwest and into northern and central Mexico proved pivotal by interlocking the regions' economies and people. The completion of a transnational railroad network in 1890 (see Map 2) fed a voracious appetite for labor in Texas and the Southwest, as well as farther east into Louisiana, and was essential to the export-oriented Mexican economy.[19] The railroads provided Mexicans an escape from the hardships of Porfirian modernization and jobs in *el norte* (the United States). For Mexican Americans, the railroads opened up new jobs in their native land. With time, more Mexicans and Mexican Americans passed through Houston on the expanding iron web, some bound for Louisiana's sugar cane and cotton fields, others imported temporarily as strikebreakers.[20] In the late 1800s and early 1900s, Mexican immigrants and Mexican Americans who filtered in and out of Houston began to stay, often earning a living as food vendors and unskilled workers in the growing city. By 1900 nearly 500 Mexican-origin people lived in Houston. By 1910 the haphazard trickle had become a steady influx as some 2,000, mostly native-born Mexican Americans, made the Bayou City their home.[21]

The transformation of Houston's economy in the early twentieth century triggered dramatic growth in the city's Mexican community and firmly established its foundation. During the nineteenth century, Houston had grown into an important commercial center by improving its port and rail facilities to serve the agricultural production of southeast Texas. The city's economy had been built around the marketing of cotton, grain, and lumber and on plentiful black labor. But in the first decades of the twentieth century, oil and gas became in-

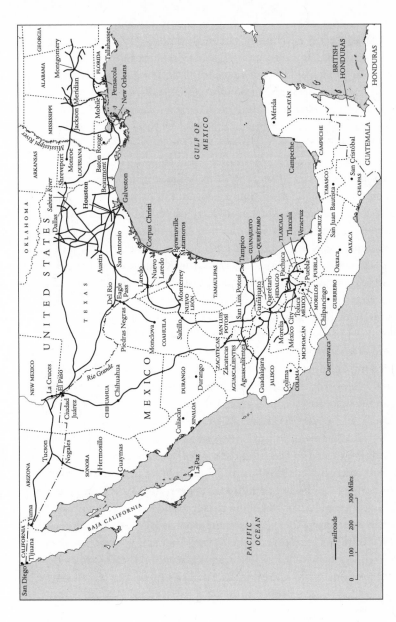

Map 2. U.S.-Mexico Railroad Connections, 1910

creasingly important to Houston's economy, as did a preference for Mexican labor.[22] Early in the twentieth century, Houston employers used Mexican Houstonians as *enganchadores* (labor agents) to recruit Mexican workers.[23] Swelling numbers of Mexican immigrants, as well as native-born Tejanos, responded to the calls for workers. They streamed into Houston during the 1910s and 1920s for several reasons. For one thing, Mexico's brutal drive to modernize culminated in the bloody Revolution of 1910, which drove large numbers of Mexicans into Texas. Meanwhile, the rise of commercial agriculture in Texas increasingly displaced rural Mexican Americans into urban employment. At about the same time, discoveries of oil near Houston gave rise to a booming petroleum industry centered in Houston and its well-developed financial and transportation infrastructure. Thus "the city where seventeen railroads meet the sea" became a magnet that attracted thousands of Mexican and Mexican American workers, offering jobs, as well as the means to reach them. World War I's labor shortages and the immigration restrictions of the 1920s (which were waived for Mexicans) also attracted workers to the Bayou City. As a result, Houston's Mexican-origin population expanded from 2,000 in 1910 to 6,000 in 1920, and then leaped to about 15,000 by 1930.[24]

Some Mexicans entered the city by way of the East Texas lumber mills owned by Houston entrepreneur John Kirby, or from places farther east. For instance, the family of Mary Villagómez worked briefly in the East Texas sawmill town of Saratoga before settling in Magnolia Park on Houston's east side in the late 1910s while Juan Rodríguez came to the city's Fifth Ward with his family from Louisiana, where his father had worked for the Southern Pacific Railroad.[25] Increasingly in the 1910s and 1920s, however, Mexicans found jobs in the new oil and gas sector of the economy and its related ship channel and railroad industries. In reality, they took jobs wherever they could. Mrs. Petra Guillén recalled, for example, that many men worked in the oil refineries and railroads while women worked as seamstresses or in food-packing plants and burlap bag companies, or they picked strawberries in the surrounding rural areas. With time, Mexican barbers, tailors, cooks, and other service workers also found a niche in the city's growing economy.[26]

These workers were part of a polyglot scene in early-twentieth-century Houston. In the 1910s and 1920s Mexican immigrants and native-born Mexican Americans jostled for jobs, housing, and cultural space in the Bayou City alongside a large black population and a smattering of various European immigrants. Blacks historically have been numerous in Houston, forming, for example, almost 40 percent of its population from the 1870s to the 1890s; between 1910 and 1970 they comprised from 21 percent to 32.7 percent of the city's inhabitants. As for its white population, Houston, like other southern cities, received some of the overflow of the "new" immigration of southern and eastern Europeans that flooded the eastern seaboard and parts of the Midwest in the late nineteenth and early twentieth centuries. In 1910 the roughly 2,000 Mexicans and Mexican Americans in Houston lived among much smaller pockets of Italians, Russians, Austro-Hungarians, Greeks, and a number of other European immigrants (plus thirty Asians—twenty Japanese, and ten Chinese). By 1930 there were almost twice as many Mexicans in the city—about 15,000—than all first- and second-generation eastern and southern Europeans combined, which totaled 8,339. Despite the diversity of the city's "new" immigrants, Houston remained numerically dominated by the northern and western European–heritage groups who founded the city, particularly Germans and British. In fact, Germans historically played a central role in Houston, far outnumbering other whites such as the British, Irish, Canadians, French, Czechs, Poles, and Scandinavian groups who historically have comprised a smaller part of the city's ethnic mosaic (see Figure 1).[27]

Thus Houston's Mexican communities took root in a society that historically had been black and white but one that increasingly became tri-ethnic—black, white, *and* brown (see Table A.1). In a city that considered them nonwhite, Mexicans stood out even though their numbers were much smaller than those in such places as San Antonio or Los Angeles. Aside from blacks, Mexicans in Houston were the only

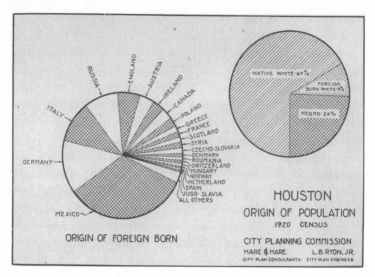

Fig. 1. Houston, Origin of Population, 1929

racial "other" present in significant and growing numbers in the early twentieth century.

In 1910 Houston's Mexicans were scattered around the margins of downtown. Most of them first congregated in what became known as El Segundo Barrio (Second Ward Neighborhood), an area just east of downtown. An enclave soon formed some two miles east of El Segundo within the Anglo suburb of Magnolia Park, sparked by the need for workers to enlarge the Houston Ship Channel between 1912 and 1914. Two smaller pockets also began to take shape during these years on the fringes of downtown, one on the north side (Fifth Ward) and another on the west side (First and Sixth Wards). These barrios became home to a steadily increasing stream of Mexican immigrants, who were joined by a small number of native-born Tejanos and Tejanas also seeking better opportunities. Most arrivals to these neighborhoods gravitated to the numerous railroad yards where jobs and cheap housing—often just railroad boxcars converted into crude shelters—were plentiful.[28]

Many Americans recoiled as thousands of Mexicans flooded Texas and the Southwest. Eventually a fierce debate embroiled the nation over the so-called Mexican problem, the dilemma of needing the Mexicans' labor but resenting their economic competition and supposed unassimilable nature.[29] In the face of hostility, this unprecedented Mexican migration to the United States in the early twentieth century clearly stamped its imprint on the Bayou City's budding *colonia*. The earlier arrivals came from Mexico's northeastern states bordering on Texas—Coahuila, Nuevo León, and Tamaulipas. The even larger flow of the 1920s streamed in from Mexico's Central Plateau, from the states of San Luis Potosí, Zacatecas, Aguascalientes, Guanajuato, Jalisco, and Michoacán. This was clearly an immigrant community, tightly knit and Mexico oriented but one in which even the Texas-born residents still identified strongly with *la patria querida* (beloved Mexico). Most important, white Houstonians, including clergy, rarely distinguished between immigrant Mexicans and native-born Mexican Americans; to most people they were all simply "Mexicans," that is, outsiders.[30] The few who tried to pass as whites drew derisive names, such as *catrines* (dandies) and *abolillados* (gringoized), in a community that tightly clung to its Mexicanness.[31]

The neighborhoods "used to be like families," a longtime resident of Second Ward recalled; close ties, reciprocity, and frequent socialization marked barrio life. Indeed, many of the residents were actually relatives, as extended families were often linked through chain migration, the practice of sequentially resettling family members by finding them jobs and housing through immigrant networks.[32] Mrs. Petra Guillén's family, for example, came to El Segundo Barrio with the help of an uncle who had preceded them. Similarly, Mary Villagómez arrived in the Magnolia barrio as part of an eleven-member extended family migration. Furthermore, the important Mexican custom of *compadrazgo* (godparentage) reinforced the neighborhood's familylike environment. Traditionally, godparents were close friends honored by parents to sponsor their child's baptism or some other important life-cycle ritual or celebration. The sponsors pledged to care for the child's spiritual and material life in the absence of the natural parents, thus becoming *comadre* and *compadre* ("coparents") to the mother and father and *madrina* and *padrino* (godmother and godfather) to the child. Through this form of kinship "by sentiment," godparents became members of the Mexican American extended family and couples created lifelong ties of mutual affection and support, something that contributed to the cohesiveness of Mexican communities. Thus, an "ethic of mutuality" suffused Houston's Mexican settlements and sustained them in an often hostile environment.[33]

In the early twentieth century, community activities and institutions also reflected an emergent *colonia*. As early as 1907, a *junta patriótica* (cultural committee) organized the traditional Mexican Independence Day celebrations, the *dieciséis de septiembre* festivities, and there was at least one mutual aid society formed by 1908.[34] Yet an important institution was lacking. In 1910 Houston's Mexican Catholics had no churches of their own. Some endured icy receptions at Anglo churches and were commonly segregated in the back of the sanctuary or forced to stand throughout the services even when some pews remained empty; many were kept out altogether.[35] Rejection was not new, but neither was the Mexicans' response of using their religion to mediate this hostility. They did this by nurturing their socioreligious traditions that were an integral part of daily life: Mexican families worshipped at their *altarcitos* (home altars) and carried on traditional Catholic devotions and celebrations in their own homes and in festive neighborhood gatherings. Soon after arriving in the city, Mexican and Mexican American Catholics launched money-raising projects to build their own places of worship, beginning with their mother church, Our Lady of Guadalupe, in 1912.[36]

Of course, Houston's *colonias* were embedded in a complex religious matrix. Virtually all the city's many ethnic groups, along with their religious institutions, could be found in any part of the Bayou

City, especially in the early decades of the twentieth century. When Mexicans first began congregating in Houston's Second Ward in the early 1910s, for instance, about half of the area residents were Jewish, almost 31 percent were black, and a mix of German and Irish immigrants, as well as native-born whites and Mexicans, made up the rest of the ward's population. As barrios formed in Houston's other five wards in the 1920s and 1930s, ethnic dispersal and the religious variety that went with it remained the pattern. Consequently, Mexicans shared a religious landscape that by 1941 included 4 synagogues, about 250 white and 268 black Protestant churches, as well as several white and 3 black Catholic churches. Baptists were the most numerous among both blacks and whites in this religious smorgasbord of twenty-two denominations and fifty-two nondenominational groups. As for Catholics, separate nationality parishes existed for the various European immigrant groups as a rule, but if they lacked churches of their own, European ethnics could attend any white Catholic church, unlike Mexicans and blacks. By the end of the 1930s, Houston's black Catholics belonged to either St. Nicholas, founded in 1887 in Third Ward; Our Mother of Mercy, established in 1929 in Frenchtown, the community of French-speaking Creoles from Louisiana who settled in the Fifth Ward in the 1920s; or Our Mother of Mercy's offshoot, St. Anne de Beaupre, started in 1937 in Houston Heights, a suburb on the city's northern fringe.[37]

Rounding out Houston's religious array were the *aleluyas*, as Mexican Protestants were commonly known. At roughly the same time that Catholic missionaries arrived in the city, various Anglo Protestant churches began taking notice of the growing Mexican population and started proselytizing in the barrios. As early as 1910, for instance, the Methodist Women's Board of City Missions pledged it would "establish a church for the Mexican people." Then came the Presbyterian missionaries, beginning in 1919, followed by Baptists in the early 1920s.[38] Thus, as Houston's Mexican ethno-Catholic communities formed, they did so alongside a sprinkling of *aleluya* neighbors and conscious of, if not socially integrated with, the Bayou City's diversity of ethnic peoples and faith traditions.

Clearly, ethnicity and religion set Mexicans apart from white and black Houstonians and, to some degree, from each other. The local press dubbed the *colonia* "A city within a city." Houston's "little Mexico" flourished as racial animosity mounted and the Great Depression loomed.[39]

CRISES AND GROWTH: 1930S–1950S

Unlike many cities, Houston weathered the Great Depression relatively well. But it was not without its problems; business stagnated at least temporarily, and joblessness afflicted many workers.[40] Mexicans and Mexican Americans in particular suffered greatly during *la crisis* (the Depression). Hundreds were unemployed, and many families lived on the edge of starvation during the 1930s, as employers often laid off Mexican workers first and government officials systematically denied them relief.[41]

In addition, Mexicans and Mexican Americans in Houston, as elsewhere, were subject to deportation. Immigration officials routinely raided construction job sites to round up Mexican nationals for repatriation, while other government agencies used various tactics to induce Mexicans to leave the United States. As the Great Depression worsened, the Mexican consul and even local Mexican organizations encouraged the departure of indigent families with promises of help from the Mexican government and by providing transportation to the border. Faced with poor prospects and nativism, at least some 2,000 Mexicans left the Houston area for Mexico during the 1930s.[42] Despite these tribulations, however, the Mexican community not only survived but grew during the 1930s, increasing from 15,000 in 1930 to 20,000 in 1940. Some of the increase came from outlying farms, as Mexican families abandoned rural life and migrated to the city. The growth of the 1930s was not dramatic, but it proved the community's viability and permanence.[43]

Moreover, continued growth also brought a shifting ethnic consciousness and increased political activism. The Depression virtually ended Mexican immigration for a time, and it engendered more antag-onism toward Mexican-origin people. In this context, a "Mexican American" ethnicity began to displace the "Mexican" orientation that had characterized southwestern *colonias* in the preceding decades.[44]

In Houston, this changing ethnicity prompted the rise of numerous civic groups, primarily among the growing middle class. These organiza-tions were active in social, political, and welfare activities for the better-ment of the Mexican community. Some were explicitly political organi-zations that held rallies and endorsed candidates; others, like the League of United Latin American Citizens (LULAC), were officially nonpartisan but vocal in their advocacy for Mexican Americans.[45] With its emphasis on political involvement, education, and the mastery of English, LULAC epitomized the emerging Mexican American mentality that saw civic responsibility as the key to accommodation to mainstream society. Sim-ilarly, a women's cultural society, the Club Chapultepec, emphasized equally its members' American citizenship and responsibilities, as well as their Mexican cultural heritage. The organization tried to smooth the way for Mexican Houstonians by educating the community at large about Mexican culture and promoting American patriotism, but it also protested the mistreatment of Mexicans in Houston.[46] Mexican Ameri-cans thus began to project a more visible profile and a changing ethnicity through these and other organizations in the 1930s.

Mexican American organizations continued to advocate for the *colonia* when better economic times returned in the 1940s. World War II created an economic bonanza for Houston as its ship channel indus-tries contributed to the war effort through the production of aviation fuel, synthetic rubber, and war vessels.[47] Mexican workers, however, often were barred from the higher-paying jobs and relegated to menial employment in the oil, petrochemical, and ship-building industries. Organizations like LULAC protested employment discrimination and inequities in the educational and judicial systems, thereby focusing more attention on the maturing Mexican community.[48] The potential strength of their growing numbers was an important part of the Mexi-can American urbanizing experience of the post–World War II years.

Like the United States in general in the later 1940s and the 1950s, Texas Mexicans became increasingly urbanized. Before World War II, most of them lived in small towns and agricultural areas, but by 1960 they were predominately an urban population. In fact, between 1940 and 1960, Mexican Americans were the most rapidly urbanizing group in the Southwest.[49] Houston's Mexican community reflected this trend. The Mexican-origin population grew from 20,000 in 1940 to 40,000 in 1950, and, by 1960, some 75,000 Mexican Americans and Mexicans lived in Houston, the great majority of whom had migrated to the city from the rural areas and small towns of Texas.[50]

An increasing social and economic stratification also characterized the expanding postwar Mexican American community. Compared to the early twentieth century, the *colonia* of the 1940s and 1950s as a whole was much more acculturated; it was a bicultural community more so than a "little Mexico." Its demographic profile reflected its changing character. By 1950, the Spanish-speaking population of the Houston area was overwhelmingly native-born, with less than 9 percent born in Mexico. In 1960, despite the near doubling of the decennial population, only 13 percent were foreign-born. In terms of economic status, however, most of Houston's Mexican-origin people ranked among the working-class poor. The poverty that had plagued many barrios since the early twentieth century attenuated only slightly in the post–World War II years. Between 1945 and 1960, many Mexicans and Mexican Americans in Houston still contended with deplorable housing, educational inequality, disease, and other social maladies. Nonetheless, working-class families and communities remained viable and continued to manifest the coping skills and endurance they had shown historically.[51]

A small middle class had also developed. These Mexican Americans were more mobile residentially than the vast majority of their counterparts; they were most likely more acculturated than other Mexican Americans as well. Home buying reflected a degree of socioeconomic improvement among the middle class as more Mexican Americans bought homes outside Houston's traditional Mexican neighborhoods.

Even though most Mexican-origin people continued to live in the old barrios in 1960, growing numbers had also moved into other parts of the city, as population expansion and a modicum of social mobility produced both a greater density of the established barrios and a dispersal of Mexicans into every part of the city in the post–World War II years. Catholic officials noted that "the Mexican population [is] moving into new subdivisions as our cities grow."[52]

The *colonia* underwent substantial changes from the 1930s through the 1950s. As their numbers grew steadily, Mexican Americans in Houston revealed their class, cultural, and generational differences and they increasingly claimed their rights as American citizens. These developments were a harbinger of greater ferment to come.

SURGE: THE 1960S AND EARLY 1970S

The 1960s and 1970s were a period of upheaval and change in America as many groups struggled to achieve social equality. Black Americans protested segregation, poverty, unemployment, and other long-standing forms of discrimination. Acting in a political climate ripe for change, other groups mounted campaigns to gain equality and self-determination: women fought to free themselves from the yoke of gender oppression; many disaffected youth sought freer lifestyles and, together with other Americans, an end to the Vietnam War; many Native American peoples demanded recognition of broken treaty promises and greater self-determination; Asian Americans forged pan-ethnic alliances to empower their communities; and Chicanos and Chicanas battled discrimination in voting, education, employment, and other areas.[53]

More than a century of struggle preceded the rise of the Chicano movement in the mid-1960s. Mexicans and Mexican Americans had resisted subjugation ever since Texas and the Southwest were wrenched from Mexico in the nineteenth century.[54] Rooted in a long tradition of resistance, *el movimiento*, as the Chicano movement came to be known, actually represented a multiplicity of efforts to redress long-standing problems stemming from social discrimination and exploitation. *El movimiento* was an explosion of different submovements that often had distinct agendas but were held together loosely by a strong undercurrent of cultural nationalism, or Chicanismo.[55]

The activities of César Chávez and Reies López Tijerina set the stage for the rise of the Chicano movement. At about the same time in the early 1960s, Chávez and Tijerina formed grassroots organizations that challenged the historical grievances of two different Mexican American constituencies. In 1962, Chávez began to organize the National Farm Workers Association to gain better working and living conditions for agricultural workers in California. In 1963, Tijerina incorporated La Alianza Federal de Mercedes (Federal Alliance of Land Grants) as a vehicle to regain the lost lands of Hispanos in New Mexico and southern Colorado. By the mid-1960s, the Gandhian persistence of Chávez and the fiery rhetoric and confrontational style of *el tigre* (as Tijerina became known) riveted national attention on Mexicans in the United States. Chávez and Tijerina catalyzed other struggles for social, political, and economic justice. In Denver, Rodolfo "Corky" Gonzales organized the Crusade for Justice to take community control of schools and foster pride among Mexican people; in Texas, José Ángel Gutiérrez became the guiding force behind La Raza Unida Party (LRUP) and its bid to harness Chicano political power; and elsewhere throughout the nation Chicanas and Chicanos spearheaded innumerable drives for social equality.[56]

As the shock waves of *el movimiento* reverberated throughout the United States, Mexican Americans used their unprecedented population expansion and political activism to demand social justice. "Mexican Americans themselves," historian Arnoldo De León noted, "used that visibility and turned to their numerical strength to attempt change in their historical condition." In Houston, the Mexican presence became ever more apparent as their number skyrocketed from 75,000 in 1960 to more than 150,000 in 1970.[57] In addition, the class, cultural, and generational differences perceptible among them in the post–World War II years became patently obvious in the 1960s and

1970s. Generally, the majority society recognized the class and cultural diversity that had developed among Mexican Houstonians, as well as their rising economic and political importance. In short, mainstream society stopped seeing Mexican Americans as exotic outsiders and "came to accept [them] as part of the city's own diverse cultural makeup."[58]

The Mexican community reflected its heterogeneity in numerous ways. On the one hand, the predominance of a bicultural way of life was evident in the proliferation of English-language and bilingual community newspapers, the abundance of English names given to "Spanish-speaking" organizations, and the prevalence of bilingualism and English-language dominance among Mexican Americans. Residential mobility continued and resulted in the formation of new Mexican American neighborhoods, mostly of the blue-collar type, outside the traditional barrios. There was also a sprinkling of Mexican American professionals in previously all-white middle-class suburbs. On the other hand, working-class Mexican Americans and a constant influx of Mexican immigrants continued to populate the old barrios; there, a few of the pre–World War II Mexicanist organizations still functioned and immigrant culture thrived.[59]

In part, the Mexican community's explosive growth in the 1960s and 1970s reflected the boom Houston experienced in its march to becoming the nation's fifth largest city and an international oil center. During this time Houston's rapidly growing oil and petrochemical industries fueled an unprecedented expansion in other sectors of the city's economy, bringing new jobs, higher wages, and a prosperity unmatched by most of the nation's urban centers.[60] But not all residents of "the oil capital of the world" shared its prosperity. Many working-class Mexican Americans still suffered chronic unemployment or were locked in low-paying dead-end jobs, despite the fact that Houston outpaced the nation in employment growth rates and showed impressive gains in per capita income during its boom years. Well-paid jobs and high-status occupations still eluded even the growing Mexican American middle class, whose members typically earned significantly less than their Anglo professional counterparts. Mexican Americans had made some gains in the 1950s, but the persistence of low incomes, poor housing, low educational levels, and other signs of marginality still marked them in the 1960s and 1970s.[61] Houston's boomtown glitz contrasted sharply with Mexican Americans' inequality, exposing the cost of their ethnicity and propelling them into social activism.

In Houston, civil rights struggles reflected the city's ethnic and religious pluralism, engaging in the tumult black, brown, and white, laity and clergy, Catholic and Protestant. The well-documented role of churches and clergy in the black civil rights struggle held true in Houston. Like their counterparts in other cities, black pastors in Houston, such as the Reverends L. H. Simpson, Earl Allen, William "Bill" Lawson, and others, exerted significant political influence from their pulpits and through their involvement in local chapters of the National Association for the Advancement of Colored People, the Southern Christian Leadership Conference, and smaller civil rights organizations.[62] Meanwhile, mostly younger Chicana and Chicano lay activists, Catholics as well as Protestants, organized outside the churches, establishing, for instance, chapters of LRUP and the Mexican American Youth Organization (MAYO), new vehicles that used confrontational tactics to challenge the older middle-class male leadership and press for social change in the Bayou City. The later 1960s and early 1970s saw Mexican Houstonians become increasingly politicized through such forums as the National Chicana Conference and by the political activism of MAYO and LRUP, and through their participation in such protests as the Texas Farm Workers' strike and the local *huelga* (strike) schools. The contagion of activism, of course, spread among Mexican American priests and sisters, as well as the city's Mexican American Protestant clergy. Leaders and organizations arose, such as Father Patricio Flores, who helped found Padres Asociados para Derechos Religiosos, Educativos y Sociales (Priests Associated for Religious, Educational and Social Rights, or PADRES); Sisters Gloria Gallardo and Gregoria Ortega, who formed Las Hermanas (Sisters), a group of militant nuns;

the Methodist pastor Rev. Arturo Fernández and other Mexican American Protestant ministers who organized the Mexican American Clergymen Association of Houston; and local Protestant attorney Benjamín Canales, assistant director of the Hispanic American Institute, a Mexican American Presbyterian advocacy organization based in Austin, Texas. And behind the scenes, highly placed white liberals in the Catholic hierarchy, such as Bishop John L. Morkovsky, Father John E. McCarthy, and Father Emile J. Farge, carried on low-profile but important activities in support of the Chicano movement.[63]

To what degree, if any, black, brown, and white Catholics made common cause for civil rights is an issue that awaits study. But, clearly, the whirlwind of protest swept up the Galveston-Houston Diocese—sometimes as an ally but often as a target of protest—as we shall see in the coming chapters. In the Bayou City, ethno-Catholicism helped sustain viable Mexican communities as they grew apace with the city but were largely shut off from its economic prosperity. It is the nature of that ethnoreligious way of life among Houston's Mexican and Mexican American Catholics to which we turn next.

Two

ETHNO-CATHOLICISM:

EMPOWERMENT AND

WAY OF LIFE

When the Revolution of 1910 made it impossible for Ramón Villa-gómez to make a living in Mexico, he decided to head north, to the United States. "*Fina, me voy al norte* [I'm going north]," he announced to his wife. But his wife quickly deflated his plans, along with his ego: "*Mira, Ramón, tú no te vas a ir al norte* [You're not going north]; *nos vamos a ir* [we are]," she countered. "You're not going to leave me behind with the family; *we're* going up there [together]!" In this family matter the wife prevailed.[1] In another time and place a bone-weary and homesick migrant farmworker, Marcos Rodríguez, sent a letter home to Houston: "When we go to church we see a garden with many flowers that the priest tends," he wrote to his sister, "and we remember that back in Houston we have a garden of flowers named Carmelitas, Rocitas, Margaritas and Lolitas," referring to his absent siblings; "that garden is cared for by *la Virgen del Rosario*."[2]

These mundane episodes illustrate two important aspects of ethno-religiosity among Mexican Catholics in Houston: its empowering na-ture and its inextricability with everyday life. This chapter will show how ethno-Catholicism played a pivotal role in sustaining generations of Mexicans and Mexican Americans by giving them a sense of cultural identity and independence, community integrity and hope in the face of adversity. In their ethno-Catholicism, people like Josefina Villagómez and Marcos Rodríguez found the strength to confront life's many travails. Moreover, their Catholicism was so thoroughly enmeshed in their lives that it was more than a set of religious beliefs and practices; indeed, it defined them. Ethno-Catholicism was a part of their very being, of how they understood themselves, related to others, and found meaning in life, as well as the means to deal with life and all it offered—the welcomed, the feared, and everything in-between. In short, Mexican ethno-Catholicism was a way of life, a "lived religion."[3]

At the heart of ethno-Catholicism were the Mexicans' deep devotion to Our Lady of Guadalupe and such vibrant community traditions as the Christmastime barrio celebrations, the *quinceañera* rite of passage, and the *altarcito* practice of home altar worship. Underpinned by a worldview in which the spiritual and the material intermingled naturally in daily life, these and other home- and community-centered faith expressions coexisted with a selective participation in the formal requirements of the church. Together all of this made up the Mexican American ethno-Catholic way of life. This chapter presents a general picture of that way of life, understanding, of course, that it had variations. As some of the following chapters will show, generational, class, and other factors influenced the way Mexicans and Mexican Americans actually lived their ethno-Catholicism.

GUADALUPE, *POSADAS*, AND *PASTORELAS*

Veneration of Our Lady of Guadalupe (or *la Guadalupana*) formed the core of Mexican Catholicism. Belief in her apparition[4] profoundly affected Mexico's religious history, resulting in the conversion of millions of indigenous and mestizo (Spanish and Indian parentage) people. Guadalupe's veneration as *la Virgen Morena* (the brown Virgin) and *la Morenita* (a typically Mexican term of endearment) underscores her ethnic connection to Mexican-origin people and helps to explain why *la Guadalupana* quickly became the central figure of the people's faith. The Roman Catholic Church recognized the fervent devotion among the masses and Guadalupe's religious and cultural centrality to the nation in naming her patron saint of Mexico. In the words of one writer, Our Lady of Guadalupe was "the greatest single influence (next to God himself) on the Mexican people."[5]

La Guadalupana offered Mexicans the solace and counsel that helped them endure their tragic and turbulent history, an Oblate explained:

> Their lot has always been one of hardship, poverty, and oppression; their beloved land has been practically under continual misrule; self-centered politicians have exploited her riches and resources; their Faith . . . has been persecuted and their clergy hounded and martyred. And through all this they have come with their faith in God and their love for His Mother undimmed. In poverty, oppression, persecution, and disease . . . Guadalupe has been their Comfort and guiding Star. She has been their Mother and their Queen, their Patroness and Protectress.[6]

Deeply stamped in the Mexican psyche, Our Lady of Guadalupe became a unifying symbol for Mexican and Mexican American Catholics everywhere. Since colonial times, followers have marched under her banner not only to express their devotion and identity but also to fight for their social and political rights. In Mexico, leaders invoked Guadalupe's help in the great revolutionary movements of 1810 and 1910; in the United States during the 1960s, César Chávez and his farmworkers struggled for economic justice under her protective gaze, as did Texas farmworkers who marched on the state capital. A militant Chicano newspaper in Houston revered *la Guadalupana* as the "Mother of the Mexican Revolution" and the "Patron of the Liberation of Aztlán [the Chicano homeland]."[7]

Not surprisingly, the barrios of Houston exploded in joyous celebration every year on the Virgin's feast day. The custom dated back to the early twentieth century. The first Fiesta Guadalupana was held on December 12, 1911, at a white parish, Annunciation, where the great mass of Mexicans amazed the pastor. "Never before had such a large gathering of Mexican Catholics been seen in Houston," a parish jour-

The main altar in the sanctuary of Our Lady of Guadalupe Church in El Segundo Barrio depicts the patron saint of Mexico and the Americas. Courtesy Houston Metropolitan Research Center, Houston Public Library.

nal revealed, noting the "great enthusiasm and fervor" the Mexicans showed on that special day commemorating the appearance of the Mother of God to one of their own.[8] Throughout the years that devotion never flagged. Our Lady of Guadalupe Parish even held two services in a futile effort to accommodate the overflow crowds every December 12. Members of different parishes fondly recalled "how important" the celebrations were to all Mexicans. But participation was a devotion, not an obligation, parishioner Mary Villagómez emphasized. Thousands of faithful turned out yearly because the event touched them deeply; it was something "very meaningful to the people."[9]

But meaningful how? On a symbolic level, la Guadalupana inspired public displays of devotion because she was the Mother of all Mexican Catholics. Although Mexican culture generally associated piety with womanliness, men, too, could openly express devotion to Guadalupe because she was their "mother" and the culture demanded men's reverence for motherhood. In other circumstances, a reinterpreted Guadalupe transgressed her ascribed religious (that is, "womanly") role and took on a political one—she became María Insurgente (Mary the Revolutionary), leading bloody wars of liberation and protest movements in rural fields and city streets. In various ways, men and women found inspiration and sustenance in la Virgen Morena.

The twelfth of December climaxed a nine-day devotional period (a novena) that involved great numbers of parishioners. In 1945 St. Patrick's pastor wrote that the parishioners "worked hard for the preparation for the feast of Our Lady of Guadalupe . . . [which] was celebrated with a solemn high mass and all the ceremonies for this great day."[10] The eight days preceding the main celebration often featured nightly preaching by guest pastors. Meanwhile, some parishioners practiced the reenactment of the apparition, others prepared food, decorated floats, or readied costumes, banners, and the church altar, while still others practiced las mañanitas, the song tribute honoring the Virgin every year just before daybreak on December 12, her feast day.[11] Typically, parishioners celebrated Our Lady of Guadalupe Day with morning and evening services. The day began with a procession around the church grounds during which the faithful honored the Virgin by singing *las mañanitas* in the crisp air of the early dawn. An early morning Mass followed, and then everyone enjoyed the traditional hot chocolate and *pan dulce* (Mexican pastry), perhaps along with a schoolchildren's play about the apparition, in the social hall.[12] In 1969 the Catholic press explained, "According to tradition the people arise early in the morning on special days such as birthdays to sing praise to the honored person, in this case Our Lady of Guadalupe."[13]

The celebrations grew in size and importance over the years. By the early 1970s an increasingly elaborate Fiesta Guadalupana instituted by the diocese supplemented events at the individual parishes. These larger affairs, initially hosted by Guadalupe Parish, included huge processions and popular mariachi masses celebrated by a bishop. A procession began in midafternoon from Blessed Sacrament Church, where 2,000 or more people gathered under the prominent image of the Virgin and made a mile-and-a-half pilgrimage through the barrio to Guadalupe Church. Decorated floats, religious banners, Mexican and American flags, and placards of barrio groups created a festive air.[14]

The celebration in 1971 was especially poignant. The Chicano press hyped the coming event weeks in advance. Parishioners read that Mexican actress and recording star Queta Jiménez and an international cast of performers were scheduled to honor the Virgin by "singing the typical Mexican *mañanitas* in a local church."[15] The faithful inundated Guadalupe Church.[16] The duet of Queta Jiménez and Adolfo Garza provided the highlight of the day with a "prayer-made-song" that moved the audience to tears. "The devotees of *la Virgen Morena*," the newspaper reported, "were delighted to see the warmth with which our compatriots honored the Queen of Mexicans."[17] The event reflected the Virgin's central place in Mexican Catholicism and revealed as well the power of a popular devotion to unite a people in celebration of their shared ethnoreligious identity.

In similar fashion, the reenactment of *las posadas*, the dramatization of Mary and Joseph seeking lodging at an inn (*posada*) on their way to

Children at Our Lady of Guadalupe Parish in the 1950s reenact the Apparition of the Virgin Mary to Juan Diego as part of the annual Virgin's Feast Day celebrations. Courtesy Houston Metropolitan Research Center, Houston Public Library.

Bethlehem for the birth of Christ, also evoked ethnic solidarity. "My mother and many of these Mexican people brought customs from Mexico," Mary Villagómez explained. "They were used to having *posadas* at Christmastime. So they would have their *posadas* in the house and they would sing and pray and carry the statues of Joseph and Mary, looking for shelter and all that." People looked forward to these festive gatherings with their neighbors. "I remember distinctly," stated Villagómez, "that we would work up to that, like a big thing was coming, you know—a *posada*! We're going to have a *posada*!"[18] Parishioners in different neighborhoods staged the event at churches or in private homes in basically the same way over the years. Like other important celebrations, the *posada* involved a novena and the drama was played out on nine consecutive nights, beginning on December 16 and ending on Christmas Eve. Groups of people carrying lanterns and statues of Mary and Joseph (or led by a costumed couple) went house to house asking for a place to rest overnight. The pilgrims sang the request for shelter, were refused, and then moved on until they were finally admitted into someone's home. Inside, parishioners prayed and sang hymns. But solemnity melded with cheer. It was a real "party atmosphere," Mrs. Hope Jiménez fondly recalled. Children squealed hysterically as they smashed a piñata, showering everyone with candy and coins and raising a roar of laughter among their parents. Late into the night a jovial buzz pulsated in barrio homes as folks feasted on steamy tamales or spicy chicken *mole* and the ubiquitous hot chocolate and *pan dulce*.[19] Some *posadas* were held at churches, merging community tradition and formal worship, but the *posadas* in the barrios predated the presence of the institutional church.[20] They were clearly an expression of community solidarity that Mexicans controlled in their own homes and communities.

Mexican and Mexican American Catholics also staged *pastorelas* during the Christmas season. These nativity plays recalled the pilgrimage by shepherds (*pastores*) to visit the infant Jesus. Amateur and semiprofessional actors performed *pastorelas* throughout Texas and the Southwest. Often the same family held the honor of representing a particular character over generations. People's backyards became barrio theaters as troupes presented a *pastorela* as a "Christmas gift to the community."[21] Guadalupe parishioner Mrs. Petra Guillén remembered that residents of Second Ward requested performances and "they would do the *pastorela* in your yard." "My uncle used to be one of the *pastores*," she recalled, "so we had to follow him wherever he went on the *pastorela*."[22] These events were not simply entertainment; they represented a sacralization of barrio space and activity. As Robert

Orsi has shown, "Religious solidarity, communion within the various expressions of popular religiosity, can precede social or communal solidarity in poor communities."[23]

Thus the *pastorelas* carried a message of resistance. In the context of Mexican American marginality, "the performance of a traditional Mexican *pastorela*—in Spanish, in the backyard of a barrio home, by a close-knit company of working-class actors—assumes a real social and political significance that extends beyond the devotional," a scholar noted. The performance of a *pastorela* was "a labor of love and devotion, in denial of the dominant notion of work as wage labor." The performers were "not 'paid' for their labor here, so much as reciprocated in gratitude (in the form of tamales, drinks, dollar bills, and so forth)."[24] Participation in a *pastorela* allowed Mexicans to express their preference for their values over those of the majority society by giving them a chance to overturn the capitalist notions of labor that pervaded their lives and to "control" their own labor, however fleetingly. This symbolic inversion of control of their labor fortified their sense of self-worth and community solidarity, and it provided a psychological victory over everyday realities of ethnic tensions and class subordination. Like the *posada*, the *pastorela* was another way that Mexican ethnoreligiosity helped to build community; by celebrating in settings of their own choosing, parishioners affirmed their Mexicanness, their style of Catholicism, and their human dignity.

QUINCEAÑERAS AND ALTARCITOS

The year 1970 was an unforgettable one for young María Quiroz. When she turned fifteen that spring, her family, friends, and community honored her with a *quinceañera*, a ceremony as elaborate as a wedding. The *quinceañera* began with a religious service, as tradition dictated. Carrying a beautiful spray of red roses, María entered St. Patrick Church dressed in a beautiful white gown, veil, and satin slippers. Her parents, godparents, eleven attendants, a page, and a flower girl accompanied her. The priest celebrated Mass and gave his blessing, and María received Communion and renewed her baptismal vows. A photo session followed the church service, and, later, a dinner and dance complete with champagne and orchestra capped the memorable day.[25]

Although laypeople and clergy alike have long disputed the *quinceañera*'s origins, meanings, and form, there is no doubt that the tradition was a great event in a young woman's life, a treasured experience often noted in local newspapers.[26] The celebration was, on one level, a gift to the fifteen-year-old from her parents and relatives. The cost was often substantial, and priests and parishioners alike complained about the "extravagance." For example, Father Patricio Flores, who became the first Mexican American bishop in the U.S. Church, worried that the *quinceañeras* had "gotten out of control" and "become too commercial." Similarly, a former pastor of St. Patrick Church warned that the tradition had "developed into a social affair with the danger of the religious aspect being forgotten."[27] Even María Quiroz's mother agreed about the expense, stating, "It's a very pretty thing, an unforgettable event, but very expensive."[28]

But several families usually bore the cost, and almost everyone involved in the ceremony shared in paying the expenses, especially the godparents, as the *Houston Chronicle* reported:

> Padrinos or godparents and relatives . . . paid for the use of the Church, split the cost of the reception dinner, paid for María's hairdo, photographs, photo albums, guest books, birthday cake, champagne for the cumpleaños participants, champagne glasses, invitations, satin pillow for the tiara and gave such gifts as the tiara, the prayer book, rosary, mantilla, religious medallion, María's bouquet, charm bracelet, ring, earrings and gloves.
>
> Attendants' dresses, shoes and headdresses totaled about $35 per girl while their escorts were responsible for renting their tuxedoes, buying their partner-attendant's bouquet and chipping in to pay for the dance.[29]

Clearly, by the 1970s celebrating a *quinceañera* was often an expensive undertaking. "Frankly," Mrs. Quiroz admitted, "if we didn't have relatives who agreed to share the expense, we couldn't do it."[30] Nonetheless, the celebration of a *quinceañera* strengthened communities by nurturing family relationships and reinvigorating the old ties of *compadrazgo*.

On another level, however, the *quinceañera* tradition was double-edged. On the one hand, the custom entailed a commitment to community service. A young woman could pledge to serve her community, for example, by finishing her education. In that way she contributed to her own material well-being, as well as that of her family and her community. She could also make a commitment to help teach catechism in her parish, thereby contributing to the spiritual life of the community.[31] The custom thus had important implications for individuals, families, and communities because it promoted family and community loyalties by cementing kinship ties and eliciting commitments from succeeding generations. On the other hand, even though the *quinceañera* promoted ethnoreligious solidarity and reflected a woman's importance in her family and culture, it also perpetuated the notion of women's inequality and constrained roles in life as primarily mothers and caretakers—the guardians of home and faith. After all, the custom marked a woman's passage into a clearly patriarchal institution, the Catholic Church, which historically tried to inculcate values of women's submissiveness and proscribed role expectations, sacralizing them through the tradition of the *quinceañera*.[32]

Nonetheless, women found ways to challenge patriarchy, one of them being through the custom of keeping private home altars, *altarcitos*. This was perhaps the most characteristic and revealing tradition among Mexican Catholics:

> The house is silent and dark. In the far corner of the living room, the flickering lights of several tall votive candles illuminate a colorful assembly of plaster saints and religious lithographs, a Spanish Bible and an arrangement of family photographs. Kneeling before this rudimentary altar, a woman prays silently over her glass rosary beads. Her eyes, wet with tears in supplication, are fixed upon an

image of Our Lady of Guadalupe. Once she has finished the rosary, she addresses herself to the saints represented by the images on her altar, petitioning or thanking each of them. She asks . . . Our Lady of St. John to intercede on behalf of her sister, who has a heart condition. In return for this favor, she makes a vow to travel to the Virgin's shrine. She requests of . . . St. Jude, patron of impossible causes, that he help her son-in-law find a job with better working hours. She invokes the Sacred Heart of Jesus and prays for . . . a recently deceased neighbor. She asks San Martín de Porres, patron saint of the poor, to look after the destitute of the world. Her last prayer . . . thanks . . . Guadalupe for her husband's improved health and for the safe delivery of her newest great-granddaughter. She closes by reminding the Virgin that, in fulfillment of her vow, the baby was given the name Guadalupe as one of her middle names.[33]

This scene was commonplace in Houston barrios. Mrs. Petra Guillén, who visited many homes during her years as a missionary catechist, remembered that most homes had an *altarcito*. Other parishioners likewise recalled that altars were a "very normal" part of home life.[34]

The normality of the *altarcito* tradition belied its profound importance in the lives of Mexican Catholic women. More than any other aspect of women's religiosity, home altar worship defined, sustained, and empowered them. This was a woman's space; it was sacred and it was hers. In this holy arena, women brought together the sacred and the here-and-now, visiting, cajoling, bargaining with, and thanking their heavenly family in the pictured presence of husbands, children, and other earthly relatives. Here women spoke first and most to *la Guadalupana*—the holiest of women and the one who best understood them *as* women. They brought to *la Virgen* and the saints all their sorrows and joys, and, bathed in the balm of a sacred presence, they emerged relieved, rejuvenated, and confident.

Parishioners disagreed about the origins of the *altarcitos*, but they were united in their attachment to them. For some, home altar worship paralleled worship in the parish church. "[W]e always kneel

Home altars, such as this one belonging to Mrs. Eloisa Garza, typically featured both heavenly and earthly family members along with religious objects. Photo from *Interiores: Aspectos Seculares de la Religión* (Houston, Tex.: Houston Public Library, 1982). Photo by Guillermo Pulido.

in front of the altar in church," Immaculate Heart parishioner Mrs. Teresa Zavala reasoned, "so we sort of carry it [the practice] into the home I guess." Others speculated that *altarcitos* evolved from the scarcity of churches; thus, having a private altar, former nun Mary Villagómez explained, was "like we're in church." Another Immaculate Heart member, Mrs. Hope Jiménez, added that the images focused a person's mind on religious matters.[35] Home altars reminded one parishioner of her upbringing, and another valued them because she felt they were part of her identity as a *"mexicana."* An integral part of daily life, *altarcitos* were taken for granted and "just enjoy[ed]."[36] The tradition of saint veneration was so entwined with Mexican American ethno-Catholicism that when priests in Houston spoke against the practice in the 1960s, parishioners felt culturally threatened and resentful.[37] But they were not about to abandon their *altarcitos*. This unbroken tradition is a clear-cut example of Mexican American resistance to religious and social assimilation pressures. Parishioners offered different explanations about the meaning and endurance of *altarcitos*, but ultimately the importance of the tradition lay in how it integrated daily life and the sacred, concretizing and voicing Mexican Catholics' understanding of their religious cosmos in an intimate, familial way. *Altarcitos* particularly empowered women, giving them access to the divine and helping them to negotiate crucial family and community relationships and to deal with gender inequality and other problems life presented.

The *altarcito* tradition revealed the vital role of women and the central place of family in Mexican American culture. The home altar tradition was, first and foremost, a family custom carried on primarily by women; women kept the tradition alive and handed it down over the years.[38] "Yes, my mother had a little altar," Eloisa Garza stated, as did her daughter and her sisters. *Altarcitos* were accepted "as something we [women] just have," Luz Vara pointed out.[39] Women believed the *altarcitos* brought the divine into the home and that the religious images of the altar represented a home's "spiritual family."[40] "[M]y grandmother used to say that the first thing that a house should have is an altar," Mrs. Janie Tijerina recalled. "That was the only way you could be in the grace of God. If God is not in the family, you're not a family," she insisted.[41]

Hence, women used home altars to invoke spiritual help as caretakers of the family. Women counted on the saints like they would earthly kin; they sought guidance, consolation, strength, protection, and other favors from the sacred persons represented in the *altarcitos*.

For instance, World War II and the Vietnam War saw many soldiers' pictures on altars, invoking a favored saint's protection.[42] Women often compared the intervention of a saint to having a legal advocate. "It's like a lawyer. When you go to a court, you don't go by yourself; you take a lawyer to represent you. So those saints are representing us," Petra Guillén explained. This analogy recalled the sixteenth-century Spanish belief that a saint represented a community to God, an advocacy described as that of an *abogado* (lawyer).[43]

The comparison also reflects a difference between Mexican-origin and other American Catholics. Like Mexican Americans, Irish, Polish, and other Euro-Americans revere particular saints. But many of those devotions may be traced back to the "devotional revolution" of the mid-nineteenth century, whereas the practice among Mexican and Mexican American Catholics reaches farther back in history. Unlike the church-sponsored devotions that developed among various Euro-American Catholic groups in the later nineteenth century—the most notable exception being southern Italians—Mexican saint veneration was forged in the caldron of *mestizaje*, the racial and cultural blending that resulted from the Spanish conquest and colonization of indigenous Mexicans in the sixteenth century. The devotion to Our Lady of Guadalupe illustrates this point. The Spanish brought with them a tradition of saint veneration to Indian Mexico, where the practice of home altar worship of indigenous deities already existed. In the New World these two customs of venerating favored sacred figures fused into popular devotions of Guadalupe and other saints.[44]

In any case, women acknowledged answered prayers by fulfilling vows made to their intermediaries. Often these *promesas* took the form of a pilgrimage to a saint's shrine, such as the one Mrs. Felix Tijerina made for the Virgin of San Juan de los Lagos, Mexico. Women also prayed novenas or made an offering of money or some sort of personal sacrifice to fulfill promises.[45] Through saint veneration, women exercised their traditional role of nurturing the family and thereby contributed to the stability of the primary institution in Mexican American life.

Yet patriarchy remained a constant companion in their lives. Despite their indispensability as caretakers of the family, many women chafed at their constrained roles and felt oppressed by the collusion of two pivotal institutions in Mexican American life, family and church. Mexican American culture expected wives and mothers to devote themselves totally to the family and put the needs of their husbands and children above their own.[46] Church representatives reinforced that subordination, as Father Antonio Marañón bluntly reminded parishioners in his local newspaper column: "If it is true that husbands and wives are equals as children of God, it is also true that they are not equal with regard to each other: the husband is the master [*jefe*] and the wife owes him submission."[47]

Confronted daily by inequality, women used their religiosity and domesticity as sources of empowerment. As keepers of religion and the home, they stood at the very center of Mexican American family and community life, a position from which they exerted significant influence, directly and indirectly, and therefore commanded respect. Women often had more control than men over family matters, their influence extending not only to religion but also to the making of important decisions concerning schooling, finances, health care, and other important matters. Historically in Mexican American communities, a woman's "strength has been exercised in the home where she has become the pillar of family life. It is just this role that has brought her leadership and her abilities to the larger community." In addition, women were primarily the ones who maintained the extended family and *compadrazgo* ties that were important to family and community well-being.[48]

Women clearly exerted their will in the domestic sphere. For example, one parishioner's mother left behind a philandering husband in Mexico City. The mother "wanted to be more independent and [have] a different life for . . . her children." She refused to live where it was acceptable for a husband to "have as many women as he wanted," the daughter recounted. So in 1956 the mother moved to Houston, taking her seven children with her; two years later the father followed.[49] In a similar vein, Mary Villagómez proudly remembered her mother's initiative and leadership in church and family matters. Villagómez described her mother as a forceful personality, a whirlwind of energy and resolve who "took the leadership that way."[50] Women's position in a mother-centered culture bolstered their dignity and assertiveness, helping them to negotiate patriarchal relationships and circumvent and temper other problems they encountered in a society that privileged men.

In asserting themselves, women drew strength from their *altarcitos*. Mrs. Janie Tijerina asserted, "I'm a great believer in my saints . . . and I believe they help me." She had been named after Our Lady of San Juan, and she always carried a small picture of the Virgin in her purse. "I think she protects me," Mrs. Tijerina stated.[51] Similarly, María López said of her favorite saint, "I have lots of faith in calling on her, [the] Virgin de San Juan," adding that "she has done many favors for me."[52] Many women prayed to the Virgin Mary and developed special lifelong relationships with her various manifestations. They revered her for her healing powers as Our Lady of St. John; sought her consolation as Our Lady of Sorrows; and saw in her a perfect role model as Our Lady of Guadalupe, a nurturing parent whose combined strength and meekness gave others vital emotional sustenance.[53]

But it is important not to exaggerate the empowering nature of home altar worship and the liberating influence of *la Guadalupana*. In reality, like other aspects of Mexican American ethno-Catholicism, this one also underscores its often contradictory nature. Saint veneration, like the tradition of the *quinceañera*, had both a positive, liberating potential, as well as a negative, constraining side. For example, while Guadalupe could inspire women to contest patriarchy, she also reinforced the pressure exerted by ethno-Catholic culture on women to emulate the "María paradox" of passivity in the face of such things as the double standard of sexual behavior.

Still, as anthropologist Kay Turner observed, Mexican American women undertook "cultural control of home and barrio life to maintain a system of values based strongly on loyalty to and respect for kin." This loyalty and sense of affiliation was "in no small way shaped and secured through an alliance formed with God and the saints, an alliance personally maintained at home by women."[54] Thus women did much more than merely assure the biological and cultural continuity of Mexican Americans. Home altar worship sustained their sense of worth, empowering them to challenge gender inequality and other harsh realities; it gave them considerable control of a crucial institution—the home—helping them to shape wholesome individuals, families, and, by extension, entire communities; and it centrally positioned them to maintain important relationships and customs that held communities together, including the *compadrazgo* networks and parish activities they dominated. In this sense, their religiosity and domesticity were hardly passive or insignificant.

INSTITUTIONAL PARTICIPATION

Mexicans and Mexican Americans attended church services less frequently than other Catholics in the United States, a source of continual complaints among clergy since the nineteenth century. Social scientists since the early twentieth century also made this observation repeatedly, and Mexican Americans themselves often confirmed it.[55] In Houston, patterns of church attendance roughly paralleled that of other Texas Mexicans. Apparently, about one-half of Mexican American parishioners regularly worshipped in their churches on a weekly basis.[56] Mexican Catholics simply did not stress frequent church attendance as heavily as the church hierarchy did, nor did they fault themselves for it. "I've always been a Catholic. I'm a very good Catholic," a prominent Houston woman insisted. "Because I don't go to church does not prove that I'm not a good Catholic. I was brought up like this."[57] Again, Mexicans defined for themselves what it was to be a good Catholic and a decent human being. Their refusal to be remade in a "better" image testified to their pride in Mexicanness and to the certainty with which they understood and lived their ethnoreligion.

Whatever their numbers, Mexican Americans who were closely

affiliated with the institutional church placed great value on attending Sunday Mass. Religion was "a main part of our lives," a dedicated churchgoer emphasized, recalling Sundays as the day at church. Before moving to the city in the 1930s, the Gonzales family rose Sunday mornings at 5 A.M. and walked five miles from their farm to the church for the 10 o'clock Mass. After services the family enjoyed "tortilla sandwiches" on the church grounds. The children then attended catechism classes before returning home at about 4 o'clock in the afternoon. This was a "commitment . . . not a sacrifice," an elderly gentleman explained, a "routine" part of family life.[58]

It was also a family tradition passed on over generations. Another parishioner, Mr. Joe Gonzales, underlined the importance of church attendance to family life. For him, going to church every Sunday was "an integral part of being a family." Grandparents, parents, and children all attended Mass together. Parents inculcated children with a sense of support for the church early in life and reinforced this value by giving weekly church attendance a high priority in the family's activities. Others recounted similar experiences of extended families worshipping together and children going to *la doctrina* (catechism classes) after services.[59]

Parents socialized their children into their ethno-Catholicism through their own modeling and by their strictness about church attendance. Children were not allowed to go anywhere else if they did not first go to Mass, a parishioner recalled. But regular churchgoing was more than a strict requirement. Esther García, a former St. Stephen's parishioner, remembered Sundays as "the highlight of the week." "[W]hen we went to church, it just made us feel good," she recalled. "I think the reason that we did practice going every Sunday was because we found . . . that *social community* that we were looking for. [T]hat was our community, and that was our way of reaching out to others . . . from other barrios, not just the one where we lived but [from] all over." Sister Agnes Rita Rodríguez, a Divine Providence nun, echoed Mrs. García's experience. The elderly nun recalled that parishioners at Our Lady of Guadalupe formed friendships and built a sense of community because the mother church in Second Ward drew Mexican worshippers from throughout the city.[60] Clearly, parishioners enjoyed Sunday Mass attendance because it reinforced the closely held cultural values of family and community. This was significant to women of the early twentieth century, whom society allowed precious few opportunities for expression and leadership. As Sister Yolanda Tarango has explained, "For my grandmother and the Hispanic women of her age, church was perceived not so much as an institution but as a community. . . . Women of this generation perceived the church as the primary means to keep the family united and cultural values alive. Their work in the church was chiefly oriented towards building the community."[61]

By the later 1960s, more clergy in the Catholic Church recognized the importance of cultural relevance in pastoral matters. Hence, one of the liturgical reforms of the Second Vatican Council was the celebration of the liturgy in the language of the people. When Spanish masses were instituted in Houston parishes, Sister Rachel Moreno noticed a positive change among parishioners at Our Lady of Guadalupe Parish in their attitudes toward the institutional church. Similarly, Immaculate Heart members indicated that they enjoyed the Mass more because they were more intimately involved by the use of their language in the service.[62]

Father Patricio Flores capitalized on the spirit of Vatican II to inject more cultural relevance into his ministry among Houston's Mexican Catholics. First, as pastor of St. Joseph–St. Stephen Parish, Flores invited the Estudiantina Guadalupana, a musical group comprised of twenty-eight girls and young women from Cuernavaca, Mexico, to perform at his church and other predominately Mexican American parishes. With their guitars, accordions, violins, and "soft hand clapping," the Estudiantina Guadalupana sang the liturgy and entertained parishioners with current popular songs after services.[63] The following year Father Flores began using a mariachi, a traditional Mexican folk band, to revive interest in poorly attended services. Flores celebrated his parish's first mariachi Mass accompanied by a local group, El Mariachi Norteño, on Sunday, October 12, 1969, during the parish's Día de la Raza (Columbus Day) festivities. The parishioners loved it. "Mariachi Masses have met with overwhelming response in two Houston churches," the Catholic press reported. Languishing services were soon "packed." Mexican American parishioners preferred the mariachi Mass, Father Flores explained, "because they feel it's their 'thing.' "[64] The innovation proved a good vehicle "for expressing the mood, temperament and emotions of the Mexican people."[65] Along with kinship networks, community ties, and language, the mariachi Mass was an important cultural ingredient that influenced patterns of church attendance among Mexicans and Mexican Americans. It also revealed how ethno-Catholic identity melded religious and social life in ways that allowed them to carve a place for themselves in the Bayou City.

Baptism and confirmation also illustrated this blending. The two sacraments ranked high among the religious duties kept by Mexican Catholics. But as with other aspects of institutional life, parishioners approached the sacraments in a distinctly Mexican way. The initiation of an infant into Catholic life was of utmost importance to Mexicans and Mexican Americans. Baptisms were great occasions, marked by a solemn ritual in the church and followed by hearty celebration in the home; they were often announced in the Spanish-language press.[66] Mexican Catholics put "all the decoration possible" into the baptism of a child. "They are accustomed to having a fiesta with tamales and beer," Father Flores explained. "If they are poor, they may have to wait a half year or a year before the baby is baptized, until they can afford the fiesta, but they consider the social aspect of the occasion very important."[67]

Baptisms were important socially because they brought together family and friends, much like the other institutional practices Mexican Catholics chose to follow. But more important, they fostered community bonds through the time-honored ritual kinship of *compadrazgo* (godparentage). In particular, *madrina* (godmother) status was much respected, given the serious commitments the relationship entailed, and it carried almost the same "social and emotional weight" as *madre*

Father Patricio Flores brought more cultural relevance to Mexican American ministry in the Galveston-Houston Diocese with such innovations as the mariachi Mass, performed here at St. Joseph–St. Stephen Parish in 1969. Courtesy *Texas Catholic Herald*.

(mother). "If the natural mother dies or is otherwise unable to care for her children," anthropologist Kay Turner has explained, "the madrina frequently takes full responsibility for raising her godchildren."[68] Thus St. Patrick parishioner María López helped rear three of her godson's children. "The three children call me Godmother. They consider me their grandmother," she explained. *Compadrazgo* had a long history and an important place in the Mexican American community, as it built ties that assured lifelong emotional and material support and reciprocity between families and "a woman's sense of power in the Texas-Mexican community."[69] In reality, the use of the term *comadrazgo* is far more appropriate than *compadrazgo*, for historically it has been women—the *comadres*—who have taken the lead in perpetuating this important Mexican American institution.

The sacrament of confirmation also held great significance. Again, however, Mexican practice differed from church expectations. "The baptism rate is very high in Mexican American areas though confirmation is quite a different thing," a bishop observed in 1970. "Interest in the last years has dwindled," he lamented, "because the Confirmation age requirement is much later in a child's life and parents either forget about it or give up on Confirmation by that time."[70] The bishop's observations reflected a long-standing difference between what the church expected and how its Mexican parishioners approached the sacrament. Historically, Mexicans in Texas and the Southwest had their children confirmed as soon as possible after baptism, without first having religious instruction and First Communion, as tradition in the U.S. Church dictated. The dearth of clergy and religious institutions in the vast region compelled bishops to give the geographically dispersed Mexicans the benefit of confirmation at an earlier age. By the twentieth century, the practice was entrenched among Houston's Mexican Catholics, and the Galveston Diocese had even condoned it since 1912.[71] With time, however, churchmen pressed to bring Mexican American practices in line with those of the majority of Catholics in yet another reflection of the hierarchy's efforts to force Mexican Catholicism into the Anglo American mold. In the late 1930s, for instance, Oblate missionaries sought to change the Mexican practice so that children could receive sufficient religious instruction and be confirmed at about age twelve. "[P]astors are fully convinced," a missionary wrote, "that valuable opportunities are being wasted because of the retention of the old Spanish custom of having the children confirmed as soon as possible after baptism." However, the author anticipated difficulty in changing the practice.[72]

By the later 1960s the church held Mexican American parishioners to the same policy as other Catholics. But for the most part, Mexican Catholics in Houston and elsewhere continued their tradition; they circumvented the policy by simply crossing the border into Mexico, where they could still confirm their children without fulfilling the requirement of First Communion. Mrs. Esther García recalled the

Particular sacraments, such as this girl's First Communion, had great social, as well as religious, importance in Mexican American communities. Courtesy Houston Metropolitan Research Center, Houston Public Library.

practice during her childhood—her grandmother and mother took several of her younger siblings to Mexico to be confirmed. Mrs. García explained that the practice remained commonplace in Houston as late as the 1970s. The Oblate father's prediction a generation earlier, that it "would be difficult . . . to change this attitude," proved correct.[73] This practice again revealed some parishioners' resistance to the pressures of the institutional church as they adjusted to life in Houston in their own way, and it revealed Mexican women's leadership and initiatives in dictating the form resistance would take in some households. That independent attitude carried over into the way Mexican Catholics participated in church organizations and in how they related to the representatives of the church.

"One of the foundations of every parish is the Parish Societies," Father Esteban de Anta asserted in 1930.[74] The priest's observation was well founded, for parish organizations served important functions both for the institutional church and the *colonia*. Parish societies enhanced spiritual and social life, provided cohesion for the community, and expressed Mexican ethno-Catholic identity.

A Mexican parish typically accommodated the entire family in its organizational life.[75] Potentially, every member of a family could belong to some parish society. There were separate men's and women's organizations; young adults', as well as boys' and girls', clubs; even societies for infants. With time there were also mixed-gender societies. Different organizations came and went over the years, but some became perennial favorites that flourished for generations. Married women traditionally joined the Guadalupanas (Society of Our Lady of Guadalupe), the Socias del Altar (Altar Society), and the Socias del Sagrado Corazón (Sacred Heart Society). Later, they formed Legions of Mary, Ladies' Councils, and Mothers' Clubs, while single young women joined the Hijas de María (Daughters of Mary), young girls the Teresitas (Society of St. Therese the Little Flower), and teens the Catholic Youth Organization (CYO). Men's societies included the Sociedad del Santo Nombre (Holy Name Society), Adoración Nocturna (Nocturnal Adoration Society), and Vasallos de Cristo Rey (Subjects of Christ the King). Boys joined a Sociedad San Luis or San José (St. Louis or St. Joseph Sodality) in the early years, and later the CYO. The youngest children found their place in the Infant Jesus of Prague Society. Women's and girls' societies were more numerous than male organizations, but parish societies offered something for everyone. These voluntary organizations provided invaluable financial sustenance for parishes through their ongoing fund-raising. Moreover, parish societies offered Mexican women one of the few arenas in which they could develop their talents outside of the home (see Table A.2).[76]

Not surprisingly, parish societies often had some intimate link to

Mexican culture and history. For example, the quintessential women's organization was the Guadalupanas, a parish society that honored Mexico's patron saint, Our Lady of Guadalupe. Similarly, the Vasallos de Cristo Rey resonated with the memory of the religious wars in Mexico during the 1920s, a time when many Catholics fought to the death against the government's oppression of the Catholic Church, which, by extension, they perceived as an attack on their very identity. Mexican parishioners in Houston routinely joined the popular annual Christ the King celebrations. The citywide affair drew thousands of Catholics in its heyday of the 1950s. The event in 1950 drew over 15,000 faithful of all ethnicities, but the strong connection between Mexican history and religiosity stood out dramatically, as the press reported:

> A bit of pathos was added in an incident involving three elderly Mexicans. During Solemn Benediction, as the bishop elevated the Ostensorium and blessed the assembled thousands, they knelt, made the Sign of the Cross, and the leader held up a small tattered banner on which was a picture of Christ the King. The three fixed their eyes on the Host, raised the banner and in unison exclaimed, "Viva Cristo rey!" They had come many miles from the Sierra range in North Mexico, where during the days of religious persecution, they and their little band of followers fled on Sundays to the fastnesses [sic] of the mountains, where, on bended knees, they recited the prayer, "O Christ Jesus, I acknowledge thee as the King of All."
>
> Here were men who had come to celebrate the Kingship of Christ, men who had suffered and had deprived themselves of many things so that they could attend the great celebration. It was a display of faith rarely paralleled.[77]

In Houston's barrios people held fast to the memory of religious and historical events that entwined to define their Mexicanness. The Cristo Rey celebrations struck a chord because they were a time to honor family members and comrades killed in the Cristero Wars, as well as an expression of identity. Events like these underscored the importance of honoring the family and protecting the faith, values that were widely shared among Mexican and Mexican American Catholics. Kept alive by parish organizations and celebrations, these events unified Mexican Catholics everywhere.

At Guadalupe Parish a men's organization, the Nocturnal Adoration Society, gained great admiration and attention and flourished for several years. Pastors, bishops, and the press marveled at this men's organization, which began in the late 1920s with two groups of twenty men taking turns praying all night, twice a month. By 1934, 120 members prayed throughout the night four times a month. Men at Guadalupe Parish were also eagerly engaged in two other societies. The pastor described the men's Sacred Heart Society as a "flourishing" confraternity "with a large membership," and he heaped praise on the church band, the Banda Guadalupana. "Day after day they practice for three hours," he wrote, "and their beautiful music lends grace and animation to all the activities of the parish."[78]

The fervent participation of men in religious activities raises questions about the gendered nature of religiosity in Mexican American Catholic culture. Conventional wisdom has long held that Mexican and Mexican American Catholic men have been minimally involved in religious matters; religion has been considered something for women and children. The notoriety the men's Nocturnal Adoration Society aroused is evidence of this; the group received so much attention precisely because it was unusual to see Mexican men show such religious fervor. Reverend De Anta called the group "rare," and in describing the men's activities he used the very telling Spanish phrase— despreciando el qué dirán (meaning "disregarding what people might say").[79] In other words, the pastor understood that these men's all-night prayer vigils transgressed ascribed gender roles, yet the men did not care what people might say about their displays of piety. This lends credence to the conventional view about gender roles and religion in Mexican and Mexican American Catholic culture.

But rather than ask if women were more involved in religious activity than men, perhaps we should ask under what circumstances was it acceptable for men to show pious devotion? Did men monopolize some parish societies because they were considered more prestigious, or because the symbolism or activities associated with particular organizations coincided more closely with the roles and behavior society ascribed to men? Maternal symbolism and the fact that Our Lady of Guadalupe represented the ideal role model for married women certainly moved many wives and mothers to join the Guadalupana societies. As was consistent with cultural mores, too, men—not women—spent the entire night away from home praying, as members of the Adoración Nocturna. Then, too, the fact that the cry "Viva Cristo Rey!" was as much a call to arms as it was a statement of religious belief prompted men to see this organization as "theirs," linked as it was to military leadership and warfare, arenas that men historically claimed.

Preparations for and participation in the many novenas, feast days, and other ceremonies their societies sponsored further involved parishioners institutionally. The month of the Virgin Mary (May) "was celebrated with enthusiasm by the Children of Mary and the Teresitas," one proud pastor wrote in 1944. The following month, the priest added, the women of the Sacred Heart Society "put their hearts into the month of June so as not to let the Children of Mary have all the honors."[80] Likewise at Guadalupe Church in the 1920s, young girls dressed in white customarily offered bouquets to the Virgin, and individuals, families, and societies took charge of particular days during the month-long devotion. The Feast of Our Lady of Guadalupe also involved many devotees.[81] In addition, parish society members reinforced their spiritual lives by corporately partaking of the sacraments. The CYO of Immaculate Heart Parish, for instance, attended Mass and received group Communion in the 1950s. At Guadalupe Parish in the 1930s, the four children's societies took turns "to appear as a unit in church." The men's Holy Name and Nocturnal Adoration Societies at different parishes also customarily took Corporate Communion.[82]

These practices undoubtedly pleased church officials, who strove to make Mexicans "better" Catholics. Like other immigrant communities, Italians in New York and Chicago, for example, Mexican Catholics in Houston felt pressured to change their style of Catholicism to conform to the Irish American model that set the standard for "acceptable" Catholicism in America.[83] Noting what in his eyes were changes for the better among Houston's Mexican Catholics, an early-twentieth-century clergyman boasted, "The Mexicanitos . . . are being transformed into a splendid unit of people who are not only practical Catholics but Catholics who are living up to the highest Christian ideals." He offered as evidence the flourishing organizational life of the parish.[84] It would be easy, but erroneous, to interpret Mexican American participation in church societies as simple conformity to Irish American Catholicism. Rather, joining parish societies was a form of accommodation, not capitulation to total assimilation. On the one hand, participation in organizations closely associated with Mexican history and identity—the Guadalupanas and Vasallos de Cristo Rey, for instance—represented yet another tie to Mexicanness and a way to bolster ethno-Catholicism. On the other hand, by being active in parish societies, Mexicans blunted church criticism and gave the impression that they were becoming "better" Catholics. In this way, Mexican parishioners met some of the demands the church hierarchy made of them while still defining their own way of being Catholic and nurturing their sense of identity and self-worth. They made do in this way, accommodating to life in the Bayou City without disappearing into it through total assimilation.[85]

Parish societies also performed important social functions. These organizations raised money, provided community service, and had the potential for social action. Organizational fund-raising enriched individuals and whole communities by fostering ethnic identity and solidarity.[86] Societies also fostered a sense of social responsibility through community service. The sixth, seventh, and eighth graders of St. Patrick's Ave María Club, for instance, helped the Red Cross and other organizations as part of their activities. At Immaculate Heart of Mary, the teenagers of the CYO distributed food baskets to indigent families, and adults also provided emergency relief through the St. Vincent de Paul Society.[87]

In addition, parish societies were potential vehicles for social action. Since the later nineteenth century, Texas Mexicans had formed secular mutual aid societies for self-help and community assistance. Similar parish-based organizations existed since at least the early twentieth century throughout Texas as Mexicans formed chapters of the Holy Mexican Union and the Liga de Protección Mexicana (Mexican Protection League) to safeguard their civic and religious interests.[88] In the early 1910s, for instance, the Liga de Protección Mexicana in Del Rio, Texas, used court action and a boycott against local newspapers' tirades about their clergy and parishioners. At Houston's Guadalupe Parish, the men's *liga* was one of the earliest parish societies established. Significantly, some of Guadalupe's parish women formed their own *liga* the next year, in 1917.[89] Separate men's and women's parish societies were customary in the early twentieth century, and, given the often political focus of the Liga de Protección, it is not surprising that men would have their own separate organization. But the existence of a separate women's society raises intriguing questions about women forming this particular kind of organization. How different or similar were the two *ligas*? Were Mexican women in early-twentieth-century Houston pushing the limits of civic participation through this organization? The sparse available evidence leaves these particular questions unanswered, as indeed many others remain about the Mexican American religious experience.

The *cursillo de cristiandad* provided another church-based organization with implications for social change. A three-day, once-in-a-lifetime experience of spiritual renewal and dedication, the "little course in Christianity" became very popular among Spanish-speaking Catholics in the early 1960s.[90] *Cursillos* brought together priests and laypeople in a retreatlike setting that imbued participants with the Christian message of dynamic self-reform and responsibility for others. The intensity of the experience fostered a sense of empowerment that potentially could be channeled into social action.[91] Church officials, however, did not intend the *cursillo* to be a separate parish society or a means of social action. They specifically instructed participants "not to form a clique or a special organization" after completing the *cursillo*. Instead, participants were supposed to volunteer their services in parish work and "leaven the parish for God."[92] However, Mexican parishioners often disregarded these instructions. Church bulletins, diocesan reports, and the local Catholic press routinely reported the activities of those who had participated in the *cursillo* (*cursillistas*) as distinct groups.[93] The *cursillistas'* insistence on maintaining a separate identity, despite the church's instructions to the contrary, again recalled the characteristic independence of Mexican American Catholics and their tendency to circumvent church authority.

Parishioners recognized the *cursillo's* potential for social change. Many Chicanos involved in social justice movements in the 1960s and 1970s were *cursillistas*, including César Chávez and many of his lay supporters, as well as vocal Chicano clerics such as Father Patricio Flores, who introduced the *cursillo* in Houston.[94] In Houston the head of the Political Association of Spanish-speaking Organizations (PASO), Manuel Crespo, believed the *cursillo* was "one of the most important efforts in the Church" to fight for racial equality. "Since I've become a cursillista I've seen how much this activity can be of tremendous help to us and the community," Crespo stated. He believed that community political leaders who were "fallen-away" Catholics could be brought back to active membership in the church through the *cursillo*. Moreover, he saw the *cursillo* as a possible avenue for "helping eliminate discrimination against us."[95]

Padres Asociados para Derechos Religiosos, Educativos y Sociales (Priests Associated for Religious, Educational and Social Rights, or PADRES), the organization of outspoken Chicano priests who sought to involve the Catholic Church in Mexican Americans' efforts for social equality, later echoed these sentiments. PADRES believed the *cursillo* was not being used to full advantage. "[S]ocial action has not been encouraged or implemented [in the *cursillo*]," the activist priests complained.

In early 1970, they demanded a separate national secretariat for Mexican Americans and culturally sensitive priests to direct the *cursillos*. Most important, PADRES called for social action to be an integral part of the *cursillo* experience.[96]

Again, Mexican American lay and religious leaders demonstrated their self-reliance and resourcefulness. The institutional church leadership had not intended the *cursillos* to be used for social action, but at least some Mexican Americans saw them as stepping stones in that direction; they recognized the possibility of using their institutional participation to challenge their outsider status in society and the church. It is important to remember that the *cursillos* were exclusively for men when they began in 1957 and that they were structured around the notion of male bonding. The *cursillo* movement radiated intensely through Mexican American communities in an era when returning Mexican American war veterans and others were asserting themselves, mounting civil rights campaigns, and struggling to take control of their lives. This aspect of Mexican American Catholicism contrasts strongly with its more feminized nature of the pre–World War II period. An assertive expression of Mexican American men willing to publicly proclaim their spirituality and apply it to social issues, the *cursillo* fit well with the political activism stirring among the post–World War II GI generation because it offered a potential arena in which they could strive for personal and community self-determination.[97]

LANGUAGE, RELATIONSHIPS, AND MEMORY

Mexican parishioners usually worshipped in parishes administered by Spanish-speaking priests and sisters, especially during the first half of the twentieth century, when most of them belonged to Mexican national parishes. Church leaders appreciated the importance of having Spanish-speaking personnel, and they tried to find native speakers or Anglos who had a working knowledge of the language, as well as experience ministering to Mexicans and Mexican Americans. Often the pastors were Spaniards and had an "American" assistant.[98]

The presence of a Spanish-speaking church staff facilitated communication but did not assure closeness and confidence between clergy and parishioners. Relations between parishioners and priests were usually cordial, but they were characterized by formality, not warmth. Parishioners' recollections revealed few endearing sentiments regarding the clerics who headed the parishes. For example, an Immaculate Heart member recalled that "[y]ears back, the Church was so private and so apart from the people." In a similar vein, a Guadalupe parishioner described relations between the churchgoers and priests as "okay" and "alright."[99]

Priests were figures of unquestioned authority who demanded respect. "[P]eople respected them as the head of the church," a woman recalled, "and what we had to do was whatever they said; that was it." Some priests kept a close watch on their church members and tried to regulate their behavior. Father Esteban de Anta often surprised parishioners with his unannounced home visits, and another priest demanded that his parishioners stay away from the *aleluyas* (Mexican Protestants). But there was limited interaction with the priest. At Immaculate Heart, the priests rarely attended the fund-raisers church members put on. Even church services afforded little contact. After a service, a parishioner explained, the priest would immediately leave the church without mingling with the members afterward. Priests had a "job to do," and "whether we like it or not we just go along with it," a parishioner summarized.[100]

The social distance between priests and parishioners reflected the ambivalent Mexican tradition of respect mixed with anticlericalism. Social scientists in the early and mid-twentieth century noted the conflicted feelings Mexicans held toward the church and the clergy.[101] Because of the great wealth and political power of the church and the great vitality of Mexican Catholicism, a later scholar wrote, no other Catholic nation "experienced such extremes of anticlericalism as Mexico."[102] The long history of church-state conflict culminated in the Cristero Rebellion of 1926–29, in which thousands of Catholics carried on a bloody resistance against the Mexican government.[103] Generations of strife between Mexican civil and religious authority undoubtedly affected attitudes in Houston's *colonia*. Mary Villagómez, with her twenty years as a nun and lifelong association with the Magnolia barrio, spoke with firsthand experience. On the one hand, Mexicans had a great reverence for the habit and the cossack, she explained, but on the other hand, many people resented the fact that the church in Mexico had sided with the rich and with the oppressive government of President Porfirio Díaz. Those parishioners blamed the church for its alliance with a dictatorship that had brought on a devastating revolution in 1910 that forced many of them to flee to the United States. But Houston's parishes were also home to large numbers of immigrants who had risked their very lives to defend the church during the Cristero Rebellion in the 1920s. The issue was a paradox because Houston's Mexican parishes harbored feelings of both estrangement and loyalty toward the Catholic Church.[104]

The gulf between priests and parishioners was also partly the result of old animosities rooted in the Spanish colonial period. Some parishioners felt that priests from Spain had a condescending attitude toward Mexicans. "I had a feeling . . . that they thought they were better than us," a woman recalled, "that our culture didn't measure up."[105] Complaints by Catholic officials about the "Spanish contempt" for Mexican Americans supported the parishioner's suspicions.[106] It was not uncommon, then, as one bishop reported in 1969, to find "some well-founded complaints about lack of rapport on the part of the Pastor."[107] The parishioners' traditional deference for the priesthood probably muted this antagonism, but at times parishioners bitterly complained and demanded the removal of priests they found unacceptable.[108] Church members also tried to dissuade the hierarchy from removing priests or nuns who had been effective and respectful.[109]

Relations between Houston's Mexican Catholics and church representatives revealed some continuity in the Texas Mexican experience. The attitudes and perceptions that colored institutional parish life were a legacy of the past, and respectful but distant relations between parishioners and clergy reinforced the tradition of tenuous links with the institutional church. These lukewarm relations also revealed the people's determination to resist treatment as second-class Catholics. When parishioners demanded sensitive and helpful church personnel, in effect they were demanding respect for themselves, their communities, and their ethnoreligious identity, asserting their cultural autonomy.

A strong carrier of culture, language richly reflected Houston's Mexican ethno-Catholic culture. Religious sentiment and symbolism suffused the peoples' language and the ordinary acts of everyday life, texturing the web of Mexican American ethnoreligious memory and identity. An Oblate priest writing about Mexico in the 1930s marveled at how thoroughly the names, events, and beliefs associated with Catholicism imbued Mexican life.[110] Such names as Providence, Faith, Hope, Guadalupe, and Santiago abounded—in people's names, the names of towns and cities, in popular songs, and in the names of businesses. "Even the amusements especially among the working classes were often of a religious nature," the cleric wrote, "such as the feast of St. John, St. James, [and] the day of Holy Innocents," in addition to the "numerous religious feasts which were the occasion of much rejoicing." He added, "There is no home no matter how humble which does not have its statue or image of our Lady of Guadalupe."[111]

The author concluded that the Spanish language was "essentially Catholic." A multitude of common sayings and proverbs exuded religious feeling. To a mother, the clatter of noisy children sounded "like the Day of Judgement." In reply to a "thank you," people responded with "Let thanks be given to God." When someone took leave, saying "see you tomorrow," the response was "If God wills it" or "If God grants us life" (*Si Dios quiere* or *Si Dios nos presta vida*). The clergyman relayed many other sayings that reflected the religious imagery typical of Mexican conversation.[112]

Similarly, Houston's Mexican Catholics often expressed their reliance on an assumed sacred presence in their lives. References to *la Virgen* and *el Señor* (God) filled family letters. Time-honored phrases included *gracias a Dios* (thanks be to God); *por voluntad de Dios* (by God's will); *que el sagrado corazón de Jesús los bendiga* (may the sacred heart of Jesus bless you); and *que la Virgen los cubra con su Santísimo manto* (may the Virgin's blessed cloak protect you).[113] To invoke the protection of a sacred intercessor for a loved one was not only a conscious act of prayer in a church or at a home altar; it was just as much an unconscious way of thinking, talking, and writing—a natural part of living. Mexican American Catholics naturally entwined familial affection and the sacred this way because theirs was a world in which the temporal and the spiritual flowed continually into each other. Parishioners emphasized that confluence. "[R]eligion was our life," Mrs. Janie Tijerina asserted. Mrs. Esther García echoed, "My spirituality has a lot to do with who I am . . . especially as a Mexican, with my background and my grandmother—she's so rooted in Aztec and Mayan blood—that part of our spirituality is who we are; we can't change that. We can't divide it; we can't separate it. That's part of our being." She added that Mexican Catholics did not separate religion from politics or other aspects of life, that when they did, "that's when we stop being who we are."[114]

At times, lay and religious alike penned verses that expressed the centrality of religion in their lives and the many ways the faith sustained them. A proud Chicano's homage to his people began, "Bronze and proud are my people from the Land of Sun, Where the Virgin Guadalupe's roses blessed us new times now begin."[115] The poem not only reflected the ethnic pride and community solidarity characteristic of the Chicano movement years, but it also underlined the continuing importance of Our Lady of Guadalupe. The author invoked this sacred intercessor at the height of the Chicano civil rights movement, as many in generations before him had done in their search for social justice. Another plea for divine intervention flowed from the pen of Blas de León, a simple farmer who lived on the outskirts of Houston in the 1920s. In *"Ante el Altar de la Virgen de los Dolores,"* De León expressed his devotion to Our Lady of Sorrows, imploring her spiritual healing.[116] Rural workers often faced a harsh life in early-twentieth-century Texas, and De León's poem spoke for many immigrants and Mexican Americans who turned to favored saints for solace from drudgery and pain. "You know how I've suffered" (*Tu sabes cuánto he sufrido*), De León reminded the Virgin. Wounded by life's rocky path (*los guijarros del camino el corazón me han herido*), he needed her peace and consolation (*dadme paz dadme consuelo*).

Many clergy and sisters recognized this universal devotion to the saints among Mexican parishioners. For example, Sister Dolores Cárdenas, who spent much of her career in Houston's barrios, always ended her newspaper column with a short tribute that reflected the span of succor devotees found in Our Lady of Guadalupe: *O Virgen de Guadalupe, la más bella de las flores; Para tí nuestros afanes, alegrías y dolores* (O Virgin Guadalupe, the most beautiful of flowers, with you we share all our troubles, joys, and sorrows).[117] In 1931 Father Esteban de Anta wrote an elegant fifteen-stanza poem titled "*A la Santísima Virgen de Guadalupe*," in honor of the 400th anniversary of the Virgin's apparition. The poem, professionally printed and featuring the image of Guadalupe, was an attractive keepsake.[118]

Mexican Americans saved commemorative holy cards and other religious mementos that reflected important religious and social events in their personal lives and in the life of their communities. The cards carried images of Christ, the Virgin, or a saint, and information about celebrated events such as special missions or novenas, the entrance of a nun or priest into religious life, anniversaries of parish societies, or special feast days. Often religious mentors inscribed the cards and gave them to parishioners. Other memories might be preserved in a tattered postcard depicting the apparition of Our Lady of Guadalupe to Juan Diego, or in a faded ribbon inscribed with the date and place of an *apadrinamiento* (a godparent sponsorship). These remembrances held important meanings for Mexican and Mexican American Catholics in Houston. As "narratives of family and communal events framed in liturgical celebrations," they were tangible symbols of binding experiences shared by many individuals and communities.[119] Stored away among a family's treasures, these mementos sacralized the collective memory of a people.

Mexican ethno-Catholicism in Houston had striking parallels with

Num. 1   Abril 1928   Año 1

Boletín Parroquial

Igl...

Ntra. Sra. de Guadalupe

Houston, T...

GUTIERREZ

Tattered but valued: parish bulletins and other religious mementos reflected a sense of identity and community among Houston's Mexican-origin Catholics. Courtesy Houston Metropolitan Research Center, Houston Public Library.

the Catholicism of southern Italian immigrants in the late nineteenth and early twentieth centuries. Church leaders ridiculed and chastised the southern Italians' pre-Tridentine way of being Catholic in much the same way they did Mexican American faith expressions. Also like the Mexicans, southern Italians had a strong anticlerical tradition and a similar pattern of infrequent church attendance; their devotional practices centered on shrines, pilgrimages, holy cards, and other sacramentals that clergy often saw as a "peculiar kind of spiritual condition" lacking in doctrinal understanding. But what church personnel saw as spiritual deficiencies southern Italians and Mexicans understood as a source of strength. For both peoples, their "peculiar" faith helped them build community and retain the identity, pride, and values that sustained them as they struggled to create a space for themselves in a society that saw them as outsiders or even outcasts.[120]

When the Oblate Fathers of Mary Immaculate arrived in Houston in 1911, they encountered the Mexican way of being Catholic described in this chapter. It was a distinct religious tradition that often clashed with their own and one that reflected the outsider status Mexicans occupied in American society and the Catholic Church. In order to understand the relationship between Mexican Americans and the institutional church, we must next examine the perceptions and attitudes church representatives revealed about their Mexican parishioners, the topic to which we now turn.

THREE

ather Esteban de Anta was appalled at what he saw in Houston in
late 1911. One of the original band of Missionary Oblates in the city,
the Spanish priest recoiled at the grinding poverty he found among
Mexicans and Mexican Americans, a "poor, ignorant and despised
people . . . eking out a miserable existence." Moreover, the cleric
shuddered at another kind of poverty that, at least in his eyes, afflicted
his parishioners—a spiritual poverty. "For many Mexicans, religion,
alas! consists of having a great many *Santitos*, and in lighting a candle
before them," De Anta decried. "It is impossible to make them realize
the importance of the Mass and of the reception of the Sacraments."[1]

Father De Anta and officials of the Catholic Church rarely spoke
about Texas Mexicans without using such phrases as "the poor Mexican" or "these poor people." But although most Texas Mexicans in the
early twentieth century were in fact poor, these descriptions reflected
more than their economic status. Indeed, the terminology revealed as
much about the views and attitudes of church representatives as it did
about the status of Mexicans in the United States. In the eyes of many
church leaders, Mexicans were poor in more than the economic sense;
they were spiritually impoverished as well. Thus Mexican Catholics
found themselves objects of both pity and scorn, and they were usually
seen as a problem for the Catholic Church.

This chapter examines changes and continuities in the way church representatives perceived Mexican parishioners in order to illustrate how those perceptions influenced and reflected the ways Mexican Catholics carved their place in Houston. Catholic officials understood the so-called Mexican problem of the early twentieth century (later called the "problem of the Spanish-speaking") as both a pastoral and a social issue. Generally, this dual perception reflected negative attitudes about Mexican Catholics, and to a large degree it contributed to their marginalization in the institutional church, especially in the early twentieth century. Over time, however, changes in the Mexican community and in societal views gradually produced attitudinal shifts among church officials. Despite a continuing tension between old stereotypes and new perceptions, by the 1960s these shifting attitudes had begun to enhance the church's ministry to Mexican and Mexican American Catholics.

THE "MEXICAN PROBLEM," 1910S–1930S

The flood of Mexican immigration in Texas and the Southwest in the early twentieth century gave rise to the so-called Mexican problem. Many Americans viewed Mexican immigrants ambivalently, as a sort of necessary evil in American society. Mexicans were wanted and needed as cheap labor, but they were also resented as economic competitors by some and as potential despoilers of the American social fabric by others. Generally, these perceptions applied equally to both native-born Mexican Americans and Mexican immigrants, for few Americans distinguished between the two groups. For the Catholic Church the "Mexican problem" was primarily a question of evangelization, a matter of combating Protestant proselytizing and making "good" (American-style) Catholics out of "nominal" ones.[2] But, in addition, church officials recognized the social side of the "Mexican problem." In the opinion of many clergy, the social aspects of the Mexicans' "problem"—their ostracism and exploitation in American society—were rooted in the racial and cultural traits of the Mexicans themselves.

Many church personnel thought of Mexicans essentially as Indians, and they often attributed to them a presumably violent "Latin temperament." However, they were also deemed polite, charming, and naturally timid.[3] Not surprisingly, some nuns felt a duty to "civilize" the Mexicans of Houston's Second Ward.[4] The perceived need to civilize Mexicans stemmed partly from the widely held view of them as nomadics.[5] Clerics noted the absence of traditional "American" values among Mexicans, especially when compared to "their more virile Northern neighbors" who were blessed, supposedly, with greater initiative. Even Bishop Christopher E. Byrne, a staunch champion of Texas Mexicans, found his flock's values deficient.[6]

In addition, it was not uncommon for representatives of the church to view Mexicans as children. The local priest was "a father indeed to the Mexicans," according to one cleric. Childlike, Mexicans were "moved more by imagination than by reason," a priest claimed, and had improvident and hedonistic tendencies.[7] An official of the Galveston Diocese, honoring a priest's work among Houston Mexicans, described his parishioners as "people who are very largely little children."[8] This tendency to infantilize the Mexican paralleled the experience of other people of color in the United States. As historian Ronald Takaki and others have shown, the ideology of the "child / savage" powerfully influenced the racialization of African Americans, Native Americans, and Asian Americans, as well as Mexican Americans.[9]

The racialization process of these groups varied, of course, depending not only on skin color but also on class, gender, geographical location, and historical era. Mexicans occupied an ambiguous place in the racial hierarchy. "As a racially mixed group," historian Neil Foley has shown, "Mexicans, like Indians and Asians, lived in a black-and-white nation that regarded them neither as black nor as white." For most white Texans, Mexicans were "a 'mongrelized' race of Indian, African, and Spanish ancestry."[10] Because of their mixed lineage, the

Mexicans' racialization experience recalls the history of other Americans whose racial classification confounded white America in the nineteenth and early twentieth centuries. Cape Verdean Americans, Afro-Portuguese Catholics from the Cape Verde Islands off West Africa, for instance, began immigrating in the 1860s mostly to southeastern New England. Considered neither white nor black in their adopted land, they came to occupy a marginal place in the Catholic Church and New England society, a situation similar to that of Mexicans in Texas.[11]

An even more striking historical parallel can be drawn between Texas Mexicans and southern Italian immigrants, especially those Italians who settled in the Deep South. Throughout the United States, Americans considered the southern Italians racially suspect and denigrated them as "kinky-haired Africans" because of their "swarthy" complexion and the fact that they were from the *mezzogiorno*, the part of Italy that is the hottest and closest to Africa. In the black and white South of the late nineteenth and early twentieth centuries, the guardians of the color line tried to keep Italian children from attending white schools and sometimes lynched adults who violated southern racial protocols by working and socializing with blacks. In the same period in Texas, Anglos treated Tejanos in much the same way and for very similar reasons. Historian Arnoldo De León has documented how whites brutalized Mexicans and held them in contempt, partly for helping slaves to escape in antebellum times but also for working, socializing, and sometimes intermarrying with blacks.[12] However, in constructing their racial views, whites emphasized the Mexicans' alleged savage Aztec Indian background.[13] This added twist distinguished the Mexicans' racialization from both the Cape Verdeans' and the Italians'. In any case, society's negative views of mixed-race people such as Mexicans existed, to some degree, in the Catholic Church in early-twentieth-century Houston. Consciously or not, these perceptions helped to perpetuate the social inequality of Mexicans in the United States.

However, racist and paternalistic clerical views nonetheless coexisted with genuine humanitarian concerns about the endemic poverty in Mexican communities. The poor were the central calling of the Oblate Fathers, a challenge reflected in the order's motto: *Evangelizare pauperibus misit me* (He hath sent me to preach the Gospel to the poor).[14] Men and women of the church agonized over the severe poverty that afflicted many Mexicans and Mexican Americans in the early twentieth century. Father Esteban de Anta observed in 1913 that Mexicans found *"[m]ucho trabajo y poco dinero"* (plenty of work but little pay) in Houston and the Southwest.[15] His superior, the Right Reverend Nicholas A. Gallagher, bishop of the Galveston Diocese, had appealed to Houston employers in 1912 for donations to ease the Mexicans' plight and carry on their evangelization. He candidly reminded "those who are benefitted most by the industrious and honest labor of this large Mexican population, namely, THE DIFFERENT RAILROADS and OTHER CORPORATIONS that employ them," of their moral duty.[16] The bishop's appeal was more than moral prodding. He recognized the importance of Mexican workers to Houston's growing economy and argued that their spiritual and temporal "uplift" was imperative for retaining them as a valuable part of the city's workforce. Contributions from area employers to the church would result in "more contented and happy" employees, the bishop reminded the corporate sector, and it would prove to Mexicans that their employers "have at heart their welfare."[17]

The Catholic hierarchy recognized the importance of the growing number of Mexicans in Houston early on and consequently began to focus more attention on their needs. But it was clear to some that the Mexicans' well-being was not a high priority among many employers. One cleric asserted that Mexicans were "more sinned against than sinning," being "heckled and brow-beaten and exploited and underpaid by avaricious and unscrupulous employers." They lived in "wretched cottages" and wore "sordid rags," another priest lamented. Sister Mary Benitia Vermeersch arrived at Our Lady of Guadalupe Parish in the summer of 1915 to find atrocious living conditions in Houston's El Segundo Barrio (Second Ward). Many railroad workers lived in company housing, usually dilapidated two- or three-room shacks. Families sometimes shared empty boxcars temporarily before finding better quarters. This dire poverty, Father L. O. Eckardt argued, made Mexican workers dependent on their employers and relegated them "to be mere machines of unskilled labor."[18]

Representatives of the church recognized that this deprivation gave rise to a panoply of other social problems. Many religious leaders criticized the indignities often heaped upon Texas Mexicans. "They came, hopeful of finding respect and love," a Houston priest observed, but found instead "only contempt and hatred. 'Greasers' they are called and looked down upon and considered as pariahs." White hostility toward Mexicans was so fierce, Bishop Byrne noted, that it sometimes exceeded that shown toward blacks.[19]

Social ostracism was widespread. "Such prejudice against the Mexicans is very strong and is shown on all sides and in hundreds of ways," a churchman reported in 1933. In an era of Jim Crow, discrimination pervaded public facilities and institutions. Mexicans were denied entry to restaurants, hotels, theaters, and other service and recreational facilities. Mary Villagómez, who grew up in Magnolia Park on Houston's east side in the 1910s and 1920s, remembered vividly that "people . . . were so prejudiced against the Mexicans." The Pine View movie theater did not even allow segregated seating, as other places sometimes did. "We could not go into Pine View," she recalled; "the Mexicans couldn't even stand at a distance to see it; no, no, you couldn't get near the place." Certain parks and residential areas were also closed to Mexicans. "We couldn't go into Mason Park . . . [or] Forest Hill; that was off limits," she recounted.[20]

Clerics readily pointed out the church's own shortcomings in this regard. "[E]ven many Catholic congregations do not want [Mexicans]," a priest wrote. Some Anglo American churches brazenly displayed signs warning, "Mexicans prohibited." Others reserved a back pew for Mexicans with a sign that read *"Mexicanos."*[21] The archbishop of San Antonio, describing a practice common throughout the Southwest, stated, "We are literally forced to erect two churches in the same localities, one for the American Catholics and the other for the Mexicans, for as one of our missionaries put it recently—'An American church for the white people and a mission church for the Helots, the Pariahs of the community, our poor Mexican Catholic people and their little ones.' "²² The archbishop's comments underscored two major aspects of the social reality of Texas Mexicans in the early twentieth century, their poverty and their status as social outcasts. The structures of the Catholic Church replicated Mexican subordination in American society.

Houston was no exception. On the city's east side, priests at Immaculate Conception, the Anglo church in Magnolia, told the neighborhood's Mexicans they had to go to the "Mexican church," Our Lady of Guadalupe, which was farther away. On the rare occasions when Mexicans were admitted into Immaculate Conception, they were allowed seating only in the back pews.²³ Newly arrived immigrants sometimes unknowingly violated this ethnic protocol. Sister Agnes Rita Rodríguez remembered her father's anguish in the late 1910s at being ordered out of Annunciation Church—the premier Anglo Catholic Church and an architectural showcase in downtown Houston. As he knelt in prayer, Mr. Rodríguez looked up to see an usher pointing to the door and saying, "You don't belong here."²⁴

On the other hand, some men and women of the church criticized racial segregation both within churches and in society. Some were particularly critical about so-called Mexican schools. The segregation of Mexican-origin children in public schools was the "norm," and Catholic officials often decried the lack of "decent" public schools for Mexican children, pointing out how "almost hopelessly ostracized" these children were. The cruelty of Anglo children toward them, one priest remarked, frequently ended in fistfights—"a race war in minature [sic]."²⁵

Mexicans stood little chance of getting a good education. In the eyes of some church leaders, this had devastating effects, both socially and spiritually. It was this denial of schooling, in the view of one priest, that doomed the Mexican to a wretched existence of backbreaking work and economic dependency. "Poverty, destitution and misery are the fruits of his uneducated condition," asserted Father Eckardt. And most important, the priest argued, the Mexican's social condition endangered his spiritual life. As long as Mexicans remained mired in poverty, the priest reasoned, their evangelization would be useless.[26] The church's main concern, after all, was saving souls, and it was evident, at least to some, that the social aspect of the "Mexican problem" was tied to the pastoral.

The pastoral side of the so-called problem, like the social, was based on perceptions about Mexicans and their culture. Church officials shared an image of Mexican religiosity that, with few exceptions, gravely disconcerted them. According to many men and women of the church, Mexican Catholics were sadly devoid of genuine piety and badly in need of spiritual rebirth. "How pitiable was their state when we first came to Houston!" an early missionary exclaimed.[27] Many clerics thought Texas Mexicans were indifferent to religion or that they were Catholics in name only. To them, the Mexicans' infrequent church attendance was proof of an irreligious nature. One priest estimated in 1938 that only 20 percent regularly complied with their religious duties. It seemed that most Mexicans were satisfied with going to church only on special occasions, such as during the Christmas season and Holy Week, or for a christening, wedding, or funeral. "He is baptized, married and buried by the priest and '¡Esto basta!' [This is enough!]," a frustrated cleric chastised.[28]

The religious laxity many church personnel saw in Mexicans often reinforced their perceptions of them as childlike. Father De Anta considered his Mexican parishioners in Houston "our friends, yes, more, our children." Seen this way, Mexican Catholics needed the constant protection of the church because they were "such easy victims" of Protestant proselytizers. Bishop Byrne agonized over his flock, especially those so widely scattered that they were only sporadically attended by a "gypsy priest," such as Father Frank Urbanovsky. The bishop wrote that when the roving priest moved on to visit other isolated Mexicans, he left "with a dread, lest the wolves of Satan come and devour his children again." In October 1948, for example, Father

Urbanovsky noted the recently built El Divino Redentor Mexican Presbyterian Church, "[l]ess than a block away" from the soon-to-be Our Lady of St. John Parish in the Bonita Gardens barrio. "Throughout the summer," Urbanovsky reported, the *aleluya* competitors had been "using every means possible to attract the [Catholic] children and through them the parents."[29]

Conscious of the ever-present Protestants, some observers tried to absolve the Mexican for his alleged irreligiosity—only to reveal their own racial bias and misconceptions. One commentator conceded that Mexicans' supposed religious deficiencies were hardly their own fault, because "by nature" Mexicans lacked energy. Religious indifference resulted because religion required energy and, the writer claimed, Mexicans were "listless to anything requiring energy." Another clergyman attributed the alleged problem to the Mexican Indian heritage, to what he vaguely called "the native mental reactions of the race."[30] More bluntly, another priest claimed that Mexicans were "to be helped because they are not of normal intelligence and therefore poor."[31] Perceptions of Mexican cultural and racial traits meshed neatly with religious ones, and societal views reverberated with clerical attitudes.

What particularly exasperated some church officials was their belief that Mexican Catholicism was "not a Faith of reason." The Mexicans' apparent inattention to some sacraments caused many to despair, and their devotion to the sacramentals of the church—*santitos*, candles, holy water, blessings, and so forth—bordered on superstition, according to one priest.[32] In a similar vein, a high official strenuously opposed a plan to build a shrine in honor of Our Lady of Guadalupe in 1936. "I certainly am not in favor of this 'shrine-business,'" the father provincial wrote pointedly. "I think that in this country we are 'overshrined, over-grotted' [*sic*] and in some cases 'over-novenad' [*sic*]," he protested. He objected on grounds that commercial motives too often replaced religious ones in these kinds of projects. But a cultural bias showed. The cleric lamented that the "beauty and purity of *American* faith and devotion" was "victimized" by these types of religious expression, practices that were commonly favored by Mexicans and other immigrants. Much more could be accomplished among the Mexicans, the father provincial suggested, "with Masses, Holy Communions, prayers and with . . . proper limited material aid."[33] Echoing the Americanizing zeal of the era, the provincial proposed an approach that might make Mexicans "better" Catholics.

Church officials and Mexicans obviously disagreed about what comprised a "good" Catholic, as an Oblate missionary revealed: "If you ask a Mexican, 'Are you a Catholic?' he will answer: 'Sí, señor, yo soy muy católico,' ('Yes sir, I am a good Catholic'), and as proof he will show you a medal that he wears, or point to the brightly-colored pictures which decorate the walls of his cottage."[34] Missionaries dreaded hearing Mexican parents say about their children, "O, sometimes they say a few prayers or light a candle before the picture of our favorite saint. So, you see, Padrecito, though they do miss Mass or Sunday-school, they are still good Catholics at home."[35] Father De Anta was understandably distressed when a religious picture he was asked to bless turned out to be that of Martin Luther! The supplicant—who insisted that the picture was not only that of a saint but of one who was muy milagrero (a great miracle-worker)—eventually admitted his error, "and Luther was cast into the devouring flames of the stove."[36]

Such observations were common, and they underscored the gulf between the style of Catholicism that predominated in the United States and the ethno-Catholicism of Mexican Americans that church officials considered a "problem." But in fact the problem was the inflexibility of the American Catholic Church. As a worldwide institution, the Roman Catholic Church evolved into various national forms, and in the United States what was deemed "Catholic" was the Irish American model, with its emphasis on regular Mass attendance and a more "intellectual," less overtly emotional, faith. American Catholicism was rigid, so much so that despite their deeply rooted Catholicism, Mexicans were objects of missionary activity. In Houston, where two Irish American bishops headed the diocese from 1892 to 1950, diocesan administrators saw the world through Irish eyes.[37] Their perceptions, furthermore, made little if any distinction between Mexicans and Mexican Americans. With few exceptions, church representatives saw them all as downtrodden "Mexicans"—poor, uneducated, laboring masses in dire need of spiritual and material uplift.

A growing awareness about differences between native-born Mexican Americans and Mexican immigrants began to emerge among church officials in the 1930s. The alleged problems posed by a burgeoning Mexican population created tremendous interest among Americans, triggering a flood of literature about Mexican-origin people in the United States from the popular press and academic and clerical writers.[38] This new knowledge coincided with a general reassessment in the scientific community about the nature of race and ethnicity and its relation to social inequality. In particular, scholars and social commentators began to doubt facile explanations that historically had attributed Mexican American poverty and social marginality simply to assumed genetic or cultural deficiencies.[39] Presumably these progressive trends sensitized some church personnel to ethnic diversity, but it was their actual day-to-day involvement with Mexicans at the parish level that forced them to reexamine their attitudes toward Mexican and Mexican American Catholics.

In the 1930s representatives of the Catholic Church began making distinctions in class, citizenship status, and civic activity among Mexican-origin people. An Oblate recognized in 1933 that immigrants were not only poor workers but middle class as well, and some had even served in the U.S. Army. Similarly, Bishop Byrne reported to the American Board of Catholic Missions in 1935 that "thousands and thousands of our 'Mexicans' have never seen the other side of the Rio Grande, nor have any desire to see it."[40] Some four years later, the prelate noted the political consciousness stirring among native-born Texas Mexicans. "A movement is on foot," Byrne reported, "to get the native Texas Mexicans more interested in citizenship; to induce them to vote, and take part in every good civic movement." In the bishop's opinion, this boded well for Mexican Americans to "command a better wage, and better living conditions."[41] The growing awareness about the differences among Mexicans and Mexican Americans slowly began to change some clerical attitudes toward Mexican parishioners. At the same time, the increased awareness helped focus more attention on them from the church.

However, some of the older attitudes persisted. For example, ideas about the volatile "Latin temperament" remained intact in some quarters. According to his bishop, the priest in charge of Immaculate Heart of Mary Church near the Port of Houston had to run his parish with "a firm hand" because "being so close to the ship docks . . . he has to deal with some rather tough people." Similarly, the Oblates did not allow priests to serve alone at Mexican missions. A provincial explained that this policy was necessary "for the safety of our priests working with these rather passionate people."[42] In addition, there were occasional signs that the historical animosities between Spain and Mexico were not completely dead and continued to plague relations between Spanish priests and Mexican parishioners. Bishop Wendelin J. Nold complained in 1955 that one priest from Spain was "inclined to treat these Mexicans with a certain degree of Spanish contempt." The bishop continued to wrestle with the problem the next year. "I do not flatter myself," he confided to an Oblate official, "that I can overcome old-country prejudices on the part of certain pastors." Nonetheless, the bishop vowed to continue to seek out priests who understood Mexican Catholics.[43]

Over time, however, changing perceptions tempered older views and attitudes. In 1945, the author of a textbook for seminarians argued earnestly that they must adopt a genuinely "wholesome attitude towards the Mexican." The writer saw this as the only solution to the church's "problem" with the Spanish-speaking. For him, Mexicans were "a loveable people, gentle, polite, docile, obedient, respectful, grateful and appreciative."[44] The particular choice of words reflected both older and emergent notions held by men and women of the church about Texas Mexicans during the World War II era, attitudinally a time of flux.

One constant factor of the times, to be sure, were the social disadvantages that continued to plague Houston's Mexican community throughout the 1940s and 1950s. Poverty persisted despite the general prosperity of the times.[45] Church officials recognized the economic roots of the "Spanish-speaking problem," though their analyses and reactions varied. Bishop Nold saw the status of Mexicans as the most recent phase in the old story of immigrant adjustment and the price newcomers paid to succeed in American society. Booming industry was remaking the Gulf Coast, he explained, and Mexicans would continue to flood into Texas to meet labor-market needs. The bishop did not minimize the Mexicans' poverty and exploitation, but he stoically concluded that "like the poor, the Spanish-speaking we will always have with us," and so he urged other church leaders to cope with the problem rather than to try to solve it.[46]

Others in the Catholic Church thought the real problem was actually the Bracero Program and the new "wetbacks." In 1942 the United States negotiated an agreement with Mexico to import workers (*braceros*, literally, those who work with their arms) under contract to ease America's labor shortage during World War II. A flood of undocumented Mexican laborers also seeking work in the prosperous postwar economy soon accompanied the legal *braceros*. By the mid-1950s, however, recessionary pressures and the public outcry against Mexican immigrants prompted the Immigration and Naturalization Service (INS) to institute a draconian program, "Operation Wetback," to stem the flood of undocumented Mexican workers. More than a million Mexican nationals consequently were rounded up and deported by INS officials between 1953 and 1956, often entangling Mexican American citizens in the process.[47] Indignant churchmen, including Archbishop Robert E. Lucey of San Antonio, railed against the injustice and suffering brought on by the new deluge of Mexican immigration of the 1940s and 1950s. Immigrant labor displaced native-born Mexican Americans and made them "second-class citizens," some church leaders argued. Rev. Frank Kilday protested that Mexican Americans were "being pushed around and manhandled because they cannot produce documentary proof of their citizenship." The angry cleric denounced the INS tactics, adding that it was impossible to know how many Mexican American citizens had been illegally deported.[48]

In the meantime, another dilemma confronted urban communities, juvenile delinquency. In the 1940s and 1950s there was an alarming public perception that youth crime was rampant throughout the nation. Historians disagree about the severity of the problem; one called the rise in juvenile delinquency "staggering," while another argued that "it was not as bad as many alarmists . . . perceived it to be." The problem was real, but, as historian Karen Anderson argued, it probably was often blown out of proportion. Wartime anxiety tended to focus more attention on crime, resulting in stricter law enforcement and more arrests, which in turn skewed public perception.[49] Nonetheless, the tragic dimensions of the problem of youth crime were strongly etched in the minds of church officials, as revealed in an entry in the journal of St. Patrick Church in 1942:

> The beginning of this year found us in the middle of gang fights. From September to February we buried 5 boys of about 17 years of age who had been killed in these fights. In February we got the boys together and formed a boys club. We were not successful in converting them entirely but by hard work we kept them from killing each other. . . . One evening when the opposing team failed to show up our boys got into several cars and went over and shot a few windows out of San Felipe Courts. . . . The boys are bad in the so called "Bloody Fifth" [Ward] but they respect the church and the priests.[50]

As church representatives worked to combat delinquency, they sometimes revealed clues to their perceptions about Mexican Americans and the social ills of the barrios. Bishop Byrne, worried that all Mexican youth in Houston were being wrongly branded as "criminally inclined," shifted the blame to public school students who lacked Catholic instruction. According to the prelate, these wayward teens sullied the reputation of Catholic schoolchildren. Similarly, clerics blamed the public schools for thwarting Father Frank Brentine's efforts among the youth at Houston's "rugged" Immaculate Heart of Mary Parish.[51] Sister Mary Dolores Cárdenas, who had long ministered to the Mexicans of Houston's Fifth Ward, likewise blamed the "bad boys" of the public school for an arson plot she apparently foiled. The feisty nun, having found gasoline cans stashed on the parish school grounds, investigated and caught a suspect. She held him and threatened not to release him "until he confessed or dried up." By the time the police arrived, a group of angry mothers surrounded and taunted her. "Parecían indias" (They were like Indians—that is, "savages"), the nun dramatically recounted, revealing with tragic irony her own prejudice evoked by the confrontation with mixed-race women—mestizas, like herself.[52]

In the eyes of some church representatives, certain negative attributes continued to shape the Mexicans' social image. Some nuns and priests blamed the Mexicans' cultural traits for the poverty in their barrios. But while this reasoning revealed pejorative clerical attitudes, it also resulted in spirited efforts by religious men and women to try to ameliorate poverty among their parishioners. An expanded consciousness about Mexicans and Mexican Americans in the 1940s and 1950s brought them greater attention from the Catholic Church, despite the unsavory attitudes it sometimes revealed among their spiritual mentors. Likewise, perceptions about Mexican spirituality also began to change despite the fact that some church officials continued to regard Mexican religiosity as suspect.

For instance, the stereotype of religious ignorance and indifference endured. "These girls do not know much about their religion," a pastor noted about his Mexican American parishioners. Priests pleaded incessantly for expanded Catholic education, for if left to themselves, clerics warned, the Mexicans would revert to being "the neglected Catholics they have been for so long." The parochial school, nuns and priests argued, was the only way to make them "real practical [C]atholics."[53] The persistent image of religious ignorance went hand-in-hand with the enduring portrayal of Mexicans' inattention to the Catholic Church. Clerics continued to see a discouraging spiritual apathy in Houston's barrios. One census report blamed mothers, at least partly, for the "lack of Catholicity" in the parish: "Mother cannot care for the family—get Children ready & come to Mass. Lack[s] sense of duty in this regard." Another pastor sensed that religious indifference posed a greater threat than Protestantism.[54] The picture of childlike irresponsibility remained entrenched in the minds of some church personnel.

Nonetheless, some church officials during the 1940s and 1950s showed a greater appreciation of Mexican Catholicism. Some defended uniquely Mexican customs. One priest insisted that Mexicans were "essentially a good people possessed of a deep religious spirit." He went on to point out that despite severe adversity, Mexican Catholics had kept the faith.[55] Another writer asserted that Americans misunderstood the Mexicans' devotion to Our Lady of Guadalupe, the central figure and foundation of Mexican Catholicism. Though most Americans dismissed this reverence as superstitious sentimentality, Brother Joseph Buckley asked: "Why should others scoff?" Furthermore, Buckley suggested that perhaps Anglo Americans' "lack of faith has not merited a like apparition." For Buckley, Mexican Catholicism was "a living faith, tangible and vibrant" and he defended the devotion to Guadalupe as "one of the most beautiful and touching incidents in a modern world of sophistication and smug unbelief."[56]

What is most significant about these changing pastoral views is the link some officials made between the Mexicans' social status and their religious "condition." Clearly, there was more understanding shown toward Mexicans and Mexican Americans and the problems they faced. There was empathy not only for the plight of native-born Mexican Americans but also for the *braceros* and "wetbacks" who often competed with them for jobs. More important, however, some men and women of the church recognized that the supposed religious shortcomings of Mexicans were largely due to historical social and economic deprivation. Church representatives explained that Mexicans' religious indifference and conversions to Protestantism grew out of changed social conditions. Mexicans and Mexican Americans had been "forced into migratory labor," church officials argued, and this had destroyed their religious ties, practices, and education.[57] To be sure, the new thinking of the 1940s and 1950s was sometimes overstated, oversimplified, and ambivalent. One account, for example, presented the Mexican as utterly transformed from a paragon of spirituality into the epitome of materialism. Before, the writer noted, "his one desire in life was to know, love and serve God"; now, the "craze for money" was his "main objective in life." Sometimes church representatives even portrayed the Mexican as a "willing and eager wanderer," despite universal acknowledgment of the drudgery of migrant life.[58] Exaggeration notwithstanding, such observations showed an increased awareness about how entwined were the social and pastoral aspects of the "Spanish-speaking problem."

These shifting views also suggested that more individuals in the Catholic hierarchy now made clear distinctions between Mexican immigrants and Mexican American citizens. Bishop Byrne distinguished native-born from immigrant early on. By the 1940s he was convinced the Texas Mexican should consider himself "neither a Spaniard nor a Mexican" but a "Texan." The distinctions had also become obvious to Catholic leaders throughout the Southwest by the mid-1940s, when some of them formed the Bishops' Committee for the Spanish-Speaking in 1945 and began convening conferences focused on both the pastoral and the material needs of Mexican Catholics.[59]

Byrne's successor in the 1950s, Bishop Wendelin J. Nold, recognized that many of the Spanish-speaking were American-born and he understood that the ongoing nature of Mexican immigration held important pastoral and social ramifications for the Spanish-speaking apostolate. Bishop Nold challenged fellow churchmen to help assimilate Mexicans and Mexican Americans more fully into mainstream society and the Catholic Church through "generous" funding, flexibility regarding language needs, and religious leadership to combat the social and economic prejudice that hampered the incorporation of Mexicans into American life.[60] The new consciousness and changing attitudes of the World War II era would expand in the coming decades, helping to fuel a gradual improvement in the pastoral and social ministry for Houston's Mexican Catholics.

INCREASED SENSITIVITY, LINGERING DOUBTS: THE 1960S–1970S

The ascendant liberalism that shook the United States in the 1960s also reverberated strongly in global Roman Catholicism. In an effort to achieve *aggiornamento*—an "updating" of the Roman Catholic Church —Pope John XXIII convened the Second Vatican Council (1962–65), an event that initiated many liberal reforms and marked a major turning point in Catholic history.[61] How far the new liberalism evidenced among the highest echelons of the church at Vatican II actually trickled down to the parish level is hard to say. The Second Vatican Council may have promoted more liberal racial attitudes among rank-and-file church representatives in Houston, particularly considering that one of the major council reforms was the enhanced status of the laity. But what stands out in the documentary record during these years is the *absence* of a discussion about race and Mexicans; what is much more obvious is a pointed awareness of the Mexican community's growing heterogeneity and its surging politicization. The liberal ethos of the 1960s and the reforms of Vatican II encouraged progressive views among men and women of the church in Houston, but what riveted their attention and forced them to reassess their attitudes about Mexican Catholics were the demands the parishioners themselves increasingly made on the institution.[62]

The 1960s and 1970s witnessed the rise of the Chicano movement, a burst of agitation for social change that challenged many mainstream institutions and assumptions, including the Catholic Church and the perceptions its representatives had of Mexicans and Mexican Americans. Under the pressures of *el movimiento*, men and women of the church developed a more realistic picture of Texas Mexicans than the monolithic image that prevailed in the early twentieth century.

By the mid-1960s church officials in Houston were clearly more discriminating in how they viewed their parishes and the people within them. In 1966, the pastor of St. Stephen Church had a realistic if blunt assessment of his parish as "bi-lingual, inner-city, [and] slummish." He was well aware that his younger parishioners spoke a mix of English and Spanish while the older ones spoke mostly Spanish, and he knew that a continual inflow of new immigrant families constantly replenished the binational, bicultural character of the parish. These traits logically suggested that the ministry in this particular parish be a bilingual one. Bishop John L. Morkovsky also recognized the class and cultural distinctions that existed in the various parishes. He observed that St. Philip's members were mostly Spanish-speaking but that "they are not at all of the inner-city type that St. Stephen's has."[63] Morkovsky also understood the need for new and flexible pastoral strategies. English masses were needed for "the rising generation," Morkovsky advised, though Spanish services remained necessary as well.[64] But others in the diocese were less flexible. As Mexican Americans increasingly dispersed into integrated neighborhoods in the 1960s and 1970s, the new ethnic mix in once segregated parishes was difficult for some priests to accept. In 1970, for instance, the pastor at the traditionally white Immaculate Conception Church asked to be reassigned. Apparently the priest felt "a more than usual worrisome burden brought on by the continuing rapid turnover of the nature of the people of the parish, from the once predominately Anglo to Mexican American."[65]

In the 1960s and 1970s, church personnel reflected more tolerant attitudes toward Mexicans and Mexican Americans, but this did not negate all the ingrained stereotypes. According to one report, for example, most of the Mexican families moving into St. Patrick Parish in 1964 were Catholics "perhaps in name only." In another case, a pastor wondered if the catechetical work among Mexican Americans in his parish had failed because the nuns "haven't enough confidence in the capacities of our Mexican people."[66] Lack of confidence in the Mexican surfaced in other ways. There were hints about irresponsibility: "It may well be that they would neglect going to any church," a provincial worried when proposing some parish boundary changes, "for the Mexicans seem blocked from their church when things like expressways, canals and distance get between them and their church." In a similar spirit, Father Anselm Walker showed little faith in the ability of "our Mexicans" to discern and resist the wiles he saw in the ecumenicalism of the sixties. The priest conceded that "the ecumenical movement may have some praiseworthy goals to offer the Anglos," but he warned that for Mexicans it surely meant "apostasy, defection and secularization."[67] Thus the old view of the Mexican "child" retained some currency.

So, too, did the corollary of Mexican "superstition." Apparently Mexican folk healers plied their trade in Houston. A St. Stephen parishioner recalled that her grandfather was a *curandero* (healer) who considered himself a "vehicle of God." In Second Ward, *curanderas* (women healers) routinely advertised in the Spanish-language newspapers. In May 1967 pastor Emile Farge reported that *hiervistas* (herbalists), *curanderos* (faith healers), and "myriads of superstitious practices" abounded in his parish. Twice, Father Farge wrote, he had been interrupted while writing his letter by parishioners wanting him to attend to two *ensalmados* (people thought to be bewitched): "One was a sick girl, the other was a boy afraid of dogs." These were not isolated incidents. "Yesterday a mother brought a boy here who 'was seeing snakes,' " the cleric wrote. In his opinion, *curanderismo* (faith healing) among parishioners could not be called "simple faith" but was a problem needing eradication.[68]

The pastor's comments were well-intentioned. He was concerned about what he saw as a dearth of Mexican American leadership in his parish and feared the children would be "brainwashed into believing they are not as good as the Anglo." Still, the priest believed the problem lay with the parishioners themselves—with their refusal to leave their Mexican church and integrate themselves into the nearby Anglo church. The parish, the cleric claimed, suffered from "Mexican American cultural inbreeding." The solution, he believed, was for parishioners to "experience a visible, definite change from a Mexican to an American environment."[69] Mexican American culture, the priest implied, could nurture little that was spiritually wholesome or socially progressive.

Such commentary recalled the prevalent attitudes of the early twentieth century, even as it reflected some of the liberalism of the civil rights era. Among some clergy, perhaps at an unconscious level, lingering doubts remained about Mexicans ever becoming "good" Catholics. But within the Catholic Church, advocates for Mexican Americans attacked these images in the 1960s and 1970s, encouraged by the political and social changes engendered by the Chicano movement. Sister Gloria Gallardo, a cofounder of the vocal nuns' organization Las Hermanas (Sisters), spoke for many when she asserted that "Anglo priests and nuns cannot identify best with the needs of the Spanish-speaking, regardless of their good intentions." "Without meaning to," Gallardo declared, "many Anglos have a paternal attitude."[70] Some nuns and priests conceded as much. For example, a pastor attributed some of his parish's problems to "the rather patronising [sic] posture that the Church has assumed toward them [Mexican Americans] in the past."[71]

In a similar vein, Father Antonio Marañón chastised the Catholic hierarchy for alienating Mexican Catholics and trying to recast them in an Anglo image. "In all the churches," Marañón decried, "what is considered a good Mexican is a well-dressed, well-behaved but thoroughly dehumanized person." Father Marañón demanded that the Catholic Church accept the Chicanos' Mexicanness: "No!" the fiery cleric insisted, "a Mexican American cannot be the mirror image of a gringo Christian."[72] Ironically, though, even Father Marañón's defense of Chicano Catholics belied the paternalism some Spanish clerics showed toward Mexicans. "The saddest part," the priest claimed, "is that it took a Spanish priest, a *gachupín* [an old slur used by Mexicans against their Spanish colonizers], to come and teach you how to be a Mexican American."[73] By the 1970s, the attitudes and perceptions held by men and women of the Catholic Church about Texas Mexicans had undergone significant change, but they continued to coexist alongside some deeply ingrained racial attitudes from the past.

Since the 1940s, Mexican American racialization had begun giving way to ethnicization, at least in some quarters. Bishop Nold, for example, saw the Mexicans as just the latest group of immigrants slowly being assimilated into the nation's mainstream. Nold and others like him used the term "Spanish-speaking" instead of "Mexican," indicating that Tejanas and Tejanos were not a separate unassimilable race permanently fated to social inequality and outsiderhood. And yet their mestizo heritage remained an important part of the Mexican American experience in Houston even into the early 1970s. A federal judge created an uproar among Mexican Americans in 1970 when he "declared" them to be white for the purpose of desegregating Houston's public schools by integrating Mexican and African American students only, leaving white schools untouched.[74] Clearly, Mexican American racial ambiguity continued to be important even in the late twentieth century, long after the racial status of nineteenth- and twentieth-century European immigrants had been settled.

As church representatives came to understand the nature of the "Mexican problem" as something that called for action beyond the spiritual realm, they faced a twin challenge: If the Catholic Church was to save the Mexicans' souls, it had to address not only their religious needs but their material ones as well. Naturally, the church responded first to basic spiritual needs. Before anything else, churches and religious schools had to be built. How that happened and what it reveals is the theme of the next chapter.

FOUR

F ather Thomas Hennessy looked out in amazement at the sea of humanity that filled his church to overflowing on December 12, 1911. Neither the reverend, pastor of Houston's most prestigious Catholic church, Annunciation, nor the city had ever seen such a large gathering of Mexican Catholics. They were there for a solemn event—indeed, a historic event—the city's first public celebration of the Mexicans' patron saint, Our Lady of Guadalupe. That special service was celebrated with "great passion and fervor," an Oblate father noted in the church journal.[1] The occasion also sent a message: Mexicans were coming to the Bayou City in large numbers and the Catholic Church needed to accommodate them.

This chapter traces the founding of Mexican parishes around the city from the 1910s to the early 1970s and shows how the Mexicans' steady population expansion and their own initiatives to build churches and parochial schools reflected their march toward greater participation in Houston's religious and social life. The Missionary Oblates who arrived in the city in 1911 found that Mexicans wanted churches of their own and would unite to bring that about. Beginning in the early twentieth century, the city's Mexican and Mexican American Catholics steadily pressed diocesan officials to increase pastoral services to them.

Over time the Catholic hierarchy responded by providing them more priests and nuns and helping to facilitate the growth of parishes to accommodate the ever-growing numbers of Mexican Catholics.

THE 1910S AND 1920S

In 1911 the bishop of the Diocese of Galveston, Nicholas A. Gallagher, entered into a contract that entrusted the spiritual care of Mexicans in Houston to the Missionary Oblates of Mary Immaculate. Bishop Gallagher chose the Oblate Fathers because their "work among the poorest of the poor along the Rio Grande [was] well known" and because apparently "so many Mexicans" in the diocese were "deprived of the consolations of Our Holy Religion on account of the scarcity of priests."[2] The understanding was that the Oblates would have "temporary charge of all Mexicans in the [D]iocese of Galveston, not otherwise provided for."[3] In Houston, this gave the Oblate Fathers a virtual monopoly on the evangelization of Mexicans in the city.

Four Oblate priests, an American, a Frenchman, an Italian, and a Spaniard, arrived in October 1911 to begin their ministry in Houston's Mexican community and to supplement the ministry to other Catholics. They established Immaculate Conception, a new parish for "American" (white) Catholics, in the suburb of Magnolia Park on the city's east side. From this "tastefully furnished" headquarters the missionaries quickly began their forays into the Mexican *colonias*, a world of stark contrast with the suburban niceties of Immaculate Conception and Magnolia Park.[4] Rev. Esteban de Anta reported that his Mexican parishioners led a "pitiful" existence, living in "sordid huts" and working for "a pittance."[5] Spiritual life, according to another priest, was equally poor. Before the Oblates arrived, the church "completely neglected" Mexican Catholics, the cleric wrote. "[D]eprived of priests who spoke their language and poorly received in the American churches," many Mexicans "lived and died without ever seeing a priest." The Oblates worked feverishly, spurred on by the ever-present Protestants, who, "[l]ike ravenous wolves," Father De Anta charged, enticed the Mexicans "with false promises . . . to abandon Mother Church."[6]

After ten months of evangelizing in the homes, stores, and meeting halls of Mexican barrios, the Oblates' labor bore fruit in the form of a two-story frame building erected to serve as a church and school for Houston's Mexican Catholics. The church was built in El Segundo Barrio at the corner of Navigation and Marsh streets. The street names perfectly suited the less-than-prime real estate where the church stood, for the area was indeed a *ciénaga*, the pastor noted, "a marsh where the runoff from the whole neighborhood collected." Undeterred, the Oblate Fathers brought in 1,500 truckloads of dirt to raise the property. Completed in August 1912, the new church was appropriately dedicated to the patron saint of Mexico, Our Lady of Guadalupe. Houston's Mexican Catholics finally had a mother church.[7]

Significantly, the dedication ceremony on September 15, 1912, coincided with the celebration of Mexican Independence Day. It took place "[w]ith a display of devotion and manifestation of zeal seldom found among even the elect and more lavishly endowed congregations," a newspaper reported. A "vast throng of Mexicans" met Bishop Gallagher when he arrived in the city, and at the parish grounds the crowd was so great that many were left outside the church, craning to see and hear what they could of the ceremony. As the prelate began the blessing of the building, parishioners formed a reverent procession behind an image of the Virgin of Guadalupe. Young girls dressed in white carried candles and accompanied the parishioners who carried *la Virgen* "in triumph" from the school to the sanctuary. "Our Lady of Guadalupe took possession of her sanctuary," the pastor wrote, "from which to protect her children, the Mexicans." A Mexican orchestra and a young women's choir added beauty and solemnity to the occasion, and the faces of the faithful beamed with pride at hearing the sermon preached in Spanish. A festive *jamaica* (bazaar) and dinner lasted long into the evening and crowned the joyous day.[8]

Toward the end of the ceremony, Bishop Gallagher administered

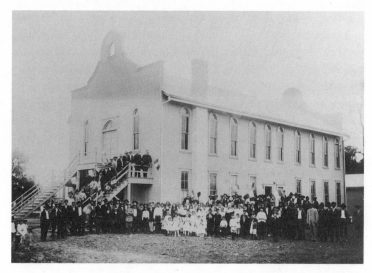

The dedication in 1912 of Our Lady of Guadalupe, the Mexican community's "mother church," was an important moment in Houston's Mexican American history. Courtesy Houston Metropolitan Research Center, Houston Public Library.

the sacrament of Confirmation to 200 men, women, and children, one of the largest such events ever held in the city. The bishop began with some revealing comments to the parishioners:

> During the thirty years I have been Bishop of this diocese, it has not seemed opportune or necessary to extend to you the privilege of having infants and children, who have not received their First Communion, receive the Sacrament of Confirmation. This privilege is always enjoyed in your own country, and now that I see your great increase in numbers in this diocese and the eagerness with which you have availed yourselves of the opportunity to advance your religious and spiritual welfare, it is with the greatest sincerity and willingness that I now grant you this right, a right to which you are entitled by reason of your loyalty to your faith amid many trials and difficulties.[9]

Bishop Gallagher's comments presaged a changing relationship between Houston Mexicans and the Catholic Church. The bishop knew that Mexicans had a different approach to the sacraments, and "granting" the parishioners the right to continue their traditional practice was more a recognition of the Mexican Catholic style than a magnanimous gesture. Before, it had not seemed "opportune or necessary" to legitimate the practice of being confirmed before having First Communion, but now their "great increase in numbers" compelled the bishop to do so. The incident showed that by insisting on defining Catholicism on their own terms Mexican parishioners could extract concessions from the church.

Mexicans' selective interest in the church's formal requirements and their initiatives to build their own places of worship became increasingly evident with time. Our Lady of Guadalupe Church became the anchor and cultural heart of the *colonia* in Houston, as a local newspaper observed in reporting that Mexican Catholics now had "a nucleus." The reporter's choice of words underlined the parishioners' self-reliance: "[T]hey seem determined to gather and to build for themselves a parish which will serve the best spiritual and temporal interests of their rapidly increasing colony."[10] The expanding community pressed for more religious services at Guadalupe Parish during the 1920s as immigration from Mexico reached unparalleled proportions. Between 1920 and 1930, Houston's Mexican population more than doubled, from about 6,000 to 15,000.[11] This obliged pastor Esteban de Anta to add two more masses each Sunday and offer Mass every day of the week, instead of only twice. Because of the availability of jobs, Father De Anta explained, "many people came to Houston and naturally following the established pattern, they flocked to the church." It became necessary to always have a priest present at the church to answer "the call of the people (*el llamamiento de la gente*)."[12] The pastor's wording was appropriate and telling because it revealed that the incessant growth and demands of the *colonia* itself prompted the increased pastoral services.

The parish school at Guadalupe also flourished. Eighty-five students enrolled during the 1912–13 school year, and this number increased to 163 by 1916–17. In the early 1920s, enrollment reached 333, and by the end of the decade some 400 students attended Guadalupe School.[13] The pastor pleaded for more teaching nuns, and with good reason because, with the exception of two school years (when there were three teachers at Guadalupe), only two teachers were assigned to the parish school during the entire decade of the 1910s. The situation improved in the 1920s, however, with an average of six teachers assigned during that decade.[14]

The growth of the Mexican community in the Second Ward prompted diocesan officials to sever Our Lady of Guadalupe from its Anglo parent church located some three miles away in Magnolia Park. In 1921, Guadalupe Church, a mission of Immaculate Conception Church since 1911, became an autonomous Mexican national parish.[15] Improvements that followed in quick succession in the early 1920s, including a convent for the resident nuns, a formidable brick church that replaced the original frame chapel, a new brick rectory, and a refurbished and expanded school, showed the vitality of the parish.[16] These initiatives reflected the parishioners' self-reliance and the importance they attached to their faith as they carved their space in the Bayou City.

Even this expansion, however, could not accommodate all those who observed the traditionally important holy days. During Semana Santa (Easter Week) in 1924, for example, the church journal noted that "the church was better with its greater space, but nonetheless it was much too small to hold the masses that turned out. Pews, aisles, sanctuary, vestries, all were filled with the faithful, and even at that many had to remain outside the church, trying to follow the services from doorways and windows."[17] Such displays of faith dramatically revealed the need for more facilities and increased Catholic officials' awareness of the Mexican presence.

As the Mexican mother church, Guadalupe brought other parishes into existence. In 1921, an Oblate superior instructed the pastor of the Anglo church in Magnolia Park to determine how many Mexicans lived within his parish. A survey discovered 230 Mexican families living "far from Father de Anta," the pastor at Our Lady of Guadalupe in Second Ward. The emergence of a barrio in Magnolia Park presented another pastoral challenge for the Catholic hierarchy in Houston. "Can you do anything?" Bishop Christopher Byrne pleaded with an Oblate superior.[18] Already since 1919 Father De Anta and other Oblates had been visiting the Magnolia Park families to administer the sacraments in their homes. Beginning in the early 1920s the Catholic leadership assigned various assistant pastors to Guadalupe specifically "to care for the growing Mexican population of Magnolia Park."[19] In 1925 one of those assistants, Father Anastacio Pérez, began holding services in a two-story family residence and business owned by Emilio Aranda at the corner of 71st Street and Navigation, in Magnolia. Aranda's property served as a temporary chapel where regular church services were held, including a daily Mass, two Sunday masses, recitation of the Rosary, baptisms, and catechism classes. In 1926 a two-story church was built in the Magnolia barrio and given the name Immaculate Heart of Mary. Two years later the Sisters of Divine Providence arrived and opened a parish school.[20]

By the mid-1920s, then, Mexican and Mexican American Catholics living on the east side of Houston had two churches and parochial schools of their own. Their counterparts in other parts of the city did not, but as they battled the difficult times of depression and war they continued to press the diocese for their own religious facilities.

The Great Depression and World War II

During the 1930s, the Catholic Church in the United States mounted a vigorous campaign to teach parishioners the essentials of Catholic doctrine. This catechetical movement was especially active in the Southwest, where the historical shortage of clergy continued. Supervised by nuns, lay volunteers established catechetical centers and taught Catholic beliefs and rituals to children, particularly those attending public schools, in any available space.[21] In Houston, several of

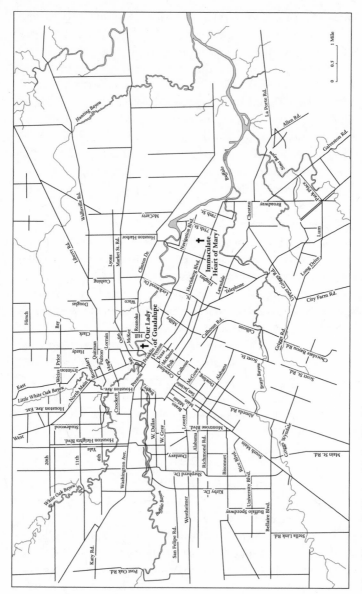

Map 3. Houston's Mexican National Parishes, 1929

these centers often became the basis for new parishes in Mexican neighborhoods.

In 1930 the school principal at Our Lady of Guadalupe, Sister Mary Benitia Vermeersch, organized a group of young Mexican American women of the parish into the Missionary Catechists of Divine Providence. Ranging in age from sixteen to twenty-two, these laywomen received religious training and, according to their bishop, had "all the zeal and consecration . . . of a nun." Initially, the group assisted the nuns in teaching catechism to public school children after school hours at Guadalupe, but their role soon expanded. The Catechists canvassed the parish territory to recruit children, and they taught catechism in several neighborhoods. In 1933 the Sisters of Divine Providence reported that eighteen "little missionaries" went out in pairs to nine catechetical centers to instruct nearly 900 children. By 1935 the Catechists had some 1,400 children under instruction in fifteen meeting places scattered throughout the city.[22] "Sister Benitia asked us if we would like to teach religion to public school Mexican children," charter Catechist Petra Guillén remembered. "So many of us volunteered to help others who were less fortunate [and] were not taught religion like we were taught in school," she explained. "I enjoyed it," another former Catechist, Rafaela Aguilar, offered. "You felt like you were giving a part of yourself to others."[23]

The Catechists brought more than the *Baltimore Catechism* to their neighbors. These lay efforts were an important part of the groundwork that preceded the spread of Catholic institutions to other Houston barrios. For instance, the second offspring of Guadalupe Parish, St. Stephen, had its beginnings as a catechetical center on Houston's west side. In 1932 the Catechists taught classes twice a week in the home of María Martínez before parishioners raised enough money to buy a property to launch St. Stephen's parish and church in their barrio.[24] In a budding area known as El Crisol, located in the Liberty Road area of northeast Houston, barrio residents repeated this pattern. There, once again the community took the initiative. José Gómez led a group that spoke with the pastor at Guadalupe Parish in 1934 and gained his

The Catechists of Divine Providence fanned out in the city to bring religious instruction and a modicum of material aid to Mexicans and Mexican Americans in the Depression era. Courtesy Mrs. Petra Guillén.

support. Soon priests were celebrating Mass and the Catechists were instructing 100 children twice a week in the Gómez home, despite some obstacles. Sister Dominic García recalled that nervous parents used to bless their children who sometimes had "to cross pastures and crawl under stalled train cars" in order to get to their religion classes. This was the beginning of Our Lady of Sorrows Parish.[25]

This pattern of religious institutional growth characterized the barrios during the 1930s and 1940s. Mexicans preserved the faith through traditional home- and community-centered worship, and their initiatives interlocked with institutional outreach efforts such as the Catechists, all of which eventually gave rise to new churches and parochial schools for Mexicans where none had existed before. While Father De Anta considered another catechetical site in the north side, the nuns and Catechists at Guadalupe sought to "broaden their field. . . to every Mexican settlement in Houston and vicinity," the press reported.[26]

As the Mexican population in Houston increased, it changed the complexion of some established neighborhoods and their parishes. St. Patrick Church on the north side is a case in point. One of the oldest parishes in Houston, St. Patrick had been the religious home of Irish Houstonians since 1880. In the 1920s Italians began moving into the area, but over the course of two decades, the number of both Irish and Italians declined as the number of Mexicans steadily increased. By the 1930s the "once fashionable" Fifth Ward was densely populated by Mexicans and Mexican Americans and most of the Irish and Italians were gone, prompting a parish history to record the "alarming" decline in St. Patrick's "English American People." The incoming pastor noted the population shift in 1941: "We found about 50 families who had belonged to the parish. There were 32 Italian grocery stores within the [parish] limits [and] about 800 [M]exican families living around about but the great majority had never seen the inside of the church."[27]

Given these circumstances, the bishop entrusted St. Patrick to his Mexican specialists, the Oblate Fathers, in 1941. St. Patrick thus became a Mexican national parish, and the Sisters of Divine Providence immediately reopened the parish school previously closed for lack of pupils.[28] St. Patrick soon exhibited a vitality that rivaled the mother church in the Second Ward. "We commenced the year 1943 with the parish on a firm footing once more," the pastor wrote. "All the societies were full of life and the school was going fine," he noted proudly. But the transition at St. Patrick may not have been entirely smooth. "The beautiful picture of Our Lady of Guadalupe was blessed and hung behind the main altar," the pastor wrote, adding that he had heard rumors "that our Italian parishioners would not have 'La Virgen Morena' behind the main altar." Apparently nothing serious developed. "The truth of the matter was that no one said a single word against the procedure," the priest wrote.[29] Were there some feathers ruffled among the Italian American parishioners? Or did the rumors originate among Mexican parishioners who feared rejection? More important than the source of the rumors or the depth of ethnic tensions is the point that the pastor noted the "incident" at all; it showed that ethnicity continued to be important as Mexicans claimed a larger place in the Bayou City. In any case, a burgeoning Mexican population, a group the Catholic hierarchy could not ignore, transformed a dying parish into a vigorous one. Despite the trying times of the Great Depression and World War II, Mexicans pressed the Catholic leadership for more institutional support, both through their continued population growth and by paving the way themselves for establishing new churches for their neighborhoods. This trend continued during the relative prosperity of the post–World War II era, and it became more evident to the church leadership when the Galveston Diocese was redesignated the Galveston-Houston Diocese and its headquarters moved to the Bayou City in 1959.[30]

Among the new enclaves of Mexicans and Mexican Americans that formed in the later 1940s and 1950s in Houston was one located just outside of the north side city limits. This neighborhood, called Bonita Gardens, had attracted the Missionary Catechists in the late 1930s. In the 1940s, the itinerant Father Frank Urbanovsky held two-week missions in the area, offering religious instruction, baptizing children, and validating marriages for area residents. Urbanovsky witnessed the fast growth of La Bonita and the "almost daily" influx of new Mexican American homeowners.[31] With the groundwork laid by the Catechists and nurtured by Padre Panchito, as parishioners called Urbanovsky, Our Lady of Sorrows Parish organized a mission chapel for the Bonita Gardens residents in 1948. The people chose to call their church Nuestra Señora de San Juan de los Lagos, honoring the Virgin's shrine in Jalisco, Mexico.[32] "As that [name] is rather long," a priest explained, "they have been using St. John of the Lakes in all business transactions." Eventually, the church's name became Our Lady of St. John, a name that pointed up the concessions some Mexican Americans made to acculturation pressures. In the end, Bonita Gardens residents gained their cultural space. They had their own church, staffed by Spanish-speaking Oblates, and named after a Mexican devotion (albeit in English). In 1957 Our Lady of St. John became a Mexican national parish, led by the only homegrown Mexican American priest in the diocese, Father Lawrence Peguero.[33]

Still more post–World War II expansion occurred on the northeast side of Houston, where a pocket of Mexican Americans formed during the 1950s on the margins of the predominately Anglo subdivision of Denver Harbor. The Anglo parish there, Resurrection, established a church mission for Mexican families in 1958. Again, the residents favored their cultural heritage in choosing a name for the church, St. Philip of Jesus, in honor of the first canonized saint of Mexico.[34] The fast growth of the city's Mexican-origin population in the 1940s and 1950s had yielded a steady expansion of churches and parochial schools in their neighborhoods, but the demographic pressures and political demands exerted by the community in the tumultuous sixties and early seventies would be unprecedented, as would the accommodations the diocese made in response.

COMING FULL CIRCLE: THE 1960S AND EARLY 1970S

The community of Jeanetta Gardens, in far southwest Houston, began as a farmworker *colonia* but was eventually swallowed up by the expanding city. Mexicans and Mexican Americans had settled in the area when farmlands were converted to modestly priced home lots in the 1940s, allowing residents to be close to agricultural jobs in the nearby towns of Rosenberg, Stafford, and Sugarland. As Houston's boundaries spread, the southwest side became affluent, surrounding Jeanetta Gardens, which remained a working-class barrio about fifteen miles from downtown and the nearest Mexican parish, St. Stephen. Maryknoll Sisters from St. Stephen held religion classes in Jeanetta Gardens homes until the mid-1950s, but the distance made the relationship untenable and an Anglo parish closer to the barrio, St. Michael, assumed the ministry to the people of Jeanetta Gardens. Eventually, community resident Francisco Aguayo donated land to the diocese for a church. The new mission church of St. Raphael was dedicated, appropriately, on the Feast of Guadalupe in December 1961. St. Raphael Parish also differed from other Mexican American parishes in its ethnic makeup. Jeanetta Gardens adjoined Piney Point, a working-class black neighborhood settled by freedmen after the Civil War. By the early 1970s, St. Raphael was 60 percent Mexican American and 40 percent black. The first black priest ordained in the diocese, Father Clifton Ransom Jr., a native Houstonian and fluent Spanish speaker, headed the parish.[35]

The creation of another mission in east Houston followed the founding of St. Raphael. In 1962 Immaculate Heart of Mary Church organized St. Alphonsus Liguori near the Port of Houston, in the Manchester addition. Mexican Catholics there had wanted pastoral services since at least the 1940s. Around 1948, Father Urbanovsky reported well-attended missions in the Manchester area. "I liked very much the spirit in general," he noted in his diary. Father Sylvester O'Toole, the priest in charge of the St. Alphonsus mission, also noted the parishioners' enthusiasm. For three years they had opened their homes to him for religion classes, prompting him to propose the mission church be elevated to parish status. "I believe that the people have worked hard for their mission Church and they have demonstrated that they will support a parish church," Father O'Toole wrote in 1966. Bishop Morkovsky responded quickly, establishing St. Alphonsus Parish within two months.[36]

The founding of St. Raphael and St. Alphonsus largely followed the established pattern of church growth in the barrios. Like their predecessors, Mexican American parishioners in the 1960s and early 1970s clearly expressed their desire to have culturally relevant religious institutions, and they laid the groundwork for them. Mexican Catholics worked to create churches that reflected their ethnic identity—by their location within the barrios, in the names they bore, through the Spanish or bilingual-bicultural services they offered, and by the communal efforts that created them. Their efforts to carve out this cultural space were yet another reflection of their ethno-Catholicism. Wherever

Mexicans and Mexican Americans set down roots, they initiated efforts that eventually prompted the church to provide pastoral services.

The evolution of St. Patrick Parish illustrated the dialectic between the changing needs and configurations of Mexican communities and accommodation by the diocese. St. Patrick had flourished in the 1940s in its Fifth Ward location on Maury Street. However, Houston's growth in the 1950s and 1960s brought changes. Progress, in the form of freeway construction and commercialization of properties, displaced Mexican families from the vicinity of the church and pushed them farther into the north side.[37] In the process, St. Patrick Church became surrounded by trains, factories, and freeway construction. "The industrialism of the section [neighborhood] has almost swallowed us up," the sisters at the parish school complained. The Oblates followed the flow of people by establishing a chapel two miles north of the parish church in 1953. By the mid-1960s, very few families remained at the parent church as the movement of parishioners toward the chapel became "a real exodus." When the last Mass was celebrated at "old" St. Patrick in 1967, only 25 families lived around the church, whereas over 400 families resided around the new chapel.[38] The late 1960s saw the construction of a new church near the chapel, as well as the reopening of the parish school and the building of a new convent and a rectory in response to the growing number of Mexican Catholics in the area. All this new construction reflected the joint efforts of parishioners and diocesan leaders "to provide adequate facilities and location where the parishioners reside."[39]

In other parts of Houston as well the expanding Mexican community compelled diocesan officials to improve existing parish facilities. The oldest parishes, Guadalupe and Immaculate Heart, undertook considerable renovation and new construction, while the more recently founded churches also upgraded their facilities.[40] Simultaneously, several Anglo congregations gradually saw their white memberships diminish as Mexican Americans became the predominate group in the parish, sometimes sparking resentment among Anglo parishioners. At Immaculate Conception Church, for instance, a white

Map 4. Houston's Majority Mexican American Parishes, 1973

Parishes
1) Our Lady of Guadalupe
2) Immaculate Heart of Mary
3) St. Stephen
4) Our Lady of Sorrows
5) St. Patrick
6) Our Lady of St. John
7) St. Alphonsus
8) St. Philip of Jesus
9) St. Raphael
10) Immaculate Conception
11) Blessed Sacrament
12) Holy Name
13) Resurrection

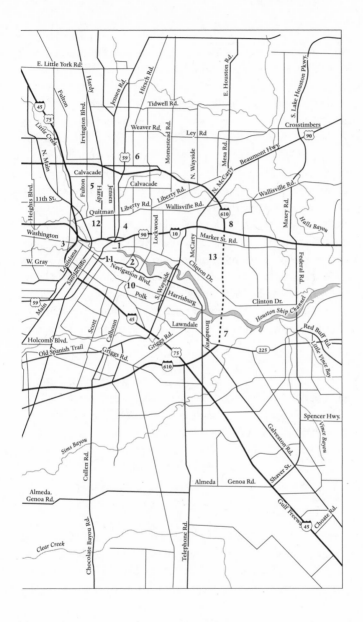

congregant complained that "the parish has gone down [because] the Spanish American people are habitating to the neighborhoods [*sic*]." The population in the Second Ward and Magnolia expanded so much during the 1960s that open land no longer separated the two barrios, a process that had been helped along by "white flight" to the suburbs.[41]

This demographic change in the East End, as the area was now called, resulted in predominately Mexican American neighborhoods, and it spurred Catholic officials to invite Mexicans to churches where previously they had been barred. During the late 1960s, the Catholic hierarchy instructed priests at Immaculate Conception to use Spanish in some of the masses "to attract the Latin-American element" to the historically all-white church.[42] By the early 1970s, the congregations of formerly "American" churches, such as Immaculate Conception, Blessed Sacrament, Resurrection, and Holy Name, were predominately Mexican and Mexican American. "Now they have actually taken over Immaculate Conception," parishioner Mary Villagómez pointed out.[43] With the integration of Immaculate Conception, the white parish where the Oblates' ministry to Houston's Mexicans began in 1911, the evangelization and institutional development of the Mexican community came full circle.

The experiences of those who participated in parish institutional life were not all the same, and belonging to one parish versus another said different things about the parishioners. At this point it is important to examine the distinctions among these parishes and what those differences reveal about Mexican American ethno-Catholicism in Houston.

National and Territorial Parishes

The Galveston Diocese promoted institutional Catholicism among Mexican parishioners by establishing national parishes exclusively for them, as church policy allowed.[44] The Catholic Church in the United States created these "foreign-language parishes" in response to the massive influx of "new immigrants" from southern and eastern Europe in the late nineteenth and early twentieth centuries. Nationality parishes had several functions. Through these structures, the church tried to meet the spiritual and cultural needs of immigrant Catholics while protecting them from proselytization. These segregated parishes were also meant to insulate native-born American Catholics from the newcomers so as to minimize interethnic conflict that might stir anti-Catholic nativism in the larger society.[45]

National parishes were also a handy tool for Americanization. In the early twentieth century, particularly during the anti-immigrant climate of the 1910s and 1920s, Catholic dioceses throughout the nation vied vigorously with Protestant denominations in a campaign to mold immigrants into "good" Americans. The U.S. Church fought to retain the loyalty of Catholic immigrants and to remake them into model Americans through a variety of activities that mixed social services and religious "uplift."[46] Thus a cleric's statement that Houston's new Guadalupe national parish presented "an opportunity of doing much more for the Mexicans" was laden with meaning.[47] It revealed a desire to provide a culturally more relevant ministry through the parishioners' language, but it also carried the implication that Mexican Catholics needed civic and religious improvement. Throughout the nation, armies of Catholic social workers, educators, and volunteers descended on barrios intent on making their residents "acceptable" Catholics and citizens. Working through parochial schools, neighborhood centers, and home visits, these Catholic crusaders for Americanization taught children and adults English and numerous vocational skills; gave them instruction in cooking, sewing, and sanitation; and exposed them to various aspects of American culture, including music and sports. All the while they tried to weave into these efforts an appreciation for a European American style of Catholicism. As one cleric put it, Mexicans were being given "a friendly and guiding hand to make them good citizens and better Catholics."[48] The national parish was central to these goals, although in practice Americanization was not monolithic and many individual church representatives did what they could to soften its implementation. In Second Ward's Guadalupe Parish, for example, Sister Benitia Vermeersch insisted that her students learn English to succeed in school, but she "did not try to strip the Mexicans of their cultural and religious practices and make them accept American customs."[49]

Nonetheless, virtually all Mexican Catholics, immigrants and native-born alike, belonged to national parishes during the first half of the twentieth century, having little choice in the matter. By the early 1940s the Oblate Fathers operated five national parishes in various Houston barrios (see Table A.3). As we have seen, the post–World War II years saw the dramatic growth and dispersal of the *colonia*, and, by the 1960s, Mexicans and Mexican Americans were scattered throughout the city and many were integrated into previously exclusively Anglo congregations. In the meantime, however, the American Catholic Church reverted to its preference for territorial parishes as European immigration waned and subsequent generations of immigrants assimilated. After the 1940s national parishes became increasingly rare throughout the United States. In the post–World War II years the dominant opinion among church leaders was that nationality parishes inhibited assimilation and that territorial, not national, parishes should be used to attract the Spanish-speaking for their eventual incorporation into American life.[50]

In Houston, these developments had mixed implications. For example, how did the Galveston Diocese respond to increasing Mexican immigration, given the trend away from establishing national parishes? And how did the increased residential mobility of post–World War II Mexican Americans affect Catholic institutional growth and pastoral services? The answers varied with episcopal administrations and communities, and they illuminate the changing nature of Mexican American ethnicity and religion in the city.

By the 1940s the Galveston hierarchy was well aware of the increasing heterogeneity of Houston's Mexican community. In the decades after World War II, the Mexican-origin population was increasingly bicultural, more Mexican American than Mexican, while it continued to absorb a steady flow of immigrants. Increased class stratification and social mobility accompanied Mexican Americans' acculturation, so that by the 1950s the church had to adjust its ministry to fit a community that neither warranted nor tolerated treatment as a "Little Mexico."

In 1953 Bishop Wendelin J. Nold recognized that the so-called problem of the Spanish-speaking posed a different challenge than European immigration had presented earlier in the century. Immigration restriction and the passage of time had resolved the problem of absorbing southern and eastern Europeans into American Catholic life, the bishop argued, but he suspected that this would not be the case with Mexican immigrants. Nold reasoned that Mexico's proximity and the demands for labor in the Texas Gulf Coast would make it unlikely that immigration barriers would be raised against Mexicans or that their influx would subside. "The Mexican is in Texas, and he is there to stay," he stated, and "[e]ach year will find him there in greater numbers." Nold believed that second- and third-generation Mexican Americans would be "absorbed into the American churches," only to be replaced by the continual stream of Mexican immigrants into the diocese.[51]

The bishop's assessment of "the problem" was partly right. But Nold's observations reflected the basic fallacy of trying to understand the experience of Mexicans in the United States through the lens of the European immigrant experience. Why did a distinctive "Mexicanness" still characterize the Catholicism of Houston's Mexicans even after the great majority of that population was native-born? Partly it was because, unlike the descendants of European immigrants, Mexicans in the United States continued to face racism and marginality. Mexican Americans retained the "Mexican" flavor of their Catholicism because it bolstered their ethnic identity and helped them come to grips with social subordination; it helped them confront the struggles inherent in their minority status, something with which the descendants of European immigrants no longer contended.

Bishop Nold was convinced that Houston still needed national parishes, and consequently the status of the original five Mexican parishes founded and staffed by the Oblates remained unchanged during the

1950s.[52] However, many clergy in the 1960s and early 1970s favored territorial over national parishes for the city's Mexican Catholics, and they suggested that new parishes in Mexican American neighborhoods be organized territorially rather than linguistically. Father Sylvester O'Toole, for example, successfully petitioned Bishop John Morkovsky to elevate St. Alphonsus Mission in east Houston to territorial parish status in 1966. Similarly, in 1971 Father Lawrence Peguero suggested that a proposed church for a predominately Mexican area in north Houston be one that "will not necessarily have to be considered a Church for Mexican Americans, but rather a territorial Church where all may go."[53]

Both cases illustrate the socioeconomic and cultural differences evident among Bayou City Mexicans in the second half of the twentieth century. In east Houston, about three miles from the old barrio of Magnolia, St. Alphonsus parishioners lived in a mixed neighborhood of whites and Mexican Americans. Father O'Toole reported that "Latin Americans" comprised the majority of Catholics in the area but that there were "a number of Anglo Catholic families who would add to our numbers in a most harmonious way since in this area the Latin Americans and Anglos associate with each other to the benefit of both groups." Similarly, the parishioners that Father Peguero identified in north Houston were mostly Mexican Americans who "speak English well and are well on the road to identifying with the Anglo community." These families had "made good in life," Peguero explained, and were "buying homes in the $16,000 level" outside the traditional barrios.[54] The same process affected old Guadalupe Parish, where younger parishioners were moving out of the Second Ward barrio. "This is a national parish and more and more the [L]atins move and become assimilated into their territorial parish," the pastor once complained. "As soon as they get an education and a better job, and they learn [E]nglish," the priest lamented, "they become a member of their territorial parish."[55]

These parishioners were likely younger Mexican Americans who were two or more generations removed from the immigrant experience, such as St. Philip's parishioners in one of the newer Mexican American neighborhoods in northeast Houston. Compared to the members of the old national parishes, St. Philip's parishioners were relatively younger and more affluent and able to operate with a surplus in their church budget.[56] On the one hand, they were "rather less than enthusiastic about having Spanish sermons," but, on the other hand, they named their church after Mexico's first canonized saint and turned out in great numbers every year in their Fiestas Patrias (Mexican Independence Day) celebration.[57] Bilingual or English-dominant, these Mexican American Catholics preferred a parish that reflected their middling social status, or aspirations, and their bicultural identity. This cultural middle ground expressed their accommodation to life in Houston; it was their way of fitting in, of finding a place for themselves in the city without totally giving up their Mexicanness.

In contrast, St. Stephen Parish and the old near west side barrio continued to be a magnet for Mexican immigrants. "St. Stephen's parish . . . still serves a definite need among the Spanish-speaking of Houston," Father Maurice Buckley wrote to his bishop, "for besides the many older people who speak very little English, new families from Mexico arrive here regularly."[58] The large presence of recent arrivals from Mexico gave the parish a more distinctly Mexican aura and made a bilingual pastoral approach necessary. When St. Stephen's parishioners defied their bishop and prevailed upon the diocese to let them keep their *iglesia mexicana* (Mexican church) and retain their status as a national parish, they showed that their adjustment to life in Houston involved more cultural resistance than accommodation.[59]

Differences among Mexican-origin Catholics revealed a variety of ethnoreligious consciousness. This heterogeneity resulted in slightly different ethnic identities and religious practices that distinguished Mexican Catholics not only from Anglo Catholics but also, to a degree, from each other. Their somewhat different ways of expressing their ethno-Catholicism fitted the parishioners' differences of class, acculturation, or nativity. In finding a place for themselves in the Bayou City, Mexican Catholics responded differently, some choosing to accommodate and others more openly resisting the forces of change and marginality they encountered in church and society. Significantly, however, the great majority wished to retain some of their Mexicanness, some degree of outsiderhood that helped them maintain a sense of ethnoreligious community and autonomy. In this sense, the story of Houston's Mexican Catholics recalls the experiences of other ethnoreligious peoples about whom historian R. Laurence Moore so perceptively wrote. Like American Jews and Mormons, Mexican ethno-Catholics "have been reluctant to let go completely of an outsider status" because "[t]oo much has been invested in it." Like other religious outsiders, Mexicans' "sense of outsiderhood helped turn their religion into something more than a religion. It became a separate culture, even an ethnic identity."[60]

Thus the challenge to the church in Houston in the second half of the twentieth century was not only to meet the needs of Mexican immigrants but also to provide pastoral services relevant to bilingual and bicultural Mexican Americans. In order to accomplish this, national parishes had to remain a part of the diocese's approach, though in Bishop Nold's opinion they were "not an ideal set-up." "I am convinced," he stated in 1953, "we must, if only because of language, continue to maintain separate churches."[61] Indeed, two decades later, in the early 1970s, the Galveston-Houston Diocese still maintained a handful of national parishes.[62]

Once parishes had been organized and churches and religious schools planted, Houston's Mexican communities bore the brunt of the financial cost of maintaining them. How they met that responsibility revealed much about the parishioners' ethnoreligious identity and way of life, as we shall see next.

FIVE

hen Mary Villagómez and her cousins were growing up in
Houston during the Great Depression, they loved going to the
jamaicas at their church in the east side barrio of Magnolia.
These festive church bazaars were something special to look
forward to in those difficult years, a way to have fun with the family,
see friends, and help the church at the same time. Across town in the
Bonita Gardens barrio a decade later, several Mexican Americans
braved snakes and mosquitos to clear some vacant lots where they
would spend many evenings after work refurbishing an old army barracks into a modest chapel for themselves.[1] In separate times and
places, these Mexican and Mexican American Catholics were doing
the same things—creating and maintaining their own places of worship. The *jamaicas* that parishioners like the Villagómez cousins enjoyed is an example of how Mexican Catholics throughout Houston
raised money to build and improve their churches and religious
schools; actually doing the work of building and remodeling the structures themselves, as the Bonita Gardens residents did, provided another means to the same end.

This chapter explains how the work of funding and expanding their
parishes was an important element in the lives of Mexican and Mexican American Catholics as they set down roots in the Bayou City.

Rather than presenting fund-raising efforts in Houston's Mexican parishes chronologically, this topical chapter describes the typical methods of fund-raising and interprets their impact on community-building. Working to raise money and maintain the parish reflected both the product and the process of Mexican ethno-Catholicism; that is, by participating in these activities, parishioners not only created churches and schools, but they also fashioned a strong sense of identity and community. Financing religious institutional development in the Mexican community posed a perennial challenge. The money raised to construct the first modest frame churches was only the beginning of a continual struggle to maintain and expand adequate church and school buildings for an ever-larger Mexican Catholic community. Diocesan officials tapped traditional sources of charity to meet some of the cost, but the financial viability of Houston's Mexican parishes depended primarily on the parishioners themselves. In order to meet their churches' financial needs, parishioners systematically gave money, donated materials and labor, and carried on endless fund-raising. Significantly, the occasional disagreements one would expect to surface remain silent in the historical record, and what is patently clear is the strong sense of community this labor of love produced among the many parishioners who carried it on year after year. Clearly, because the parishioners' fund-raising revealed their distinctly Mexican ethno-Catholicism and the beliefs and values that defined them as a people, this ongoing activity did far more than pay for the costs of operating the parish; it also constantly rejuvenated Mexican American culture, provided socialization, and reinforced ethnoreligious identity and cohesion in Mexican communities.

GETTING STARTED

Early in 1912 the newly arrived Missionary Oblates began planning a theatrical performance to be held on Sunday evening, February 25, in downtown Houston's Saengerbund Hall. The Oblate Fathers intended to use the proceeds of this "Dramático-Musical" to help build Houston's first Mexican Catholic church. But then tragedy struck. On February 21 a fire, one-and-a-half miles long and half a mile wide, devastated a large part of the city's Fifth Ward, jumped Buffalo Bayou, and burned down a small part of neighboring Second Ward as well. The conflagration razed some forty city blocks, leaving hundreds homeless and jobless, including many Mexicans and Mexican Americans. Flyers addressed to "MEJICANOS" soon circulated in the barrios calling for a large turn-out at the coming Saengerbund Hall performance to help their compatriots "survive the vicious blow they have just suffered." The handbills explained that the funds raised by the theatrical event would be diverted to the fire victims but that activities to raise money for a Mexican church would continue.[2]

This event in the early history of Mexican Catholicism in Houston foreshadowed a pattern of enthusiastic support among Mexicans for religious fund-raising. Entries in the Guadalupe Church journal, for example, revealed that parishioner contributions through pledges and *jamaicas* amounted to $1,354, an amount that almost matched the $1,500 seed money received from the Catholic Church Extension Society. Parishioner Dolores Ramos collected a large portion of the contributions, which financed many of the basic needs of the infant church —the painting, heating, electricity, furniture, and so forth.[3]

In subsequent years, Mexican Catholics in other barrios proved equally eager to pay for their own churches. One congregant recalled that before Mexicans in Magnolia Park had a place of worship, the Oblate Fathers encouraged them to raise money to build a church, and neighborhood residents responded enthusiastically. Mary Villagómez pointed out that her mother was "a go-getter" for the church. She and other Magnolia residents worked diligently to collect money to build the first Immaculate Heart of Mary Church in the mid-1920s.[4] This self-reliant spirit was evident in other parts of the city. In the 1930s, for instance, residents of El Crisol barrio quickly gathered $600 and located the property on which to build the first church and school of what became Our Lady of Sorrows Parish.[5]

In a similar manner, the circuit priest Father Frank Urbanovsky

MEJICANOS

1912

Considerando las circunstancias en que nos encontramos y la catastrofe de que han sidi victimas muchos de nuestros compatriotas en esta ciudad de Houston el Domingo 21 de 1912 hemos acordado dedicar los productos de la velada Dramatico-Musical, del Domingo 25 de Febrero, a las 7.30 P. M. que iba a ser dada en beneficio del proyectado TEMPLO CATOLICO para remediar en cuanto sea posible los sufrimientos de que esos infelices son objeto.

No dudamos de que todos los Mejicanos daran muestra de su amor patrio y de su caridad cristiana acudiendo numeros.

Bien poco mostrariamos que somos verdaderos hijos de Mexico, si en estas horas de tribulacion y de prueba, no nos compadecieramos de nuestros hermanos, los consolaremos ayudandoles a sobrellevar el rudo golpe que acaban de experimentar.

Sin embargo no queremos abandonar el proyecto comenzado de levantar un TEMPLO CATOLICO a la gloria de Dios y para ello daremos otra velada del mismo genero.

Con objeto de obtener mas fondos, hemos reservado algunos puestos, que podran obtenerse al precio de 50c. Admicion General 25c. niños 15c.

Salon Saengerbund
Esquina Preston y San Jacinto
Segundo piso.

Encargados | *Padres Oblatos*
J. Gutierrez
y
C. Solsona

A flyer announcing a fund-raiser. Mexican Catholics diverted funds intended for building their first church to help people recover from a fire that razed a large section of Fifth Ward and part of Second Ward in 1912. Courtesy Southwestern Oblate Historical Archives.

noted the efforts of Bonita Gardens residents to acquire their own church in the 1940s. In mid-1947, Father Panchito reported that Mexican Americans there were "paying off the lots they bought for the future church." By the following year they had obtained four acres and two houses and were well on their way to establishing a temporary church. Urbanovsky also observed another kind of contribution typically made by parishioners—donated labor. Every bit of the work to build the first San Juan de los Lagos Church was donated by area residents. First, some twenty boys and men cleaned up the entire property, then an old army barracks was brought in sections to be reconstructed and refurbished by the men of the community. A church bell hung from a mesquite tree called volunteers to work on the project from six to eleven each evening, and, after a worker hand-fashioned an altar, the community's faithful knelt in their "new" chapel four months after setting to work.[6]

Some ten years later in another part of Houston, the people of Jeanetta Gardens launched St. Raphael Parish with equal fervor. The women of the neighborhood organized a Guadalupana Society immediately after the priest at a nearby Anglo church showed an interest in their barrio in 1958. The Guadalupanas collected money for the new church by holding dinners and rummage sales in the community. Before long, a local resident donated the land on which to build St. Raphael Church.[7] In varying degrees, outside financial sources augmented these barrio initiatives.

Catholic mission-aid societies helped finance many of the first chapels and parochial schools in Mexican communities throughout the Southwest. Organizations such as the Catholic Church Extension Society, the American Board of Catholic Missions (ABCM), and Our Sunday Visitor raised millions of dollars to fund church growth during the twentieth century. This practice followed the precedent set by the French Society for the Propagation of the Faith during the nineteenth century.[8] The founding of Our Lady of Guadalupe Church illustrates the role of institutional charity in Mexican parish development. In 1912, the Extension Society designated a gift of $1,000 toward the erection of

Guadalupe. The parish journal recorded the cost of construction at $4,515—"unpainted"—almost half of which was paid for by the Extension Society and the Oblate Fathers. Between 1915 and 1918, the Society provided an additional $1,400 to pay the interest on the remaining debt and meet other needs of the struggling infant church.[9]

Other parishes received similar aid. Churches required altars and pews, school materials, and living quarters for religious personnel, and at various times mission-aid organizations helped pay for some of these necessities.[10] From 1905 to 1950, for instance, the Extension Society gave $129,136 to the Galveston Diocese. Similarly, the American Board of Catholic Missions donated $1.5 million to the church in Texas between 1925 and 1951. Yearly sums of $15,000 to $20,000 from the ABCM were specifically designated for "Mexican work" in the Galveston Diocese from the mid-1940s to the mid-1950s.

But while the aggregate sums were substantial, they were thinly spread across many parishes and over several decades. For example, sixty-six towns and cities shared the amount given by the Extension Society to the diocese between 1905 and 1950. Houston's portion was $7,840, but, spread over some forty-five years, it averaged less than $175 per year and was parceled out to as many as six Mexican churches. In comparison, the ABCM contributions were larger, especially in the early 1950s, when donations specified for Mexican centers averaged $15,000 per year.[11] But again, Mexicans in Houston formed only a fraction of the Spanish-speaking apostolate in the large diocese.

On the one hand, Mexican parishes welcomed any help that lightened their financial loads. The contributions by mission-aid societies were, after all, an improvement over the neglect the church had shown for them in the past. On the other hand, though, the distribution of these funds showed how the pastoral needs of Mexicans took a back seat to that of Anglos. Concerning the $1.5 million distributed by the ABCM in Texas during 1925–51, historian Jay Dolan pointed out that "the Catholic population of Texas was heavily Mexican, with about two of every three Catholics being Mexican. Nevertheless, English-speaking parishes received $980,866 and the Spanish-speaking $390,000, or about one quarter of the total funds distributed by the Board. Such a distinction clearly indicated that the apostolate to the Mexicans came in a distant second to that of the Anglos."[12] Clearly, inequality still haunted Mexican Catholics in the form of the economic discrimination they faced within the church well into the twentieth century.

Institutional charity was supplemented by individuals who contributed money for the pastoral and material growth of Mexican parishes. From time to time the Catholic hierarchy made pleas for financial assistance from employers and the community at large and enlisted the support of some well-to-do individuals.[13] For example, Abe Silverman, known simply as the "Man of Providence" until after his death, contributed money anonymously to Guadalupe Parish for many years. Similarly, Mr. A. A. Hirst contributed the lion's share of funds to build the first house for the nuns at Guadalupe; Agnes Hamilton made possible the construction of a two-story convent; and the Scanlan family was a source of long-term aid to Guadalupe School.[14]

Like institutional charity, private philanthropy helped the development of religious institutions in the Mexican community. Donations of these kinds, however, hardly matched the spiraling cost of providing places of worship and religious instruction. Building costs were staggering in light of the meager financial resources of the Mexican community. In 1912, for example, Guadalupe's first frame church cost $4,515; its permanent brick structure built in 1923 cost $33,420; and a new parish school built in 1949 cost $88,000. Similarly, St. Patrick's pastor estimated the cost of a new church at $30,000 in 1944; two years later the estimate was revised upward to $40,000. By the time the new church was constructed in the mid-1960s, the land itself cost $30,000 and the building was estimated to cost $150,000.[15] Thus, given the limits of institutional and individual charity, Mexican Catholics relied on their own efforts to maintain the financial viability and continued growth of their parishes.

Mexican parishioners clearly demonstrated their willingness to contribute their money, property, and labor for the sake of having their
own churches and parochial schools. The initial phases of parish development were successful in large part because of the work and
financial contributions of countless parishioners, coupled with some
outside support. However, this was only a beginning. The task of
maintaining adequate facilities for a growing community posed an
even greater challenge. Once parishes were organized and the first
chapel-schools opened, church members faced the cost of upkeep and
further expansion. The first frame buildings were often refurbished,
but eventually they were replaced with permanent brick structures. In
addition to larger churches and schools, rectories and convents had to
be built and salaries and maintenance costs met. Pastors looked to
their parishioners—not to the diocese or outside support—to finance
most of these needs.

The construction in the early twentieth century of the Mexican
mother church, Our Lady of Guadalupe, illustrates the success with
which parishioners cooperated to expand their religious facilities. The
parish quickly paid off its debt on the first church and collected the
money to build the second church in 1923. The diocesan hierarchy
made no mention of the parishioners' role in the financial success of
the parish but instead lauded the "indefatigable zeal and self sacrifice"
of the pastor.[16] Despite a lack of official acknowledgment, the material
progress of Guadalupe Parish came largely from the parishioners' own
sweat and sacrifice, as their struggles and successes continued to show
over time.

Building programs at Our Lady of Guadalupe and St. Patrick in the
1940s illustrate this trend. For example, the new Guadalupe Parish
School originally cost $88,000, of which a debt of $39,000 remained in
1949. Of the $49,000 already paid, all but $2,000 had been paid by
church members themselves. The funds for the school were very
quickly gathered and "given willingly" but at great sacrifice by the

low-income parishioners. The pastor, Father Agapito Santos, realized that "money came hard" in his barrio, but he showed great confidence in the *colonia*, estimating that the debt would be paid in two years.[17] Similarly, St. Patrick's pastor confidently launched a fund drive for a new $30,000 church in the mid-1940s. The cleric sought 400 families to donate $25 or more to the project. "The donations are coming in slowly but surely and I believe that by next June we will have $15,000 in the bank," the priest noted in the parish journal. As it turned out, his optimism was justified; by 1946, some $16,000 had been raised.[18]

Raising money this way continued throughout the diocese over the years, and through the constant toil and sacrifice, several Mexican parishes achieved financial stability and self-sufficiency. But while several churches operated in the black, some of the poorer ones struggled to service large debts in the face of escalating costs and shrinking parish revenues. Our Lady of Guadalupe, for instance, had trouble paying a diocesan loan in 1971. The pastor explained that "tight money and inflation," as well as the inability to charge much for school tuition, posed serious financial problems for the parish. This was complicated by the fact that younger parishioners were moving out of the neighborhood, leaving older, less affluent members behind to support the church. "Little by little we are becoming a parish of the old whose only income is a pension or S.S. [Social Security] check which is never very much," the priest lamented. Significantly, though, the pastor reported that collections had not gone down, despite high unemployment in the parish.[19] Guadalupe's faithful still scraped together significant amounts of money for their church, as they had done traditionally. Other low-income parishes faced similar situations. At St. Raphael and Our Lady of St. John, for example, income and expenditures alternately exceeded each other in the 1960s and early 1970s.[20] As the 1970s began, the poorer parishes met their financial challenges with their customary relentless efforts and varying degrees of success.

In contrast, other parishes fared considerably better. For instance, Blessed Sacrament had a balance of nearly $4,000 at the end of 1971. Similarly, Our Lady of Sorrows Parish finished 1965 with a balance of more than $4,000, while St. Philip, another "vigorous mission," reported a balance exceeding $7,000 in 1966. Even more impressively, St. Patrick Parish had a balance of over $23,000 in 1965.[21] Hence, several Mexican parishes not only survived but flourished over the course of the twentieth century primarily through their own efforts. Spanish-speaking parishioners successfully harnessed the cooperation and meager resources of innumerable barrio residents at every stage of parish development, and, despite some setbacks, the funding strategies that Mexican Catholics used largely succeeded. How did they do it and what did their particular approaches reveal about their ethno-religion?

For many years church officials complained that "[t]he Mexican is not a collection box or envelope giver." The lament pervaded church correspondence and literature, but it revealed more about institutional racism and neglect than the reality of finances in Mexican parishes.[22] Despite this negative stereotype, the fact is that the mainstay of revenue in Houston's Mexican parishes was the regular collection of offerings on Sundays and holy days. Though the traditional (10 percent) tithe was not customary, many Mexican Catholics systematically made cash contributions to their parishes.

Parishioners recalled that parents and children regularly gave an offering at church services. Children eagerly waited to be given nickels, dimes, and quarters to "throw . . . in the basket" each week, a woman recalled. And her family was not unique in this regard; even the "truly poor" added to the collection plate: "They would say, 'Well, I only have five dollars but . . . las monjitas [the nuns], they need it.' And there was the five dollars in the basket, and I knew that was their last five dollars," a parishioner recounted.[23] Some families also gave money through the "envelope system" since the early twentieth century. In the late 1920s, the Guadalupe Parish bulletin listed the names of individuals who had "faithfully paid their monthly subscriptions." During January and February 1928, the paid pledges of 177 parishioners ranged from fifty cents to ten dollars, with most averaging about one or two dollars. The next year, as the economy worsened, contributions declined sharply; most donations were reduced by half, and several congregants were unable to pay the full amounts they pledged.[24] Nonetheless, regular contributions continued over the years, and by the 1960s the envelope system was part of the parochial reports, indicating the reliability and importance of this type of parishioner donation.[25] Sunday and holy day collections were by far the largest source of income reported by the Mexican parishes during the mid-1960s and early 1970s, averaging roughly one-half to three-fourths of the annual parish income.[26] But regular contributions had to be supplemented in other ways.

Pledging money for specific building projects was yet another important way of raising revenue. A member of Immaculate Heart of Mary Church explained that this was how Magnolia residents "accumulated enough to buy the land to begin with, and then to build the first church, and then again to build the big church and the school." Another member recalled "selling bricks"—soliciting pledges for construction materials—to raise money to build the new church erected in 1950. Similarly, many parish families individually or jointly sponsored the cost of stained glass windows and other items, such as religious objects and sanctuary furniture.[27] The amount of the contributions varied, from modest individual and family donations to gifts of over a thousand dollars from groups of parishioners and parish societies.[28]

All these forms of financial support were augmented by numerous smaller activities that formed an unending cycle of raising money in the parishes. Some children sold newspapers; others put on cake sales. *Rifas* (raffles) were a perennial favorite in all parishes, and some churches sponsored weekly breakfasts and lunches, bingo games, and an occasional *Gran Baile* (big dance) to fund specific parish projects.[29] Another long-standing tradition was parish "teatro," plays put on in the church hall that often featured the children of the parish. At Guadalupe Church during the late 1930s, parishioners enjoyed a nineteen-act variety show for an admission price of twenty cents for adults and ten cents for children. In addition to raising needed money, this *fiesta*

Children often performed musical numbers and plays in Our Lady of Guadalupe Church's social hall as part of their school activities, as well as for the ongoing fund-raising of the parish. Courtesy Mrs. Petra Guillén.

teatral had the added benefit, clergy and nuns pointed out, of "attract[ing] the parents and grown-up members of the family who might not otherwise attend the services." Flyers and bulletins reminded the community of upcoming events and urged the barrio residents to support the work of the church.[30]

These were valuable barrio customs. On one level, they sustained the economic life of the parish and contributed substantially to the institutional presence of the Catholic Church in Mexican communities. But equally important, fund-raising fostered ethnic solidarity. The projects involved large numbers of neighborhood residents and church members in experiences that reinforced their ethnic identity and sense of community because they were often culturally based and greatly invested with their time, money, and labor.

One particular type of fund-raising, the *jamaicas*, best revealed the implications of Mexican ethno-Catholicism. These festivals varied in size and frequency and were sometimes called *kermesses, noches mexicanas*, or simply fiestas. Some churches held several bazaars regularly throughout the year. At Guadalupe Church they were a "standard operating procedure" for generating parish revenue. Similarly, members of Immaculate Heart of Mary recalled that *jamaicas* were staged "every Sunday" during the Great Depression.[31] Often a series of small bazaars led up to a well-publicized annual affair that entailed extensive preparations, even the closing of city streets. A newspaper described one such event:

> Designers Friday were completing plans for an old Mexican village to be built in replica on the grounds of Our Lady of Guadalupe parish. . . . Gay decorations will transform the village into scenes of color and beauty for fiesta time. There will be no charge for admission to the village. Almost continuous entertainments, including typical songs and dances of old Mexico, will be staged.
>
> Refreshments will be served. Visitors may sit at tables while enjoying fast-changing spectacles of amusements.
>
> Huge loads of confetti, enough to strew Main Street from beginning to end . . . has [*sic*] been provided for revelry and merrymaking at the carnival.[32]

The *jamaicas* were a way for Mexican Catholics to enjoy and propagate their culture on various levels, as the preparations involved individuals, families, and whole neighborhoods in cooperation. "Everyone would pitch in with whatever they could," one woman recalled; "everyone took part in it."[33] In the process, many of the relationships and values that undergirded Mexican American life were expressed and confirmed. For example, some of the preparations for the bazaar reinforced gender roles, as men usually did the organizing—contacting parishioners and rounding up food and other items—while women did the "dirty jobs" of food preparation and cleaning.[34]

Women often held *tamaladas*, get-togethers of family and close friends for the particularly arduous task of making tamales to sell at the *jamaicas*. "My grandmother would make tamales [for the bazaars]," a church member related. "It was a family affair; we would all help her."[35] The *tamalada* was an important occasion for both family socializing and socialization, and this tradition offers an opportunity to further examine the role of women "as agents in the production of religion."[36] The *tamalada* involved women, men, and children in long hours (even days) of intensive, gender-defined work. An assembly-line process orchestrated by a mother or grandmother, the most demanding and skilled work was carried out by women while men generally had less taxing responsibilities. Typically, storytelling, jokes, and *chisme* (gossip) punctuated the drudgery, and elders inevitably handed down their generation's wisdom to youngsters in cooking instructions laced with admonitions about proper behavior. The *tamalada* thus imparted many of the core values of Mexican American family and community life, although, like the tradition of the *quinceañera*, it, too, was a double-edged sword. On the one hand, the *tamalada* clearly illustrated the Mexican cultural norm of relegating women to food preparation. On the other hand, women's control of food—and their intimate linking of it to the religiosity they were modeling for children and community —gave them a source of domestic power and community stature. Sister Yolanda Tarango reminds us that women passed down traditions "in a uniquely female manner, teaching through stories, rituals, and example."[37] *Tamaladas* for church fund-raising illustrate this, and they reveal as well another way that women found to exert family and community influence while they propagated ethno-Catholicism. Through the *tamaladas*, then, children learned about work, internalized gender roles, and imbibed religious and other cultural values. Women thus socialized and rooted children in their ethnoreligious culture, teaching them by example that to work for the church in this way was part and parcel of being a member of a Mexican Catholic family and community. Such lessons played a crucial role in maintaining viable Mexican American communities in Houston.[38]

On another level, the preparations for the *jamaicas* linked individuals and families to the larger Mexican community through the extensive cooperation that was needed to carry out a profitable church bazaar. St. Stephen did not have "rich people," Aurora Gonzales explained, "but we had a lot of people who were willing to do the work. And we had, at the bazaars, from the little young girls who were eight or ten years old working to create something with their hands to the older ladies who could hardly walk that would come in to make tamales—the support as a group, *as a people* was fantastic."[39] Parishioners made candies, cookies, cakes, *raspas* (snow cones), and paper flowers to sell. For two or three days before the bazaar, children cut up newspapers and magazines to make confetti to sell and others solicited contributions from barrio merchants and store owners in the downtown area. Churches sponsored annual parish queen contests in which teenaged girls campaigned for cash "votes." The highly touted crowning of the parish queen culminated the laborious efforts of many neighborhood residents who contributed to a successful *jamaica*.[40]

The frequent mention of the bazaars in various parish records testified to their financial importance.[41] During the 1920s, Guadalupe Parish collected amounts of $500 to more than $3,000 a year from *jamaicas*. By 1971, the annual bazaar at Guadalupe gathered $12,000, while the event at nearby Blessed Sacrament Church brought in just under $22,000.[42] Aside from the Sunday and holy day collections, festivals were often the largest source of parish income.

But the importance of the *jamaicas* went beyond finances. Rich in human warmth, they were a true celebration of community. At these events, familiar Mexican music wafted through the evening air, creating a carefree atmosphere as people chatted and strolled around the festively decorated booths and attractions, their senses tantalized by the delicious aroma of steaming tamales, *arroz con frijoles* (rice and beans), and *mole*. Happy shouts of children pierced the night as they greeted cousins and friends, and hearty calls of *¡Quehúbole!* (How are you?) rang out when compadres exchanged strong *abrazos* (embraces). Our Lady of Guadalupe Parish had its own band that regaled many *jamaicas* over the years. Similarly, many Second Ward and Magnolia

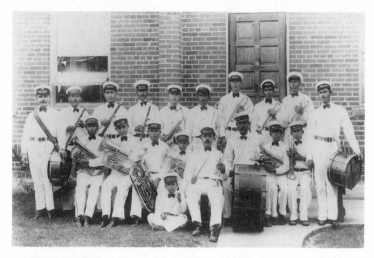

The church band of Our Lady of Guadalupe was a popular and important ingredient of the religious and social life of the Second Ward parish and barrio. Courtesy Houston Metropolitan Research Center, Houston Public Library.

Processions such as this one at Our Lady of Guadalupe Parish in the 1940s were an integral part of ethno-Catholicism. Courtesy Houston Metropolitan Research Center, Houston Public Library.

railroad workers played in the Southern Pacific Band. One parishioner proudly recounted that her *padrino* (godfather) played the tuba in the "SP" Band. "I loved to just sit there and watch him," she recalled.[43] These bazaars nurtured the important custom of godparentage by giving godparents and godchildren a chance to talk and enjoy each other's company. Mexicans preserved affectionate ties with family and friends this way, bonds of mutual support that strengthened families and sustained communities. Furthermore, the *jamaicas* introduced children to Mexican courting rituals: "The boys would stand on the outer line and the girls would walk around and the boys would throw confetti at us," a woman reminisced.[44] Thus these parish celebrations facilitated courtship and marriage, providing generational continuity among Mexican Catholics.

Clearly, the *jamaicas*, and indeed all their fund-raising efforts, served Mexican Catholics in many ways, by providing an important part of the financial base of their parishes and cementing the links between faith, identity, and community. Of course, this approach was distinctly Mexican but not unique; other Catholics had similar ways of fostering community through religion. The fusion of sacred and secular activity in Houston's barrios strongly parallels the central role Catholicism played in the lives of southern Italian immigrants in the late nineteenth and early twentieth centuries. Robert Orsi has beautifully shown how the Catholicism of New York's southern Italians totally permeated their lives and overflowed exuberantly from their homes into Harlem's streets during the feast of Our Lady of Mount Carmel. In Houston, too, Sicilian immigrants who had settled on the rural fringes northwest of the city held similar celebrations each year, complete with fireworks, processions, and bazaars.[45] In the early to mid-twentieth century, Italian American and Mexican American Catholics shared similar ways of cementing their ethnoreligious identity and sense of community.

Houston's Mexican Catholics clearly showed the depth of the connection they felt between their identity and their religious life when diocesan authorities unilaterally decided to dissolve St. Stephen, a

Mexican national parish dating back to the 1930s, and merge its members with a nearby Anglo church, St. Joseph. Seeing this as an affront to their dignity and a threat to their identity, St. Stephen's parishioners revolted.

THE ST. JOSEPH–ST. STEPHEN CONTROVERSY

In 1966 a five-year battle erupted between members of St. Stephen Church and the diocesan leadership that illustrates important links between fund-raising and Mexican ethno-Catholic identity. That fall Bishop John Morkovsky began an ill-fated attempt to merge St. Stephen, in Houston's near west side, with the historically Anglo St. Joseph Church some four blocks away. Bishop Morkovsky thought the consolidation would streamline administration and make more efficient use of resources and personnel. St. Stephen would continue to provide services and have a resident priest, but it would revert to mission status and be incorporated into the territorial parish of St. Joseph. In effect, Mexicans and Mexican Americans who historically had been barred from white churches now were the key to saving one of them from financial ruin. Apparently unmindful of the cruel irony involved, the bishop predicted that the practical effect of the merger would "probably be imperceptible." To the hierarchy, the plan seemed reasonable.[46] But St. Stephen's parishioners saw the merger very differently. Like their parents and grandparents before them, they had worked hard to raise money to build and maintain their own church. Now it seemed all their efforts might be erased, along with the bonds and memories those efforts had created over many years.

The merger took effect in early 1967. Father Patricio Flores took the helm at the new St. Joseph–St. Stephen Parish, and the diocese assigned an assistant to reside at St. Stephen's rectory. Services continued at both churches, and the new administration conducted the business of the combined parish from the Anglo church. But not even the appointment of the highly regarded Father Flores appeased St. Stephen's parishioners, and their dissatisfaction soon surfaced. On May 9,

1967, the new priest at St. Stephen confided to Bishop Morkovsky that fear and intimidation were rife in the parish. "The fear is of integration," Father Emile Farge reported, "of our people here not having *nuestra Iglesia Mexicana* (our Mexican church)." Father Farge warned the bishop that three parishioners were intimidating others into signing a petition by telling them that they would not be accepted at St. Joseph. The priest dismissed the petition drive as parish politics; the organizers feared being "dethroned" by the merger, Farge explained.[47] Father Farge also suggested a strategy to force St. Stephen's members to meld into St. Joseph: operate the mission from St. Joseph, remove the resident priest, and reduce Sunday masses from five to two or three. "I know we can't anglacize [sic] the Mexican but we must [A]mericanize him," the priest insisted.[48]

Three hundred signatures voicing the pleas of St. Stephen's petitioners did nothing to alter the situation, nor did they move the bishop to reappoint their former pastor as they asked. Father Farge's suggestions, in contrast, apparently carried more weight, for parishioners continued to complain about the lack of a resident priest at St. Stephen, a discord that smoldered into the next year.[49] Seeking to end the turmoil, the joint parish council agreed in October 1968 to sell both churches and begin congregational life anew under another name in a central location in the neighborhood. In early March 1969, diocesan officials announced plans to reorganize the parish at nearby Washington Avenue under the name of St. Martín de Porres, the patron saint of social justice. The proposal ignited more loud protests from both churches. Thirty "angry protestors" from St. Joseph confronted the bishop after the announcement, and, once again, over 300 members of St. Stephen signed a petition asking the bishop to let them express their feelings about the merger and the plan to relocate. At a subsequent meeting that month, "bedlam" reigned over the proposed changes.[50]

In the wake of the parishioners' opposition, Bishop Morkovsky appeared to suspend the planned sale of the churches. "There has been no decision yet on whether or not the property will be sold," the bishop stated in early March 1969. But other plans went forward. Throughout 1969 there were numerous fund-raising activities to benefit the proposed church of St. Martín de Porres. For example, Pastor Flores issued a letter soliciting donations for the proposed church on August 12. Also, in September the local Catholic newspaper reported on the *Rey Feo* (Ugly King) contest being held among the clergy to raise money for the new church. In the end, however, the plan to build a new church at a different location was laid aside.[51]

But harmony still eluded the parish. St. Stephen's parishioners remained dissatisfied with their mission status, and emotions erupted again in 1971. The congregation at St. Stephen bitterly resented not having their own pastor, wrote Mr. Raymond Lomas to the bishop. Lomas also complained that St. Stephen's members felt abandoned by the administration at St. Joseph. Poignantly he revealed the anguish that afflicted the troubled parish:

> Please forgive my boldness at writing this letter, but it must be done in order to tell you about the misfortune we find ourselves in at St. Stephen's Church. Although I imagine that you already know. As you know, since Father Buckley [the pastor prior to the merger] left, we have been without a pastor. We have had them, but not living at St. Stephen, which is what the people of the parish protest. That is why I am letting you know about this, before things deteriorate further. At this point the priests at St. Joseph apparently have a great deal of work and most of the time they're at St. Joseph and many parishioners come here asking for a priest and there is none. They [the St. Joseph priests] come here only when they celebrate a mass and then they quickly return to St. Joseph.
>
> . . . Because of this, our Reverend Bishop Morkovsky, I wish you would place your holy hand on your heart and be compassionate and send us a pastor here at St. Stephen. We have everything, thanks to God. A good house [rectory] with air conditioning and we are ready to work to support our church and the pastor who would come here. Which is all we ask of you, a pastor at St. Stephen.[52]

Lomas closed his letter rather bluntly, revealing the flip side of Mexicans' traditional reverence for the clergy, a deference now strained by a threat to their way of being Catholic: "Answer me quickly so I'll know your opinion," Lomas demanded.[53]

Bishop Morkovsky may still have been contemplating the Lomas letter when tensions flared again. St. Stephen's representatives, led by layman John Alderete, walked out of the joint parish council meeting in protest and met on their own. At their "Special Meeting" held on April 6, 1971, St. Stephen's parishioners discussed "the situation which prevails in the parishes of St. Stephens [sic] and St. Joseph."[54] Significantly, the letter to the bishop referred not to the merged parish of "St. Joseph–St. Stephen" but rather to the separate parishes. Still very much attached psychologically to their former parish, the St. Stephen's council representatives clung to their identity as an independent Mexican church. The meeting produced six resolutions that were forwarded to the bishop, along with the signatures of 309 members of St. Stephen Church. The parishioners declared that the rumored closing of St. Stephen Church had polarized the membership. They wanted to avoid any further hindrance of "the progress of our Holy Catholic Church" but were adamant about keeping their own house of worship, stating that "under no circumstances shall we accept the closing of our church." The parishioners pressed the bishop to "use his influence, as spiritual leader of the Diocese," to keep St. Stephen open. They also sought the assignment of a permanent resident pastor at St. Stephen and the continuation of the church "to the service of the Spanish-Speaking Community." In effect, St. Stephen's members called for the restoration of their previous status as an independent Mexican national parish.[55]

Scarcely two months passed before St. Stephen's members wrote to their bishop again.[56] Matters had worsened, with tensions between some parishioners and a priest reportedly escalating to an altercation. On June 25 the *Houston Chronicle* reported that Father Patout had "denied an observer's report that he had a physical scuffle" with some St. Stephen parishioners whom the priest said had been "passing out their own church bulletin at Sunday Mass, as a replacement for the official bulletin."[57] The tone and candor of the parishioners' letter to the bishop reflected the degenerating state of affairs. They poured out their indignation, accusing specific priests of "unjust and undignified" behavior. The petitioners also claimed that St. Joseph's priests slighted them. St. Stephen had not been provided the weekly parish bulletins for several weeks, the parishioners complained, and the priests offered neither explanations nor apologies.[58] Worse yet, the new schedule of reduced services at St. Stephen greatly restricted their right to receive the sacrament of confession. The letter also claimed that the clergy had misled the parishioners regarding the handling of parish funds.[59] Finally, the petitioners charged priests with unbecoming behavior. "Week after week . . . the Pastor . . . takes the opportunity [of the sermon] to hurl insults and even improprieties at the congregation," the petitioners complained, adding that the "gossiping" clergy even maligned St. Stephen's members when they visited other churches.[60]

St. Stephen's petitioners wrote that they wished to avoid any further incidents that might bring "serious calamities." Thus they issued the bishop their strongest demands to date, a "final" resolution: "FIRST: that from this date on, for no reason will the presence of Father Patout be permitted in the Church of St. Stephen, where he has been the main instigator of the recent events that afflict the bosom of our parish." The petitioners also demanded action on a long-standing complaint: "SECOND: that you are given a period of two weeks, beginning with the date of this memorandum, to provide our parish of St. Stephen with its own 'PASTOR.' "[61] St. Stephen's parishioners spoke clearly and unequivocally, and it was up to the leader of the diocese to respond. They counted on Bishop Morkovsky, who had told the parish council he "would try to do what was best for the people."[62]

On July 1, 1971, about three weeks after the St. Stephen ultimatum was issued, the diocese reorganized the administration of St. Joseph–St. Stephen Parish. A new pastor and assistant were appointed, and although the merger remained, the assignment of new priests seemed to assuage the disgruntled parishioners. A relative calm descended on the joint parish. The local Catholic press noted a "revitalized" spirit in the combined parish and reported that the two congregations were cooperating, a visible enthusiasm having returned to parish organizations and activities. Many credited the tranquility to the self-effacing new pastor, Father Maurice Dho. Mr. Raymond Lomas, who earlier had appealed to the bishop, stated simply, "We are working better now because we have a better priest." More to the point, Mrs. Raymond Canales, another St. Stephen member, revealed, "We have a priest who stays here all the time, ready to serve the people." Lastly, parishioners no doubt were pleased that plans to sell the two churches and relocate were finally dropped.[63] The church hierarchy's changes apparently brought calm to the beleaguered parish. The new parish administration appeared to be to the parishioners' liking, and they had a resident priest at St. Stephen Church, something that reflected at least part of their former structure and status as an independent parish.

Still, things had not completely reverted to their former status; St. Stephen was still a mission subsumed in a territorial parish, not the autonomous *Mexican* parish it had once been. Despite the easing of tensions, both Bishop Morkovsky and Father Dho sensed a continuing dissatisfaction. On May 24, 1973, the bishop confided to the priest that, "for the good of souls," the two churches might need to be separated. Two weeks later Father Dho formally proposed "that St. Stephen be reinstated to its status, as before being united to St. Joseph and that a priest be assigned there permanently." Bishop Morkovsky concurred. "Four or five years ago," he explained, "it was thought that the people of the area of St. Joseph's and St. Stephen's could best be served from one rectory, and perhaps even as one congregation." But, the bishop conceded, "it appears now that the people will be better served by returning to the former status." Without fanfare Bishop Morkovsky restored "the dissident parish" to its original form on July 1, 1973.[64] St. Stephen once again became an independent parish for the Spanish-speaking, with its own resident pastor. St. Stephen's parishioners regained what they had temporarily lost, their cherished *iglesia mexicana*.

The merging of St. Joseph and St. Stephen embroiled parishioners and diocesan leaders in bitter controversy for six years. Throughout the painful episode, the members of St. Stephen Church refused to yield their original demands. Why did they not compromise? Why was it so important to have their own Mexican church? The answers to these questions involved notions of honor and economic justice, but, most important, they had to do with how deeply entwined were the parishioners' sense of identity and their parish life.

The controversy had to do partly with respect, or the lack of it, in the opinion of St. Stephen's members. They were surely rankled at their demotion from independent parish to mission. Moreover, the parishioners believed they were being treated as second-class Catholics —ignored, misinformed, and even maligned by the parish clergy. St. Stephen's members understood that the diocesan plan to integrate them into a white church was essentially an effort to force them to accept a different Catholic tradition—an attempt to make them "better" Catholics. Forced Americanization insulted them. Furthermore, the way in which it was carried out offended their sense of the sacred. The defiant parishioners accused one priest of behavior "unworthy of the Representative of GOD OUR LORD." The clergy's purported gossip not only tarnished "the prestige and good name" of St. Stephen's members, but, worse, it soiled "the HOUSE OF GOD."[65] In the eyes of the parishioners, these priests had violated both sacred roles and sacred space, and the affair tore deeply at their social and religious sensibilities.

The affair also had to do with economic justice. St. Stephen, like other Mexican parishes, had been built through dint of hard work and sacrifice by the parishioners. Now their efforts and money were being used to save another church and, to add insult to injury, a church whose doors had always been closed to them because they were Mexicans. The saving of St. Joseph Church, the second oldest parish in Houston, was a strong motive for consolidating the two congregations, though Bishop Morkovsky had emphasized other reasons for the merger. In the late 1960s, St. Joseph's membership had declined to the point that the weekly collections were far less than the operating expenses. At the end of the 1967–68 academic year, the parish school had to close "for economic reasons," and the church was "in dire need of repairs." Meanwhile, St. Stephen Parish "flourished," with collections sufficient to meet all its expenses.[66] Thus, in order "[t]o save St. Joseph's from the wrecker's ball," the press later reported, "diocesan officials merged St. Joseph's and St. Stephen's into one parish." St. Stephen's parishioners felt they were being used. "We have discovered," they wrote to the bishop, "that all [our] weekly collections are deposited directly in the name of St. Joseph Church, ignoring that these funds come from our Parish."[67] St. Stephen's members chafed in their roles as pawns in an economic injustice.

Aside from these questions, however, the controversy hinged on the issue of identity. Shortly after being assigned pastor of the joint parish in July 1971, Father Dho recognized the futility of trying to establish a merged parish in a new location. "It is unrealistic and too early now to try and unite St. Joseph and St. Stephen's into a third church building," he observed. Dho concluded that "[t]he two congregations—especially St. Stephen's—are not ready to give up their identities."[68] Father Dho's sense of the situation was right. When Bishop Morkovsky merged St. Stephen's and St. Joseph's parishes, he unintentionally jeopardized the sense of community and way of life among Mexican Catholics on Houston's near west side. This cultural trauma could only be righted by restoring the original status of the *iglesia mexicana*.

Mexican American Catholics developed strong bonds with their parishes not only because of the efforts they exerted to establish and maintain them but also because of the cultural nourishment they derived from the institution-building process itself. Sociologist Harvey Newman notes that parishioners have a sense of "preciousness" about their churches partly because they do not view them as commodities to be negotiated. Rather, they develop a "special relationship" with the place of worship based on the "material and psychic rewards" they associate with it.[69] Such practical things as nearness to one's home and friends and access to important services provided by social networks associated with the church contribute to a sense of community among church members and neighborhood residents. Parishioners' ties to their place of worship are "a source of identification with the status of the group and its position within the community," and "there is the sense of joining together with others who share common traits of social status and background to form an organization which stands together against others."[70]

Newman's observations capture some of the embedded meanings and relationships associated with St. Stephen Parish, and they help explain why its members fought to keep its Mexican identity. Clearly, St. Stephen's parishioners derived "material and psychic rewards" from their Mexican church. Apart from the spiritual sustenance the *iglesia mexicana* imparted, it also offered significant material and social benefits, such as access to social services and the support networks represented by nearby friends and family. All of this, to borrow anthropologist Deborah Reed-Danahay's phrase, helped them "make do."[71] The *iglesia mexicana* gave a marginalized ethnic community the wherewithal to "stand together against others"—those who wished to make them "better" Catholics or otherwise impugned their dignity.

St. Stephen Church represented a large part of the social and cultural life of Houston's near west side barrio. Church members and neighborhood residents had strong associations with St. Stephen Parish—vivid memories of their sacrifices to establish and maintain the church, and a tapestry of relationships woven together by the countless solemn and joyous events that took place there over the years, the baptisms, *quinceañeras*, *jamaicas*, and more. "Memory locates the individual in a community" and "men and women discover who they are in their memories," Robert Orsi reminds us.[72] The *iglesia mexicana* embodied the collective memory of the parishioners of the near west side community, its symbolism fused with the people's self-image. St. Stephen expressed not only the community's style of Catholicism but also its members' identity as Mexican-origin people; it was an expression of the people themselves. Thus, giving up St. Stephen was tantamount to surrendering their spiritual and cultural self-expression and losing part of what made them who they were. Keeping their independent parish, on the other hand, was a way of resisting forces that sought to remake them. Fortified by their ethno-Catholicism, St. Stephen's parishioners successfully resisted the hierarchy's coercion, however well-intentioned, to abandon their Mexicanness and adopt an "American" way of being Catholic. When St. Stephen's members regained control of their Mexican church, they preserved their ethnoreligious identity and their dignity, both of which helped them face the inequality that marked their lives as ethnic Mexicans in Houston.

As the Catholic Church expanded its pastoral ministry among Houston's Mexicans and Mexican Americans, it also began to focus more on the parishioners' social needs. Nuns and priests familiar with Mexican poverty began to go beyond their pastoral responsibilities to help parishioners gain a better material life, as the next chapter illustrates.

SIX

THE CHURCH IN THE BARRIO: THE EVOLUTION OF CATHOLIC SOCIAL ACTION

Sister Mary Benitia Vermeersch often trudged Houston's back alleys and streets late at night—alone. This was unheard of! Her night outings were not only dangerous, but they also flew in the face of what society expected of women, especially nuns. But Sister Benitia was well known for putting the welfare of others before her own, and neither the dangers of the streets nor the tongue-wagging of those who considered her evening forays unbecoming kept her from doing what she had to do. Sister Benitia had a mission: she was determined to do something about the crushing poverty she saw all around her in Guadalupe Parish and other poor neighborhoods in Houston. Giving fleeting thought to her personal safety and reputation, Sister Benitia went beyond her strictly religious duties and brought badly needed food, clothing, and medical attention to many indigent Mexicans and Mexican Americans in the city during the decades of the 1910s, 1920s, and 1930s.[1]

Sister Benitia's "charity work" was one way the Catholic Church in Houston responded to the material needs of Mexican parishioners from the 1910s to the mid-1960s. This chapter focuses on the changing nature of this social ministry and its impact on the Mexican ethno-Catholics living in the Bayou City. Encompassing many aspects of

parishioners' lives, including the personal, vocational, financial, educational, and recreational, Catholic social ministry had implications for
individuals, as well as entire communities, making it a form of social
action or social reform. During the early twentieth century, Catholic
Church representatives in Houston who tried to improve their parishioners' material lives worked individualistically and unsystematically,
while, at the same time, Mexican Catholics had their own tradition of
self-help. Over time, however, Catholic social ministry evolved from ad
hoc humanitarian efforts to more systematic institutional approaches
that, by the 1940s, clearly distinguished between mere charity and the
need to engage the structures of society to bring about meaningful
social change. Driving these changes were church leaders' awareness
of an expanding and increasingly politicized Mexican American community, their continued sensitivity to Protestant proselytizing, and
their evolving vision of Catholic social action as a leaven for social
change.

Ad Hoc Social Action

During the first half of the twentieth century, the Catholic Church in
Houston addressed the material needs of Mexicans and Mexican
Americans mainly through the charitable works of individual clergy
and nuns. This individual social action was wide-ranging, involving
men and women of the church in making job referrals, interceding
with employers on behalf of workers, helping with legal and financial
matters, notifying relatives in family emergencies, and many other
kinds of "personal action."[2]

Personal and family counseling formed a large part of a priest's
duties. Parishioner Mary C. Villagómez recalled how people in the
early twentieth century depended on the advice of local priests. Her
brother, for example, sought his pastor's counsel about bringing his
fiancée from Mexico to Houston. In a similar vein, when it came time
to build the family house, Ms. Villagómez's father, not knowing anything about home construction or anyone who did, had the reverend

look at a sketch of what he planned to build. "In other words, they looked to the priest to be not only a spiritual leader but also a material [one]," Ms. Villagómez explained. His parishioners confided in him and sought him out in times of need, Father Esteban de Anta reported in 1930. "How many 'marital differences' have thus been smoothed out!" the cleric exclaimed. "How many tears dried!"[3]

Social ministry of this kind entailed personal sacrifice, as nuns, in particular, often shared their own meager resources with needy parishioners.[4] More than any other representatives of the church, nuns seized the initiative and made personal social action an integral part of their ministry. In Houston, Mary Benitia Vermeersch and Mary Dolores Cárdenas of the Sisters of Divine Providence epitomized individual social action through their tireless work to alleviate the effects of poverty among the city's Mexicans.

Sister Benitia's ministry in Houston spanned twenty-three years as principal of Our Lady of Guadalupe School. When she arrived in the summer of 1915, the city's suffocating heat and humidity aptly symbolized the poverty that engulfed her new mission in El Segundo Barrio. Undeterred, she immediately began canvassing the parish and coordinating relief for the needy from various local sources. She firmly believed, according to one of her protégées, that people would be more receptive to the church's message if first their hunger and oppressive living conditions were alleviated. Tirelessly she trekked Houston's streets making contacts all over the city with merchants, the well-to-do, and anyone else she could enlist in her effort to meet some of the basic material needs of her students and their families. As resourceful as she was relentless, Sister Benitia salvaged discarded rugs for parishioners who often slept on cotton-picking sacks on bare floors, and she solicited food from grocers and packing houses, clothing and other provisions from affluent homes, as well as useful gifts from local charities. With seemingly endless energy she even made time to supervise the cultivation of small vegetable plots on the parish grounds for use by neighborhood families, and part of her arsenal of food included a poultry and cow yard on the church property.[5] Sister Benitia's efforts also brought medical services into the Second Ward when an influenza epidemic devastated the Mexican community in 1918–19.[6]

From 1915 to 1938, "La Madre Benita," as she was called, carried on her personal brand of social action and won the hearts of the parishioners in Houston's Second Ward and beyond. She characterized her material aid to the poor not as begging but as simply reminding others of their Christian duty. "[She] was a very compassionate person," Mrs. Petra Guillén, a longtime parishioner, recalled. "Food was given to her and she fed the poor."[7] When tensions developed between Sister Benitia and the new pastor at Guadalupe Parish, the local bishop had her transferred out of the diocese at the end of the school year in 1938 despite a petition of protest signed by more than 600 dismayed parishioners.[8]

Sister Benitia managed to work well with Father Esteban de Anta, the longtime pastor of Guadalupe Parish, despite her legendary independence. "In all of her intrepidness, she had done many things that few nuns would dare to do in those days," Missionary Catechist historian Sister Mary Paul Valdez wrote. Historian Stephen A. Privett, who described Sister Benitia as "something of an anomaly within the rigidly controlled and highly centralized structures," reported that a highly placed clergyman once marveled, "How Benitia ever got loose is an absolute miracle, given the structures and traditions of her order." Father De Anta apparently accepted her maverick style, and the two worked "unselfishly to build the parish materially as well as spiritually" for seventeen years.[9]

But that was not to be with the new pastor, Father Ladislao López. Father López apparently butted heads with Sister Benitia from the very start after arriving at the parish in late summer 1936, and he enlisted his superiors to have the nun removed. The year 1937 passed "with constant criticism and account requesting by Father López," Sister Valdez wrote. In early 1938 Bishop Christopher Byrne wrote to the superior of the Oblate Fathers in San Antonio, "I heard today that Sister Benitia of Houston still rules at Guadalupe; if you can hasten her removal I think all things would be helped." As was often the case when nuns exerted any independence, priests perceived them as a threat to their authority. Such is the tone of the correspondence between the bishop and the Oblate superior—the nun "still rules," the bishop remarked, as if the intrepid Benitia had completely taken over control of the parish; "there is some danger of her promoting herself from Vicar General to Bishop," the Oblate superior jokingly responded. In such cases, mother superiors usually obeyed a bishop's decision, but often not without resistance. In Sister Benitia's case, her mother superior stalled the pastor, his Oblate superior, and the bishop for some time. "I have had two calls from the Mother Superioress" [who] "left me with the impression that Sister would be removed, as soon as possible," Bishop Byrne wrote to the Oblate superior. "She promised to remove her when her term as Superior ended," the Oblate superior wrote to the bishop, but he added, "I could not ascertain from her when that particular time was."[10] From the time of his arrival until he was rid of Sister Benitia, Father López had to endure her way of doing things for two years. Of course, tensions like these were common between nuns and clergy. They point up not only gender-based frictions within the Catholic Church but also the uphill institutional battles individuals faced when they took on the burden of social action of an individualistic and unconventional nature. They also testify to the depth of the religious convictions that drove Sister Benitia's action on behalf of others.

In much the same style, Sister Mary Dolores Cárdenas attended to the material needs of St. Patrick parishioners in Fifth Ward, on Houston's north side. Sister Dolores was well prepared for the twenty-two years she struggled at St. Patrick; she had previously spent thirteen years doing "all kinds of jobs besides teaching" at Our Lady of Guadalupe during the years Sister Benitia was in charge.[11] "In Houston I took advantage of all the offers that came my way," she recalled. She regularly tapped government sources for surplus food to provide free lunches at St. Patrick School in the 1940s, but the government's peanut butter and similar items needed to be supplemented. So she would rise early and have a neighborhood teen take her to the wholesale produce

Nuns like Sister Dolores Cárdenas, shown here distributing clothing during the Great Depression, took the lead in ministering to the material needs of parishioners. Note the three Catechists (two behind the nun's left shoulder and one to her far right). Courtesy Houston Metropolitan Research Center, Houston Public Library.

market to try to get any leftover vegetables. A soup bone paid for with her own money completed the hot meal she gave her students. When St. Patrick's cafeteria had to be given up in favor of more classroom space, the determined nun still managed to provide free milk for her students.[12]

Providing food and other basic needs was but one form of personal social action. Often, priests and nuns also served as character references for parishioners trying to find jobs. The Southern Pacific Railroad, being a major employer of Houston Mexicans, received many letters from priests and nuns recommending "honest" and "trustworthy" workers. Sister Dolores was particularly zealous at this task. She suspected that the "SP" paid relatively better wages than other employers, so with typical inquisitiveness she looked into what was needed to apply. Soon she was hard at work tutoring young men in the barrio in math and otherwise preparing them to pass the required tests, much to the chagrin of the people in the Southern Pacific employment office, whom she exasperated and overwhelmed with referrals.[13]

Church representatives of course were very familiar with the precarious finances of many parish families, and they understood that everyone was expected to contribute to a family's income. Both Sister Benitia and Sister Dolores cajoled many potential employers, plaintively appealing to their "kind hearts" to hire students from their parishes who badly needed to work in order to help their families.[14] Clearly, many nuns thought helping parishioners find jobs was an important part of their social ministry, and they had some success at this: "Many of the young men of the parish, and even a good number of the parents of her present-day pupils," a parishioner testified about Sister Benitia, "now hold jobs obtained through her recommendations."[15]

The efforts of Sisters Benitia and Dolores were part of the long tradition of Catholic nuns and other women in U.S. history who used religious and gender ideologies "to justify, define, and expand their role in American society." Nuns like Benitia and Dolores, like all other women of their generation, had to find ways to work within the constraints imposed by a patriarchal society and church. They exploited women's ascribed role (and implicit power) as mothers— feeding, clothing, and otherwise being nurturers and caretakers of children and the poor—because these were gender-appropriate activities that paralleled women's domestic roles in the family. This "maternal feminism" allowed nuns to provide material assistance to Mexican families as they struggled to overcome marginality and make a life in Houston. It also provided avenues for nuns to develop their individual skills and to wield a certain amount of influence wherever they ministered.[16]

It would be easy but wrong to dismiss these nuns' gutsy efforts on behalf of Mexicans in the early to mid-twentieth century. Amid the widespread poverty of Houston's barrios, these women worked creatively to bring food, clothing, and other material aid to hard-pressed families. Their efforts helped to sustain many families over the years and inspired individuals to persevere in the face of inequality and discrimination. The nuns' personal interventions sometimes proved pivotal in helping individuals succeed educationally and rise above a life of poverty, later to lead the way for others. For example, Bishop Patricio Flores, a major civil rights leader during the Chicano movement, often acknowledged Sister Benitia as an important mentor in his life. Sister Benitia paved the way for Flores to become a priest, despite his disadvantage as a high school dropout. After hearing that clergymen had rebuffed Flores's idea of becoming a priest, Sister Benitia characteristically said to him: "In the Church you don't start at the bottom. You go straight to the top." With that she had the teenager drive her to Bishop Christopher Byrne's office, where she introduced him and persuaded the prelate to give the young dropout a chance at a seminary education.[17] However apolitical nuns who undertook "charity work" might seem by today's standards, they were precursors of social change who prepared the soil and planted the seeds for greater social change in the future.[18]

In addition to the efforts of Sister Benitia, Sister Dolores, and other nuns, priests also came to the aid of the working poor and the unemployed. This outreach had long-standing papal approval. In the 1891 encyclical, *Rerum Novarum*, Pope Leo XIII had ordered: "Go to the workingman, especially where he is poor; and in general, go to the poor." In 1931, Pope Pius XI decreed in *Quadragesimo Anno*: "Let our parish priests . . . dedicate the better part of their endeavors and their zeal to winning the laboring masses to Christ and to His Church." These words especially resonated among the Oblate Fathers, whose raison d'être was ministry to the poor.[19]

The outreach of bishops to the larger community complemented the initiatives of nuns and priests. Bishop Nicholas A. Gallagher appealed in early 1912 to the major employers of Mexicans in Houston to help finance the church's efforts to ease their plight. His successor, Bishop Byrne, likewise instructed pastors throughout the Galveston Diocese to solicit a special Sunday collection specifically for the work at Our Lady of Guadalupe Parish. Sometimes these appeals struck a responsive chord in the community at large. In September 1915, for example, a railroad official made an open appeal to Houstonians to help repair damage to Guadalupe Parish facilities caused by the hurricane of August 16, 1915.[20]

Bishop Byrne also voiced his support for unionization. In 1942 the prelate instructed his pastors not to be strangers to the labor unions, which, after all, were comprised of men from their neighborhoods. Byrne instructed his priests to identify and get to know any union leaders in their parishes. As the spiritual leader of the diocese, Bishop Byrne wanted to show workers that "the Church is the defender and friend of Labor," and he strongly urged pastors to convey this message.[21]

In the early twentieth century, however, church support for the working classes was mostly rhetorical. This stance was in tune with the conservative political heritage of Texas. Indeed, even in cities like San Antonio and El Paso, with their greater concentrations of Mexican workers and closer ties to American and Mexican labor unions, Mexicans and Mexican Americans struggled gamely but made few advances against powerful anti-union sentiment and tradition. Houston's Mexican workers, being fewer and less closely tied to organized labor, worked under even greater disadvantages than their counterparts elsewhere in the state. In the 1910s and 1920s, there was minimal labor activism among Mexicans in the city. It increased somewhat during the 1930s, though it apparently did not approach the scope of efforts in San Antonio and other cities.[22] Not surprisingly, the leadership in the Galveston Diocese did not move beyond verbal support for Mexican labor in the first half of the twentieth century, and thus social action in the labor arena was even more circumscribed than the personal intervention of parish priests and nuns on behalf of individual workers.

Individual efforts blended with many group activities at the parish level aimed at social needs in the barrios. Parishes implemented ongoing and ad hoc projects that, for the most part, involved the same aims and church personnel as the individual initiatives described earlier. In fact, much of the organized social work of the parishes was carried out by nuns, using the parochial school as their main vehicle. The *Houston Chronicle* noted in 1935, for example, that over 500 " 'little Americans,' members of Houston's Mexican colony [were] served with food, clothing and educational facilities at Our Lady of Guadalupe parochial school." When the Great Depression exhausted parish resources, Father De Anta appealed for the first time to the community at large. Civic and social welfare leaders joined with the parish to stage an elaborate four-day carnival and bazaar on the church grounds in December 1935 so that Guadalupe could "continue its social welfare and educational work." Similarly, funds were raised in April 1940 for the Mexican Catholic Community Center operated by Guadalupe Church on the west side of the city.[23]

Catholic schools also contributed to helping the poor; some sponsored government-subsidized lunch programs that became relatively stable features of their programs beginning in the 1940s. Though some pastors balked at the red tape involved, their superiors insisted that Mexican parishes take advantage of government assistance "to consult the good health of their children." Needy families paid minimal cafeteria charges, and church bulletins reminded parishioners that adjustments would be made for children who could not pay.[24] Concern for the welfare of parish children spurred church leaders to attack other social evils that arose from time to time. In 1932, for instance, Bishop Byrne proudly remarked that a priest's campaign against an "evil dance hall" would be long remembered. In a similar vein, Father Agapito Santos enlisted the help of the director of the Houston Settlement Association to shut down a brothel that was operating too close to Our Lady of Guadalupe Church. As one magazine article aptly stated, the Oblate Fathers in Houston were "on patrol."[25]

The clergy were particularly vigilant about juvenile delinquency in the barrios, which was a widespread concern in Houston, especially from the early 1940s to the mid-1950s. Some Mexican youths formed gangs, such as the Magnolia gang, the Scorpions, the Long-Hair gang, and others, and local authorities associated them with the rise of juvenile violence and crime that afflicted the nation during this time. By chance, the notorious "zoot-suit riots" that shook Los Angeles in the summer of 1943 coincided with a sensational murder trial involving members of the Long-Hair gang in Houston. In response to increased crime among Mexican teenagers, civic groups, such as the Federación de Sociedades Mexicanas y Latino Americanas (Federation of Mexican and Latin American Organizations), joined city officials and other groups to combat juvenile delinquency.[26]

Catholic officials entered the fray fully aware of public perceptions. "There is a cry going up and it is found in Houston," Bishop Byrne lamented, "against the Mexican youth that they are criminally inclined."[27] The diocese tried to focus more attention on parish youth as tragedies struck various barrios in the 1940s and 1950s. St. Patrick Parish buried five teenaged victims of gang fights in a span of less than six months in 1942, and Our Lady of Guadalupe Parish also suffered from gang violence. Nearby Immaculate Heart of Mary Church struggled with the same situation, as did Our Lady of Sorrows and Our Lady of St. John.[28]

But despite the gravity of the problem, the cooperation of some priests was less than their superiors expected. In 1942 an Oblate provincial heartily agreed with Bishop Byrne's idea about increasing the "boy work" in Houston's Mexican parishes. But, unfortunately, the provincial complained, "In all our parishes where the Spanish Fathers are in charge, they have refused to cooperate." The Oblate superior believed the Spanish priests in Mexican parishes generally gave "too much time to the 'Hijas de Maria' [Daughters of Mary, a parish society], and having no time for the boys, these consequently became 'Hijos del diablo' [Sons of the Devil]."[29] More than a decade later, a different bishop and provincial grappled with the same problem that, the bishop concluded, stemmed from the "old-country prejudices" that some Spanish priests had against Mexican parishioners.[30]

Efforts to eradicate delinquency had strong support at the highest levels of the Galveston Diocese. In fact, by the mid-1950s, Bishop Wendelin J. Nold considered reaching the youth the top priority in the ministry for the Spanish-speaking. Despite some priestly recalcitrance, church officials earnestly tried to find the right mix of experienced personnel and proven tactics to fight delinquency in Houston parishes.[31]

The strategies varied. Many parishes channeled youthful energy and free time into organized athletics. The nuns at the "Summer School of Catholic Action" at Guadalupe Church featured very successful football and basketball teams. Even the itinerant Padre Panchito harnessed the vigor of barrio teens. On one visit to the Bonita Gardens area, the "gypsy priest" recruited twenty boys to help with the heavy labor of clearing a lot for the future church of Our Lady of St. John. This done, he persuaded county officials to level part of the area to use as a baseball diamond.[32] Priests and nuns believed that gangs could be wiped out if only they could find more recreational facilities for neighborhood youth, and they worked hard to provide this. But sometimes their efforts were stymied. For example, Father Santos and the sisters at Guadalupe Parish wanted desperately to expand the parish playground by relocating a long-abandoned cemetery adjacent to the rectory. This "big dream" never materialized, however, for one of the few bodies that remained interned was that of Confederate war hero Dick Dowling. A local group's plans for making the cemetery a shrine for the legendary Texan overrode the need for a playground. "But what better shrine could there be to Lieutenant Dowling . . . than a playground for these Latin-American citizens?" asked a reporter who agreed with the parish's priorities. Others in the community at large disagreed.[33]

Protestant proselytizing among Mexicans also spurred Catholic social action. The competition for Mexican souls was real and long-standing. Despite the historical predominance of Catholicism, some Mexicans and Mexican Americans had been converting to Protestantism since the nineteenth century. By the twentieth century, a small but stable portion of the Mexican community, perhaps 5 to 10 percent, belonged to Protestant denominations.[34] In all of Houston's barrios, a number of small Mexican American Protestant churches existed alongside the Mexican parishes, their presence in the city dating back at least to the early 1920s. As Houston's Mexican population grew, so did the number of *aleluyas*, as the Mexican Protestants were called. In fact, by 1940 there were at least ten Baptist, Methodist, Presbyterian, Lutheran, Pentecostal, and other Mexican Protestant churches scattered among the city's barrios. The number of non-Catholic churches continued to increase in the 1950s. In the area around St. Patrick the pastor reported two Mexican Protestant churches in 1951 (Baptist and Lutheran) and a Latter-day Saints church two years later. St. Patrick's census reported five Mexican Protestant churches (two Baptist, an Assembly of God, a Church of Christ, and a Methodist), as well as a Latter-day Saints church. Catholic officials constantly agonized about the "great leakage" in the Catholic Church, that Mexicans were straying from their traditional faith.[35]

In addition to the Mexican Protestant churches, Catholic clergy worried about the Protestant "Houses of Neighborliness" and other community centers that combined social services in the barrios with proselytizing. For example, the Methodist Church sponsored the Wesley Community House, which opened in 1930 to offer recreational and other social services to the Mexicans of the near north side, while Anglo Presbyterian women operated similar centers in other barrios.[36] Of course, not all of Houston's community centers were directly affiliated with Protestant churches. The Rusk Settlement House had provided an array of social services to the residents of Second Ward since 1907. Like most settlement houses throughout the United States, Rusk Settlement purported to be a secular institution. Nonetheless, as historian María Cristina García noted, "Most settlement workers . . . came from middle-class families, their values shaped by Calvinist morality and the Social Gospel movement."[37]

No wonder, then, that Bishop Byrne grew uneasy in 1942 when he learned that the Young Men's Christian Association (YMCA) was "flirting" with "our Mexican boys." He pointed out that the YMCA had recently spent $11,000 to build a boys' club house near Our Lady of Sorrows Church, and he ordered the priests at St. Stephen and Our Lady of Sorrows to "get interested in that."[38] In a similar manner, an Oblate

Both Catholic and Protestant churches vied for the attention of Mexican American teenagers such as these pictured in Houston's Fifth Ward in the 1940s. Courtesy Houston Metropolitan Research Center, Houston Public Library.

provincial took a strong interest in the work being done by the Houston Junior Forum Community House in the late 1950s. The director seemed "a very capable woman, and at the same time most considerate even though not a Catholic." For the Catholic hierarchy, involvement in this project presented an opportunity to combat social problems, as well as shore up Catholicism in the Second Ward. Thus the hierarchy assigned Father Frank Brentine to work with the Community House director, "to direct [her] in a favorable manner."[39] Houston's predominately Protestant ethos and institutions challenged the Catholic Church to redouble its own social work in the barrios.

During the early to mid-twentieth century representatives of the Catholic Church approached social issues and material needs in Mexican communities in an indirect and individualistic manner, mainly through the personal efforts of priests and nuns acting on their own.

But an ever-growing Mexican population and shifting attitudes within the church hierarchy focused greater attention on Mexican Catholics. At the same time, Protestant proselytizing among Mexicans spurred the church to increase its social services to them in an attempt to keep them within the Catholic fold. Mexicans and Mexican Americans accepted this aid, and at the same time they continued to rely on each other, as they always had.

The Mexican Tradition of Self-Help

The Mexican community had a long-established tradition of self-reliance reaching back to the Spanish and Mexican eras when a catastrophic fire struck Houston in 1912. The conflagration razed over forty city blocks and destroyed about $7 million of property in an area roughly half a mile wide and one and a half miles long. Fifth Ward suffered most of the damage, and there was some destruction in Second Ward as well, leaving many Mexicans among the hundreds of homeless and jobless victims. In a display of ethnic solidarity, the money that had been gathered by the community for its first church was diverted to the victims of the fire. As important as the projected new church was to Houston's Mexicans, the suffering of their fellow compatriots took precedence.[40]

Mexican communities throughout the Southwest had always banded together for self-preservation through mutual aid societies and other organizations. Some, like the Liga de Protección Mexicana, were fully grounded in Oblate parishes and enjoyed the blessing of the church.[41] At Houston's Guadalupe Parish, men formed a Liga de Protección Mexicana in 1917 and the following year the women there started their own chapter. Also at Guadalupe, a secular organization called the Asamblea Mejicana Pro-Raza (Pro-Mexican Congress), whose goal was "to protect Mexicans against the insults and abuses of which they are often victims," tried to recruit members by advertising in the church bulletin.[42] Little is known about these protective societies at Guadalupe Parish, but, given the Oblates' active involvement with *ligas* throughout Texas, these chapters probably pursued a mutual aid–type of social action with the blessing of the pastor. However, it is important to emphasize that this reflected traditional Mexican self-reliance and community organization, not dependency on the church. In fact, Mexican self-help organizations predated any Catholic institutional presence in the city's *colonia*.[43]

While church leaders helped to channel food and other basic needs into Mexican parishes, these same parishes, despite their own poverty, did what they could to ease the plight of others. "Although money is scarce at the church," a newspaper reported about Guadalupe Parish, "sometimes Father Agapito Santos, the pastor, must refuse cash donations because he knows the givers can't afford them." Parishioners regularly contributed to communitywide charities, such as the Community Chest and Red Cross, to the amazement of the nuns who knew the extent of poverty among them. "They somehow manage to bring a can of food for every drive," a nun pointed out.[44]

Operation Relief reflected well the parishioners' magnanimity and the church's role in helping to coordinate it. When two hurricanes devastated Tampico, Mexico, in 1955, the five Mexican national parishes of Houston responded quickly and generously. Oblate Father John Sauvageau, pastor of St. Stephen Church, coordinated the effort. Over radio and television, he appealed for donations eleven times a day while the priests of the other four Mexican parishes informed their church members. "After only a five-day campaign," Father Sauvageau recalled, "we had received $5,642.00."[45] In Mexico Father Sauvageau personally supervised the distribution of the food and medicine purchased with the contributions, while efforts continued in Houston to raise more money. The Bonita Bar donated proceeds from a barrel of beer, local musicians staged a benefit dance at the Acapulco Night Club, and the director of the Morales Funeral Home facilitated the discounted purchase of a $10,000 ambulance that was loaded with supplies and driven to Tampico by Father Sauvageau.[46]

When disasters struck, Mexicans and Mexican Americans put aside religious differences. The summer before the Tampico disaster, in July

1954, flooding along the Rio Grande devastated Mexican communities in Laredo, Eagle Pass, and Del Rio, Texas, along with their neighboring cities of Nuevo Laredo, Piedras Negras, and Ciudad Acuña in Mexico. In this case a Mexican American Baptist pastor, Reverend James L. Novarro, organized a relief drive in Houston. Reverend Novarro coordinated the collection of more than 300,000 pounds of food and clothing, as well as $5,800 in cash for medical supplies, and he personally supervised the distribution of the aid on both sides of the U.S.-Mexico border.[47]

Church leaders gave important guidance to self-help efforts, but it was the parishioners who made most of the sacrifices necessary to carry on the work. In 1957, for instance, St. Stephen's parishioners started a credit union with thirty-five members and $136.00; less than two years later the credit union had 400 members and had loaned out over $29,000. The success "was made possible by the savings of our people —25¢ . . . $1.00 . . . , and in a few rare cases, $5.00," Father Edward Murray explained, and because the parishioners themselves "were willing to utilize their talents and time to protect our people from the loan shark."[48] St. Stephen's credit union differed significantly from earlier church social action in that it combined clerical guidance with Mexican American leadership; it was not passive charity. Priests motivated by the goal of economic redemption of the working classes understood their role as nurturing self-reliance among their parishioners.[49]

The parish school also cooperated with outside groups interested in attacking educational problems in the barrios. In the late 1950s Houston's well-known entrepreneur and civic activist Félix Tijerina started a program of preschool classes for Spanish-speaking children throughout Texas. In Houston several Mexican parishes disseminated information about the program in a highly successful media blitz in April 1960.[50]

Clearly, Mexican and Mexican American Catholics in Houston maintained a tradition of self-sufficiency that often involved cooperation with the institutional church. Self-help efforts involving clergy and nuns expressed the long-standing practice of Mexicans availing themselves of church services while maintaining some distance from the institution. It also underscored the dialectical nature of their ethno-Catholicism.

Toward Institutional Social Action

By the 1940s the Catholic Church began to bureaucratize and institutionalize its social ministry, though piecemeal charity continued. The Bishops' Committee for the Spanish-Speaking (BCSS), launched in 1945, exemplified this new approach to Catholic social action. Under the firm control of the progressive archbishop of San Antonio, Robert E. Lucey, the BCSS sought the cooperation of bishops throughout the Southwest to exert a concerted "spiritual and temporal welfare work" for Mexicans and Mexican Americans.[51]

Bishop Byrne of the Galveston Diocese played at least an indirect role in the formation of the BCSS. For years he had decried the exploitation of Texas Mexicans and cast about for support. "What do you think of the idea of asking the Fathers [in Houston] to get the Mexican people more interested in the Civil life of which they are a part?" he asked an Oblate provincial. Several years before the BCSS came into being, Bishop Byrne called for action by the church. "I think, we have a field for Catholic Action," he wrote, referring to the need for an increased social ministry, "and a battle for Social Justice that we can not any longer neglect."[52] The bishop's comments reflected the more progressive attitudes that were becoming evident among some men and women of the church in the 1940s, as well as an awareness of the political implications of the growing Mexican population. Equally important, the statement was also a call to redress some of the past failures of the church.

Byrne continued emphasizing the citizenship rights of Mexican Americans as a way to end their exploitation. "I think the sooner we get these who are called Mexicans, to vote, and to use their American citizenship, they will all the sooner be regarded with greater respect and they will be accorded better wages for their work," the bishop urged. The aging prelate challenged the "energetic young Arch-bishop" Robert E. Lucey to take up the cause.[53] Indeed, the dynamic and influential Lucey eventually developed the BCSS as a new phase of Catholic social action. Bishop Byrne died before the committee began its tenure in Houston during 1953–55 at Immaculate Heart of Mary Parish, but he had been an important precursor of the liberal Anglo Catholics who would have significant roles in the impending civil rights era.[54]

The Bishops' Committee, it should be noted, was first and foremost Archbishop Lucey's personal vehicle for farmworker advocacy. None-theless, it also brought some needed services to urban Mexican Ameri-cans. In various cities the BCSS established child-care programs and clinics, promoted youth work and public housing, and worked to bring a variety of city services to neglected Mexican American neighbor-hoods.[55] In Houston the BCSS had slight impact, according to a former executive secretary. "I don't think that our presence in Houston had a tremendous impact on the Hispanic community there," Father Wil-liam O'Connor recalled.[56] This is not surprising considering Bishop Lucey's rigid control over the committee, its primary focus on migra-tory workers, and the fact that Houston was not part of the "Big Swing," the perennial route made by migrant farmworkers. Still, the committee organized voter-registration drives and English classes in Mexican parishes, and it had ceremonies for those who trekked north from Houston; priests blessed the workers and their vehicles on their departure and welcomed them upon returning to their parishes.[57]

Part of the BCSS strategy was to have each diocese establish its own Catholic Committee for the Spanish-Speaking, to continue its advo-cacy after the regional office moved on to another diocese in its rotat-ing schedule.[58] In spring 1964, under a newly created Catholic Commu-nity Relations Council (CCRC), the Galveston-Houston Diocese named Father Patricio Flores to head its new Committee for the Spanish-Speaking.[59] Together, the CCRC and the Committee for the Spanish-Speaking embodied Catholic social action in Houston during the 1960s.

The CCRC's director carefully stated the role of the church in social action. Father John E. McCarthy explained that the council would bring to bear the moral influence of the church on critical social problems. Significantly, however, the council would play an indirect role. Rather than offer concrete solutions to problems, it sought to clarify the ethical issues involved in disputes. "Each of these areas is one in which leadership properly belongs in the hands of the laity," Father McCarthy emphasized, partly echoing the past, as well as hinting at the direction that institutional social action would take in the future. A church representative's role in social action would be to work closely with trained and dedicated laypeople who would themselves lead efforts for social justice.[60]

The Community Relations Council, created at the height of the civil rights movement, was clearly prompted mostly by black, rather than Mexican American, concerns.[61] Nonetheless, the formation of a Committee for the Spanish-Speaking signaled an important change in the Galveston-Houston Diocese. It indicated Bishop John Morkovsky's desire for a stronger social ministry and a more systematic means of seeking social justice for Mexicans and Mexican Americans. Furthermore, the appointment of Father Flores—a former migrant farmworker keenly aware of Mexican Americans' needs and an outspoken critic of the church's treatment of Mexicans—clearly signaled a response to the increasing social and political activism among Mexican Americans in the years after World War II.[62]

Of course, it could be argued that these developments only reflected the national trend toward greater bureaucratization of charitable work and the professionalization of social action under way since the Progressive Era, evidenced in the creation of the National Conference of Catholic Charities (1910) and the National Catholic Welfare Conference (1919).[63] However, despite their prominence, these kinds of efforts did not trickle down and ignite movements for significant social change. For one thing, as late as 1960, three-fourths of American seminarians lacked training in the social teachings of the church.[64] Rather than the church changing society, the reverse occurred. As other historians have recognized, social justice movements triggered great changes in the U.S. Catholic Church.[65] This is the pattern Houston reflected in the post–World War II years. Earlier, Bishop Byrne's support for the BCSS revealed changing clerical attitudes toward Texas Mexicans in the late 1930s and early 1940s. By the 1950s, this increased awareness about the rapidly growing Mexican community and its increasing politicization moved Catholic leaders to do more to fight discrimination against Mexicans and Mexican Americans. Mexican Americans' burgeoning numbers and political agitation magnified their presence and increased the pressure on the church in Houston to provide a more effective social ministry for Mexican Catholics, as evidenced in the naming of Father Flores to head the Committee for the Spanish-Speaking.

Father Flores scheduled the first meeting of the committee to be held in Houston on October 11, 1964, announcing that education would be its major focus. The committee sought to help develop college scholarships and vocational training programs and to encourage parents to keep their children in school. Poor academic preparation denied factory and industrial jobs to many Mexicans and Mexican Americans, Father Flores stated, and was a link in the chain of poverty: "Low income forces them to take the worse [sic] in housing and poor housing conditions create many other serious problems."[66]

The Galveston-Houston Diocese moved quickly to attack the problem of education in the barrios through the Catholic Community Relations Council and other groups. In January 1965 the CCRC began a program to provide remedial instruction in math and reading at St. Stephen, Immaculate Heart, and St. Raphael nationality parishes, hoping to "eliminate academic deficiencies that lead to school drop-outs." Soon after, the diocese implemented Head Start programs at twenty-two centers, including several of the traditionally Mexican parishes in Houston. Adult education followed, with literacy classes offered by the Diocesan Council of Catholic Women at St. Stephen Parish and St. Raphael mission during the mid-1960s.[67]

The Catholic Community Relations Council, the Committee for the Spanish-Speaking, and other diocesan-level organizations, then, reflected the institutionalization of social action in the Galveston-Houston Diocese by the mid-1960s. A more coherent and systematized social ministry had developed in the post–World War II era. By the mid-1960s, with the rise of the Chicano movement, there were forces at work that eventually would propel the church in Houston into unprecedented turmoil and involvement in social issues in Mexican American communities. It is that aspect of the church's social role that we turn to next.

SEVEN

"May God protect us from guys like you," an angry young Chicano yelled at the priest. Others who had come to the meeting with the pastor also spewed bitterness as their parents watched "with glassy eyes of disbelief." The activists left Resurrection Catholic Church unable to convince the pastor to let them hold their school boycott classes at the church. "The Shepherd Refuses His Flock," a Chicano newspaper railed, adding that "the majority of the Catholic Schools, in time of need, have refused to help the people that they should be serving."[1]

This scene from a chapter in the Chicano civil rights movement (*el movimiento*) in Houston illustrates how the tumultuous years of the civil rights era rocked the Galveston-Houston Diocese. This chapter's focus is on the response of the Catholic Church to the turmoil of the Chicano movement during the mid-1960s to early 1970s, when the Mexican American quest for self-definition and inclusion in Houston climaxed. During the Chicano movement representatives of the church in Houston alternately resisted and embraced the cause for Mexican American equality. *El movimiento* unleashed a fury of demands for more social action by the church. The diocesan administration responded to many petitions in traditional ways, but the unprecedented internal and external pressures for reform forced the church hierarchy to respond in new ways as well. As individual clerics and nuns pushed efforts for Mexican American equality within the church and in society, the leadership of the Galveston-Houston Diocese cautiously supported and followed the vanguard.

THE CHURCH IS CHALLENGED

During the civil rights era many people questioned American values and institutions, and religious institutions were no exception. Indeed, churches often came under fierce attack as disaffected groups challenged their subordinate status in society.[2] Mexican Americans also questioned the role of religious institutions in their lives. Local and national leaders frequently looked to the church for help in addressing pressing social issues. For instance, when labor organizer César Chávez emerged as a national symbol of the Chicano movement in 1965, the institutional church figured prominently in his struggle for economic justice for California farmworkers. Though many individual clergy and nuns actively supported his cause, Chávez challenged the church hierarchy to throw its formidable influence and resources behind the striking agricultural workers. "We don't ask for more cathedrals," he stated, "We ask the Church to sacrifice with the people for social change, for justice."[3]

Calls for the Galveston-Houston Diocese to step up its social activism came from many quarters as hometown politicians, congressional representatives, local barrio activists, and other Chicanas and Chicanos increasingly prodded the institution. In 1965 Manuel Crespo, chair of the Houston chapter of the Political Association of Spanish-speaking Organizations (PASO), called on church leaders to do more to encourage Mexican American interest and participation in politics. Clergy "could help Latin Americans very much by mixing more with them, talk[ing] to them and encourag[ing] them in their political obligations," Crespo urged. Similarly, Texas congressman Henry B. González, in Houston to address the annual meeting of the Society of St. Vincent de Paul, a major Catholic charitable organization, suggested that clergy "redefine" and bring more relevance to their social-action programs. Likewise, local activist William Gutiérrez called for church officials to stop taking Mexican Catholics for granted and urged priests to "become deeply involved and active in the plight of the Mexican American."[4]

Over time, the voices of protest became increasingly strident. At a Houston conference in October 1969, for example, Herman Gallegos, the executive director of the Southwest Council of La Raza, a coordinating organization of Mexican American advocacy groups, denounced the institutional church's failure toward Mexicans. He charged that the institution was "too far removed" from Chicanos and Chicanas and that it was at least partly to blame for some of the social problems facing them. Gallegos challenged the representatives of Catholic charities to help remedy some of these ills by creating housing, education, and economic development programs for Mexican Americans.[5]

Others used angrier language. Lalo Delgado, a Chicano academic and activist, told a gathering of lay and clerical officials in Houston that the Catholic Church was a racist institution, that "bishops, priests and Sisters have turned it into an ugly church." Yolanda Garza Birdwell, a Mexican American Youth Organization (MAYO) leader in Houston, similarly assailed the church in a newspaper interview. "[W]hen the dogs in River Oaks [Houston's most affluent neighborhood] are eating more meat than a lot of her northside friends," the *Houston Chronicle* reported, "a woman has a right to fight back." "So it's a sin to stop having children?" Birdwell asked rhetorically. "Okay, mothers have more children and there's malnutrition and a great injustice is done. I have no doubt the Church is very responsible for this situation," Birdwell charged as she pointed the finger of blame for the poverty in Houston barrios.[6] Chicanas who attended the Conferencia de Mujeres por la Raza (National Chicana Conference), held in Houston May 28–30, 1971, echoed this anger. Many denounced the oppression of Mexican American women by men at home and in the church, and a resolution defiantly "recognize[d] the Catholic Church as an oppressive institution." The conference went on record in support of abortion and resolved "to break away" from the Catholic Church.[7]

The Chicano press voiced virulent attacks on the church during the late 1960s and early 1970s, publishing scathing editorials that condemned the failings of institutional Christianity. Chicano journalists, for example, accused church personnel of hypocrisy and insensitivity toward Mexican American parishioners. On one occasion the editor of *Compass* likened the clergy to "[p]arrots, who do not know or understand the seriousness of the doctrine being taught." In another editorial, the paper charged that clerics would rather dedicate themselves to building beautiful structures than to speaking out against discrimination and economic injustice.[8]

Another community newspaper, *Papel Chicano*, aimed most of its ire at Protestants, but it also reminded readers that "the Catholic Church [was] unmindful of the needs of the Chicano." The paper criticized the institutional church for neglecting social issues that affected both the spiritual and material welfare of its parishioners, claiming that priests did more harm than good and were "such cowards" that they were afraid to denounce bigotry, racism, and discrimination. Church officials who lacked the courage or ability "to relate Christian teachings to the community's everyday life and problems should find other vocations," the article continued, "where they will not do such damage to the parishioners' spiritual lives." The newspaper's denunciations revealed not only disillusion but also the historical anticlericalism and self-sufficiency of Mexican Catholics, who, the paper asserted, owed no allegiance to an institutional church "that pretends to teach doctrines which are alien to the spirit of the Chicano," notions such as turning the other cheek and being long-suffering.[9]

An anonymous poem in one of Houston's Chicano newspapers reflected the disillusionment many felt with the Catholic Church:

> I was hungry
> and you formed a humanities club

and discussed my hunger.
Thank you.
I was imprisoned
and you crept off quietly
to your chapel in the cellar
and prayed for my release.
I was naked
and in your mind
you debated the morality of my appearance.
I was sick
and you knelt and thanked God for your health.
I was homeless
and you preached to me
of the spiritual shelter of the love of God.
I was lonely
and you left me alone
to pray for me.
You seem so holy;
so close to God.
But I'm still very hungry,
and lonely,
and cold.
So where have your prayers gone?
What have they done?
What does it profit a man
to page through his book of prayers
when the rest of the world
is crying for his help?[10]

During the 1960s and 1970s many Chicanas and Chicanos vented a palpable anger and estrangement they felt toward the church. They lashed out at the institution's historical relationship with Mexicans— some seeing it as blatantly racist, others as paternalistic and insensitive at best—and they accused the church leadership of perpetuating their inequality. These Chicanos and Chicanas wanted more than just spiritual comfort from the institutional church; they expected it to be their ally, not their oppressor through its inaction in social matters. Prayers without social action, many Chicano Catholics felt, left them "still very hungry, and lonely, and cold." For them the institution was out of step with their struggle for social change.[11]

Some parishioners expected their churches to work for social justice in the barrios. In the fall of 1970, parishioner Eduardo López sought his bishop's support on a divisive issue. López explained to Bishop John Morkovsky that the members of Our Lady of Sorrows Parish were polarized over whether "a church [should] bury its head in the sands of complacency or . . . try to aleviate [sic] the everyday problems of the community."[12] López described what he and other members thought their church should be and do:

> We feel that a church or a religion is not judged by the beautiful buildings in the parish or by the amount of money raised or the amount of money in the bank. We feel a church should be judged by the amount of faithful who participate in church activities. By the amount of faithful who are allowed to participate in its government. We feel that to preach of charity and brotherlly [sic] love is not sufficient . . . that it is imperative that we go out and actually put into practice those beautiful [C]hristian teachings; especially in the poverty level community in which we live.[13]

These parishioners urged their parish council to get involved in issues affecting their neighborhood. "We wanted to tell them how deeply we feel that our community has no recreational activities for our children, no parks, no boy scouts, no girl scouts, [that] our teenagers have no place to go," the parishioner explained. "We told them of the drug addiction problem amoung [sic] our school children; the necessity of more and better police protection." The group pleaded with their parish council for permission to use church facilities for activities "that would not only deal with the spiritual but also the material needs of our community." But those who controlled the parish council and day-to-day church activities disagreed completely with the petitioners' vision of the church, asserting that it "is a spiritual body that must not get involved in the civic affairs of the community."[14] Although this particular attempt to involve a church in social issues was staved off for the time being, the efforts of López and like-minded parishioners at Our Lady of Sorrows sent a strong message to the diocesan leadership. Chicana and Chicano laypeople increasingly stepped forward and pressed the Catholic hierarchy in Houston to join their quest for social justice.

THE CHALLENGE WITHIN: ACTIVIST PRIESTS AND NUNS

By the later 1960s the Galveston-Houston Diocese also felt pressured from within its own ranks to support Chicano social causes. The most outspoken local cleric was Father Patricio Flores, who had long ministered to Mexican Catholics in and around Houston before diocesan officials selected him in 1964 to head the local Bishop's Committee for the Spanish-Speaking.[15] Reverend Flores warned that there would be a mass exodus of Mexicans from the church unless it showed more concern and sensitivity toward them. "We, as a big body [the institutional church] are not doing enough," the priest admonished. His message was clear: Despite the fact that the great majority of Mexican Americans were Catholics, "the Church has not really been sympathetic or sensitive to us in our social, economic or educational struggle." On another occasion, the outspoken cleric decried that Mexican Americans "have been victims of . . . semi-slavery . . . , lived in conditions sometimes worse than animals in the zoo and yet the Church keeps silent."[16]

In October 1969, Father Flores was among fifty or so Chicano priests who met in San Antonio to form an organization called Padres Asociados para Derechos Religiosos, Educativos y Sociales (Priests Associated for Religious, Educational and Social Rights, or PADRES). These Chicano clerics vowed to take "the cry of our people" to the hierarchy of the church, and to involve the institution in *el movimiento*.

The formation of PADRES owed much to the pressures exerted by the Mexican American laity. Their awareness of the Chicano movement, the group's information officer told the press, was "one of the principal reasons the priests had come together."[17] Father Ralph Ruiz, the first national chairman of PADRES, explained that Mexican American Catholics resented the fact that "the Church is not Mexican American oriented." PADRES would "have to make the Church cognizant of the fact that we exist and that we wish no longer to be ignored or taken for granted," the cleric declared.[18]

A group of Chicana nuns soon joined the drive to gain the institution's attention and support. Two activist sisters, Gregoria Ortega and Gloria Gallardo, founded Las Hermanas (Sisters) in a conference held in Houston in April 1971. Gallardo and Ortega were elected president and vice-president, respectively, of the new organization dedicated to promoting social change, cultural pride, and Chicana leadership.[19] Similar to PADRES (which Gallardo also helped establish in Houston), Las Hermanas declared that they sought "revolutionary" changes within and outside of the church. Refusing to be constrained by the notion of separate sacred and secular spheres, Gallardo declared, "We agree that there should no longer be a dichotomy between religion and social aspects."[20] At the initial meeting of Las Hermanas, the conference program tantalized the participants with such questions as "Do Politics Turn You On?"; "How Do Sisters Promote Social Justice?"; and "What Is the Church's Role with La Raza?" At a national conference the sisters discussed how they might help raise the economic status of Mexicans and Mexican Americans in the United States and develop barrio leadership. In Houston they appeared at community center meetings to publicize their message and were active in barrio issues.[21]

Las Hermanas aimed to bring the Mexican community's needs "more forcibly" to the attention of the church hierarchy, declaring that they would not be ignored. If the hierarchy did not support Las Hermanas, a sister warned, it would "hear from us."[22] Clearly, these Chicana nuns had developed far beyond the "maternal feminism" that

Sister Gloria Gallardo, Chicana activist and co-founder of Las Hermanas, was one of the leaders of the Mexican American community's boycott of Houston's public schools in 1971. Courtesy Houston Metropolitan Research Center, Houston Public Library.

characterized precursors such as Sisters Benitia Vermeersch and Dolores Cárdenas in the early to mid-twentieth century. Sisters active in Las Hermanas understood themselves as political agents. In the early 1970s they understood, as activist sisters recently recognized, that being "political" did not necessarily "mean being a registered member of the Democratic or Republican party . . . [or] running for public office." Rather, it meant "to grasp one's elemental kinship with a 'people' . . . to discern, however inchoately, that one is *of* the people, which is to say that little in one's life is ever wholly private and that one's most personal spaces have import for the public weal." Las Hermanas paved the way for today's activist sisters who understand that "to be political is to incorporate into one's self-identification the fact of one's rootedness in a people and to make and act on choices that contribute to the welfare (good journeying) of that people."[23] They were important actors and companions in the Mexican Catholic pilgrimage in the Bayou City. The church clearly heard the rising chant of protest and the calls for support of the Chicano movement both from within and from outside its ranks, and began to respond.

THE INSTITUTIONAL RATIONALE

Church involvement in the Chicano movement in Houston took two forms. Institutionally, the Galveston-Houston Diocese played the role of supportive ally of *el movimiento*, albeit within cautiously prescribed limits. Significantly, however, the catalysts for social change were individual priests and nuns, many acting alone or through newly formed organizations like PADRES and Las Hermanas. Political activism by religious personnel dramatically departed from the traditional patterns of church activities in Houston's Mexican communities. While some individuals within the church had long worked to improve the material lives of Mexican Americans, they had never led efforts to mobilize their parishioners on a large scale for social and political change. Nor had the diocesan leadership ever supported a movement for social change to the extent that it did in the 1960s and 1970s. The unfolding of *el movimiento* did not wait for the church's blessing. Rather, Chicanas and Chicanos were in the vanguard of social change, and the church hierarchy followed with its support.

The institutional role the church would play began to take shape in the early 1960s. During all the masses conducted on Sunday, August 25, 1963, for instance, Houston Catholics heard an explanation of the church's official position on "the race question." Pastors were instructed to read a three-page pastoral letter to their parishioners from the bishops in the United States that eloquently declared that "[d]iscrimination based on the accidental fact of race or color, and as such injurious to human rights, . . . cannot be reconciled with the truth that God has created all men with equal rights and equal dignity." The following year, the Galveston-Houston Diocese instituted "Social Justice Sunday," an annual "day of prayer focused on human rights and human dignity." In the ensuing years, Bishop John Morkovsky established committees and sponsored forums to address racial unrest and social inequality in Houston. Although these developments arose in response to the black freedom struggle, the church also recognized "the disabilities visited upon other racial and national groups."[24] The policy set forth in the early 1960s in response to the black civil rights struggle thus had a direct bearing on the diocese's response to the Chicano movement.

The declarations of the U.S. bishops and the activities of Bishop Morkovsky in Houston outlined the stance of the institutional church on social change. Although church leaders eloquently denounced social oppression, they left it to those outside the institution to actually initiate changes; the role of the church was that of moral suasion in support of progressive change. "We should do our part," the U.S. bishops stated, "to see that voting, jobs, housing, education and public facilities are freely available to every American." In the same spirit, Bishop Morkovsky declared that minority grievances in Houston were moral issues and "definitely concerned" the church. But official church policy made it very clear that "civic action" in defense of human rights was primarily the concern of the laity and, particularly, of course, the prime duty of civil authorities.[25]

In Houston, the Bishop's Interracial Committee promoted interracial justice by working with Catholic lay organizations in the city. The committee "[did] not feel that it should . . . react toward civic problems or enter into the field of community relations" because it recognized "that there were already existing organizations which were formed to react to interracial injustice in the community." The role of the Interracial Committee was, therefore, "to use every persuasive means available to bring about interracial justice." "Necessary persuasion" then demanded "action on the part of the committee and its lay working group." This approach implied a strictly facilitatory role for the institutional church, such as providing forums, finding ways to air issues, and bringing together parties in conflict. Thus the U.S. bishops suggested that Catholics work for social justice "through various lay organizations . . . as well as with civic groups of every type," and that the places to discuss social issues should be the parish and diocesan societies, political gatherings, and civic and neighborhood associations.[26] This policy of guidance and facilitation recalled the position church personnel took in the past, when they encouraged the formation of parish-based mutual aid societies like the Liga de Protección Mexicana and other self-help organizations. It was within this framework that the Catholic Church in Houston responded to *el movimiento*. In the meantime, individual sisters and priests seized opportunities to spearhead social causes themselves, beginning with the key events of 1966.

INDIVIDUAL RESPONSES OF CLERGY AND NUNS

The Chicano movement in Texas was sparked by *La Marcha*, a dramatic protest march staged by striking farmworkers from the Rio Grande Valley of South Texas to the state capitol in Austin during the summer of 1966. The march originally aimed to publicize the strikers' demands by staging a pilgrimage from Rio Grande City to nearby San Juan Shrine Church, a place of special religious significance for Mexican American Catholics. However, it quickly assumed a broader purpose with larger ramifications; it became instead the "Minimum Wage March," a 490-mile trek to the capitol steps that marked a pivotal event for Texas Mexicans. Father Antonio Gonzales, the assistant pastor of Houston's Immaculate Heart of Mary Church, co-led the march, along with labor organizer Eugene Nelson, of the National Farm Workers Association, and Rev. James L. Novarro, the Mexican American pastor of Houston's Kashmere Baptist Temple.[27]

As the farmworkers' strike unfolded in Starr County in June 1966, Gonzales and Father Lawrence Peguero of Our Lady of St. John visited the area to assess the conditions surrounding the conflict. Father Gonzales reported that there was a dire shortage of basic necessities among farm laborers and that families were "going hungry."[28] The two priests collected food and clothing among their parishioners in Houston for the strikers, and delivered still more donations as the strike garnered support from Houston labor unions.[29] A Valley Workers Assistance

Committee was soon formed in Houston, and, with Father Gonzales as its chairman, the group held rallies at different parishes and coordinated the flow of support from Houston to the strikers.[30]

On July 4, seventy-five farmworkers began the pilgrimage to San Juan Shrine, accompanied by Father Gonzales and some forty supporters from Houston. Four days later in San Juan, the strikers and other state leaders decided to march to the state capital to demand that the Texas legislature include farmworkers in a new minimum wage law of $1.25 per hour. The purpose of the protest thus shifted from the demands of a fledgling farmworkers' union to the larger issue of economic justice for Mexican Americans. Gonzales agreed to remain with the farmworkers until Labor Day (when they planned to present their demands on the steps of the capitol), and thus he emerged as one of the leaders of the "march for justice."[31]

As the marchers inched their way toward the capital under the scorching Texas sun, tremendous demonstrations of support buoyed their spirits. Hundreds of Chicanos and Chicanas joined the caravan at different points, and thousands attended the rallies in the larger cities along the way. But five days before reaching their destination, Governor John Connally and an entourage of officials suddenly confronted the marchers on the highway. Father Gonzales and co-leader Reverend James Novarro warmly greeted the governor but were soon disappointed. Although he complimented the peaceful nature of the protest, the governor lectured the marchers on the possibility of violence if they continued. Furthermore, he bluntly told them he would not meet with them in Austin or call a special session of the legislature to consider a minimum wage bill. The governor's words stunned Father Gonzales like a slap to the face. "We feel that the lamentation and the sufferings of so many poor people in Texas were directed to the governor and . . . they were not heard," the dejected priest reported. Another marching cleric noted that Connally's demeanor was "a pat on the head, a great white father-type of thing" that angered the marchers. The governor's rebuff backfired and only strengthened the protesters' resolve. The march continued.[32]

Striking Texas farmworkers and supporters march to the state capital in summer 1966. Note woman (middle) carrying a picture of Our Lady of Guadalupe. Courtesy Houston Metropolitan Research Center, Houston Public Library.

Supporters listen to leaders of the Texas farmworkers' Minimum Wage March of 1966. Father Antonio Gonzales (holding crucifix) is flanked by co-leaders Rev. James Novarro to his right and Eugene Nelson on his left. Courtesy Migrant Farm Workers Organizing Movement Collection, University of Texas at Arlington Libraries.

The demonstrators finally reached the state capitol in Austin on September 5, 1966 (Labor Day), where they were greeted by some 10,000 clamoring supporters. Drama and poignancy reigned that afternoon. A former farmworker himself, Father Gonzales visibly moved the crowd when he introduced his parents, migrant workers for forty years. His mother had borne eighteen children and his father recently had been stricken with cancer, the priest revealed, and yet they still depended on back-breaking migrant work for a living, earning wages that were a "disgrace" to Texas and the nation. Gonzales then declared a "Vigil for Justice." He would bless two farmworkers—"two of the poorest of the poor"—and station them in front of the capitol, where they would remain until the state legislature passed a minimum wage law. Amid thunderous cheers that afternoon, César Chávez and other labor, political, and religious leaders demanded social justice for Mexican Americans, loudly echoing the success of the "march in the sun."[33]

Father Gonzales and Reverend Novarro moved quickly after the march to capitalize on their success. Gonzales met with Governor Connally three days after the rally and reported that the governor had agreed to cooperate. The same week the Valley Workers Assistance Committee met at Immaculate Heart of Mary Church in Houston and announced the next stage of the struggle for fair wages. Stating that their work had "just begun," Gonzales and Novarro outlined an ambitious agenda. First of all, they planned to organize thirty-six secondary assistance committees to help impoverished workers in South Texas. In addition, the clerics announced that before 1968 they hoped to organize Mexican and other workers in sixteen states throughout the Southwest and Midwest.[34]

But despite the success and momentum of *La Marcha*, its immediate goals were lost: the farmworkers' strike failed, and in their next session the state legislature failed to pass a minimum wage law. Yet in a more important sense the minimum wage march produced profound results and proved to be a pivotal historical moment. During and after the march Mexican Americans across the state showed an increased political awareness and a heightened ethnic consciousness that gave

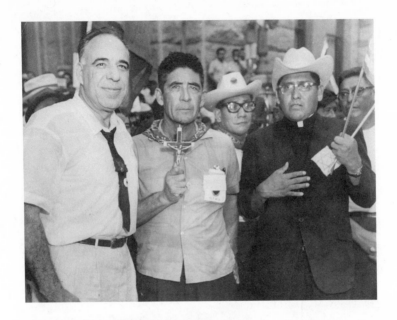

Above: Father Antonio Gonzales (right) with one of "the poorest of the poor" (farmworker holding crucifix) and Texas congressman Henry B. González at the culminating rally of *La Marcha* in 1966. Courtesy Houston Metropolitan Research Center, Houston Public Library.

Left: Chicano lay and clerical activists. Father Patricio Flores (left) meets with labor organizer César Chávez in Houston in 1969. Courtesy *Texas Catholic Herald*.

direction to their long-held resentments and energized the budding Chicano movement in Texas.[35] Strike organizer Eugene Nelson neatly summed up the new mood when he observed, "The Tejanos no longer tip their hats to the *gabachos* (Anglos)."[36] Mexican deference to the white establishment crumbled in the aftermath of the march. Early in *el movimiento*, clerical leadership fueled the fire of Chicano resistance to subordination.

In addition to Gonzales, another priest, Father Patricio Flores, earned a reputation as a leading social activist and advocate of Mexican Americans in Houston. He forcefully reminded his colleagues and the public, for example, not to let the plight of farmworkers be "swept under the rug."[37] Many of his fellow priests disapproved of Flores's support of César Chávez and the United Farm Workers' grape boycott, but the cleric stood firm. He encouraged the Houston grape boycott committee to meet at his parish, and at rallies and meetings he eloquently defended the strikers, whom he felt worked under "inhumane conditions."[38]

As director of the Committee for the Spanish-Speaking in Houston, Flores demanded greater material support from the diocese for programs for Mexican Americans. But many of Houston's Catholic churches refused to allow the use of their parish facilities to implement federal antipoverty programs, and even his own committee, Flores complained, lacked sufficient staffing and cooperation from the diocese.[39] Flores particularly decried the lack of educational opportunities for Mexican Americans and he tried to focus church attention on it. Like other social reformers, Flores realized that low educational achievement locked Mexican Americans out of good jobs and in turn created other serious problems. In addition, educational underachievement precluded the development of a significant body of homegrown priests and sisters to serve their own people.[40] Himself a high school dropout, Flores understandably placed frequent and heavy emphasis on education as a key to social progress. Father Flores also worked for change through his involvement in PADRES, though his activities in this regard were not in Houston proper. PADRES was not established in

Houston until about a year after its founding and after Flores departed to the episcopy in San Antonio.[41] Flores escalated his advocacy after his elevation to bishop and as PADRES national chairman in the early 1970s. The Houston PADRES, bereft of a powerful leader, never evolved into an activist organization comparable to its counterparts elsewhere in Texas and the Southwest.[42]

While priests like Gonzales and Flores agitated for Chicano rights, Chicana nuns also confronted the Catholic hierarchy and society with demands for social change. Sister Gloria Graciela Gallardo, for example, went to Houston in early 1970 after being active in community organizing in her native San Antonio. Recruited by Father Flores to help in his work in Houston, Gallardo became a coordinator for the Bishop's Committee for the Spanish-Speaking in the Galveston-Houston Diocese and immediately took up various Chicano causes.[43] In autumn of 1970 Houston public school officials subverted a court-ordered desegregation plan by integrating schools that were predominately black and Mexican American, leaving Anglo schools virtually unaffected. Outraged, community leaders formed the Mexican American Education Council (MAEC), headed by prominent lay activist Leonel Castillo. MAEC quickly organized a boycott of Houston's public schools and set up a number of *huelga* (strike) schools to tutor the boycotting students.[44] Sister Gallardo played an integral role in the lengthy campaign that followed. Reinterpreting the traditional role of a nun and her ascribed role as a Mexican American woman, she participated in protest rallies and spoke publicly for MAEC, for a time serving as its acting director.[45]

The activities of Father Gonzales, Las Hermanas, and PADRES were clearly a break from any social action undertaken in the past by church personnel on behalf of Mexicans in Houston. Unlike the individual efforts of nuns and priests in the past, these religious activists mobilized Mexican Americans on a large scale for social change. Acting on their own initiative, they sought social justice by engaging in political protest and by using church facilities and religious forums to help propel the Chicano movement. Individually and in concert, these religious men and women played an important part in moving the Catholic Church toward its role as an ally of *el movimiento*. Thus pressured, the Galveston-Houston Diocese responded with institutional programs that complemented the individual actions of religious personnel.

INSTITUTIONAL ACTIONS

One of the ways the Galveston-Houston Diocese responded to the Chicano movement was by continuing its charitable works among Mexican parishioners. During the 1960s and 1970s, the diocese expanded some of its long-standing social services to barrio residents, particularly health services of various kinds. For example, one of the oldest Catholic charitable institutions in Houston was the San José Clinic. Started in 1924 as the "Mexican Clinic," San José provided free medical services to all the poor but was begun specifically to stem the alarming mortality rates among Mexican children in El Segundo Barrio during the 1920s. In 1970, the diocese significantly expanded the clinic's services, doubling the size of the facility and adding new medical and social services. Appropriately, newly appointed Bishop Patricio Flores presided over the dedication ceremonies.[46] The diocese also sponsored many ad hoc projects at predominately Mexican American parishes, including nutrition programs, tutoring and cultural enrichment activities, and summer recreation programs. Coordinated with public agencies and community groups, these efforts channeled more money to "less fortunate" parishes through Bishop Morkovsky's personal initiatives and a greater emphasis on the Christian obligation of charity.[47]

Some of these efforts were ecumenical and cross-ethnic. In the post–Vatican II years, the Galveston-Houston Diocese joined with various white, brown, and black Protestant groups to attack poverty in Houston barrios. One such initiative was the Latin American Community (LAC) Project, sponsored originally by the United Church of Christ and Houston Metropolitan Ministries but soon designated a project of Volunteers in Service to America (VISTA). The LAC Project aimed to empower the "hard core poor" of Houston's East End, a predominately Mexican American section of the city. Between 1965 and 1972, LAC tried to organize residents "to attack the root causes of deprivation, alienation and discrimination." Its operations included educational and employment services, coordination of emergency relief and recreational services, as well as nonpartisan political activities. LAC's programs involved local church personnel and facilities, including some of the Catholic parishes in the targeted ship channel area, Guadalupe, Immaculate Heart, Blessed Sacrament, and St. Alphonsus.[48] These parishes and others provided volunteer workers, trustees, and material and moral support for LAC projects.[49]

By far the most ambitious ecumenical and interethnic venture was the building of Oxford Place, a $2.7 million interfaith housing project cosponsored with the Episcopal Church. The apartment complex in Houston's north side offered government-subsidized rent and a number of social services for its residents (the majority of whom were Mexican Americans and blacks), including English lessons, basic education, and child care. The diocese also helped to sponsor the Centro de la Raza community center, which had aims and activities similar to the LAC Project.[50]

Projects like Oxford Place and some of the social services provided by the diocese were in keeping with established practices yet different in an important respect. Church-sponsored social services had a long history, but the idea of developing self-help in the barrios was more recent. Hence, a project director insisted that a literacy program for Mexican Americans was "not looked upon as a handout, but rather as one that will train them to develop leadership within their own community."[51] Similarly, the LAC Project claimed it was vastly different from "traditional welfare agencies" in that it aimed to "help people break their dependency on 'charity,' paternalism and on the welfare system."[52] The church's support for self-help projects meshed with its policy of indirectly nurturing social change rather than leading frontal assaults on social problems. As evidenced by the religious and ethnic diversity of the Oxford Place staff, led by Baptist Reverend Lupe Maciel, it also reflected a shift from competition to more cooperation with local Protestants and other ethnic communities.

The Texas farmworkers' strike of 1966 illustrated the church's policy of indirectly supporting social change. When Father Antonio Gonzales became a co-leader of the Minimum Wage March in July 1966, the Galveston-Houston Diocese explicitly gave him its blessing. "I am happy to have you take leave of absence from Immaculate Heart of Mary until Labor Day," wrote Bishop Morkovsky to Gonzales, "to represent myself and this diocese in the efforts for just wages for the working man in the Valley Marchers' project." The prelate even authorized the priest to use the parish car and credit card in these activities. Gonzales's religious order, the Oblates, also approved his participation, thanking Bishop Morkovsky for his support of "the cause of the underdog."[53]

Soon after the beginning of the strikers' march, the Galveston-Houston Diocese and four other Texas dioceses publicly supported the farmworkers' right to unionize. Bishop Morkovsky gave his "blessing to the efforts of those who are directly concerned with the problems of justice and the dignity of man."[54] Less publicly, Anglo diocesan officials carried on behind-the-scenes activities to support the Chicano movement. For example, the diocese gave some direct financial and material support to the farmworkers' cause. Bishop Morkovsky donated money to help with Eugene Nelson's living expenses while he was in Houston in early 1966 organizing a grape boycott to support striking California farmworkers, and Father John McCarthy and other Houston priests guaranteed Nelson a small monthly income during his organizing efforts among the Rio Grande farmworkers. Father McCarthy also headed the diocesan Community Relations Council, which brought together the handful of religious and labor leaders in Houston, San Antonio, and Amarillo to form the Valley Workers Assistance Committee used to channel money and supplies to the strikers in South Texas. McCarthy gave important support to the farmworkers' cause even though he purposely kept a low profile because, as he explained, "I was always very sensitive about being an Anglo cleric who did not even speak Spanish."[55]

These actions by Catholic officials in Houston revealed their stance on social issues. Bishop Morkovsky was careful to emphasize the intermediary role of the church. The first step toward settling the Rio Grande Valley strike was "the voicing of problems by the people involved," Morkovsky explained, and "an appraisal of the problems by mutual trust and communication."[56] On the one hand, such wording reflected the hierarchy's belief that both labor and management had the right to organize to protect their interests, a position that had encyclical precedent. On the other hand, this position also expressed the diocesan leadership's desire to facilitate, rather than directly lead, efforts for social change. The diocese consistently reflected this position in the ensuing years. As the farmworkers' strike wore on in the Rio Grande Valley, the Community Relations Council under Father Emile Farge continued to send aid to the strikers from Houston parishes.[57] On another front, Bishop Morkovsky joined other Houston clerics who voiced support of the California farmworkers' grape strike. Again, Houston's highest Catholic cleric reiterated that church teachings and papal encyclicals emphasized the right of workers to organize collectively.[58] The limits of this policy became quite clear, however, when Father Gonzales overstepped the boundary set by the hierarchy for political activism among its clergy.

THE LIMITS OF CHURCH SUPPORT

Gonzales continued to be active in political circles in Houston after the Minimum Wage March. In an address to a PASO convention in August 1967, however, he incurred the wrath of the political establishment when he called for more Chicano militancy. "PASSO doesn't throw bricks and cause riots, but some Negroes have caused some riots, and I compliment them because they stirred up the cities," the priest reportedly declared. Gonzales could not condone violence but he understood the reasons why it occurred. Father Gonzales also called for Chicanos and blacks to form a powerful political coalition. He believed his work toward this goal would be supported by his superiors.[59] But he was mistaken.

Democrats and Republicans alike quickly attacked Gonzales in the press. Within a day of the press accounts, Bishop Morkovsky mildly reprimanded the activist priest and explained the church's position. The bishop stated that he did not intend to curb efforts to promote "Christian principles of justice and charity" but that it was "to the disadvantage of justice and charity for the Church or its leaders to engage in political controversy." The priest's role was to teach laypeople Christian principles, the bishop explained, and "it is up to the lay people to put these in practice in the political arena."[60] The prelate also rebuked Gonzales for attacking politicians "by name." The local press had reported that Gonzales had "swapped verbal blows" with the former Texas attorney general who had been in the entourage that tried to dissuade the farmworkers' march on the capital.[61] "Whether they needed this criticism of yours or not," the bishop lectured Gonzales, "it was not fitting nor is it going to help the promotion of Christian principles for the Church or its representatives to take up this kind of attack."[62]

Bishop Morkovsky offered a contemporary example to explain his reasoning. In Morkovsky's opinion, the Reverend Martin Luther King Jr. had "lost some of his effectiveness by publicly expressing himself against the government policies in Viet Nam." "His cause for peace may certainly be right," Morkovsky argued, "but possibly it was a mistake in leadership on his part to publicly adopt one side of a concrete application of principles in which there are sincere Christians on both sides." The bishop reiterated that Gonzales could be most effective by giving his people "spiritual guidance" and "in this way help to develop leadership among them." After this incident, Father Gonzales was ordered to clear his public appearances beforehand with his superior and the bishop's office.[63]

Gonzales's predicament illustrated that the Galveston-Houston Diocese would pursue social justice within clearly defined limits and protocol. The diocese supported the Chicano movement by allowing and even encouraging some activism among its clergy, such as Father Gonzales's involvement in the Minimum Wage March. It also took a public stand on certain principles, such as the right of workers to organize and strike, and it even gave some financial and material support to the striking farmworkers. But Father Gonzales's remarks at the PASO convention went beyond what the church leadership in Houston saw as its proper role in social issues, and, consequently, the priest's activities were reined in. After his controversial speech, Gonzales was reassigned to a rural outpost in East Texas, "to help him settle down to the regular parochial duties." In February 1968, the priest's superior wrote to Bishop Morkovsky that Gonzales now recognized "his limitations in the social action field and in the jungle world of politics."[64]

The church hierarchy wanted to remain above "the jungle world of politics," to seek out high-minded influential people upon whom to exert moral persuasion in order to effect social change. In 1966, the Catholic Community Relations Council (CCRC) moved into the chancery (the main headquarters building of the diocese) and was integrated into the diocesan structure, thereby gaining "more of a handle on power than before," according to Father Farge, the CCRC director.[65] Father Farge claimed he alone controlled social action activities in the diocese, that neither the bishop nor the diocesan chancellor had tried to "keep this office out of delicate or possible explosive affairs." Still, Farge admitted that "[t]he difficulty with this alliance is that one must act in a socially acceptable way."[66] Bishop Morkovsky sought "to get people influential in the establishment to meet together and to find that they have the same high ideals." This circle of people would then be "broadened step-by-step so that the establishment would be influenced."[67] Obviously, maverick political actions by individuals like Gonzales fitted neither the philosophy nor the strategy of institutional social action in the Galveston-Houston Diocese.

FAILING TO DELIVER?
THE HUELGA SCHOOLS AND OXFORD PLACE

During the Chicano boycott of Houston public schools, the Catholic Church failed its children, at least in the opinion of one community newspaper, *Papel Chicano*. The newspaper was bitterly disappointed by pastors who refused to allow religious facilities to be used as *huelga* schools. In 1971 the paper reported that one parish wanted $400 a month rent, plus cost of utilities, which prompted the editor to charge that the church put "exploitation" ahead of the education of children.[68] Another article assailed a pastor as "a racist gringo priest" who had "no right" ministering to Mexican Americans, and claimed that the majority of the Catholic schools had refused to support the school boycott.[69] Although several parishes and individual priests did help the boycott in different ways, backing for the *huelga* schools was uneven, and some Chicanas and Chicanos obviously resented the lukewarm support.[70]

Papel Chicano also considered the diocese's involvement in Oxford Place harmful to Chicano interests in Houston. About a year and a half after the opening of the housing project, the newspaper denounced it as "Another Well-Meaning Instant Slum." *Papel Chicano* argued that Oxford Place was an example of misguided thinking by churches "who were very rapidly destroying the very people [they] sought to help." The newspaper charged that the project was plagued by overwhelming problems: poor race relations between Chicanos and blacks in the complex and in the surrounding white neighborhood, high unemployment and student dropout rates, and lack of public transportation to outside areas with good jobs. *Papel Chicano* further argued that the church-related managing agency (and by association the Galveston-Houston Diocese) was to blame for not providing the necessary support to ensure success for Oxford Place residents.[71]

The project administration had failed to provide tutoring for students to succeed in the white schools of the area, the newspaper charged, and there had been no leadership training, no education in race relations, and no programs to organize the residents to protect themselves from the racism of the surrounding community. "To have done this kind of work would have caused the people in Oxford Place to stand up for themselves in the schools and community," the editorial asserted, "and neither of these two religious sects [Catholic and Episcopalian] want any whites to actually know these minorities are living in 'their' communities." Ultimately, the writer argued, the problem at Oxford Place was "the unwillingness of the churches to really break the poverty cycle."[72]

At least some Chicanos considered the diocese's indirect approach to social change a failure. Some of the more disaffected voices in the community charged that it was not only ineffective but also disingenuous—not only did it not work, but it was not really *supposed* to work, they implied. However, that conclusion reflected more the time's political hyperbole and personal estrangement some felt toward the church than it did an accurate understanding of the diocese's policies and actions toward Chicano social issues. Clearly, racial conflict between Chicanos and blacks had marred the early history of Oxford Place.[73] That is not to say, though, that the Catholic Church in Houston had conspired to thwart Chicano aspirations for equality. The church had indeed been supporting *el movimiento*, albeit through more conservative means than appealed, understandably, to more militant Chicanas and Chicanos.

LEGITIMATION OR CONTROL? THE *ENCUENTROS*

The activism of the late 1960s and early 1970s culminated in an institutional response by the hierarchy of the U.S. Catholic Church called an *encuentro*, a meeting to address problems. Father Edgard Beltrán, an activist priest from Latin America, suggested the idea in the fall of 1971 while visiting the Archdiocese of New York. The idea soon gained support in the U.S. hierarchy and thus the first Encuentro Hispano de Pastoral (Pastoral Congress for the Spanish-Speaking) became a reality in June 1972. For the first time, the Catholic Church in the United States provided a national forum for leaders of Spanish-speaking communities throughout the nation to air their grievances. Two hundred and fifty delegates met in Washington, D.C., to examine the place of the Spanish-speaking in the church. "It was a meeting," said Bishop Patricio Flores, "called by the [C]hurch not to praise, but to make a self-evaluation and correct what is wrong." What was "wrong," essentially, was that Mexican-origin and other Spanish-speaking peoples—25 percent of the U.S. Catholic population—had virtually no voice in the institutional church and were not adequately served by it, pastorally or socially. Adequate representation was the central theme of the national *encuentro*: "[I]f we are 25 per cent of the church, we should participate in 25 per cent of . . . the committees of the national church," Bishop Flores demanded.[74] The three-day meeting produced seventy-eight conclusions and demands calling for "greater participation of the Spanish-speaking in leadership and decision-making roles at all levels within the American church."[75]

The crescendo of Chicano demands struck a responsive chord within the U.S. Catholic Church. On the national level, for instance, the church responded by naming more Mexican American bishops.[76] Locally, Houston's Bishop Morkovsky opened the door to greater Mexican American participation and voice in the church. In the months after the national *encuentro*, similar regional and diocesan meetings took place, and the findings of these smaller forums and the motions of the national meeting were then presented to the U.S. bishops in November 1972 to serve as a basis for a comprehensive pastoral plan for Spanish-speaking Catholics.[77] Houston hosted the Southwest regional *encuentro* in October 1972. Prior to the meeting, in July, Bishop Morkovsky named Father John McGrath, the Oblate pastor of St. Patrick Parish, as interim coordinator of the ministry for the Spanish-speaking. In appointing an Anglo to this position, Bishop Morkovsky was not slighting Chicanos or their social activism. Morkovsky made clear to Father McGrath that his was a temporary position, one meant to start discussions about developing a "pastoral" plan; "the social part" of the ministry remained in the hands of such people as the well-known activist sister Gloria Gallardo and Father John McCarthy, who earlier had facilitated much of the diocese's support for the striking farmworkers. In addition, Bishop Morkovsky ordained more Mexican American laymen as permanent deacons in Houston's predominately Mexican parishes. In July 1972 the local Catholic newspaper featured three such appointees, Manuel Betancourt, Benigno Pardo, and Valeriano Leija, proudly posing in surplice and cassock. Coming in the wake of the national *encuentro*, Bishop Morkovsky's actions signaled his recognition that Chicanas and Chicanos comprised at least 25 percent of the diocese and, therefore, their needs were one of the hierarchy's "special areas of concern."[78]

As the year 1972 drew to a close, Mexican Catholics in Houston and throughout the nation entered a changed relationship with the institutional church, especially as it affected their struggle for social equality. The Galveston-Houston Diocese, like the national church leadership, had begun to respond systematically to pressures from Chicanas and Chicanos. It had put in place the *encuentro*, an institutional structure that could serve as a springboard for further changes. It now seemed possible to build a critical mass of homegrown clergy and sisters who could leverage their power in the struggle for social justice. Those who interpreted these developments optimistically saw in the *encuentros* legitimation of Chicano protest and concessions from the Catholic Church in the United States; some even called the *encuentro* process the "Magna Charta of Hispanic Catholics."[79]

But others were less optimistic. Had the church co-opted the Chicano movement, channeling protest into a controlled environment of its own creation? At the Houston regional *encuentro*, poet Lalo Delgado extemporaneously harangued attendees for seventy minutes about the long-standing neglect of Mexicans by the Catholic Church in the United States and the festering discord many Chicanas and Chicanos felt toward the institution. At the same meeting, national lay leader Pablo Sedillo hinted at co-optation, reminding listeners that similar meetings had taken place before, with nearly identical conclusions, yet nothing had changed. Sedillo voiced what many Mexican Catholics had experienced historically: "To date there has been a com-

The Diocese of Galveston-Houston responded to Mexican American pastoral needs in part by ordaining more permanent lay deacons. Here (left to right) Manuel Betancourt, Benigno Pardo, and Valeriano Leija pose outside St. Mary's Seminary in 1972. Courtesy *Texas Catholic Herald.*

mitment of words, lip service, but no real action."[80] Ultimately Sedillo offered a cautiously optimistic assessment of the *encuentros* and the juncture Mexican Catholics and the institutional church had reached. Although he did not see the *encuentros* as a panacea, Sedillo perceived a significantly altered relationship between Mexican Americans and the institution in 1972. "The Mexican Americans are not asking for pity, for handouts, for a box of groceries. We're beyond that traditional help," Sedillo explained. The Catholic Church in the United States was "beginning to respond" to the needs of Mexican Catholics, Sedillo stated, adding that he hoped the rhetoric would beget meaningful action.[81] The lay leader viewed the reactions of the church hierarchy in the 1960s and early 1970s in historical perspective and correctly recognized them for what they were, a response to activism by Chicanas and Chicanos.

In 1972 Mexican and Mexican American Catholics in Houston faced the future with mixed feelings. Some looked forward to brighter times; for others, the clouds of the past darkened the vista. But few would deny that their particular way of being Catholic and their relationship with the Catholic Church had been deeply entwined as they journeyed toward greater self-determination.

EPILOGUE

N ational and international developments in the last three decades
of the twentieth century brought significant changes to Houston
and the nation. In particular, three overlapping developments
underscore striking changes in the social and religious landscape
of the Bayou City that have affected ethno-Catholicism since the 1970s:
the dramatic increase in Latin American immigration, the waning of
liberal politics, and the rise of Latino evangelical Protestantism.

A new wave of Latin American immigration to the United States
began in the 1970s. Driven by economic crises in Mexico, civil wars and
political violence in Central and South America, and changes in U.S.
immigration laws that stimulated Latin American migration, this rising tide of migrants sharply increased and diversified the nation's Hispanic population in the last three decades of the twentieth century.[1] By
the year 2000, Latinos in the United States numbered some 35.3 million, accounting for 12.5 percent of the country's 281.4 million residents. The 20.6 million Mexican-origin people in the United States
comprised the largest group of Hispanics, or 58.5 percent of the total
Latino population. At 3.4 million, Puerto Ricans, who made up 9.6
percent of the Latino population, remained the second largest group,
while Central Americans (1.7 million) and South Americans (1.4 million) eclipsed the number of Cuban Americans (1.2 million).[2]

In Houston, the 1970s saw an increase of 88 percent in the city's
Hispanic residents (from 149,727 to 281,331), making them 17.6 percent
of the city's population by 1980. In the early 1980s, droves of Central
Americans began fleeing their war-torn homelands. Of this exodus
from Guatemala, Honduras, and especially El Salvador, only Los An-

geles received more immigrants than Houston. By 1990, Houston's Hispanics numbered 450,483 (or 27.6 percent) of the city's population of 1.6. million. Latino growth and diversity persisted, and by 2002 Houston was a city of about 2 million people whose roughly 772,000 Hispanic residents represented 39 percent of the city's population, while whites made up 29 percent and blacks 26 percent, reflecting a pattern evident in many urban areas throughout the country.[3]

As the number of Central and South Americans has grown in Houston, their distinct dialects, foods, and folkways have also become more evident alongside those of the Mexican community. Today, vendors of Salvadoran *pupusas* (a popular tacolike food) are as easily found as Mexican taco stands, and a variety of music pulsates in many city streets and homes—from Mexican *música norteña* to Caribbean salsa beats to Colombian *cumbias* and Latin rock—mirroring a changing Latino community. In today's shifting ethnic landscape, Houston's roughly 568,000 Mexicans and Mexican Americans remain a large numerical majority of the city's Hispanic population (73 percent). But they share the city with a significant number of other Latinos (some 205,000) who trace their roots to Central and South America or the Caribbean.[4] In light of this increased Hispanic diversity, what has happened to ethno-Catholicism in Houston and other places where "Spanish-speaking" historically has meant "Mexican"?

For one thing, it is abundantly clear that Mexican American ethno-Catholicism continues to flourish in Houston and the Southwest. In the decades since the 1970s, newspapers, popular literature, and scholarly studies consistently have reported a vibrant lived religion among Mexican American ethno-Catholics.[5] For example, Our Lady of Guadalupe still commands a fervent following. As parishioner Petra Guillén noted, the annual December 12 Guadalupe Feast Day celebrations at Our Lady of Guadalupe Church in Houston's Second Ward have grown "more and more" in recent years; in the year 2003 some 15,000 to 20,000 devotees jostled for seating space at the masses held in honor of *la Morenita*. "We keep the church open from the eleventh at night until the twelfth at midnight," Mrs. Guillén recounted. "It's open with mariachis all night through, *matachines* (Indian dancers) all night through . . . it's open regardless—whether it's raining or freezing, they are there."[6] Similarly, talk of a divine sign from *la Guadalupana* can electrify a community, sending legions of faithful to the site of a reported apparition, as has twice been the case in recent years in the Bayou City.[7] And, as they did in the past, Mexican and Mexican American Catholics in Houston and other cities in Texas and the Southwest continue to make pilgrimages, raise funds to maintain their parishes, and in other ways distinguish and celebrate their Mexican ethnoreligious identity and way of life.[8]

In addition, the 2000 census showed a significant Mexican presence outside of the Southwest, where ethno-Catholicism has begun to reveal its importance in new settings such as New York City and Washington, D.C., as well as in the Carolinas, Georgia, and other places in the Deep South. In Chicago's Mexican American community, which, like Houston's, dates back to the early twentieth century, religious traditions in barrio homes and streets echo those of Houston.[9] Similarly, in New York City—where the 2000 census reported a Mexican population of more than 186,000 (plus some 100,000 undocumented immigrants)—"[Mexican] music, dance and street festivals are often intertwined with religion, politics and the struggle for legal rights."[10] Thus significant growth and continuity have characterized the lived religion of Mexican and Mexican American ethno-Catholics since the 1970s. Especially as it structures family and community life and expresses ethnic identity, ethno-Catholicism continues to play an important role in helping immigrants and native-born alike meet the daily challenges of modern urban life.

In the process, of course, some aspects of ethno-Catholicism show signs of change and adaptation. According to Luís León, for example, Mexican American *curanderismo* (faith healing) in Los Angeles "has shifted from the familiar intimate space of home to the public space of commodity consumption." In today's urban capitalist culture, *curanderismo*, "once restricted to private homes and kinship networks," may be evolving into a tradition that is as concerned with folk healing as it is with profit-seeking, as entrepreneurs establish *botánicas* (stores) in which contracted *curanderas* (faith healers) perform their traditional healing services and "both religious and secular items are bought from a wholesale distributor, marked up, sectioned off into discrete display areas, tagged with prices, and sold for profit."[11] Clearly, as folklorist Ilana Harlow states, "You have to look at how people have to adapt their culture to survive in the new environment, but also how they adapt the new environment to support their culture."[12] Ethno-Catholicism historically has provided ways for Mexicans to adjust to U.S. society, and it continues to do so. Mexican and Mexican American Catholics still celebrate *quinceañeras*, kneel before *altarcitos*, and otherwise conserve age-old traditions that define them as a people and help them make sense of life, even as some aspects of those traditions undergo change. However altered and evolving, ethno-Catholicism still functions in much the same way it has historically, and it continues to be a foundational element of the Mexican American urban experience.

Ironically, however, despite the vitality of their ethno-Catholicism and even as their numbers have grown dramatically in the U.S. Catholic Church and society, in one sense, the influence of Mexican Americans within the structures of the church has lessened. In the post–civil rights era, Mexican American pastoral and social concerns have been diluted by the institutional church's approach that treats them as "Hispanic"—and increasingly as "multicultural"—issues rather than as Mexican American concerns per se. In the heyday of civil rights, Chicanas and Chicanos awakened the Catholic Church to their needs and gained concessions from it, including the naming of more Mexican American bishops, the creation of the Mexican American Cultural Center in San Antonio, and the elevation of the Division of the Spanish-speaking to Secretariat of Hispanic Affairs.[13]

However, the subsequent *encuentros* took place against the background of increasing U.S. Latino diversity and interethnic tensions as Mexican Americans and other Latinos competed for the church's resources.[14] By the time of the Second National Encuentro, held August 18–22, 1977, in Washington, D.C., the perception existed "that Mexican Americans, because of their numbers, were dominating the other Latino groups."[15] Consequently, church historian Moisés Sandoval has argued, the church hierarchy "appropriated the process of the *encuentro*" so that "it could no longer be considered part of the *movimiento* [the Chicano movement], coming from and controlled by the people."[16] Thus, despite eloquent rhetoric about resolving "to correct injustices both inside and outside the Church," the concrete actions that resulted from the Second Encuentro were clearly pastoral, not social.[17]

The church hierarchy's control of the *encuentro* process and the primacy of pastoral over social justice concerns became even clearer when Washington, D.C., hosted the Third National Encuentro during August 15–18, 1985.[18] By that time Latinos other than Mexican Americans had increasingly captured the attention of the church leadership. Moreover, the country's political climate had shifted dramatically by the 1980s—the backlash against minority demands that had started in the 1970s stood clearly ascendant and embodied in the neoconservative policies of the so-called Reagan Revolution. In an atmosphere in which minority demands for equality were increasingly labeled "reverse discrimination," the resolutions of the Third Encuentro focused not on social justice but at finally developing a national pastoral plan for Hispanics. But even that important achievement reflected a lack of urgency as the church presented the plan as "a beautiful new car without wheels," a mandate without funds to implement it.[19]

Encuentro 2000 took place July 6–9 in Los Angeles. With the title "Many Faces in God's House" and multiculturalism as its hallmark, this latest *encuentro* focused on "the richness of the Church's racial, ethnic and cultural diversity." Indeed, ethnic diversity reigned—mariachi music and Native American drumbeats opened the celebration as 5,000 Catholics representing 150 dioceses and 153 ethnic backgrounds streamed into the Los Angeles Convention Center. In the ensuing days the press highlighted the proceedings' sensory and ethnic richness—the sounds of conch shells announcing prayer services, the wail of Celtic bagpipes, the tempo of African American hymns, the aroma of Asian incense, and the striking colors of Korean, Polish, Filipino, Middle Eastern, and other dance spectacles.[20] Amid this rainbow of humanity, the U.S. bishops urged the participants to confront the challenges of Catholic diversity, and pastoral matters clearly occupied center stage, although some individuals made eloquent statements about social justice.[21]

The decline of PADRES as a Chicano activist organization also reflected the more conservative tenor of the post–civil rights era and paralleled the multiculturalist and pastoral trajectory of the post-1972 *encuentros*. Since its founding in 1969, PADRES had aggressively promoted Mexican American equality in both the church and the larger society. But after some gains in the 1970s, the organization became increasingly polarized into two camps, the pastoralists who focused on reforming the structures of the church and the liberationists who wanted to concentrate on changing oppressive societal structures. Despite liberationists' insistence that "the major thrust of PADRES should not be in trying to get more Hispanos appointed bishops but in political action on behalf of the poor," they found themselves increasingly isolated in the conservative climate of the 1980s as the organization adopted a more cooperative and conciliatory stance toward the church leadership.[22] Not surprisingly, the decline of liberal politics and the conservative papacy of John Paul II coincided with the death of PADRES. In 1990 the organization ceased to exist when it merged with two other groups made up mostly of foreign-born Spanish and Latin American clerics to form Asociación Nacional de Sacerdotes Hispanos (National Association of Hispanic Priests, or ANSH), an organization that, at least in some eyes, "seems intent on avoiding" social and political issues in favor of concerns that "directly affect the priests themselves."[23] The disappearance of PADRES into ANSH undoubtedly further submerged Mexican American social concerns in the U.S. Catholic Church.

Unlike PADRES, the activist sisters' organization, Las Hermanas, weathered repressive forces and changing times and has been able to continue its mission of championing Latina equality both within the church and in society at large.[24] Although the Chicano movement fueled both organizations and shaped their liberationist postures and goals, Las Hermanas made changes in its identity and mission that proved crucial to its survival. While PADRES remained exclusively an organization of Chicano priests, Las Hermanas started as a Chicana nuns' group but soon expanded its membership to include not only other Spanish-speaking sisters but also Catholic laywomen. Moreover, Las Hermanas evolved from a group that sought primarily their own empowerment as Chicana nuns within the Catholic Church to one that struggles for a broader goal, "the promotion of the Hispanic woman." These changes allowed the organization to find support outside the male-dominated institutional church and to become a larger and more diverse group that promoted Latina issues, not only within the Catholic Church, but also in a number of social and political arenas.[25] Las Hermanas has thus continued as a voice for Mexican Americans in the face of the changes of the last thirty years.

And potentially the most far-reaching of those changes has been the prolific increase of evangelical Protestantism among U.S. Latinos. What the New York Times called "a huge cultural transformation that is changing the face of religion in the United States" understandably has led to much hand-wringing among Catholic clergy and laity alike. It is "a sad thing," conceded Bishop Joseph A. Fiorenza of the Galveston-Houston Diocese, "a serious problem" that is difficult to combat given the lack of homegrown Hispanic priests. The marked increase of Latino evangelical Protestants is also quite evident to parishioners who resent their more frequent and aggressive proselytizing in Houston's Mexican American neighborhoods.[26] Estimates vary, but probably at least one million Hispanics had left the Catholic Church by the beginning of the twenty-first century. Whereas historically "Mexican American" and "Spanish-speaking" invariably meant "Catholic," today perhaps only 65 percent to 75 percent of U.S. Latinos are Catholics.[27] Only time will tell if the "great leakage" will continue.

However, there are at least two factors counteracting this trend, the continuing vitality of Mexican American ethno-Catholicism and the fact that the relationship between the church and Mexican Americans has been irrevocably altered. Clearly, the lived religion of Mexican American Catholics is flourishing and spreading throughout the United States, and, given Mexico's proximity and historical ties to the United States, this will continue. Equally important, Mexican American and Latino Catholics have created their own church within the larger U.S. Church. This is no small matter, as it has reversed the church's historical stance of strongly promoting assimilation at the expense of ethnic consciousness and traditions.[28] Consequently, today's Catholic leadership is more acutely aware than ever of the Mexican American presence, and church representatives point to initiatives such as a new Hispanic ministry plan and the appointment in the Galveston-Houston Diocese of Bishop James Anthony Tamayo, a native Tejano, as evidence of their increased responsiveness to Mexican American pastoral needs.[29]

But what of social justice? How have the political shifts to the right and the growth of evangelical Protestantism—a faith expression not known for its engagement in social issues—affected the quest for Latino social equality? At first glance, the developments of the last thirty years do not augur well for progress on the social and political front, particularly the fight to tame the beasts of poverty and racism that still tear at Latino communities. The prospects appear dim in a time when "American Catholics in general do not put much support behind efforts specifically designed to help members of minority groups" and, arguably, the institutional Catholic Church promotes a type of "multiculturalism without a transformative political agenda [that] can be just another form of accommodation to the larger social order."[30] Who will provide the leadership for an effective social ministry in the twenty-first century?

The struggle for Latino social equality will continue much as it has in the past, that is, largely through lay initiatives that enlist the support of the churches. Not all the organizations rooted in the activism of the 1960s and 1970s have disappeared, nor has their capacity to inspire new recruits totally faded. The fire of liberation theology still fuels the efforts of many Latino Catholic activists working in behalf of the most vulnerable of barrio residents; the San Antonio–based Communities Organized for Public Service (COPS) and the West Coast–based Pacific Institute for Community Organizing (PICO) are but two examples.[31] In Houston, Mexican American Catholics continue to seek social justice through The Metropolitan Organization (TMO). Since the late 1970s, several predominately Mexican parishes have successfully used "the not-so-gentle prodding" of this interdenominational grassroots organization to gain better city services, establish antidrug campaigns, and otherwise improve their low-income neighborhoods; more recently they have turned their attention to helping poor immigrants.[32] At St. Philip of Jesus Parish on Houston's East End, TMO leader Lillian Quiñones recently launched a crime-fighting effort in the surrounding El Dorado barrio, and at Our Lady of Guadalupe Parish, a twenty-five-year tradition of feisty community activism continues.[33]

In addition to these continuing efforts, there will be—indeed, there already are—new configurations in religious-based social activism among Mexican Americans and Latinos. One of the fruits of the rise of Latino evangelical Protestantism is, surprisingly, evidence of a budding social consciousness.[34] According to recent studies, Latino Pentecostals in particular have been developing a ministry to attack social ills that plague urban Mexican Americans and Puerto Ricans since at least the 1970s. The rise of the Religious Right, sociologists Ana María Díaz-Stevens and Anthony Stevens-Arroyo argue, "moved Latino Pentecostal and Evangelical congregations toward direct political engagement" as they sought to stem drug abuse and other problems that threatened their communities. Evidence of a Pentecostal social ministry is seen in the work of individuals and organizations from Los Angeles to Philadelphia and New York.[35] Pentecostal women have been especially active in these efforts, even to the point of transgressing the strict gender restrictions often imposed on them by their faith traditions.[36] Finally, in recent years Latino Pentecostalism has begun to elaborate the theological underpinnings for social action, as well as the organizational vehicles, such as the Alianza de Ministerios Evangélicos Nacionales

(National Alliance of Evangelical Ministries, or AMEN), to implement it—recalling the elaboration of liberation theology and the founding of PADRES and Las Hermanas in an earlier era.[37]

Still, Latinos sorely lack decision-making power in today's institutional Catholic Church, and they lack the political clout to significantly improve their status in society. This is ironic, given the profound changes they have brought to the American religious scene and the fact that they are the nation's largest minority. Anthropologist Peggy Levitt sums it up well: "Latinos enjoy greater power and autonomy with respect to their own church-based activities, but this has not translated into greater power within the institution as a whole or into a more prominent role in the political arena."[38]

The developments of the last thirty years, then, have had mixed effects on ethno-Catholicism in Houston and throughout the United States. On the one hand, Mexican Americans have left the church in large numbers and their influence as a separate ethnic group within the institution seems to have waned. Coupled with the unfolding sexual abuse scandals, these developments may not bode well for continued church funding for Mexican American ministries. On the other hand, the lived religion of the people remains vibrant, and although political conservatism threatens to undo hard-fought victories of the civil rights era, Mexican American aspirations and efforts for greater self-determination have hardly been stamped out. To understand the effects the developments of the last three decades have had on Mexican American ethno-Catholicism requires more in-depth study; these closing pages merely sketch a preliminary understanding. Conceivably, the last thirty years were a prelude to a great social transformation that will be played out in the twenty-first century. When the history of the "browning of America" is written, that story will have been significantly shaped by the concurrent rise of conservative politics and Latino Evangelicalism, as well as an enduring Mexican American ethno-Catholicism.

APPENDIX

TABLE A.1. Houston's White, Black, and
Mexican-Origin Populations, 1910–1970

Year	Total City Population	White (% of Total)	Black (% of Total)	Mexican-Origin (% of Total)
1910	78,800	52,832 (67.0%)	23,929 (30.4%)	2,000 (2.5%)
1920	138,276	98,268 (71.0%)	33,960 (24.6%)	6,000 (4.3%)
1930	292,352	214,687 (73.4%)	63,337 (21.7%)	15,000 (5.1%)
1940	384,514	277,959 (72.3%)	86,302 (22.4%)	20,000 (5.2%)
1950	596,163	430,503 (72.2%)	124,766 (20.9%)	40,000 (6.7%)
1960	938,219	645,547 (68.8%)	215,037 (22.9%)	75,000 (7.9%)
1970	1,232,802	754,889 (61.2%)	316,551 (25.7%)	150,000 (12.2%)

SOURCES: U.S. Bureau of the Census, *Census of the United States* (reports for 1910–70): for 1910: vol. 3, p. 852; 1920: vol. 3, p. 108; 1930: vol. 3, pt. 2, pp. 1015, 1023, and vol. 6, supplement, p. 97; 1940: vol. 2, pt. 6, pp. 1044, 1045, 1047; 1950: vol. 2, pt. 43, pp. 102, 350; 1960: Final Report PHC(1)-63, p. 15; and 1970: vol. 1, pt. 45, sec. 1, pp. 97, 118, 158. Estimates for the Mexican-origin population for each decennial year are from De León, *Ethnicity in the Sunbelt*, 7, 23, 55, 98, 147, and include other Hispanics. However, Houston's Spanish-speaking population historically has been overwhelmingly of Mexican origin (88 percent as late as 1980); see Shelton et al., *Houston*, 96. Total percentages may slightly exceed 100 percent because of rounding of numbers.

TABLE A.2. Mexican American Parish Societies,
1910s–1970s[a]

Society	Membership	Focus[b]	Active[c]
Adoración Nocturna	men	devotion to Jesus	OLG: 1928–30s, 1960s OLS: 1950s–60s OLJ: 1960s
Apostolado	adults	devotion to Jesus	OLG: 1919 OLS: 1950s
Banda Guadalupana	men	music for parish events	OLG: 1930s
Blessed Sacrament	adults	devotion to Jesus	OLG: 1919
Catholic Young Adults	young adults	socializing; religious study	OLG: 1960s Resurrection: 1970s
Catholic Youth Organization	teenagers	socializing; community service	St. Patrick: 1940s, 1960s OLS: 1950s IHM: 1960s OLG: 1960s St. Joseph: 1960s Resurrection: 1970s
Cursillo	men, later integrated	parish and civic activism	St. Stephen: 1960s–70s OLS: 1960s OLJ: 1960s St. Patrick: 1960s St. Alphonsus: 1960s
Guadalupanas	married women	devotion to Our Lady of Guadalupe	St. Patrick: 1940s, 1960s OLG: 1960s St. Stephen: 1960s–70s
Hijas de María	single women	devotion to Virgin Mary	OLG: 1917–30s St. Patrick: 1940s, 1960s OLS: 1950s–60s OLJ: 1960s
Hombres Católicos	men	parish service	St. Patrick: 1960s

Society	Membership	Focus[b]	Active[c]
Infant Jesus of Prague	young children	devotion to Jesus	OLG: 1930s St. Patrick: 1950s
Ladies' Council	women	governance	St. Alphonsus: 1960s
Legion of Mary	women	catechism instruction	OLS: 1950s St. Patrick: 1950s
Liga de Protección Mexicana	men women	social issues social issues	OLG: 1916 OLG: 1917
Men's Choir	men	religious music	OLG: 1960s
Men's Society	men	parish service	St. Patrick: 1960s
Mother's Club	mothers	parish service	St. Patrick: 1950s–60s
Movimiento Familiar Cristiano	married couples	religious study for family support	St. Patrick: 1960s
Sagrado Corazón	women	devotion to Jesus	OLG: 1920s–30s OLS: 1960s St. Patrick: 1940s, 1960s St. Stephen: 1960s
Santo Nombre	men	devotion to Jesus	OLS: 1950s–60s St. Stephen: 1960s–70s OLG: 1960s OLJ: 1960s St. Patrick: 1960s–70s
Socias / Sociedad del Altar	women	altar maintenance	OLG: 1960s St. Patrick: 1960s St. Stephen: 1960s–70s
Sociedad San José	boys	saint devotion	OLG: 1930s
Sociedad San Luis	boys	saint devotion	OLG: 1917

Society	Membership	Focus[b]	Active[c]
Sodality of Our Lady	adults	devotion to Virgin Mary	OLG: 1960s
St. Vincent de Paul	adults	charity	IHM: 1950s–70s St. Alphonsus: 1960s
Teresitas–St. Therese the Little Flower	younger girls	saint devotion	OLG: 1930s St. Patrick: 1940s OLS: 1950s–60s
Vasallos de Cristo Rey	men	Cristo Rey celebrations	St. Patrick: 1940s OLG: 1960s
Vela Perpétua	adults	devotion to Jesus	OLG: 1912 OLS: 1950s–60s St. John: 1960s
Youth Club	teenagers	socializing; service	St. Alphonsus: 1960s

SOURCES: Parish records, Archives of the Oblates of Mary Immaculate, San Antonio; Archives of the Congregation of Divine Providence, San Antonio; Archives of the Diocese of Galveston-Houston, Houston; and author's oral history interviews.

[a]Incomplete records preclude a full recovery of parish societies; this list is representative but not exhaustive. Some of the more popular societies (e.g., Guadalupanas, Hijas de María, Santo Nombre, Sagrado Corazón, etc.) likely had a continuous existence in most parishes.

[b]In addition to other activities, all societies raised money for the parish.

[c]Parish abbreviations: OLG = Our Lady of Guadalupe; OLS = Our Lady of Sorrows; OLJ = Our Lady of St. John; IHM = Immaculate Heart of Mary. Exact dates indicate founding.

TABLE A.3. Mexican American Parishes in Houston,
1910s–1970s

Parish	City Area / Barrio Name	Oblate Missionary Activity Since	Parish Type and Founding Date	Changes
Our Lady of Guadalupe	Second Ward El Segundo	1911	Mexican mission, 1912	Mexican national parish, 1921
Immaculate Heart of Mary	East End La Magnolia	ca. 1919	Mexican national parish, 1926	
St. Stephen	Near West Side	ca. 1930	Mexican national parish, 1932	dissolved, 1967 restored, 1973
Our Lady of Sorrows	Northeast El Crisol	ca. 1934	Mexican national parish, 1936	
St. Patrick	Fifth Ward El Quinto		Mexican national parish, 1941	reverted to territorial, 1968
Our Lady of St. John	Northeast La Bonita	1948	Mexican national parish, 1957	changed to territorial, 1964
St. Alphonsus Liguori	East End La Magnolia	ca. 1948	territorial parish, 1966	
St. Philip of Jesus	East End El Dorado	1958	territorial parish, 1967	
St. Raphael	Southwest	1950s	territorial mission, 1970	1972: 60% / 40% Mexican / Black
Immaculate Conception	East End La Magnolia		white territorial parish, 1911	mostly Mexican, ca. 1970

Parish	City Area / Barrio Name	Oblate Missionary Activity Since	Parish Type and Founding Date	Changes
Blessed Sacrament	East End		white territorial parish, 1908	mostly Mexican, ca. 1970
Holy Name	Near North Side El North Side		white territorial parish, 1919	mostly Mexican, ca. 1970
Resurrection	East End		white territorial parish, 1920	mostly Mexican, ca. 1970

SOURCES: Giles, *Changing Times*; documents, Archives of the Diocese of Galveston-Houston, Houston; and Archives of the Oblates of Mary Immaculate, San Antonio.

NOTES

ABBREVIATIONS

ABCM: American Board of Catholic Missions

ACDP: Archives of the Congregation of Divine Providence, San Antonio, Texas

ADGH: Archives of the Diocese of Galveston-Houston, Houston, Texas

ALUC: Archives of Loyola University of Chicago, Chicago, Illinois

AOMI: Archives of the Oblates of Mary Immaculate, San Antonio, Texas

CAT: Catholic Archives of Texas, Austin, Texas

FC: *Family Circular* (Sisters of Divine Providence newsletter)

HC: *Houston Chronicle*

HMRC: Houston Metropolitan Research Center, Houston, Texas

MI: *Mary Immaculate* (Oblates of Mary Immaculate magazine)

OLG *Boletín*: Our Lady of Guadalupe Parish *Boletín Parroquial*, Juan P. Rodríguez
    Family Collection, Houston Metropolitan Research Center, Houston, Texas

OLG *Codex*: *Codex Historicus* of Our Lady of Guadalupe Parish (Houston), Archives
    of the Oblates of Mary Immaculate, San Antonio, Texas

SP *Codex*: *Codex Historicus* of St. Patrick Parish (Houston), Archives of the Oblates of
    Mary Immaculate, San Antonio, Texas

TCH: *Texas Catholic Herald* (Galveston-Houston diocesan newspaper)

INTRODUCTION

1   David McLemore, "A Spirited Catholicism," *Gazette Telegraph*, May 18, 1996, E1,
    E3 (reprinted from the *Dallas Morning News*).

2   Frank Trejo, "Faithful Swarm to Mexican Shrine to Ask for Help," *Gazette
    Telegraph*, May 18, 1996, E1, E3 (reprinted from the *Dallas Morning News*).

3   Rev. Allan Figueroa Deck quoted in McLemore, "Spirited Catholicism," E3.

4   A note about terminology: I use the terms "Mexican" and "Mexican American"
    interchangeably since both native-born and immigrants make up Mexican

American communities. I also use "Texas Mexican" and "Tejano" and "Tejana" synonymously in reference to Mexican-origin residents of Texas. The euphemism "Spanish-speaking" (for "Mexican") is used in its 1940s–50s context, and "Chicana" and "Chicano" refer to politically militant Americans of Mexican descent during the 1960s and 1970s. Where the generic terms "Hispanic" and "Latino" appear, referring to any Spanish-speaking person of Latin American heritage in the United States, the discussion will place them in their proper post-1970s context. "Anglo," "Anglo American," and "Euro-American" have distinct historical meanings, but for stylistic convenience I use them interchangeably in reference to white Americans. Lastly, I use "Chicano" and "Mexican American" synonymously in discussing historiography.

5   Roberto S. Goizueta, "The Symbolic World of Mexican American Religion," in Matovina and Riebe-Estrella, eds., *Horizons of the Sacred*, 119–38, quote on 121.

6   Cogent discussions about "popular" religion include Davis, "From 'Popular Religion' to Religious Cultures," 321–41; Orsi, *Madonna of 115th Street*, xiii–xxiii; and Hall, ed., *Lived Religion in America*, vii–xiii. See also the excellent essay by theologian Orlando O. Espín, "Popular Catholicism," 308–59; the social science and theological essays in Stevens-Arroyo and Díaz-Stevens, eds., *Enduring Flame*; and Goizueta, *Caminemos con Jesús*, ch. 2.

7   On this point, see Wright, "If It's Official," and Bornstein, *Bianchi of 1399*, 3–7. See also Wright, "Popular and Official Religiosity," 1–175.

8   James C. Scott, *Weapons of the Weak*; Levine, *Black Culture*; Genovese, *Roll, Jordon, Roll*; Raboteau, *Slave Religion*; R. Laurence Moore, *Religious Outsiders*; Reed-Danahay, "Talking about Resistance"; Gibson, *Accommodation Without Assimilation*.

9   Reed-Danahay, "Talking about Resistance"; Gibson, *Accommodation without Assimilation*.

10 Timothy M. Matovina, "Hispanic Faith and Theology," *Theology Today* 54 (January 1998): 510.

11 For example, see Elizondo, *Galilean Journey*.

12 Matovina, *Tejano Religion and Ethnicity*.

13 Of the thirteen parishes in the Galveston-Houston Diocese that were predominately Mexican American by the early 1970s, six had been canonically established as Mexican national parishes between 1921 and 1957; the rest had become de facto Mexican parishes as the city's Mexican-origin populations expanded greatly in the decades after World War II. See Table A.3.

14 Grebler et al., *Mexican American People*, 456–57 (my emphasis).

15 For the revival of American religious history, see May, "Recovery of American Religious History"; Dolan, "New Religious History"; and Tentler, "On the Margins." On the growth of Chicano history, see Saragoza, "Significance of Recent Chicano-Related Historical Writing." On the dearth of studies about Latino religions, see Marty, "Editors' Bookshelf," 104, and Tentler, "On the Margins," 119–20.

16 Dolan and Hinojosa, eds., *Mexican Americans and the Catholic Church*; Matovina, *Tejano Religion and Ethnicity*.

17 Matovina and Poyo, eds., *¡Presente!*; Carroll, *Penitente Brotherhood*; Matovina and Riebe-Estrella, eds., *Horizons of the Sacred*.

18 A pioneering effort that begins to identify the basic contours of the history of Mexican American, Puerto Rican, and Cuban American Catholics is the *Notre Dame History of Hispanic Catholics in the U.S.*, 3 vols.: Dolan and Hinojosa, eds., *Mexican Americans and the Catholic Church*; Dolan and Vidal, eds., *Puerto Rican and Cuban Catholics in the U.S.*; and Dolan and Deck, eds., *Hispanic Catholic Culture in the U.S.* See also the collection of sociological and theological research contained in Stevens-Arroyo, ed., *Program for the Analysis of Religion among Latinos Series.* On the Southwest see Hinojosa, "Mexican American Faith Communities"; Sheridan, *Los Tucsonenses*; and Deutsch, *No Separate Refuge.* On the Midwest see Badillo, "Catholic Church and the Making of Mexican-American Parish Communities"; García and Cal, "*El Círculo de Obreros Católicos 'San José'*"; Crocker, "Gary Mexicans"; and Rogers, "Role of Our Lady of Guadalupe Parish."

19 Vidal, "Citizens Yet Strangers"; Lisandro Pérez, "Cuban Catholics."

20 Vidal, "Citizens Yet Strangers"; Díaz-Stevens, *Oxcart Catholicism*, 47–48.

21 Vidal, "Citizens Yet Strangers"; Díaz-Stevens, *Oxcart Catholicism*.

22 Dolan, *American Catholic Experience*, 204–8, 302–3; see also Shaw, *Catholic Parish as a Way-Station*, and Gleason, "Immigrant Assimilation."

23 Dolan, *American Catholic Experience*, 176–78, 372–76; Vidal, "Citizens Yet Strangers"; Díaz-Stevens, *Oxcart Catholicism*.

24 Lisandro Pérez, "Cuban Catholics." For more on the Cuban perspective, see Tweed, *Our Lady of the Exile*; McNally, *Catholicism in South Florida*; and McNally, *Catholic Parish Life on Florida's West Coast.*

25 Dolan and Deck, eds., *Hispanic Catholic Culture in the U.S.*, 454.

26 See Raboteau, "Black Church" and *Slave Religion*; Baer and Singer, *African-American Religion*; Lincoln and Mamiya, *Black Church*; and Sandoval, *On the Move*, 135–36.

27 In addition to the historiographical essays cited in note 6, see Stout, "Eth-

nicity"; Marty, "Ethnicity"; Butler, "Future of American Religious History"; and Hackett, "Sociology of Religion."

CHAPTER ONE

1 Juárez, *"La Iglesia Católica,"* 229–32, 239. For the English version, see Juárez, *"Los Padres Rancheristas."* The bishop defused the crisis with a false promise, proffered through the mayor, to bring back the sisters sometime.

2 De León, *Mexican Americans in Texas*, 7–8, 19–20.

3 Weber, *Mexican Frontier*, 160, 44–45, 70–73.

4 Ibid., 162–77; De León, *Mexican Americans in Texas*, 27–28.

5 Doyon, *Cavalry of Christ*; James T. Moore, *Through Fire and Flood*; Diekemper, "French Clergy," 34.

6 Juárez, *"La Iglesia Católica"*; Dolan, *American Catholic Experience*, 177. See also Tafolla, "Church in Texas."

7 De León, *Tejano Community*, ch. 6; see also Doyon, *Cavalry of Christ*, 133–35, and Tafolla, "Expansion of the Church," 231–32.

8 Espín, "Popular Catholicism." See also Deck, *Second Wave*, 55–56. Quote in Dolan, *American Catholic Experience*, 16–17.

9 Hinojosa, "Mexican American Faith Communities," 19–23; Juárez, *"La Iglesia Católica."* See also De León, *They Called Them Greasers*, 1–7.

10 De León, *Tejano Community*, 153.

11 Espín, "Popular Catholicism," 338; Josef J. Barton, "Land, Labor, and Community," 198–200. On socioreligious traditions and community-building in the Spanish and Mexican eras, see De la Teja, *San Antonio de Béxar*, 146–52, and Matovina, *Tejano Religion and Ethnicity*.

12 Diekemper, "French Clergy," 29–38; Juárez, *"La Iglesia Católica,"* 241–43.

13 Dolan, *American Catholic Experience*, 373, referring to Los Angeles, but the same held for Texas; see Juárez, *"La Iglesia Católica,"* 241–42.

14 Tafolla, "Expansion of the Church," 225–28; Juárez, *"La Iglesia Católica,"* 242–43; Sandoval, *On the Move*, 42–43; Dolan, *American Catholic Experience*, 372, 374.

15 McComb, *Houston*, 10–18; Shelton et al., *Houston*, 5.

16 Kreneck, *Del Pueblo*, 20–21; De León, *Ethnicity in the Sunbelt*, 4–5.

17 Stewart and De León, *Not Room Enough*, 29–31.

18 De León, *Ethnicity in the Sunbelt*, 6. By the late 1880s Mexicans represented only about 4 percent of the Texas population. See Jordan, "Century and a Half of Ethnic Change," 393–94.

19   Cardoso, *Mexican Emigration*, 1–17; Montejano, *Anglos and Mexicans*, 106–7; Coatsworth, *Growth Against Development*.

20   Montejano, *Anglos and Mexicans*, 91; Clark, "Mexican Labor," 476, 485; De León, *Ethnicity in the Sunbelt*, 6.

21   The census enumerated 476 "foreign-born whites" from Mexico living in Houston in 1910 (U.S. Bureau of the Census, *Thirteenth Census*, 852); De León, *Ethnicity in the Sunbelt*, 6–7.

22   McComb, *Houston*, 19–51, 92–123; Feagin, *Free Enterprise City*, 48–54; De León, *Ethnicity in the Sunbelt*, 7. A wealthy Mexican refugee passing through Houston in 1914 noted that Negroes "are being displaced by Mexican workers." See Torres, *Memorias de mi viaje*, 68.

23   *Houston Chronicle*, January 22, 1906, 8; August 10, 1908, 5; November 11, 1904, 22. For the recruitment of Mexican labor, see Cardoso, *Mexican Emigration*, 14, 27–29, 85–86, and Clark, "Mexican Labor," 475–76.

24   Shelton et al., *Houston*, 9–14; De León, *Ethnicity in the Sunbelt*, 7–8, 23; Cardoso, *Mexican Emigration*, 38–54, 71–95; Montejano, *Anglos and Mexicans*, 113–14; quote in Kreneck, *Del Pueblo*, 28.

25   Villagómez October 25, 1990, interview; Mary Catherine Villagómez, "Memorias de mi infancia," handwritten ms., Villagómez Family Collection, HMRC; Juan and Isidra Rodríguez interview. Lumber king John Henry Kirby transported Mexicans to his East Texas lumber mills not far from Houston. See Sitton and Conrad, *Nameless Towns*, 107. Ruth A. Allen documents a small Mexican presence in the East Texas lumber industry in the first decade of the twentieth century in *East Texas Lumber Workers*, 53, 55; see also Sitton and Conrad, *Nameless Towns*, 47, 60–61, 71, 76–77, 107–8, 122, 126, 189.

26   Guillén 1990 interview; Juan and Isidra Rodríguez interview; De León, *Ethnicity in the Sunbelt*, 9; Zamora, *World of the Mexican Worker*, 26.

27   Cary D. Wintz, "Blacks," in Von der Mehden, ed., *Ethnic Groups of Houston*, 20, table 1; U.S. Bureau of the Census, *Thirteenth Census*, 852; U.S. Bureau of the Census, *Fifteenth Census, 1930. Population*, 1023; Theodore G. Gish, "Germans," in Von der Mehden, ed., *Ethnic Groups of Houston*, 159–78. On other ethnic groups in Houston, see Von de Mehden, ed., *Ethnic Groups of Houston*; Maas, *Jews of Houston*; Collins, *Ethnic Identification*; and Beeth and Wintz, eds., *Black Dixie*.

28   De León, *Ethnicity in the Sunbelt*, 8–12, 14–16.

29   Montejano, *Anglos and Mexicans*, 179–96; Romo, "Responses to Mexican Immigration." For contemporary American and Mexican perspectives see, respec-

tively, Bogardus, *Mexican in the United States*, and Gamio, *Mexican Immigrant*, ch. 5.

30 Rosales, "Mexican Immigrant Experience," 60–61; De León, *Ethnicity in the Sunbelt*, 13–14, 18; Rosales, "Shifting Self Perceptions."

31 Zavala / Jiménez interview. The scorn for Mexicans who denied their heritage is seen in the poem *"Los abolillados,"* in *Gaceta Mexicana*, April 15, 1928, 12; see also Treviño, *"Prensa y Patria."*

32 Guillén 1990 interview; Grebler et al., *Mexican American People*, 83–84; Tilly, "Transplanted Networks."

33 Guillén 1990 interview; Villagómez October 25, 1990, interview. For *compadrazgo*, see Norma Williams, *Mexican American Family*, 23–27. Karen Mary Dávalos describes godparents as "members of the family . . . by sentiment" in her article *"La Quinceañera,"* 117–18. I have borrowed the phrase "ethic of mutuality" from Zamora, *World of the Mexican Worker*, which treats its implications for Texas Mexican labor and political struggles in the early twentieth century. For the continuing importance of *compadrazgo* see Beatriz Terrazas, "Godparents . . . and More," *Dallas Morning News*, July 11, 2001, C1–2.

34 De León, *Ethnicity in the Sunbelt*, 7, 9–10.

35 Villagómez October 25, 1990, interview; Sister Agnes Rita Rodríguez interview; Zavala / Jiménez interview; Guillén 1990 interview. The barring of Mexicans from "American" churches was commonplace; see Eph A. Kaye, "A Speedy Glimpse at Texas Oblate Work," *MI*, July 1925, 35; and Rev. G. Mongeau, "Mexicans in Our Midst," *MI*, December 1933, 345.

36 Villagómez October 25, 1990, interview; Guillén 1990 interview. Religious institutional development and worship patterns are discussed in subsequent chapters.

37 De León, *Ethnicity in the Sunbelt*, 8, 12; Beeth and Wintz, *Black Dixie*, 23, table 1; Maas, *Jews of Houston*, 34–41; Work Projects Administration, *Houston*, 189; Catholic Youth Organization Centennial Book Committee, *Centennial*, 75, 143, 150.

38 Armstrong, *Room to Grow*, 7; Bello interview; Pizaña, "Hispanic Baptists in Houston," 95.

39 "Houston's 'Little Mexico' Is a City Within a City," *Houston Chronicle*, November 9, 1930, 9.

40 Shelton et al., *Houston*, 9; McComb, *Houston*, 167–68; Rhinehart and Kreneck, " 'In the Shadow of Uncertainty,' " 23–24.

41 De León, *Ethnicity in the Sunbelt*, 45–51; McComb, *Houston*, 168.

42 Rhinehart and Kreneck, " 'In the Shadow of Uncertainty.' " For broader studies

of the repatriations, see Hoffman, *Unwanted Mexican Americans*, and Balderrama and Rodríguez, *Decade of Betrayal*.

43 Gonzales interview; De León, *Ethnicity in the Sunbelt*, 54–55.

44 On the elusive nature of the shift from "Mexican" to "Mexican American" ethnic consciousness, see Richard A. García, "Mexican American Mind"; George J. Sánchez, *Becoming Mexican American*; Rosales, "Shifting Self Perceptions"; and De León, *Ethnicity in the Sunbelt*, chs. 4–6.

45 De León, *Ethnicity in the Sunbelt*, ch. 5.

46 Weeks, "League of United Latin American Citizens"; Kreneck, "Letter from Chapultepec."

47 Shelton et al., *Houston*, 16–18; De León, *Ethnicity in the Sunbelt*, 90–91.

48 De León, *Ethnicity in the Sunbelt*, 91–92; San Miguel, *Let All of Them Take Heed*, 139–63; Zamora, "Failed Promise."

49 De León, *Ethnicity in the Sunbelt*, 98; Grebler et al., *Mexican American People*, 112–13.

50 De León, *Ethnicity in the Sunbelt*, 98–99. Father Frank Urbanovsky, a missionary who worked chiefly among rural Mexicans in the Galveston Diocese, witnessed the rural-to-urban shift. After retiring from his missions, Urbanovsky pastored Houston-area parishes where he met many people he had known previously in outlying rural communities. See Urbanovsky interview.

51 De León, *Ethnicity in the Sunbelt*, 99–104.

52 Ibid., 104–5; letter to Bishop Wendelin J. Nold, July 26, 1956, Our Lady of St. John File, ADGH; Father Nicholas [Tanaskovic] to Bishop Nold, March 12, 1952, Provincial Records, AOMI.

53 For overviews of the civil rights era, see Matusow, *Unraveling of America*, and Morgan, *Sixties Experience*.

54 Acuña, *Occupied America*.

55 Muñoz, *Youth, Identity, Power*; Ignacio M. García, *Chicanismo*.

56 Gómez-Quiñones, *Chicano Politics*, 101–53; Acuña, *Occupied America*, ch. 9; Muñoz, *Youth, Identity, Power*.

57 De León, *Ethnicity in the Sunbelt*, 147.

58 Goodman et al., *Mexican American Population*, 6–16; De León, *Ethnicity in the Sunbelt*, ch. 8; quote on 147.

59 De León, *Ethnicity in the Sunbelt*, 149–56; Goodman et al., *Mexican American Population*, 17–111, passim.

60 Shelton et al., *Houston*, 17–28; Feagin, *Free Enterprise City*, 73–96; Kaplan, "Houston."

61   De León, *Ethnicity in the Sunbelt*, 156–59; Feagin, *Free Enterprise City*, 76; Kaplan, "Houston," 203; Grebler et al., *Mexican American People*, 13–34.

62   Davidson, *Biracial Politics*, 36–40; Bullard, *Invisible Houston*, 115–17; Cecile E. Harrison and Alice K. Laine, "Operation Breadbasket in Houston, 1966–78," in Beeth and Wintz, eds., *Black Dixie*, 223–35.

63   De León, *Ethnicity in the Sunbelt*, chs. 9 and 10, esp. 172–74, 185–89, and 195–98; Ignacio M. García, *United We Win*, 178–80; San Miguel, *Brown, Not White*; "Dedicated to Community Action"; "To the Houston City Council and to [t]he Houston Independent School District Board," typed ms., Huelga Schools Coll., HMRC; Brackenridge and García-Treto, *Iglesia Presbiteriana*, 204.

Chapter Two

1   Villagómez November 9, 1990, interview.

2   Marcos Rodríguez to María Carmelita Rodríguez, June 16, 1941, Rodríguez Family Collection, HMRC.

3   See Orsi, *Madonna of 115th Street*, xix–xxiv, and Hall, ed., *Lived Religion in America*.

4   According to pious tradition, the Virgin Mary appeared to an Indian named Juan Diego outside Mexico City in 1531. On December 9 and again on December 10, the Virgin sent Juan Diego to the bishop with a request that a shrine be built in her honor. The prelate wanted proof of the apparitions, however, and so the Virgin told Juan Diego to return the next day, when she would provide a sign for the bishop. But Juan Diego's uncle became deathly ill and he did not meet the Virgin the next day as she asked. On the following day, December 12, Juan Diego went to bring a priest for his dying uncle. The Virgin again appeared to him, telling him she had made his uncle well and sending him yet again to the bishop, this time sending roses wrapped in Juan Diego's mantle as proof for the bishop. When Juan Diego revealed the roses, a portrait of the Virgin miraculously appeared imprinted on the mantle. Convinced, the bishop built Guadalupe's shrine on Tepeyac hill, the site of the apparitions. Because she appeared to one of their own, the Mexican masses made Guadalupe the center of their religious devotions and her Basilica in Mexico City became the most important pilgrimage site of her legions. Moreover, Guadalupe became "a central symbol of the Mexican nation and its destiny." See Harrington, "Mother of Death, Mother of Rebirth," 27. A classic interpretation of Guadalupe's importance is Wolf, "Virgin of Guadalupe." For an introduction into the vast literature, see the citations in the revisionist article by William B. Taylor, "Virgin of Guadalupe."

5   Francis A. Kilday, "Guadalupe is Mexico's REAL Heart!" *MI*, December 1952, 296–98, 320; Rev. G. Mongeau, "A Catholic People," *MI*, January 1934, 10–12; Joseph Buckley, "Mexicans Have a Queen," *MI*, January 1940, 12–13; see also Elizondo, *La Morenita* and *Guadalupe*.

6   Buckley, "Mexicans Have a Queen," 13.

7   Elizondo, *La Morenita*, 87–92; Meier, "María Insurgente"; Chandler, "Mexican-American Protest Movement," 237; *Papel Chicano*, December 12, 1970, 1; see also Rivera, "Power and Symbol."

8   OLG *Codex*, 2.

9   Guillén 1990 interview; Zavala / Jiménez interview; Gonzales interview; Villagómez November 9, 1990, interview.

10 SP *Codex*, 35.

11 Ibid.; Zavala / Jiménez interview; Gonzales interview; see also "Fiesta Guadalupana," *TCH*, December 10, 1976, and *TCH*, November 21, 1980, 6.

12 Guillén 1990 interview; Gonzales interview; Zavala / Jiménez interview; see also *Papel Chicano*, January 13, 1972, 12; and *El Sol*, November 17, 1972, 3.

13 "Two Masses Scheduled for Guadalupe," *TCH*, December 5, 1969, 1.

14 "Fiesta Guadalupana"; "Bishop Morkovsky Recalls," *TCH*, November 21, 1980, 6; Guillén telephone interview.

15 *Papel Chicano*, October 28, 1971, 11.

16 Ibid., January 13, 1972, 12.

17 Ibid.

18 Villagómez November 9, 1990, interview.

19 Ibid.; Zavala / Jiménez interview; Gonzales interview; Guillén 1990 interview. See also *TCH*, December 10, 1964; December 26, 1969, 1, 5; December 24, 1971, 2; and West, *Mexican-American Folklore*, 159–60, 177–78.

20 Villagómez November 9, 1990, interview; Zavala / Jiménez interview.

21 West, *Mexican-American Folklore*, 173–76; see also Waugh, *Silver Cradle*.

22 Guillén 1990 interview.

23 Orsi, *Madonna of 115th Street*, 178–80.

24 John Wheat, "*Los Pastores*: Continuity and Change in a Texas-Mexican Nativity Drama," *Journal of Texas Catholic History and Culture* 5 (1994): 51–52, explaining anthropologist Richard R. Flores's interpretation of the *pastorela* tradition. For the full and cogent analysis, see Flores, *Los Pastores*.

25 *HC*, March 22, 1970, 7–10 ("Texas Magazine"). Customarily the number of attendants is fourteen (one for each year of the girl's life), and the celebrant who is now fifteen years old (*quince años*) embodies the fifteenth birthday, or *quinceañera*.

26 See Dávalos, "*La Quinceañera*," esp. 107–13; *HC*, March 22, 1970, 7–10; *El Puerto*, October 1959, 9; and *El Sol*, March 22, 1968, 2.

27 *TCH*, October 2, 1970, 11; *HC*, March 22, 1970, 7–8; Villagómez November 9, 1990, interview.

28 *HC*, March 22, 1970, 10.

29 Ibid.

30 Ibid.

31 C. Gilbert Romero, *Hispanic Devotional Piety*, 72–73; Arturo Pérez, *Popular Catholicism*, 22–23.

32 On the contradictory nature of the tradition's meanings, see Dávalos, "*La Quinceañera*." Men and women alike recounted the ways male privilege dominated church life in Houston's parishes. See Zavala / Jiménez interview and Gonzales interview. For a perspective on Aztec and Spanish colonial influences vis-à-vis women and religion, see Mirandé and Enríquez, *La Chicana*, 37–38.

33 Flores and Novo-Pena, *Interiores*, 21.

34 Guillén 1990 interview; Gonzales interview; García 1990 interview; Zavala / Jiménez interview.

35 Flores and Novo-Pena, *Interiores*, 30; Zavala / Jiménez interview. Anthropologist Kay Turner ("Mexican-American Women's Home Altars," 25–27, 68–71 nn. 20–22) suggests that home altars have their origins in the syncretism of Mexican indigenous and pre-Christian European religious practices.

36 Zavala / Jiménez interview; García 1990 interview; Guillén 1990 interview.

37 Gonzales interview.

38 Turner, "Mexican-American Women's Home Altars," ch. 1; Flores and Novo-Pena, *Interiores*, 21.

39 Quoted in Flores and Novo-Pena, *Interiores*, 24, 30.

40 García 1990 interview; Guillén 1990 interview.

41 Quoted in Flores and Novo-Pena, *Interiores*, 29.

42 Guerra and Goodman, *Content Assessment of "El Sol,"* 18; Flores and Novo-Pena, *Interiores*, 29; Zavala / Jiménez interview; García 1990 interview; Guillén 1990 interview.

43 Guillén 1990 interview; Flores and Novo-Pena, *Interiores*, 27; Christian, *Local Religion*, 55–59.

44 See Rodríguez, *Our Lady of Guadalupe*, 45–46; Espín, "Popular Catholicism," 325–32; and Turner, "Mexican-American Women's Home Altars," 25–26. On the devotional revolution see Larkin, "Devotional Revolution," and Taves, *Household of Faith*.

45 Turner, "Mexican-American Women's Home Altars," 38–50, 395; Rodríguez, "Impact of Our Lady of Guadalupe," ch. 4; Flores and Novo-Pena, *Interiores*, 28–29. For the continuing importance of saint veneration in Texas and Mexico, see David McLemore, "A Spirited Catholicism," and Frank Trejo, "Faithful Swarm to Mexican Shrines to Ask for Help," both in *Colorado Springs Gazette Telegraph*, May 18, 1996, E1, E3; see also Simons and Morales, "Churches, Chapels, and Shrines," 116–18.

46 Cotera, "La Conferencia De Mujeres Por La Raza: Houston, Texas, 1971," in Alma M. García, ed., *Chicana Feminist Thought*, 155–57. See also Francisca Flores, "Conference of Mexican Women in Houston—*Un Remolino*," in ibid., 157–61.

47 "Jerarquía en el matrimonio," *TCH*, November 29, 1968, 12.

48 Turner, "Mexican-American Women's Home Altars," 38–50; Rodríguez, "Impact of Our Lady of Guadalupe," 86–91; Consuelo Nieto, "Chicanas and the Womens Rights Movement," *Civil Rights Digest* (Spring 1974), quoted in Maxine Baca Zinn, "Chicanas: Power and Control in the Domestic Sphere," *De Colores* 2, no. 3 (1976): 25. This portrait of empowered domesticity is based on recent social science research (not historical studies), but Mexican American women's influential position in the culture has long been a given in Chicano oral tradition. Mirandé and Enríquez (*La Chicana*, 116) state, "Anyone who has grown up in a Chicano family would scoff at the notion that the woman is weak, quiet, or submissive. If there is a persistent image of the woman in Chicano culture, it is that she is a strong and enduring figure." For a historical study, see Griswold del Castillo, *La Familia*. Studies since the 1970s amply contradict the stereotypical image of the Mexican American family as pathologically authoritarian and patriarchal; a good review essay is Zinn, "Chicano Family Research."

49 García 1990 interview.

50 Villagómez November 9, 1990, interview.

51 Flores and Novo-Pena, *Interiores*, 27.

52 Ibid., 25–26.

53 García 1990 interview; Gonzales interview; Guillén 1990 interview; Flores and Novo-Pena, *Interiores*; Rodríguez, "Impact of Our Lady of Guadalupe," 118–23; Turner, "Mexican-American Women's Home Altars."

54 Turner, "Mexican-American Women's Home Altars," 17–18.

55 Numerous studies and oral tradition suggest that Mexicans traditionally have attended church services less frequently than other Catholics (10–20 percent under the national average). See Stoddard, *Mexican Americans*, 90–91. See also Gamio, *Mexican Immigrant*, and Grebler et al., *Mexican American People*, 473–77.

For Mexican Americans confirming low affiliation, see Gonzales interview; Sister Mary Rachel Moreno to author, July 11, 1990; and "Need Adult Education," *TCH*, October 2, 1970.

56 In 1965–66, one study found that 58 percent of Mexican parishioners in San Antonio attended Sunday services weekly. See Grebler et al., *Mexican American People*, 472, table 19-1. In Houston between 1959 and 1966, about 54 percent of the estimated population of four parishes attended Sunday Mass weekly. See Reports on the Status Animarum, 1959–66, in Our Lady of Guadalupe, Our Lady of Sorrows, St. Patrick, and St. Alphonsus Files, ADGH. There is no definitive figure regarding church attendance; studies have shown considerable variation, and many are simply estimates.

57 Mrs. Janie Tijerina, quoted in Flores and Novo-Pena, *Interiores*, 29.

58 Gonzales interview.

59 Ibid.; Zavala / Jiménez interview; García 1990 interview.

60 García 1990 interview; Sister Agnes Rita Rodríguez interview.

61 Tarango, "Hispanic Woman."

62 *New Catholic Encyclopedia*, 1967 ed., s.v. "Vatican Council II," by R. F. Trisco; ibid., s.v. "Liturgical Participation," by P. Murray; Sister Mary Rachel Moreno to author, July 11, 1990; Zavala / Jiménez interview.

63 "Mexican Señoritas to Sing the Liturgy," clipping, *TCH*, October 25, 1968, in *TCH* Photograph Files, St. Patrick File, Chancery, ADGH.

64 Press release, March 23, 1970, PADRES Collection, CAT.

65 "Mariachi Masses," *TCH*, December 12, 1969, 6. For the importance of the innovation, see also *TCH*, October 3, 1969, 1; Rev. P. F. Flores to Bishop John Morkovsky, October 5, 1969, St. Stephen File, ADGH; and *Día de la Raza* flier, October 12, 1969, St. Stephen File, ADGH.

66 *La Gaceta Mexicana*, June 1, 1928, 11; see announcements in other issues in Mexican American Small Collections, Box 2, HMRC.

67 "Need Adult Education."

68 Turner, "Mexican-American Women's Home Altars," 44.

69 Norma Williams, *Mexican American Family*, 23–27; De la Teja, *San Antonio de Béxar*, 150–51. First quote in Flores and Novo-Pena, *Interiores*, 27; second quote in Turner, "Mexican-American Women's Home Altars," 44.

70 "Need Adult Education."

71 Villagómez telephone interview; see also Rev. Charles Serodes, "The Works and Wants of a Mexican Parish," *MI*, October 1922, 117; and "Dedication at Houston," *Southern Messenger*, September 19, 1912.

72 Rev. G. Mongeau, "The Mexicans," *MI*, March 1938, 79–80.

73 Ibid., 80; García 1990 interview.

74 Rev. Esteban de Anta, "Houston, Texas," *MI*, January 1930, 14.

75 The following summary of parish societies is a composite based on a review of documents spanning the twentieth century and oral history interviews. For specifics, see the SP *Codex* and OLG *Codex*, the annual Status Animarum reports, and *Mary Immaculate* magazine (1930s), all in AOMI; see also *Family Circular* (1930s–50s); *Texas Catholic Herald* (Houston, 1964–70); and Guillén 1990, García 1990, Villagómez, Zavala / Jiménez, and Gonzales interviews.

76 Tarango, "Hispanic Woman," 58.

77 "Greatest Religious Demonstration Ever Held," *Southern Messenger*, November 2, 1950, clipping in vertical file, CAT; see also the many references to Mexican American participation in Christ the King celebrations in *FC*, ACDP.

78 See De Anta, "Houston, Texas," 14; "Notes from Houston," *MI*, May 1931, 146; *HC*, September 9, 1934, clipping in Rodríguez Family Collection, HMRC; ABCM *Reports*, 1930, 1931, ALUC; OLG *Boletín*, July 1929, 8; Guillén 1990 interview; Zavala / Jiménez interview.

79 OLG *Boletín*, July 1929, 8.

80 SP *Codex*, 33, 35.

81 OLG *Boletín*, July 1929, 7.

82 *MI*, March 1959, 16–20; *FC*, December 1937, 61; *TCH*, November 27, 1970, 3; "Notes from Houston," 146–47.

83 See Orsi, *Madonna of 115th Street*, and Shaw, *Catholic Parish as a Way-Station*.

84 "Notes from Houston," 146–47.

85 See Reed-Danahay, "Talking about Resistance," and Gibson, *Accommodation Without Assimilation*.

86 The importance of fund-raising is treated in Chapter 5.

87 *FC*, March 1952, 116–17; Don LeBlanc, "Waterfront Priest," *MI*, March 1959, 16–20; Villagómez November 9, 1990, interview.

88 De León, *Tejano Community*, 194–96; Gamio, *Mexican Immigration*, 121–22. The tradition of self-help is more fully discussed in Chapter 6.

89 Zamora, *World of the Mexican Worker*, 80; OLG *Codex*, 8.

90 The *cursillo de cristiandad* originated in Spain in the late 1940s and was brought to the United States in 1957 by two Spanish air cadets temporarily stationed in Texas. Father Patricio Flores, a pioneer in the cursillo movement, held the first cursillo in the Galveston-Houston Diocese at the predominately Mexican Guardian Angel Parish in Pasadena, a Houston suburb. See "Just Six Years

Ago," *TCH*, October 29, 1964, 2; "Hundreds Attend," *TCH*, November 12, 1964, 2; and *New Catholic Encyclopedia*, 1967 ed., s.v. "Cursillo," by J. F. Byron.

91   Grebler et al., *Mexican American People*, 467; Hough, "Religion and Pluralism," 188–89.

92   Typescript, ca. 1963, Provincial Records, AOMI; Grebler et al., *Mexican American People*, 467.

93   St. Stephen Parish Bulletin, June 6, 1971; Status Animarum, 1966, St. Alphonsus File; and Status Animarum, 1964, Our Lady of Sorrows File, all in ADGH; *TCH*, November 5, 1964, 12; November 12, 1964, 12; December 10, 1964, 10; January 7, 1965, 8.

94   Grebler et al., *Mexican American People*, 467; Sandoval, *On the Move*, 84.

95   *TCH*, February 11, 1965, 10.

96   Tucson Convention Resolution, PADRES Collection, CAT.

97   Significantly, women began participating in cursillos in 1963, showing yet again that Mexican American women's agency and initiatives predated the feminism of the Chicano movement (*TCH*, October 29, 1964, 2).

98   The correspondence between religious orders and bishops of Galveston-Houston is filled with discussions about the importance of having Spanish-speaking personnel, especially priests, in Houston's Mexican parishes. Besides the Oblates, other priests in the diocese were beginning to enroll in classes to learn Spanish by the early 1970s. For references to Spanish-speaking priests, see Rev. A. Antoine to Bishop Christopher Byrne, January 21, 1919; Rev. E. Lecourtour to Byrne, August 9, 1922; Rev. Theodore Laboure to Byrne, September 27, 1931; Rev. Walter Arnold to Byrne, June 10, 1943; Rev. Nicholas Tanaskovic to Bishop Wendelin Nold, October 20, 1951; and Rev. John Hakey to Bishop John Morkovsky, January 31, 1967, all in Provincial Records, AOMI; and *TCH*, May 28, 1971, 2. For references to sisters, see Father Nicholas [Tanaskovic] to Bishop Nold, February 2, 1951, Provincial Records, AOMI; Father Augustine Pérez to Nold, February 25, 1953, Our Lady of Sorrows File, ADGH; Rev. M. Buckley to Bishop Morkovsky, June 24, 1966, St. Stephen File, ADGH; and Father A. Goossens to Buckley, July 4, 1966, St. Stephen File, ADGH. See also Villagómez interviews; Guillén 1990 interview; and García 1990 interview.

99   Zavala / Jiménez interview; Guillén 1990 interview.

100   Zavala / Jiménez interview; Guillén 1990 interview. Parishioners added, however, that priests tended to interact more with the people in the post–Vatican II years.

101   Gamio, *Mexican Immigrant*; Woods, *Mexican Ethnic Leadership*.

102 José M. Sánchez, *Anticlericalism*, 183.

103 See Meyer, *Cristero Rebellion*; James W. Wilkie, "The Meaning of the Cristero Religious War against the Mexican Revolution," *Journal of Church and State* (Spring 1966): 214–33; for a contemporary assessment, see Galarza, *Roman Catholic Church*.

104 Villagómez November 9, 1990, interview. The deference Mexicans showed toward priests and nuns is evident in a diary of Sister Delphine Marie [Mary Villagómez], 1944, photocopy in author's possession. See also F. Arturo Rosales, "Mexicans in Houston: The Struggle to Survive, 1908–1975," *Houston Review* 3, no. 2 (Summer 1981): 234; and Rosales, "Mexican Immigrant Experience," 62.

105 Zavala / Jiménez interview.

106 See Bishop W. J. Nold to Rev. Father Nicholas [Tanaskovic], October 19, 1955; Tanaskovic to Nold, October 22, 1955; and Nold to Tanaskovic, May 21, 1956, all in Provincial Records, AOMI; see also Gamio, *Mexican Immigrant*, 163. Grebler et al., *Mexican American People*, 451, reported "a fairly widespread impression" of Spanish priests as "authoritarian."

107 Bishop John L. Morkovsky to Rev. Clifford Blackburn, December 1, 1969, Provincial Records, AOMI.

108 See the explicit complaints against some clerics' undignified and insulting behavior in Resolution, June 10, 1971, St. Stephen File, ADGH.

109 For example, over 650 parishioners signed a petition protesting the transfer of the highly regarded Sister Benitia Vermeersch; see Toribio Cano, President of Diocesan Council, to Mother Superior M. Philothea, May 16, 1938, Our Lady of Guadalupe File, ACDP. Similarly, children from St. Patrick petitioned their bishop to keep a popular priest, Father Anthony Moreno; see Mr. Ralph R. Vásquez, basketball coach, to Bishop Wendelin Nold, March 23, 1963, and St. Patrick children's choir to Nold, March 23, 1963, both in Provincial Records, AOMI.

110 Mongeau, "Catholic People."

111 Ibid., 12.

112 Ibid., 11–12.

113 Ángela Pérez de Rodríguez to Carmelita and Margarita Rodríguez, August 14, 1939; Marcos Rodríguez to Carmelita Rodríguez, August 29, 1939; Ángela Pérez de Rodríguez to Carmelita Rodríguez, July 8, 1940; and Marcos Rodríguez to María Carmelita Rodríguez, June 16, 1941, all in Rodríguez Family Collection, HMRC.

114 Flores and Novo-Pena, *Interiores*, 29; García 1990 interview. See also Gonzales interview for similar comments about religion and identity.

115 Roberto Santoya, "Bronze and Proud—My People," *Papel Chicano*, February 20, 1971, 8.

116 Blas de León Poetry File, Mexican American Small Collections, Box 3, HMRC. I am thankful to Thomas H. Kreneck for this information.

117 *El Sol*, November 17, 1972, 3.

118 Folding commemorative, Rodríguez Family Collection, HMRC.

119 See the numerous holy cards and other religious mementos in the Rodríguez Family Collection and the Gómez Family Collection, HMRC; religious postcard and "Apadrinamiento" ribbon, Villagómez Family Collection, Box 1, folder 7, HMRC; quoted phrase from Tarango, "Hispanic Woman," 57.

120 See Orsi, *Madonna of 115th Street*, xvi–xvii; 55 and passim.

CHAPTER THREE

1 Rev. Esteban de Anta, "Missionary Work in the Diocese of Galveston," *Extension Magazine*, August 1913, 5, 22.

2 Montejano, *Anglos and Mexicans*, 179–96. For a Catholic perspective on the "problem" see Charles J. Taylor, "The Mexicans of Texas," *MI*, December 1915, 7–8; Taylor, "Our Mexican Problem in Texas," *MI*, June 1923, 30–32; and Rev. G. Mongeau, "The Mexicans—A Rural Problem of the Catholic Church in the Southwest," *MI*, March 1938, 78–81, 94–95.

3 "Among our Brethren Exiled from Mexico," *Extension Magazine*, January 1915, 9; Rev. Esteban de Anta, "A Missionary Tour among the Mexicans," *MI*, December 1924, 101. See also Most Reverend Arthur J. Drossaerts, "The Children of Guadalupe," *Extension Magazine*, October 1937, 4; and Mongeau, "Mexicans," 78.

4 *FC*, November 1912, 23.

5 Rev. L. O. Eckardt, "The Oblate Fathers in Texas," *MI*, June 1917, 137; Mongeau, "Mexicans," 78.

6 Taylor, "Our Mexican Problem," 32; ABCM *Reports*, 1929, 63, ALUC.

7 Rev. Esteban de Anta, "Houston, Texas," *MI*, January 1930, 14; Mongeau, "Mexicans," 78; Rev. Charles Serodes, "The Works and Wants of a Mexican Parish," *MI*, October 1922, 117.

8 "Honored by Churchmen," *HC*, April 30, 1935, 9.

9 Takaki, *Iron Cages*, 101, 106, 187, 113–17, 125–26, 223, 269, 275.

10 Foley, *White Scourge*, quote on 5. See also Foley, "Becoming Hispanic," 53–70.

11   Halter, *Between Race and Ethnicity*.

12   Orsi, "Religious Boundaries"; De León, *They Called Them Greasers*.

13   De León, *They Called Them Greasers*, 65–66, 69. See also De León, *Racial Frontiers*, 31–32.

14   Very Reverend H. A. Constantineau to Bishop Nicholas A. Gallagher, August 26, 1911, Provincial Records, AOMI; De Anta, "Missionary Work," 22.

15   De Anta, "Missionary Work," 22. The poverty in Mexican American communities is documented in Clark, "Mexican Labor in the United States," and Selden C. Menefee, *Mexican Migratory Workers of South Texas* (1941), reprinted in Cortés, ed., *Mexican Labor in the United States*; for Houston, see De León, *Ethnicity in the Sunbelt*, 11–12, 16–17, 26–27, 46–56.

16   Bishop Gallagher, form letter, January 9, 1912, File 8H59, AOMI (emphasis in original). Many of Houston's Mexicans, perhaps as many as 25 percent, worked for the numerous railroad lines. See De León, *Ethnicity in the Sunbelt*, 8–9.

17   Gallagher letter, January 9, 1912, File 8H59, AOMI.

18   Taylor, "Our Mexican Problem," 32; Rev. L. O. Eckardt, "Conditions in Our Missions," *MI*, December 1922, 176; Valdez, *History of the Missionary Catechists*, 5–6. See also De León, *Ethnicity in the Sunbelt*, 12. For Mexican immigrant labor in this period see Reisler, *By the Sweat of Their Brow*.

19   De Anta, "Missionary Work," 6; Bishop C. E. Byrne to Very Reverend A. C. Dusseau, June 11, 1938, Provincial Records, AOMI. See also Tafolla, "Expansion of the Church," 235.

20   Rev. G. Mongeau, "Mexicans in Our Midst," *MI*, December 1933, 327, 345; Zavala / Jiménez interview. See also Montejano, *Anglos and Mexicans*, 157–254, and De León, *Ethnicity in the Sunbelt*, 26–27.

21   Mongeau, "Mexicans in Our Midst," 345.

22   Drossaerts, "Children of Guadalupe," 4.

23   Villagómez October 25 and November 9, 1990, interviews; Zavala / Jiménez interview.

24   Sister Agnes Rita Rodríguez interview. See also Cárdenas interview and Guillén 1990 interview.

25   Drossaerts, "Children of Guadalupe," 4; "The Growing Need for Mission Schools," *Extension Magazine*, February 1916, 5; Mongeau, "Mexicans in Our Midst," 327. For the Mexican American struggle against segregated schools see San Miguel, *Let All of Them Take Heed*; for Houston's Mexican schools see De León, *Ethnicity in the Sunbelt*, 12–13, 27–28, 57–58.

26   Taylor, "Our Mexican Problem," 32; Eckardt, "Conditions in Our Missions," 176.

27 Gallagher letter, January 9, 1912, File 8H59, AOMI; De Anta, "Missionary Work," 5, 22.

28 Serodes, "Works and Wants," 117; Mongeau, "Mexicans," 78; Eph A. Kaye, "Texas Talking," *MI*, April 1924, 4–5.

29 De Anta, "Missionary Work," 5; Byrne to Dusseau, June 11, 1938, AOMI. Between 1937 and 1954, Father Frank Urbanovsky ministered to the Mexicans in isolated rural areas of central and southeast Texas in his trailer-chapel, *Espíritu Santo* Mission. He periodically visited Houston to attend to scattered pockets of Mexicans who had no churches of their own. Endearingly called Padre Panchito by parishioners—the nickname for Francisco, or Frank, is Pancho—Father Urbanovsky eventually settled in Houston and pastored Resurrection Parish, in the predominately Mexican American neighborhood of Denver Harbor, where he died in 1991. See Urbanovsky diary, CAT, and obituary, *TCH*, February 22, 1991, 10.

30 Kaye, "Texas Talking," 5; Mongeau, "Mexicans," 78.

31 Monsignor A. Verhagen to Archbishop Arthur J. Drossaerts, October 18, 1937, Religious Congregations of Women Collection, Hermanas Guadalupanas File, 1930–40, Archives of the Archdiocese of San Antonio, San Antonio, Texas.

32 Eckardt, "Conditions in Our Missions," 176; Serodes, "Works and Wants," 118; Mongeau, "Mexicans," 78.

33 Letter to Bishop Byrne, February 14, 1936, Provincial Records, AOMI (emphasis added). Father José A. Prieto wanted to erect a shrine for Texas Mexicans in Austin, Texas, modeled after the great Basilica of Our Lady of Guadalupe in Mexico City. See Rev. José A. Prieto to Rt. Rev. E. E. Byrne, February 12, 1936, Provincial Records, AOMI.

34 Eckardt, "Conditions in Our Missions," 176.

35 Serodes, "Works and Wants," 118.

36 De Anta, "Missionary Work," 22.

37 On the dominance of Irish Catholicism and the adjustment of various ethnic groups to that model, see Dolan, *American Catholic Experience*, 143–44, 294–303, and passim. On Irish prelates in the Galveston-Houston Diocese see Giles, *Changing Times*, 28–29, 56–59.

38 Mongeau, "Mexicans in Our Midst," 345. For a sampling of clerical and academic literature see Linna E. Bresette, *Mexicans in the United States*; Manuel, "Mexican Population of Texas," 29–51; Paul S. Taylor, *American-Mexican Frontier*; and Gamio, *Mexican Immigration*.

39 Anthropologist Franz Boas and sociologist Robert Park were instrumental in

shaping the discourse on race. See Gossett, *Race*, and Matthews, *Quest for an American Sociology*.

40 Mongeau, "Mexicans in Our Midst," 327; ABCM *Reports*, 1934–35, 75, ALUC.

41 ABCM *Reports*, 1939–40, 58, ALUC.

42 Bishop C. E. Byrne to Very Reverend Walter Arnold, November 29, 1940, Provincial Records, AOMI; Arnold to Byrne, March 22, 1942, Provincial Records, AOMI.

43 Bishop Wendelin J. Nold to Very Reverend Father Nicholas (J. Tanaskovic), October 19, 1955, Provincial Records, AOMI; Nold to Tanaskovic, May 21, 1956, Provincial Records, AOMI.

44 Simon, *Pastoral Spanish*, xviii, xxiii.

45 De León, *Ethnicity in the Sunbelt*, 99–104.

46 "Spanish Speaking Problems," *TC*, July 25, 1953, clipping, Nold File, Episcopal Collection, CAT.

47 Galarza, *Merchants of Labor*; Juan Ramón García, *Operation Wetback*.

48 Rev. Frank A. Kilday, "Second Class Citizens," *MI*, July–August 1953, 2–3; Kilday, "The New Challenge," *MI*, January–February 1956, 16; Sandoval, "Effects of World War II," 350–51. On the varied responses to the Bracero Program and Operation Wetback, see Mario T. García, *Mexican Americans* and *Memories of Chicano History*; and Gutiérrez, *Walls and Mirrors*.

49 See Perrett, *Days of Sadness*, 347–49; Karen Anderson, *Wartime Women*, 95–105; De León, *Ethnicity in the Sunbelt*, 105–10; and Mazón, *Zoot-Suit Riots*, 60–61.

50 SP *Codex*, 24. Longtime parishioners Juan and Isidra Rodríguez recalled that Mexican Americans used to refer to the Fifth Ward as the *Quinto Infierno* (the hellish Fifth or, literally, the fifth hell). See Juan and Isidra Rodríguez interview.

51 Bishop Byrne to Very Reverend Walter Arnold, June 11, 1943, Provincial Records, AOMI; Don LeBlanc, "Waterfront Priest," *MI*, March 1959, 16–20. For references to delinquency in other Mexican neighborhoods see Bishop W. J. Nold to Very Reverend Lawrence J. Seidel, July 9, 1957, and Seidel to Nold, August 13, 1957, Provincial Records, AOMI.

52 Cárdenas interview. On the issue of color sensitivity among Mexican-origin people see Gamio, *Mexican Immigration*, ch. 4; Paul S. Taylor, *American-Mexican Frontier*, passim; McWilliams, *North from Mexico*, ch. 2; and Forbes, "Race and Color."

53 SP *Codex*, April 19, 1945, 33; Rev. F. A. Santos to Rev. Mother Angelique, July 12, 1948, Our Lady of Guadalupe File, ACDP; Rev. Augustine Pérez to Bishop Wendelin J. Nold, November 21, 1955, Our Lady of Sorrows File, ADGH. See also Mother Angelique to Fr. A. Santos, September 11, 1951; letter from Sr. M. of

the Nativity, December 4, 1943; and Rev. F. A. Santos to Rev. Mother Angelique, May 4, 1948, all in Our Lady of Guadalupe File, ACDP.

54 Census, 1951, St. Patrick File, ADGH; Census, 1953, St. Stephen File, ADGH.

55 Simon, *Pastoral Spanish*, xv, xxi. Positive views of Mexican Catholicism existed before the World War II era, of course, but they did not appear as frequently. See Rev. G. Mongeau, "A Catholic People," *MI*, January 1934, 10–12; for more paternalistic views see Drossaerts, "Children of Guadalupe," 34, and *FC*, November 1935, 34–35.

56 Brother Joseph Buckley, "Mexicans Have a Queen," *MI*, January 1940, 12–13.

57 Kilday, "Second Class Citizens"; Kilday, "New Challenge"; Sandoval, "Effects of World War II," 350–51; Simon, *Pastoral Spanish*, xvi–xvii, xxii.

58 Kilday, "New Challenge," 16.

59 Bishop Byrne to Most Reverend Walter Arnold, June 16, 1943, Provincial Records, AOMI; National Catholic Welfare Conference, *Spanish Speaking*, 10; Dolan, *American Catholic Experience*, 377.

60 "Spanish Speaking Problems."

61 Dolan, *American Catholic Experience*, ch. 15.

62 Historian Jay P. Dolan has argued that civil rights agitation in the later twentieth century more profoundly affected changes in the Catholic Church than did the Second Vatican Council. See "Religion and Social Change."

63 Rev. M. Buckley to Bishop John L. Morkovsky, June 24, 1966, St. Stephen File, ADGH; Morkovsky to Very Reverend John A. Hakey, February 24, 1967, Provincial Records, AOMI. See also Morkovsky to Hakey, February 9, 1967, Provincial Records, AOMI.

64 Morkovsky to Hakey, September 19, 1966, Provincial Records, AOMI; Pastoral Letter from Bishop Morkovsky, January 8, 1965, Provincial Records, AOMI.

65 Letter to Bishop Morkovsky, August 28, 1970, Provincial Records, AOMI.

66 Letter to Monsignor Harris, April 27, 1964, St. Patrick File, ADGH; Father A. Goossens to Father Buckley, July 4, 1966, St. Stephen File, ADGH.

67 Hakey to Morkovsky, March 8, 1967, Provincial Records, AOMI; "Ecumenical Movement Offers Little to the Texas Mexicans," *TCH*, October 31, 1969, 5. See also Father Anselm Walker, "Texas Mexicans: Target for Marxist Revolution," *TCH*, October 24, 1969, 5, for similar perspective.

68 García 1990 interview; *El Sol*, October 31, 1969, 2; Father Emile J. Farge to Bishop Morkovsky, May 9, 1967, St. Stephen File, ADGH. See also Romano, "Charismatic Medicine," and Trotter and Chavira, *Curanderismo*.

69 Farge to Morkovsky, May 9, 1967, St. Stephen File, ADGH.

70 *Houston Post*, April 21, 1971, clipping in Joe Torres / Huelga Schools Collection, HMRC.

71 "Synopsis of Problems," January 30, 1971, St. Raphael File, ADGH.

72 *Papel Chicano*, June 1, 1972, 12.

73 Ibid.

74 San Miguel, *Brown, Not White*.

Chapter Four

1 OLG *Codex*, 2.

2 Copy of contract, October 5, 1911, Provincial Records, AOMI; Oblate Provincial H. A. Constantineau to Bishop N. A. Gallagher, August 26, 1911, Provincial Records, AOMI.

3 Memorandum from Bishop Gallagher, December 18, 1911, Provincial Records, AOMI; see also October 26, 1911, clipping in Oblata File, AOMI; and "Parish History of Our Lady of Guadalupe, Houston, Texas," Parish Collection, CAT.

4 Rev. Esteban de Anta, "Missionary Work in the Diocese of Galveston," *Extension Magazine*, August 1913, 5–6, 22; OLG *Codex*, 1.

5 Rev. Esteban de Anta, "Houston, Texas," *MI*, January 1930, 13.

6 "This Is Our Story," typewritten document (copy in French), Box 4, Mexican American Small Collections, HMRC; De Anta, "Missionary Work," 6.

7 De Anta, "Houston, Texas," 13; "House of Houston," *MI*, October 1929, 306; OLG *Boletín*, April 1928, 2; OLG *Codex*, 5.

8 "Dedication at Houston," *Southern Messenger*, September 19, 1912; OLG *Codex*, 4–5.

9 "Dedication at Houston."

10 Ibid.

11 Cardoso, *Mexican Emigration*, ch. 2; De León, *Ethnicity in the Sunbelt*, 23, 55.

12 OLG *Codex*, 10–12.

13 Sister M. Lucinda Schuler and Sister M. Rachel Moreno, comps., "History of Our Lady of Guadalupe School," ACDP; Chancery office questionnaire, ca. 1929, Parish Collection, CAT.

14 Rev. E. de Anta to Mother Superior Florence, May 1, 1923, and Faculty list, both in Our Lady of Guadalupe File, ACDP.

15 Giles, *Changing Times*, 123; "House of Houston," 306. Our Lady of Guadalupe became the first of several "national" parishes exclusively for Spanish-speaking parishioners in Houston.

16 OLG *Codex*, 18, 28; "House of Houston," 306–7; see also Valdez, *History of the Missionary Catechists*, 12.

17 OLG *Codex*, 29.

18 Letter to Father Tonson, November 30, 1921, Provincial Records, AOMI; Bishop C. E. Byrne to Father Lecourtour, August 12, 1922, Provincial Records, AOMI.

19 Chancery office questionnaire, Immaculate Heart of Mary (Houston) File, Parish Collection, CAT; Villagómez October 25, 1990, interview; letters to Bishop Byrne, January 9, 1924, August 9, 1922, August 22, 1922; and letter to J. M. Kirwin, August 22, 1925, all in Provincial Records, AOMI.

20 Giles, *Changing Times*, 138–39; "House of Houston," 307; ABCM *Reports*, 1930, 57, ALUC.

21 Dolan, *American Catholic Experience*, 377.

22 "The Catechists in Houston," *MI*, May 1933, 151–52; "Silver Jubilee," *MI*, June 1935, 181; "Modern Lay Apostles," *MI*, September 1935, 233–34; ABCM *Reports*, 1931–35, ALUC; *FC*, March 1933, 128. The Catechists received papal approval and became an adjunct of the Sisters of Divine Providence in 1946; see Valdez, *History of the Missionary Catechists*.

23 "Missionary Catechist: Sister Benitia," *TCH*, January 11, 1980, clipping in files of ACDP; Guillén interview.

24 "New Parochial School," *HC*, October 9, 1932, 9; "The Poor Will Have the Gospel Preached to Them," *MI*, January 1938, 16–17; Giles, *Changing Times*, 101.

25 Giles, *Changing Times*, 149; "Poor Will Have the Gospel," 16–17; Bob Giles, "Our Lady of Sorrows Parish," *TCH*, September 14, 1984, 28. The barrio of *El Crisol* took its name from the constant odor of creosote, a weathering agent used on railroad ties that was manufactured in a plant in the neighborhood; see Urbanovsky diary, May 1947, 306, CAT.

26 "Starving Kids Get Lift," *HC*, September 11, 1932, 14; ibid., October 9, 1932, 9.

27 "Their History," *HC*, January 16, 1950, 15; Giles, *Changing Times*, 98–99; handwritten ms., ca. 1950, St. Patrick School File, ACDP; last quote in SP *Codex*, 20.

28 Bishop C. E. Byrne to Rev. Walter Arnold, January 30, 1941, Provincial Records, AOMI; "Old Parish to Be Taken Over by Oblates," *HC*, February 6, 1941, 17; Mother M. Philothea to Rev. L. A. Ferrero, May 15, 1941, and Contract, September 28, 1943, both in SP *Codex*; Giles, *Changing Times*, 99.

29 SP *Codex*, 1943, 25–26.

30 Giles, *Changing Times*, 61.

31 "Poor Will Have the Gospel," 17; Urbanovsky diary, April 28–May 11, 1947, 304;

May 21–June 6, 1948, 121; October 1948, 166, CAT; "Bishop Blesses New Statue," *TCH* clipping, Our Lady of St. John (Houston) File, Parish Collection, CAT.

32 "Capsule History of Our Lady of St. John Church," and "Pertinent Data for Parish History," both in St. John File, ADGH; Urbanovsky diary, April 28–May 12, 1947, 304, CAT.

33 Rev. C. Conaty to bishop of Galveston Diocese, June 6, 1949, and Decree of Erection, June 28, 1957, both in Our Lady of St. John File, ADGH; Giles, *Changing Times*, 166.

34 Giles, *Changing Times*, 211; *TCH*, April 28, 1967.

35 See "St. Raphael Celebrates," commemorative in St. Raphael File, ADGH; Giles, *Changing Times*, 194–95; "Emphasizes Dignity," *TCH*, 11; and parish history form, St. Raphael File, ADGH.

36 Giles, *Changing Times*, 205; Urbanovsky diary, May 10–21 [ca. 1948], 118, CAT; Fr. Sylvester O'Toole to Bishop Morkovsky, April 26, 1966; and "St. Aphonsus Parish," *TCH*, June 17, 1966, clipping, both in St. Alphonsus File, ADGH.

37 Giles, *Changing Times*, 99; See also Feagin, *Free Enterprise City*, 257.

38 *FC*, April 1956, 146; Giles, *Changing Times*, 99; Father A. Goossens to bishop of Galveston Diocese, June 6, 1966, St. Patrick File, ADGH. See also letter to Monsignor Harris, April 27, 1964, St. Patrick File, ADGH; *TCH*, December 10, 1964, 10; and *TCH*, September 29, 1967, clipping in Parish Collection, CAT.

39 Giles, *Changing Times*, 99.

40 Ibid., 139, 149–50; De León, *Ethnicity in the Sunbelt*, 150–52.

41 Letter to bishop of Galveston-Houston Diocese, June 29, 1971, Immaculate Conception File, ADGH; De León, *Ethnicity in the Sunbelt*, 150.

42 Bishop John L. Morkovsky to Rev. John A. Hakey, March 13, 1967, Provincial Records, AOMI; Hakey to Rev. James Meagher, September 5, 1968, Immaculate Conception File, ADGH; see also Morkovsky to Meagher, March 19, 1969, Immaculate Conception File, ADGH.

43 Giles, *Changing Times*, 114, 133; "Houston Parish," *TCH*, April 24, 1970, 1; letter to Bishop John Morkovsky, August 28, 1970, Provincial Records, AOMI; quote in Zavala / Jiménez interview.

44 Traditionally, parishes have been defined by geographical boundaries, with all Catholics living within a specified area (e.g., a neighborhood) being members of that "territorial" parish. Membership in so-called national parishes (also known as "nationality" and "foreign-language" parishes) is based on language rather than place of residence. The Catholic Church historically has preferred

territorial parishes but has used nationality parishes to accommodate immigrants. See Harte, "Racial and National Parishes."

45   Olson, *Catholic Immigrants*, 101–67.

46   Dolan, *American Catholic Experience*, 295–303, 363–65; Shaw, *Catholic Parish as a Way-Station*.

47   Letter to Bishop Christopher Byrne, July 19, 1921, Provincial Records, AOMI.

48   Archbishop John J. Cantwell quoted in Sánchez, *Becoming Mexican American*, 159. See also Mario T. García, *Desert Immigrants*, 212–19; Richard A. García, *Rise of the Mexican American Middle Class*, 196–98; De León, *Ethnicity in the Sunbelt*, 28; Romo, *East Los Angeles*, 145–48; and George J. Sánchez, *Becoming Mexican American*, 156–61.

49   Valdez, *History of the Missionary Catechists*, 14. For a balanced discussion of the double-edged nature of Americanization and national parishes among Mexican Catholics in California, see Burns, "Mexican Catholic Community," 148–69.

50   In 1940 there were fifty-seven Mexican national parishes in the United States; eight years later there were forty-four; and by 1960 there were only twenty-two. See Olson, *Catholic Immigrants*, 147, 122, and Harte, "Racial and National Parishes," 162.

51   "Spanish Speaking Problems," *TC*, July 25, 1953, clipping in Nold File, Episcopal Collection, CAT.

52   "Memorandum of Visit of Provincial with Bishop of Galveston," ca. April 30, 1955, Provincial Records, AOMI.

53   Sylvester R. O'Toole to Bishop John Morkovsky, April 26, 1966, St. Alphonsus File, ADGH; "St. Alphonsus Parish," *TCH*, June 17, 1966, clipping in St. Alphonsus File, ADGH; Rev. Lawrence Peguero to Morkovsky, July 12, 1971, Our Lady of St. John File, ADGH.

54   O'Toole to Morkovsky, April 26, 1966; Peguero to Morkovsky, July 12, 1971.

55   Rev. B. A. Waggner to Miss Rickert, Chancery office, December 28, 1971, Our Lady of Guadalupe File, ADGH.

56   Bishop John L. Morkovsky to Oblate Provincial Reverend John A. Hakey, February 9, 1967, and Morkovsky to Hakey, February 24, 1967, both in Provincial Records, AOMI.

57   Morkovsky to Hakey, February 24, 1967, and Rev. M. [Maurice] Buckley to Morkovsky, August 2, 1967, both in St. Philip File, ADGH.

58   Rev. Buckley to Bishop Morkovsky, June 24, 1966, St. Stephen File, ADGH.

59   Bishop John L. Morkovsky to Rev. John A. Hakey, February 9, 1967, Provincial

Records, AOMI; Rev. M. Buckley to Bishop Morkovsky, June 24, 1966, St. Stephen File, ADGH. The story of the St. Stephen revolt is told below.

60 R. Laurence Moore, *Religious Outsiders*, 100.

61 "Spanish Speaking Problems."

62 Starting in the 1960s the Galveston-Houston Diocese began redesignating some of the city's national parishes as territorial ones. Hence Our Lady of St. John, which had been designated a national parish in 1957, was changed to territorial status in 1964; St. Patrick ceased to be a nationality parish in 1968, and plans to convert Immaculate Heart of Mary from a national to a territorial parish were discussed in 1969. See *TCH*, January 7, 1965, 8; Decree of Erection, June 18, 1968, St. Patrick File, ADGH; and Bishop Morkovsky to Rev. James Meagher, March 19, 1969, Immaculate Conception File, ADGH. On the knotty problem of changing the status of the Mexican parishes, see Father Nicholas [Tanaskovic] to Bishop Nold, June 5, 1952, Provincial Records, AOMI; and Oblate Provincial's letter to Bishop Nold, July 26, 1956, Our Lady of St. John File, ADGH.

Chapter Five

1 Villagómez October 25, 1990, interview; Zavala / Jiménez interview; "Capsule History of Our Lady of St. John Church," Our Lady of St. John File, ADGH.

2 "Mejicanos," flyer in OLG *Codex*.

3 OLG *Codex*, 6–7.

4 Villagómez October 25, 1990, interview; Zavala / Jiménez interview.

5 "The Poor Will Have the Gospel Preached to Them," *MI*, January 1938, 16–17.

6 Urbanovsky diary, April 28–May 12, 1947, 304–5, and May 21–June 6, 1948, 121–22, CAT; Urbanovsky interview; "Capsule History of Our Lady of St. John Church."

7 "Saint Raphael Celebrates," commemorative in St. Raphael File, ADGH.

8 Dolan, *American Catholic Experience*, 375; Hegarty, *Serving with Gladness*, 157–58. Hegarty (158) writes that the Society for the Propagation of the Faith gave the Galveston Diocese $249,000 between 1846 and 1901, "the largest sum contributed to any single diocese in the United States, just as the diocese was probably one of the poorest."

9 F. C. Kelley to Rev. N. A. Gallagher, August 19, 1912, Parish Collection, CAT; OLG *Codex*, 6, 7–8; "Appeal for Assistance," microfilm roll no. 11, Extension Society Records, ALUC.

10   "Appeal for Assistance," February 11, 1937, and Bishop W. J. Nold to Rev. Richard R. St. John, March 21, 1951, both in Diocesan Correspondence, Extension Society Records, ALUC; Rev. Joseph A. Cusack to Bishop John L. Morkovsky, April 7, 1966, St. Patrick File, ADGH; Cárdenas interview; see also Rev. E. B. Ledvina to Bishop Gallagher, October 17, 1912, and Ledvina to Gallagher, May 19, 1917, both in Gallagher File no. 5, Episcopal Collection, CAT.

11   "Gifts of the Catholic Church Extension Society to the Diocese of Galveston," Diocesan Chancery Collection, CAT; Dolan, *American Catholic Experience*, 375; ABCM *Reports*, 1940–55, ALUC.

12   Dolan, *American Catholic Experience*, 375.

13   Appeals for donations, Bishop N. A. Gallagher, January 9, 1912, and G. W. La Lumiere, railroad official, September 7, 1915, both in Immaculate Conception (Houston) File, AOMI; see also Pastoral Letter from Bishop Byrne, ca. 1924, Provincial Records, AOMI.

14   Valdez, *History of the Missionary Catechists*, 20, 36–39; OLG *Codex*, 6–8; Kelley, *Story of Extension*, 200; Sister M. Lucinda Schuler and Sister M. Rachel Moreno, "History of Our Lady of Guadalupe School," TMs, ACDP; letters of October 6, 1972, Scalan Foundation to Bishop Morkovsky and to sisters at Guadalupe School, Our Lady of Guadalupe File, ADGH.

15   Chancery Office Questionnaire, ca. 1929, Our Lady of Guadalupe File, Parish Collection, CAT; "Father Santos," *Houston Post*, April 23, 1949, clipping in Our Lady of Guadalupe File, ADGH; "Desde el quinto barrio," *TCH*, December 10, 1964, 10.

16   Jubilee program souvenir, 1935, Our Lady of Guadalupe File, ACDP.

17   "Father Santos," *Houston Post*, April 23, 1949, clipping in Our Lady of Guadalupe File, ADGH.

18   SP *Codex*, 29, 36.

19   Irene Rickert to Rev. B. A. Wagner, December 9, 1971, and Wagner to Rickert, December 28, 1971, both in Our Lady of Guadalupe File, ADGH.

20   Similar in socioeconomic makeup, the two parishes alternated between deficits and small surpluses of $1,000–$2,000 (typewritten document, January 30, 1971, St. Raphael File, ADGH; "Emphasizes Dignity," *TCH*, October 23, 1970, 11; Financial Report, 1969, St. Raphael File, ADGH; Financial Report, 1965, Our Lady of St. John File, ADGH).

21   Financial Report, 1971, Blessed Sacrament File, ADGH; Financial Report, 1965, Our Lady of Sorrows File, ADGH; Bishop John L. Morkovsky to Rev. John A. Hakey, February 9 and February 24, 1967, Provincial Records, AOMI; Financial Report, 1965, St. Patrick File, ADGH.

22 Bishop Byrne to Rev. Laboure, June 19, 1930, Provincial Records, AOMI; see any issue of *MI*.

23 Gonzales interview.

24 Ibid.; OLG *Boletín*, April 1928, 9–10; and July 1929, 10.

25 In the early 1950s, about 200 out of some 614 member families at St. Stephen used the envelope system. Census, 1953, St. Stephen File, ADGH. At St. Patrick, 425 out of some 1,500 families used the envelopes. St. Patrick Annual Parochial Report, 1960, File 8H64, AOMI; at Blessed Sacrament, 500 of 1,235 did so. Financial Report, 1971, Blessed Sacrament File, ADGH. See also Financial Report, 1965, Our Lady of Sorrows File, ADGH.

26 St. John Financial Report, 1965; St. Patrick Financial Report, 1965; Our Lady of Sorrows Financial Report, 1965; St. Raphael Financial Report, 1969; and Blessed Sacrament Financial Report, 1971, all in ADGH.

27 Parishioners sponsored the stained glass windows of the first Immaculate Heart Church, in 1926; the ones for the first Guadalupe Church were also paid for this way. See Zavala / Jiménez interview; OLG *Codex*, 6.

28 Immaculate Heart of Mary Church Commemorative Program, January 29, 1950, Villagómez Family Collection, HMRC. Apart from other contributions, the commemorative listed paid cash pledges from individuals and families totaling $8,255 in denominations of $25 (1); $50 (145); $60 (2); $80 (2); $100 (5); and $200 (1).

29 "Father Santos"; *FC*, March 1952, 116–17; parish bulletin, March 5, 1972, Our Lady of St. John File, ADGH; parish bulletin, June 6, 1971, St. Stephen File, ADGH; parish bulletin, May 30, 1971, St. Joseph–St. Stephen File, AGHD; Financial Report, 1965, Our Lady of St. John File, ADGH; Gonzales interview; Zavala / Jiménez interview.

30 OLG *Boletín*, April 1928, July 1929; *FC*, December 1944, 67–68; February 1946, 87–88; January 1950, 66; broadsides, January 23, 1938, and June 16, 1940, Rodríguez Family Collection, HMRC; parish bulletin, June 6, 1971, St. Stephen File, ADGH.

31 Villagómez October 25, 1990, interview; Gonzales interview; Zavala / Jiménez interview.

32 "Mexican Village," *HC*, December 13, 1935, 6; see also *HC*, November 30, 1935, 5; September 29, 1933, 18; November 27, 1935, 22; December 3, 1935, 2; April 20, 1940, 6A; April 26, 1940, 1D.

33 Zavala / Jiménez interview.

34 Ibid.; Gonzales interview.

35 Zavala / Jiménez interview.

36 This phrase is borrowed from León, "Born Again in East LA," 170.

37 Tarango, "Hispanic Woman," 57.

38 Although virtually nonexistent for Mexican Americans, food studies would seem a fertile field for historians interested in the study of ethnicity. A suggestive article is Brett Williams, "Why Migrant Women Feed Their Husbands Tamales." The word *tamalada* can refer either to the making of tamales or to a festive meal of tamales. Either way, the dish is often associated with religious celebration. A social worker's telling observation in 1930s Los Angeles reveals its ethnoreligious significance:

> On Christmas Eve in old Mexico it is customary among the families to hold a tamalada after the Midnight Mass. One family will make great preparation for such an occasion and will invite all its relations and perhaps one other family to be present at the festivities. . . . The tamaladas here [in Los Angeles] are not of that type. Instead of a private home, they are held in a rented dance hall. Everyone goes. There is not much order and a great deal of confusion. The girls sometimes smoke and drink, which would never be tolerated in Mexico. The older people consider this *a desecration of a sacred custom.* (Quoted in Sánchez, *Becoming Mexican American*, 167; emphasis added)

39 Gonzales interview.

40 Ibid.; clipping, SP *Codex*, 36. See also the parish queen photos in the Guillén Family Collection and Medellín Family Collection, HMRC. The *Family Circular*, the Sisters of Divine Providence newsletter, often mentioned the parish queen contests.

41 OLG *Codex* and SP *Codex*; *FC*, ACDP; see also *Día de la raza* flier, October 12, 1969, St. Stephen File, ADGH; and church bulletins, St. Joseph–St. Stephen Parish, May 30, 1971; St. Stephen Parish, June 6, 1971; and Our Lady of St. John Parish, March 5, 1972, all in ADGH. Local newspapers also frequently noted the *jamaicas*; see *HC*, September 29, 1933, 18; November 27, 1935, 22; November 30, 1935, 5; December 3, 1935, 2; December 13, 1935, 6; April 20, 1940, 6A; and April 26, 1940, 1D.

42 Financial Reports, Our Lady of St. John, 1965; Our Lady of Sorrows, 1965; St. Patrick, 1965; St. Raphael, 1969; and Blessed Sacrament, 1971, all in ADGH; OLG *Boletín*, July 1929, 8.

43 Our Lady of Guadalupe Band photo, 1930, Petra Guillén File, Mexican American Family and Photograph Collection, HMRC; Southern Pacific Lines Band photo, 1926, Gómez Family Collection, HMRC; Zavala / Jiménez interview.

44 Zavala / Jiménez interview.

45 Orsi, *Madonna of 115th Street*; Giles, *Changing Times*, 127–28.

46 Bishop John L. Morkovsky to Rev. John A. Hakey, September 19, 1966, Provincial Records, AOMI; "Surviving a Century of Storms," *TCH*, August 25, 1978, 6.

47 "Controversial Parish Here Split in Two," *HC*, July 20, 1973, sec. 3, 21; Father Emile J. Farge to Bishop Morkovsky, May 9, 1967, St. Stephen File, ADGH.

48 Father Emile J. Farge to Bishop Morkovsky, May 9, 1967, St. Stephen File, ADGH.

49 Petition from St. Stephen's parishioners to Bishop Morkovsky, ca. May 25, 1967; Resolution from St. Stephen Parish to Bishop Morkovsky, April 1971; and Resolution from St. Stephen Parish to Bishop Morkovsky, June 10, 1971, all in St. Stephen File, ADGH.

50 Chancellor Bernard J. Ganter to Mr. Joseph F. Montalbano, October 9, 1968, St. Stephen File, ADGH; "Angry Parishioners," *HC*, March 7, 1969, clipping in St. Stephen File, ADGH; "The Spirit of St. Joseph–St. Stephen," *TCH*, February 4, 1972, clipping in St. Stephen File, ADGH; "Surviving a Century of Storms."

51 "Angry Parishioners"; *El Sol*, May 23, 1969, 1; Memorandum, June 17, 1969, St. Stephen File, ADGH; *Noche Mexicana* advertisement, *TCH*, July 18, 1969, 11; *TCH*, August 1, 1969, 3; solicitation letter from Rev. P. F. Flores, August 12, 1969, copy in *TCH* Photograph Files (St. Joseph–St. Stephen), Chancery, ADGH; "Three Priests Compete," *TCH*, September 26, 1969, 3; *Día de la Raza* flier, October 12, 1969, St. Stephen File, ADGH.

52 Raymond Lomas to Bishop John L. Morkovsky, March 23, 1971, St. Stephen File, ADGH.

53 Ibid.

54 Resolution, April 1971, St. Stephen File, ADGH; "Dispute Surfaces in Joint Parish," *HC*, June 25, 1971, sec. 3, 7.

55 Resolution, April 1971, St. Stephen File, ADGH.

56 Resolution, June 10, 1971, St. Stephen File, ADGH.

57 "Dispute Surfaces."

58 As an example of how they were not taken seriously, the petitioners claimed that their priests did not believe they had met with the bishop but that the priests did listen to some nonparishioners who proposed an incredible scheme

to raise $400,000 within thirty-six hours for the proposed new church. See Resolution, June 10, 1971, and St. Joseph–St. Stephen Parish Council Meeting Report, May 16, 1971, St. Stephen File, ADGH.

59   St. Stephen's parishioners submitted documents they claimed proved that Sunday collections from the two churches were in fact being pooled, despite being told they were kept in separate accounts. See attachments to the Resolution, June 10, 1971, St. Stephen File, ADGH.

60   Resolution, June 10, 1971, St. Stephen File, ADGH.

61   Ibid.

62   St. Joseph–St. Stephen Parish Council Meeting Report, May 16, 1971, St. Stephen File, ADGH.

63   "Controversial Parish"; "The Spirit of St. Joseph–St. Stephen"; "Surviving a Century of Storms."

64   Copies of letters, Bishop John Morkovsky to Father Maurice Dho, May 24, 1973, Dho to Morkovsky, June 7, 1973, and Morkovsky to Dho, June 8, 1973, all in *TCH* Photograph Files (St. Joseph), Chancery, ADGH; "Surviving a Century of Storms."

65   Resolution, June 10, 1971, St. Stephen File, ADGH.

66   "Surviving a Century of Storms."

67   Ibid.; Resolution, June 10, 1971, St. Stephen File, ADGH.

68   "Surviving a Century of Storms."

69   On the concept of "use value" as applied to religious institutions, see Newman, "God and the Growth Machine." Newman (238) argues that, unlike the "exchange value" that property holds for entrepreneurs, congregants do not view their churches as commodities to be bought and sold. Instead, their "special relationship . . . with a place such as a church building [is] based on the use value of the place itself as well as the access it gives to other use values." I am indebted to my colleague Professor Kee Warner, of UC–Colorado Springs, for bringing this article to my attention.

70   Ibid., 238–39.

71   Reed-Danahay, "Talking about Resistance," 221–29.

72   Orsi, *Madonna of 115th Street*, 153.

CHAPTER SIX

1   Privett, *U.S. Catholic Church*, 127; Valdez, *History of the Missionary Catechists*, 5–12, 19–20; Guillén interview.

2   Paul Decker, "Catholic Action and Social Action in the Oblate Southwest," *MI*, December 1949, 344; Villagómez November 9, 1990, interview.

3   Villagómez November 9, 1990, interview; Rev. Esteban de Anta, "Houston, Texas," *MI*, January 1930, 14.

4   Decker, "Catholic Action," 334; De Anta, "Houston, Texas," 14. This type of social action continued into the contemporary period. Sister Mary Rachel Moreno, C.D.P., a social worker who was principal of Our Lady of Guadalupe Parish School in 1965–66, tried to find jobs for parishioners through Houston employment agencies. She wanted them "to grow spiritually, intellectually [and] materially if possible." Letter to the author, July 11, 1990.

5   Valdez, *History of the Missionary Catechists*, 5–12, 19–20; *FC*, January 1916, 73; November 1916, 37; November 1934, 60; February 1935, 146–47; December 1937, 61; *HC*, September 11, 1932, 14.

6   Valdez, *History of the Missionary Catechists*, 8. Although Monsignor George T. Walsh is credited with starting the "Mexican Clinic" in 1924, Sr. Benitia's groundwork in the later 1910s most likely helped bring about the founding of this important health resource for Houston's Mexicans. For the clinic see "San Jose Clinic," typewritten manuscript, Mexican American Small Collections, Box 2, HMRC; see also De León, *Ethnicity in the Sunbelt*, 30.

7   Valdez, *History of the Missionary Catechists*, 5–12, 19–20; Guillén interview; *Today's Catholic* (San Antonio), June 20, 1980, clipping in Women Religious Orders Collection, CAT; quote in *TCH*, January 11, 1980, clipping in Catechists File, ACDP; see also Antonio Rodríguez, "In Tribute to Sister Benitia," *Southern Messenger*, June 23, 1938.

8   Bishop C. E. Byrne to Rev. A. C. Dusseau, January 28, 1938; Dusseau to Byrne, January 31, 1938; and Byrne to Dusseau, February 1, 1938, all in Provincial Records, AOMI; Mr. Toribio Cano, President of Diocesan Council, to Rev. Mother Philothea, May 16, 1938, Our Lady of Guadalupe File, ACDP; see also Valdez, *History of the Missionary Catechists*, 44–45.

9   Valdez, *History of the Missionary Catechists*, 36, 43; Privett, *U.S. Catholic Church*, 127.

10 Valdez, *History of the Missionary Catechists*, 43–45, quote on 44; Byrne to Dusseau, January 28, 1938; Dusseau to Byrne, January 31, 1938; Byrne to Dusseau, February 1, 1938, Provincial Records, AOMI.

11 "History of Our Lady of Guadalupe School," MS, ACDP; Cárdenas, *Meditaciones*.

12 Cárdenas interview; *FC*, January 1942, 114; December 1942, 69; *El Buen Vecino* (Houston), March 8, 1946, clipping in St. Patrick File, ADGH.

13 Cárdenas interview.

14 Sister Mary [Benitia] to Mr. Deden, S.P. Shops, February 7, 1934; and Sister M. Dolores to Daves Loan Office, December 2, 1927, Rodríguez Collection, HMRC; see also several other letters of this kind in ibid.

15 Rodríguez, "Tribute to Sister Benitia."

16 Coburn and Smith, "Creating Community and Identity," quote on 92. On the ideology of maternal feminism, see Gordon, "Putting Children First," and "Maternalism as a Paradigm." See also Coburn and Smith, *Spirited Lives.*

17 Martin McMurtrey, *Mariachi Bishop*, 35–38, 121, quote on 36. On Flores's historic stature, see David McLemore, "Beyond the Pulpit," *Dallas Morning News*, June 25, 2001, A1, A12.

18 Griffin, "Sisters of Divine Providence." See also Roberto R. Treviño, "Facing Jim Crow: Catholic Sisters and the 'Mexican Problem' in Texas," *Western Historical Quarterly* 34, no. 2 (Summer 2003): 139–64.

19 Decker, "Catholic Action," 345, 348; see also *New Catholic Encyclopedia*, 1967 ed., s.v. "Rerum Novarum," by J. Newman; and s.v., "Quadragesimo Anno," by R. J. Miller.

20 Appeal for donations, Bishop Nicholas A. Gallagher, January 9, 1912, Immaculate Conception (Houston) File, AOMI; Pastoral Letter from Bishop Byrne, ca. 1924, Provincial Records, AOMI; appeal for donations, G. W. La Lumiere, September 7, 1915, Provincial Records, AOMI.

21 Pastoral Letter from Bishop C. E. Byrne, April 15, 1942, Episcopal Collection, CAT.

22 See Richard A. García, *Rise of the Mexican American Middle Class*, ch. 2, ch. 5, esp. 167–73; Mario T. García, *Desert Immigrants*, 96–106; De León, *Ethnicity in the Sunbelt*, 17–18, 55; Zamora, *World of the Mexican Worker*, 49–50, 194.

23 *HC*, November 27, 1935, 22; November 30, 1935, 5; December 3, 1935, 2; December 13, 1935, 6; April 20, 1940, 6A; April 26, 1940, 1D.

24 *El Buen Vecino* (Houston), clipping in St. Patrick File, ADGH; Cárdenas interview; "Notes from Houston," *MI*, May 1931, 147; *FC*, April 1939, 130; April 1940, 173; March 1942, 158; December 1942, 69; Bishop Nold to Very Reverend Nicholas Tanaskovic, July 19, 1954, and Tanaskovic to Nold, July 27, 1954, Provincial Records, AOMI; "History of Our Lady of Guadalupe School."

25 Bishop Byrne to Rev. Theodore Laboure, May 21, 1932, Provincial Records, AOMI; Rev. A. Santos to Franklin Harbach, February 1, 1949, and Harbach to Santos, February 14, 1949, Harbach Papers, HMRC; Don Le Blanc, "Waterfront Priest," *MI*, March 1959, 16.

26   De León, *Ethnicity in the Sunbelt*, 105–10.

27   Bishop Byrne to Very Reverend Walter Arnold, June 11, 1943, Provincial Records, AOMI.

28   SP *Codex*, 1942, 24; *Houston Post*, April 23, 1949, clipping in Our Lady of Guadalupe File, ADGH; Le Blanc, "Waterfront Priest," 16–20; Bishop Wendelin Nold to Very Reverend Lawrence J. Seidel, July 9, 1957, Our Lady of St. John File, ADGH; see also letter to Bishop Byrne, April 24, 1942; Bishop Nold to Very Reverend Father Nicholas, May 21, 1956; and Seidel to Nold, August 9 and 13, 1957, all in Provincial Records, AOMI.

29   Letter to Bishop Byrne, April 24, 1942, Provincial Records, AOMI.

30   Bishop Nold to Father Nicholas, May 21, 1956, Provincial Records, AOMI.

31   Ibid. One proposal was to replace Father Santos at Our Lady of Sorrows Parish with Father Emmet Walsh, whose boys' club in Laredo was lauded by city officials there; see letter to Bishop Byrne, April 24, 1942, Provincial Records, AOMI.

32   *FC*, April 1957, 145; Urbanovsky diary, May 21–June 6, 1948, CAT.

33   *Houston Post*, April 23, 1949, clipping in Our Lady of Guadalupe File, ADGH.

34   The actual size of the Mexican American Protestant community at any given time is unclear, but the most often-cited figure until recently has been 5 to 10 percent. See Sánchez, *Becoming Mexican American*, 163 and 306 n. 51. A recent study funded by the Pew Charitable Trusts, "Hispanic Churches in American Public Life," found that "about 70 percent of the country's 35.4 million Hispanics are Roman Catholic, and 22 percent are Protestant." See Ted Parks, "Study Tallies Where Hispanics Worship, How They Vote," *Star-Telegram*, May 11, 2001, available from <http://www.star-telegram.com/new/doc/1047/1:FAITH20511101.html> (accessed May 17, 2001).

35   De León, *Ethnicity in the Sunbelt*, 28, 50–51, 57; Parish census, 1951, St. Patrick File, ADGH; "Census of St. Patrick Church 1953," typed ms., St. Patrick File, ADGH. For overviews of Mexican American Protestantism see Sylvest, "Hispanic American Protestantism," and Grebler et al., *Mexican American People*, 486–512. For samples of the abundant Catholic discussions about Protestant proselytization see Rev. F. Bormann, "Schools and the Children of the Missions," *Extension Magazine*, February 1916, 13; Rev. Gerard Mongeau, "A Chat with a Texas Missionary," *MI*, June 1926, 18–20; Mongeau, "Mexican Youth for Christ," *MI*, July 1934, 214–16; Frank A. Kilday, "The New Challenge," *MI*, January–February 1956, 14–18, 22; Jim Collison, "The Baptists," *MI*, October 1961, 23–25; and "Testigos de Jehova," *TCH*, December 19, 1969, 11. See also Gamio, *Mexican Immigrant*, 195–209.

36   De León, *Ethnicity in the Sunbelt*, 50–51.

37   María Cristina García, "Agents of Americanization," 122.

38   Bishop Byrne to Very Reverend Walter Arnold, April 15, 1942, Provincial Records, AOMI; De León, *Ethnicity in the Sunbelt*, 51.

39   Oblate Provincial Seidel to Bishop Nold, April 21 and June 16, 1958, Provincial Records, AOMI.

40   "Mejicanos" flier, OLG *Codex*; *HC*, February 22, 1912; see also *HC*, February 23, 1912, 27; and February 27, 1912, 10.

41   See José Hernández, *Mutual Aid for Survival*; for Houston see De León, *Ethnicity in the Sunbelt*, 31–33; on Oblates fostering the Liga de Protección Mexicana, see Carmen Tafolla, "Expansion of the Church," 234–35. Mutual aid societies had papal approval; see Decker, "Catholic Action," 344.

42   OLG *Codex*, 8; OLG *Boletín*, April 1928, Rodríguez Family Collection, HMRC.

43   De León, *Ethnicity in the Sunbelt*, 32 and 41 n. 36.

44   *FC*, November 1943, 36; March 1945, 144; March 1952, 116–17; *Houston Post*, 23 April 1949, clipping in Our Lady of Guadalupe File, ADGH.

45   "Christmas Came Early in Houston," *MI*, December 1955, 16. Father Sauvageau reported religious, social, and financial news to his parishioners via the local Spanish-language radio station, KLVL; see "Dial 1480 and the Rosary," *MI*, December 1954, 12–15.

46   "Christmas Came Early," 16, 18, 19.

47   "Rain and Relief," photo and caption, *HC*, July 7, 1954, 1A; "Flood Relief," photo and caption, in ibid., 8A.

48   Fr. Edward J. Murray, "A Parish That Licked the Loan Shark!" *MI*, June 1959, 2–3. See also García 1990 interview.

49   Murray, "Parish That Licked the Loan Shark," 5; Decker, "Catholic Action," 344.

50   Letter and pulpit announcement, April 28, 1960, Provincial Records, AOMI; for Tijerina's "little school of the 400" see Kreneck, *Mexican American Odyssey*, 198–203 and passim.

51   Bronder, *Social Justice and Church Authority*, 75.

52   ABCM *Reports*, 1939–40, 58, ALUC; Bishop Byrne to Very Reverend Walter Arnold, November 29, 1940; December 2, 1940; June 11, 1943, Provincial Records, AOMI.

53   Byrne to Arnold, June 11 and 16, 1943, Provincial Records, AOMI.

54   Very Reverend Nicholas Tanaskovic to Bishop Wendelin J. Nold, February 11, 1953; Nold to Tanaskovic, February 16, 1953; Archbishop Robert E. Lucey to

Nold, February 24, 1955; and Nold to Tanaskovic, February 28, 1955, all in Provincial Records, AOMI.

55 Bronder, *Social Justice and Church Authority*, 75–76; Sandoval, *On the Move*, 48. See also Walsh, "Work of the Catholic Bishops' Committee."

56 Letter to the author from Father William O'Connor, O.M.I., August 26, 1991. The same appeared to be true for Los Angeles and San Antonio; see Grebler et al., *Mexican American People*, 482–83 n. 56.

57 Father O'Connor to the author, August 26, 1991; De León, *Ethnicity in the Sunbelt*, 55.

58 Bronder, *Social Justice and Church Authority*, 75.

59 "Community Relations Unit Set Up," *TCH*, May 14, 1964, 2.

60 Ibid.

61 See the specific reference to "the rights and opportunities of our Negro brethren [*sic*]," in Pastoral Letter from the Bishops of the United States, August 25, 1963, Provincial Records, AOMI. Also note the absence of any references to Chicanos and the focus on black issues and speakers at a church-sponsored civil rights conference in Houston in 1966, in *TCH*, October 14, 1966, clipping in Diocesan Chancery Collection, CAT.

62 For background on Father Flores see McMurtrey, *Mariachi Bishop*.

63 O'Brien, "American Priest." See also Brown and McKeown, *Poor Belong to Us*.

64 O'Brien, "American Priest," 448.

65 For example, Dolan, "Religion and Social Change."

66 *TCH*, October 1, 1964, 2.

67 *TCH*, January 28, 1965, 9; May 27, 1965, 1, 10; July 29, 1965, 3; clipping, November 12, 1965, St. Stephen File, ADGH.

Chapter Seven

1 *Papel Chicano*, September 16, 1971.

2 Cox, " 'New Breed' "; McNamara, "Social Action Priests."

3 Chávez quoted in Sandoval, *Fronteras*, 384.

4 *TCH*, February 11, 1965, 10. A Spanish immigrant, Crespo was well known for his civic involvement and business activities in the Mexican community since the 1930s; see Kreneck, *Mexican American Odyssey*, 67, 69, 71; and De León, *Ethnicity in the Sunbelt*, 74, 83. See also *TCH*, October 3, 1969, 1; September 18, 1970, 1, 11.

5 *TCH*, October 3, 1969, 1, 6. For similar sentiments, see Carrillo, "Sociological Failure."

6   *TCH*, October 13, 1972, 10; *HC*, February 19, 1970, 1, 4 (sec. 3).

7   See Document no. 43, Marta Cotera, "La Conferencia De Mujeres Por La Raza: Houston, Texas, 1971"; Document no. 44, Francisca Flores, "Conference of Mexican Women in Houston—Un Remolino [A Whirlwind]"; and Document no. 45, Anna NietoGomez and Elma Barrera, "Chicana Encounter," in Alma García, *Chicana Feminist Thought*, 155–64.

8   Editorial, *Compass*, October 1967, 4; October 1968, 10–11.

9   *Papel Chicano*, February 3, 1971, 9; February 29, 1972, 11.

10   "Listen, Christian," *Compass*, October 1968, 4. Some internet sources attribute slightly varying versions of this poem to Bob Rowland.

11   For studies and essays from the 1970s that focus on institutional racism and discrimination within the Catholic Church, see Hurtado, "Attitudinal Study"; Soto, "Chicano and the Church"; Carrillo, "Sociological Failure"; Juárez\ "La Iglesia Católica"; and Isais-A., "Chicano and the American Catholic Church." More recent works include Mirandé, *Chicano Experience*, ch. 6, and Pulido, "Race Relations."

12   Eduardo N. López to Bishop John L. Morkovsky, ca. November 1970, Our Lady of Sorrows File, ADGH.

13   Ibid.

14   Ibid. While some parishioners at Our Lady of Sorrows fought to get other laity involved in social issues, the situation at St. Raphael's Parish in far southwest Houston was slightly different. There, a concerned priest complained he could not get working-class adults involved in the problems that afflicted their children—teen pregnancy, alcohol and drug abuse, and high school dropout rates. He explained, "Our people are workers, for the most part. They are not inclined to attend meetings. . . . The difficulty is that when the priest has most time for visiting the people, they just arn't [*sic*] at home." See typewritten manuscript, "St. Raphael's Church," January 30, 1971, St. Raphael File, AGHD.

15   For details of Flores's life see McMurtrey, *Mariachi Bishop*.

16   *TCH*, October 24, 1969, 1; June 30, 1972, 7.

17   McMurtrey, *Mariachi Bishop*, 55; Sandoval, *Fronteras*, 397–98; *TCH*, October 24, 1969, 1. See also Juan Romero, "Charism and Power."

18   Rev. Ralph Ruiz to Rev. L. C. Reyes, December 8, 1970, PADRES Collection, CAT.

19   Las Hermanas Proposal, Castillo Collection, HMRC; Sandoval, *Fronteras*, 405–7.

20   *Houston Post*, April 21, 1971, clipping in Joe Torres / Huelga Schools Collection, HMRC; "Qué Pasó Sheet," PADRES Collection, CAT. See also Basso, "Emerging 'Chicana' Sister."

21 Las Hermanas Conference Program, Joe Torres / Huelga Schools Collection, HMRC; *TCH*, November 26, 1971, 12; December 10, 1971, 1; *Papel Chicano*, October 28, 1971, 11; November 9, 1971, 2. For an in-depth study of the national organization see Medina, *Las Hermanas*.

22 Clipping, *Houston Post*, April 21, 1971, Joe Torres / Huelga Schools Collection, HMRC; "Spanish-speaking Sisters Unite," *TCH*, April 8, 1971.

23 Quotes from Quiñónez and Turner, *Transformation of American Catholic Sisters*, 72–73.

24 Pastoral Letter from the Bishops of the United States, August 25, 1963, Provincial Records, AOMI; clippings, *TCH*, October 14, 1966, June 23, 1967, and September 15, 1967, in Diocesan Chancery Collection, CAT.

25 Pastoral Letter from the Bishops; clipping, *TCH*, June 23, 1967, Diocesan Chancery Collection, CAT.

26 *TCH*, June 23, 1967, clipping in Diocesan Chancery Collection, CAT; Pastoral Letter from the Bishops.

27 For a fuller account see Rhinehart and Kreneck, "Minimum Wage March"; Joan Hart Cohen, "To See Christ in Our Brothers"; and Chandler, "Mexican American Protest Movement."

28 *TCH*, June 24, 1966, 1.

29 "La Marcha . . . Valley Farm Workers' 491-Mile March for Justice," in *Harris County PASO 5th Anniversary and Salute to Valley Farm Workers* (Houston: Harris County PASO, 1966), pamphlet in Mexican American Small Collections, HMRC.

30 *TCH*, July 1, 1966, 1, 6.

31 "La Marcha"; *HC*, July 5, 1966, 6.

32 "La Marcha"; *HC*, September 1, 1966, 19 (sec. 1), September 4, 1966, 10 (sec. 1); Chandler, "Mexican American Protest Movement," 244.

33 "La Marcha"; *HC*, September 5, 1966, 1, 18 (sec. 1), September 6, 1966, 1 (sec. 1).

34 *HC*, September 7, 1966, 13 (sec. 1), September 9, 1966, 11 (sec. 1); *TCH*, September 9, 1966, 1, 6.

35 Rhinehart and Kreneck, "Minimum Wage March," 39–44; Chandler, "Mexican American Protest Movement," 245; for similar assessments see De León, *Ethnicity in the Sunbelt*, 173–74; and Montejano, *Anglos and Mexicans*, 284–85.

36 Quoted in Rhinehart and Kreneck, "Minimum Wage March," 44.

37 Bishop P. F. Flores, "Mission and Vision, Mexican American Apostolate," typewritten manuscript (mimeographed), n.d. [ca. 1971], García Collection, HMRC.

38 *TCH*, December 5, 1969, 1; *HC*, April 8, 1970, 1 (sec. 4); clipping, *TCH*, February, 5, 1971, PADRES Collection, CAT; McMurtrey, *Mariachi Bishop*, 57–58.

39 *TCH*, October 24, 1969, 1.

40 *TCH*, October 1, 1964, 2; October 24, 1969, 1; October 2, 1970, 1; Flores, "Mission and Vision."

41 Flores became auxiliary bishop of San Antonio on May 5, 1970. Later that year, in December, a PADRES "action group" was initiated in Houston. See Sandoval, *On the Move*, 72, and "Qué Pasó Sheet."

42 Father Lawrence Peguero was PADRES diocesan director in Houston during the early 1970s, but his bootstraps philosophy contrasted dramatically with the outlook of more militant priests like Flores. While Flores attacked societal barriers, Peguero described himself as "a firm believer in the American system." A contemporary recalled that Houston PADRES was insignificant in the social arena and that Peguero was simply "not interested in social issues." Father Peguero believed that the function of the church was "strictly a moral one," that it was "not the function of a priest to be a leader in social work." Though at times he expressed support for some Chicano causes, Peguero's career and philosophy were summed up in the Franklinesque homilies he was fond of repeating: "We don't have any poor people in our neighborhood—only lazy ones" and "The only thing that has not been tried against poverty is work." See PADRES booklet (undated, ca. 1971), PADRES Collection, CAT; *Houston Post*, March 5, 1970 (Close-up sec.), clipping in Our Lady of St. John File, ADGH; *HC*, October 2, 1970, 5 (sec. 2); and McCarthy 1991 interview. See Sandoval, *Fronteras*, 401–2, for social activism of PADRES elsewhere; De León, *Ethnicity in the Sunbelt*, 206, briefly mentions PADRES emergency relief activities in Houston in the 1970s.

43 *National Catholic Reporter*, August 13, 1971, 1; résumé of Gloria Graciela Gallardo, Castillo Collection, HMRC.

44 De León, *Ethnicity in the Sunbelt*, 185–89; "MAEC preparing," *TCH*, August 6, 1971, 1. See also San Miguel, *Brown, Not White*. Leonel Castillo parlayed his high-profile activism into a successful run for the office of city controller and later served as the first Mexican American director of the Immigration and Naturalization Service in the Carter administration (Kreneck, *Del Pueblo*, 201–2).

45 *Papel Chicano*, September 26, 1970, 3, 5; October 24, 1970, 5; January 16, 1971, 7; February 20, 1971, 5; April 1, 1971; clipping, *Houston Post*, April 21, 1971, Joe Torres / Huelga Schools Collection, HMRC.

46 "San Jose Clinic," typewritten manuscript, Mexican American Small Collections, Box 2, HMRC; *TCH*, April 17, 1970, 12.

47 Much of the effort was carried out through the Bishop's Committee on the Inner City, the Council on Community Relations, and the Council of Catholic

Women. See Catholic Charities of the Diocese of Galveston-Houston 1967 Annual Report, Provincial Records, AOMI; Morkovsky memorandum to Monsignor Ganter, May 22, 1968, Blessed Sacrament File, ADGH; clipping, *TCH*, November 12, 1965, St. Stephen File, ADGH; clipping, *TCH*, June 19, 1970, Diocesan Chancery Collection, CAT; *TCH*, April 3, 1970, 6; May 3, 1970, 3; clipping, *TCH*, June 17, 1966, *TCH* Photograph Files (St. Stephen), ADGH; clippings, *TCH*, March 17 and 31, 1972, *TCH* Photograph Files (Immaculate Heart of Mary), ADGH; Bishop's Pastoral Letter, September 23, 1968, Provincial Records, AOMI; and clipping, *TCH*, December 5, 1969, Diocesan Chancery Collection, CAT.

48   *Houston Post*, November 13, 1965, clipping in Latin American Community Project (LAC) scrapbook; typewritten manuscript in LAC scrapbook; "Minister's Quarterly Report," Folder 2, Box 1; and "History, Structure and Purposes of the LACK Project," Box 2, Folder 1, all in VISTA Collection, HMRC. The LAC Project was also known as "LACK."

49   Flier in LAC scrapbook; LACK Project *Voice*, Box 1; and LACK Project Director's Report, Box 2, Folder 2, all in VISTA Coll., HMRC. An offshoot organization of LAC that involved some East End priests was The East End Mission (TEEM). See *TCH*, January 23, 1970, 12.

50   Oxford Place was managed by an "interfaith and interracial staff" led by director Lupe Maciel, a Baptist, and four Spanish- and non-Spanish-surnamed office personnel, two Catholics and two Baptists. See *TCH*, April 24, 1970, 2; and "Report of Self-Study Committee of Houston Metropolitan Ministries," undated, ca. August 1970, Organizations File, Castillo Collection, HMRC. The Galveston-Houston Diocese entered into two other ecumenical agreements to provide low-cost housing, Pleasantville Village in 1967 and Houston Home Ownership Corporation in 1969, though these were not exclusively aimed at Mexican Americans. Giles, *Changing Times*, 63.

51   *TCH*, April 3, 1970, 6.

52   LAC Project Director's Report, September 1967, Box 2, Folder 2, VISTA Collection, HMRC. On the national level, the hierarchy of the church in the United States formed the Campaign for Human Development in 1969 to empower the poor and attack root causes of inequality. See Evans, "Campaign for Human Development."

53   Bishop John L. Morkovsky to Rev. Antonio Gonzales, July 28, 1966, and Provincial John A. Hakey to Morkovsky, August 6, 1966, both in Provincial Records, AOMI.

54   *TCH*, July 15, 1966, 3.

55   Joan Hart Cohen, "To See Christ in Our Brothers," 24–25; McCarthy 1991
     interview; quote in McCarthy 1972 interview. See also "Begin Aid Collections
     for Strikers," *TCH* clipping, June 24, 1966, and "Strikebreaking Aliens Decried
     by Texas Priest," *TCH* clipping, August 29, 1969, both in Bishop McCarthy Files,
     TCH Photograph Files, ADGH.

56   *TCH*, July 15, 1966, 3.

57   *TCH*, March 24, 1967, 3.

58   *Alamo Messenger* (San Antonio), February 7, 1969, clipping in Episcopal Collec-
     tion, CAT; see also *TCH*, December 5, 1969, 1.

59   *HC*, August 20, 1967, 24 (sec. 1).

60   Bishop John L. Morkovsky to Rev. Antonio Gonzales, August 21, 1967, Provin-
     cial Records, AOMI.

61   *HC*, August 20, 1967, 24 (sec. 1).

62   Morkovsky to Gonzales, August 21, 1967.

63   Ibid.

64   Provincial John A. Hakey to Bishop John L. Morkovsky, February 13, 1968, Pro-
     vincial Records, AOMI. In February 1968, Father Gonzales was reassigned to
     Houston. Back in the city, the priest renewed his political activities. His interest
     ranged from PASO and the Democratic Party to La Raza Unida Party, and even-
     tually even the Republicans. In the opinion of a contemporary, Gonzales "lost
     touch with reality in the heady world of the Chicano movement" and was
     "used" by politicians. Within six months of his return to Houston, Gonzales was
     again in trouble with his bishop, and his association with the diocese was tempo-
     rarily suspended while he explained reports of "irresponsible" behavior. This
     episode was apparently smoothed over, since within a week he was back at his
     post and communicating with the bishop regarding his latest political activity, a
     meeting with a representative of the incoming Nixon administration. Father
     Gonzales eventually left the priesthood. See Provincial John A. Hakey to Bishop
     John L. Morkovsky, February 13, 1968; Morkovsky to Gonzales, February 14,
     1968; Morkovsky to Gonzales, November 27, 1968; and Gonzales to Morkovsky,
     December 5, 1968, all in Provincial Records, AOMI; *El Sol*, March 22, 1968; April 26,
     1968; May 3, 1968; and McCarthy 1991 interview. Co-leader Rev. James Novarro
     similarly came under severe criticism. When newspaper pictures showed him
     carrying Father Gonzales's crucifix in a show of ecumenical solidarity in the
     priest's absence, many of his fellow Baptists were outraged; he eventually lost his
     pulpit because of his political activities. See Novarro interview.

65 Undated memorandum from Father Emile Farge (ca. August 1968), Organizations File, Castillo Collection, HMRC.

66 Ibid. Farge described his job as social action director as one of "exposing people to people [through the Catholic Interracial Committee]," maintaining contact with grassroots organizations, and "political activities, especially pushing the good legislation, good political candidates." In the late 1960s, he led an effort to build an ecumenical social action coalition, the Joint Strategy and Action Committee, which was "motivated by the common knowledge of the problem that many in our Greater Houston area are disenfranchised from real participation in the life of the city." He described the effort as "the only realistic ecumenical group working on the race-culture crises." See Farge letters and memoranda from 1968 to 1969 in Organizations File, Castillo Collection, HMRC.

67 Memorandum from Bishop Morkovsky to Father Farge, February 14, 1969, Organizations File, Castillo Collection, HMRC.

68 *Papel Chicano*, February 20, 1971, 2.

69 Ibid., September 16, 1971.

70 Ibid., August 22, 1970, 4; November 21, 1970, 2; January 16, 1971, 7; February 20, 1971, 5; *TCH*, September 11, 1970, 8.

71 "Oxford Place, Another Well-Meaning Instant Slum," *Papel Chicano*, September 16, 1971.

72 Ibid.

73 Houston Council on Human Relations, *Black / Mexican-American Project Report*, 6.

74 Sandoval, "Organization of a Hispanic Church," 141–42; Bishop Flores quoted in *National Catholic Reporter*, July 7, 1972, 1, 2.

75 *TCH*, November 3, 1972. See also National Conference of Catholic Bishops, *Hispanic Ministry*, 8, 29; Sandoval, *On the Move*, 79–82.

76 Sandoval, *On the Move*, 74–79.

77 Ibid., 79–82; *National Catholic Reporter*, July 7, 1972, 2; *Compass*, October 1972, 4.

78 *Compass*, October 1972, 4; Bishop John L. Morkovsky to Rev. Robert J. McGrath, July 11, 1972, St. Patrick File, ADGH; Morkovsky to Rev. Edward F. Brauman, June 3, 1971, Immaculate Heart of Mary File, ADGH; photo, *TCH* Photograph Files (Immaculate Heart of Mary), ADGH.

79 Sandoval, *Fronteras*, 429.

80 *TCH*, October 20, 1972, 2; October 13, 1972, 10.

81 Sandoval, *On the Move*, 81; *TCH*, October 20, 1972, 2.

1   Ueda, *Postwar Immigrant America*, 44–57, 68–71; Shelton et al., *Houston*, 103–6; Néstor Rodríguez, "Hispanic and Asian Immigration Waves," 32–37.

2   Betty Guzmán, "The Hispanic Population: Census 2000 Brief," May 2001, <http://www.census.gov/population/www/cen2000/briefs.html> (accessed May 2, 2004).

3   De León, *Ethnicity in the Sunbelt*, 221, 233; Shelton et al., *Houston*, 96, 98; <http://www.census.gov/2002/ACS/Tabular/160> (accessed April 21, 2004); <http://www.census.gov/2002/ACS/Narrative/160> (accessed April 21, 2004).

4   De León, *Ethnicity in the Sunbelt*, 221–22, 239–40; Shelton et al., *Houston*, 109–10; <http://www.census.gov/2002/ACS/Narrative/160>.

5   For newspaper reports, see notes 6, 7, and 8 below; for examples of scholarly studies, see Matovina and Riebe-Estrella, ed., *Horizons of the Sacred*, and Jeanette Rodríguez, *Our Lady of Guadalupe*; also see "In the Hispanic Tradition, the Reverence of the Season Reigns," in *American Country Christmas, 1992*, ed. Patricia D. Wilson and Brenda W. Kolb (Birmingham, AL: Oxmoor House, n.d.), 72; and "Hidden Houston: The City You See on the Surface Is Not All the City There Is," interview of Petra Guillén by David Theis in *Cite: The Architecture and Design Review of Houston* 50 (Spring 2001): 24.

6   Guillén 2004 interview; Elena Vega, "Thousands Celebrate Virgin of Guadalupe," *HC*, December 18, 2003, <http://continuum.uta.edu> (accessed August 3, 2004).

7   Megan K. Stack, "A TREAT FOR BELIEVERS: Visitors Flock to See Ice Cream Stain Some Say Is Image of Virgin," *Dallas Morning News*, January 14, 2000, 29A, 30A; Richard Vara, " 'Lady of the Light': Reflected Image Attracts Pilgrims to Houston Driveway," *HC*, August 4, 2001, <http://continuum.uta.edu> (accessed August 4, 2004).

8   Zelie Pollon, "HEALING PILGRIMAGE: Thousands Flock to Small Church Known for Its Restorative Powers," *Dallas Morning News*, April 23, 2000, 36A; Tara Dooley, "A Walk of Faith: Church Group Re-creates Jesus' Journey to Crucifixion," *HC*, April 18, 2003, <http://continuum.uta.edu> (accessed January 4, 2005); Richard Vara, "Beacon in the Barrio: WE'RE FAMILY SPIRIT BUILDS GROWTH AND A NEW CHAPEL AT LA DIVINA PROVIDENCIA IN PORT HOUSTON," *HC*, September 20, 2003, <http://continuum.uta.edu> (accessed August 4, 2004); Rhea Davis, "Church's Warm Greeting Stifling This Time of Year: Parishioners Are Trying to Raise Money for an Air Conditioner," *HC*, July 17, 2004, B1, B7; David Mc-

Lemore, "A Spirited Catholicism: Connecting to the Invisible World Includes Making Bargains with God," *Gazette Telegraph*, May 18, 1996, E1, E3; Richard Vara, "Hispanic-Catholic Tradition Runs Deep," *HC*, July 12, 1990, 19A; Mercedes Olivera, "Exhibit Shows Vast Ties to Virgin of Guadalupe," *Dallas Morning News*, November 27, 2004, 30; John Hillman, "Church to Celebrate All Souls Day with Spanish Service," *Arlington Morning News*, October 30, 1999, 1A, 5A; Joey Guerra, "Jessica's Big Day: Today's *Quinceañeras* Add Modern Flourish to an Old Tradition," *HC*, December 19, 2004, <http://continuum.uta.edu> (accessed January 3, 2005).

9   See Dávalos, *"La Quinceañera,"* and Dávalos, " 'The Real Way of Praying': The Via Crucis, *Mexicano* Sacred Space, and the Architecture of Domination," in Matovina and Riebe-Estrella, ed., *Horizons of the Sacred*, 41–68.

10   Julie Salamon, "Celebrating Mexican Life in New York," *New York Times*, December 8, 2004, <http://www.nytimes.com/2004/12/08/arts/08mexc .html> (accessed December 8, 2004).

11   Luis D. León, " '*Soy una Curandera y soy una Católica*': The Poetics of a Mexican Healing Tradition," in Matovina and Riebe-Estrella, ed., *Horizons of the Sacred*, 95–118, quotes on 115. See also David McLemore, "Day of the Dead Becoming Increasingly Commercialized," *Dallas Morning News*, October 25, 1999, 17A, 20A.

12   Quoted in Salamon, "Celebrating Mexican Life in New York."

13   Sandoval, "Organization of a Hispanic Church," 142–43; Díaz-Stevens and Stevens-Arroyo, *Recognizing the Latino Resurgence*, 172–73.

14   Díaz-Stevens and Stevens-Arroyo, *Recognizing the Latino Resurgence*, 172–76; Sandoval, *On the Move*, 82–83; Poyo, " 'Integration Without Assimilation,' " 106.

15   Díaz-Stevens and Stevens-Arroyo, *Recognizing the Latino Resurgence*, 175.

16   Sandoval, "Organization of a Hispanic Church," 144.

17   Sandoval, *On the Move*, 82–83; Díaz-Stevens and Stevens-Arroyo, *Recognizing the Latino Resurgence*, 189–91.

18   Sandoval, "Organization of a Hispanic Church," 145.

19   Sandoval, *On the Move*, 83.

20   Secretariat for Hispanic Affairs, "Encuentro 2000," June 3, 2003, <http://www .usccb.org/hispanicaffairs/encuentro.htm> (accessed April 4, 2004); Araceli M. Cantero, *"Encuentro 2000 celebró la diversidad,"* La Voz Católica, <http://www .vozcatolica.org/31/particip.htm> (accessed April 4, 2004); Agostino Bono, " 'Encuentro 2000' Gets Underway in Los Angeles," *Denver Catholic Register*, 12 July 2000, <http://www.archden.org/dcr/archive/20000712/2000071204wn

.htm> (accessed April 4, 2004); Pamela Schaeffer, "Catholics Show Their Diversity," *National Catholic Reporter*, 28 July 2000, <http://www.findarticles.com/cf—dls/m1141/35—36/63973888/print.jhtml> (accessed April 4, 2004).

21   Bono, "'Encuentro 2000' Gets Underway"; Schaeffer, "Catholics Show Their Diversity."

22   Stevens-Arroyo, "Emergence of a Social Identity," 13–15; Matovina, "Representation and the Reconstruction of Power," 226–27, quote on 226.

23   Stevens-Arroyo, "Emergence of a Social Identity," 115–17; Edmundo Rodríguez, "Hispanic Community," 225–27, quote on 227.

24   On Las Hermanas see the groundbreaking study Medina, *Las Hermanas*.

25   Matovina, "Representation and the Reconstruction of Power," 229–33.

26   Fiorenza interview; Guillén 2004 interview; Juan and Isidra Rodríguez interview; Julia Duin, "The Hispanic Exodus: Thousands Abandon Catholic Church for Other Faiths," *HC*, September 16, 1989, and Richard Vara, "The Spanish-Speaking Spirit: Growth among Hispanic Pentecostal Churches Continuing," *HC*, March 29, 1997, both at <http://continuum.uta.edu> (accessed August 4, 2004). Quote from the *New York Times* in Edwin H. Hernández, "Moving from the Cathedral to Storefront Churches," 216.

27   Edwin H. Hernández, "Moving from the Cathedral," 222; Díaz-Stevens and Stevens-Arroyo, *Recognizing the Latino Resurgence*, 35.

28   Díaz-Stevens and Stevens-Arroyo, *Recognizing the Latino Resurgence*, 190–91; Jay P. Dolan, *Hispanic Catholic Culture in the U.S.*, 449–50. Dolan sees the creation of a Latino church within the U.S. church as something that "far surpasses in scope and permanence" what large and well-established ethnic groups like Poles and Germans were able to achieve despite their prominence in U.S. Catholic history.

29   Fiorenza interview; Cecile Holmes White, "New Prelate to Serve Houston Diocese: A Bilingual, Bicultural Bishop," *HC*, January 30, 1993; Cecile Holmes White, "Catholics Plan Hispanic Outreach," *HC*, June 18, 1994; Richard Vara, "Se Habla Espanol: AUXILIARY CATHOLIC BISHOP SIGN OF GROWING HISPANIC INFLUENCE," *HC*, February 9, 2002; and Larry B. Stammer and Richard Vara, "U.S. Bishops Give More Attention to Hispanics," *HC*, November 16, 2002, all available at <http://continuum.uta.edu> (accessed August 4, 2004). See also Rossi and May, eds., *Recall, Rejoice, Renew*, 102–4.

30   Riebe-Estrella, "Strategies on the Left," 205, 215.

31   Díaz-Stevens and Stevens-Arroyo, *Recognizing the Latino Resurgence*, 202, 214–15.

32   Jim Morris, "TMO Gets More Clout with Age," *HC*, October 14, 1990, <http://

continuum.uta.edu> (accessed August 3, 2004); Betty L. Martin, "TMO Leaders Speak Up, Extract Officials' Plans," *HC*, March 18, 2004, <http://continuum .uta.edu> (accessed January 3, 2005). See also Kim Cobb, "East End Residents Oppose Plans to Build Trash Burner," *HC*, February 5, 1987, <http://continuum .uta.edu> (accessed August 4, 2004); Stephen Johnson, "TROUBLE WITHIN, TROUBLE WITHOUT: Cantinas Spill Violence and Noise into Surrounding Neighborhoods," *HC*, June 24, 1991; "Politicians Get Religion at Meeting: Church Leaders Seek Help on Social Issues," *HC*, May 7, 2001, <http://continuum.uta.edu> (accessed August 3, 2004); Fiorenza interview; and Guillén 2004 interview. On the history of TMO in Houston, see Mary Beth Rogers, *Cold Anger*, and Warren, *Dry Bones Rattling*, 61–65.

33 Betty L. Martin, "El Dorado Neighbors Want to Take Back Their Streets," *HC*, November 20, 2003, <http://continuum.uta.edu> (accessed August 3, 2004); Jo Ann Zúñiga, "James D. Steffes, 66, 'Unusually Dedicated'" (obituary), *HC*, September 26, 2001, <http://continuum.uta.edu> (accessed August 3, 2004); Guillén 2004 interview.

34 Díaz-Stevens and Stevens-Arroyo, *Recognizing the Latino Resurgence*, 205–10; Edwin H. Hernández, "Moving from the Cathedral," 232–34. See also Arlene M. Sánchez Walsh, *Latino Pentecostal Identity*.

35 Díaz-Stevens and Stevens-Arroyo, *Recognizing the Latino Resurgence*, 206–7.

36 Ibid., 209–10.

37 Ibid., 206.

38 Levitt, "Two Nations under God?" 157.

BIBLIOGRAPHY

ARCHIVAL AND MANUSCRIPT SOURCES

Austin, Texas
    Catholic Archives of Texas
        Diary of Father Frank Urbanovsky
        Diocesan Chancery Collection
        Episcopal Collection
        PADRES Collection
        Parish Collection
        Women Religious Orders Collection

Chicago, Illinois
    Archives of Loyola University of Chicago
        American Board of Catholic Missions *Reports*
        Catholic Church Extension Society Records

Houston, Texas
    Archives of the Diocese of Galveston-Houston
        Blessed Sacrament Parish Files
        Immaculate Conception Parish Files
        Our Lady of Guadalupe Parish Files
        Our Lady of St. John Parish Files
        Our Lady of Sorrows Parish Files
        St. Alphonsus Parish Files
        St. Joseph–St. Stephen Parish Files
        St. Patrick Parish Files
        St. Philip Parish Files
        St. Raphael Parish Files
        St. Stephen Parish Files
        Texas Catholic Herald Photograph Files

Houston Metropolitan Research Center, Houston Public Library
  Leonel Castillo Collection
  Hector García Collection
  Melesio Gómez Family Collection
  Petra Guillén Family Collection
  Franklin Harbach Papers
  Medellín Family Collection
  Mexican American Family and Photograph Collection
  Mexican American Small Collections
  Juan P. Rodríguez Family Collection
  Joe Torres / Huelga Schools Collection
  Ramón and Delfina Villagómez Family Collection
  VISTA Collection

San Antonio, Texas
  Archives of the Archdiocese of San Antonio
    Religious Congregations of Women Collections
  Archives of the Congregation of Divine Providence
    Catechists File
    Our Lady of Guadalupe Parish (Houston) File
    St. Patrick School (Houston) File
  Archives of the Oblates of Mary Immaculate
    Codex Historicus of Our Lady of Guadalupe Parish (Houston)
    Codex Historicus of St. Patrick Parish (Houston)
    Immaculate Conception Parish (Houston) File
    Immaculate Heart of Mary Parish (Houston) File
    Oblata File
    Provincial Records
    File 8H59

GOVERNMENT DOCUMENTS

U.S. Bureau of the Census. *Thirteenth Census of the United States, 1910. Population.* Vol. 3. Washington, D.C.: Government Printing Office, 1913.
———. *Fourteenth Census of the United States, 1920. Population.* Vol. 3. Washington, D.C.: Government Printing Office, 1923.
———. *Fifteenth Census of the United States, 1930. Population.* Vol. 3, pt. 2. Washington, D.C.: Government Printing Office, 1932.

——. *Fifteenth Census of the United States, 1930. Special Report on Foreign-Born White Families . . . with an Appendix Giving Statistics for Mexican, Indian, Chinese, and Japanese Families*. Vol. 6, supplement. Washington, D.C.: Government Printing Office, 1933.

——. *Sixteenth Census of the United States, 1940. Population*. Vol. 2, pt. 6. Washington, D.C.: Government Printing Office, 1943.

——. *Seventeenth Census of the United States, 1950. Population*. Vol. 2, pt. 43. Washington, D.C.: Government Printing Office, 1952.

——. *Eighteenth Census of the United States, 1960. Census Tracts, Houston, Texas*. Final Report PHC(1)-63. Washington, D.C.: Government Printing Office, 1962.

——. *Nineteenth Census of the United States, 1970. Population*. Vol. 1, pt. 45, sec. 1. Washington, D.C.: Government Printing Office, 1973.

INTERVIEWS

The original tape recordings and notes of oral history interviews conducted by the author are held in the Houston Metropolitan Research Center, Houston, Texas.

Bello, Reverend E. Z. Interview by Ruth T. Bello, August 12, 1986, Houston, Texas. Tape recording. Ruth T. Bello Collection. Houston Metropolitan Research Center, Houston, Texas.

Cárdenas, Sister Mary Dolores. Interview by the author, April 17, 1990, San Antonio, Texas. Tape recording.

Fiorenza, Bishop Joseph A. Interview by the author, July 30, 2004, Houston, Texas. Tape recording.

García, Mrs. Esther. Director, Galveston-Houston Diocese Office of Hispanic Ministries. Interview by the author, November 14, 1990, Houston, Texas. Tape recording.

——. Interview by the author, June 3, 1992, Redwood City, California. Telephone interview.

Gonzales, Joe E., Raquel A. Gonzales, and anonymous participant. Interview by the author, December 16, 1990, Houston, Texas. Tape recording.

Guillén, Mrs. Petra R. Interview by the author, October 22, 1990, Houston, Texas. Tape recording.

——. Interview by the author, June 16, 1992, Redwood City, California. Telephone interview.

——. Interview by the author, July 29, 2004, Houston, Texas. Tape recording.

McCarthy, Bishop John E. Interview by the author, October 18, 1991, Austin, Texas. Tape recording.

——. Interview by Jan H. Cohen, March 10, 1972, Houston, Texas. OH 27, Texas Labor Archives, University of Texas at Arlington Special Collections Division.

Moreno, Sister Mary Rachel. Interview by the author, April 18, 1990, San Antonio, Texas. Typescript.

Novarro, Reverend James. Interview by Thomas H. Kreneck, December 13, 1984. Tape recording. Houston Metropolitan Research Center Oral History Collection, Houston, Texas.

Rodríguez, Sister Agnes Rita. Interview by Diana Torres. N.d. Mexican American Studies Oral History Collection, Our Lady of the Lake University, San Antonio, Texas.

Rodríguez, Juan and Isidra. Interview by the author, July 29, 2004, Houston, Texas. Tape recording.

Urbanovsky, Father Frank. Interview by Thomas H. Kreneck, 1979. Tape recording. Houston Metropolitan Research Center Oral History Collection, Houston, Texas.

Villagómez, Mary C. Interviews by the author, October 25 and November 9, 1990, Houston, Texas. Tape recording.

——. Interview by the author, June 3, 1992, Redwood City, California. Telephone interview.

Zavala, Mrs. Teresa Villagómez, and Mrs. Hope G. Jiménez. Interview by the author, December 12, 1990, Houston, Texas. Tape recording.

Periodicals

Compass, Houston, Texas, 1967–69, 1972.

Dallas Morning News, June 25, July 11, 2001.

El Puerto, Houston, Texas, 1959.

El Sol, Houston, Texas, 1968–72.

Extension Magazine (Catholic Church Extension Society), 1907–68 ca.

Family Circular (Sisters of Divine Providence newsletter), 1912–60.

Gazette Telegraph, Colorado Springs, Colorado, May 18, 1996.

Houston Chronicle, Houston, Texas, 1910–72.

La Gaceta Mexicana, Houston, Texas, April 15, June 1, 1928.

Mary Immaculate (Oblate Fathers' magazine), 1915–67.

National Catholic Reporter, Kansas City, Missouri, 1964–72.

Papel Chicano, Houston, Texas, 1970–72.

Southern Messenger, San Antonio, Texas, September 19, 1912, June 23, 1938, and November 2, 1950.

Star-Telegram, Fort Worth, Texas, May 11, 2001.

BOOKS, ARTICLES, ESSAYS, AND PAMPHLETS

Abramson, Harold J. *Ethnic Diversity in Catholic America*. New York: John Wiley & Sons, 1973.

Acuña, Rodolfo. *Occupied America: A History of Chicanos*. 3d ed. New York: Harper Collins, 1988.

Ahlstrom, Sidney E. *A Religious History of the American People*. New Haven, CT: Yale University Press, 1972.

Alba, Richard D. *Ethnic Identity: The Transformation of White America*. New Haven, CT: Yale University Press, 1990.

Alexander, June Granatir. "Religion and Ethnic Identity in a Slavic Community: Pittsburg's Slovak Catholics and Protestants." *Studi Emigrazione* 103 (September 1991): 423–41.

Allen, Ruth A. *East Texas Lumber Workers: An Economic and Social Picture, 1870–1950*. Austin: University of Texas Press, 1961.

Anderson, Karen. *Wartime Women: Sex Roles, Family Relations, and the Status of Women during World War II*. Westport, CT: Greenwood Press, 1981.

Armstrong, Reverend Walter W. *Room to Grow: A History of Houston Methodist Missions*. Houston, TX: privately printed, 1963.

Badillo, David A. "The Catholic Church and the Making of Mexican-American Parish Communities in the Midwest." In *Mexican Americans and the Catholic Church, 1900–1965*, edited by Jay P. Dolan and Gilberto M. Hinojosa, 235–308. Notre Dame, IN: University of Notre Dame Press, 1994.

Baer, Hans A., and Merrill Singer, *African-American Religion in the Twentieth Century: Varieties of Protest and Accommodation*. Knoxville: University of Tennessee Press, 1992.

Balderrama, Francisco E., and Raymond Rodríguez, *Decade of Betrayal: Mexican Repatriation in the 1930s*. Albuquerque: University of New Mexico Press, 1995.

Barton, Josef J. "Land, Labor, and Community in Nueces: Czech Farmers and Mexican Laborers in South Texas, 1880–1930." In *Ethnicity on the Great Plains*, edited by Frederick C. Luebke, 190–209. Lincoln: University of Nebraska Press, 1980.

Bass, Dorothy C., and Sandra Hughes Boyd. *Women in American Religious History: An Annotated Bibliography and Guide to Sources*. Boston: G. K. Hall, 1986.

Basso, Sister Teresita. "The Emerging 'Chicana' Sister." *Review for Religious* 30 (1971): 1019–28.

Bayard, Ralph. *Lone Star Vanguard: The Catholic Re-occupation of Texas, 1838–1848*. St. Louis: Vincentian Press, 1945.

Bean, Frank D., and Marta Tienda. "The Structuring of Hispanic Ethnicity: Theoretical and Historical Considerations." In *The Hispanic Population of the United
States*, edited by Frank D. Bean and Marta Tienda, 7–35. New York: Sage, 1987.

Beeth, Howard, and Cary D. Wintz, eds. *Black Dixie: Afro-Texan History and Culture
in Houston*. College Station: Texas A&M University Press, 1992.

Bogardus, Emory S. *The Mexican in the United States*. Los Angeles: University of
Southern California Press, 1934; reprint, San Francisco: R & E Research Associ-
ates, 1970.

Bornstein, Daniel E. *The Bianchi of 1399: Popular Devotion in Late Medieval Italy*.
Ithaca, NY: Cornell University Press, 1993.

Boyer, Paul, and Janet Wilson James, eds. *Women in American Religion*. Philadelphia:
University of Pennsylvania Press, 1980.

Brackenridge, R. Douglas, and Francisco O. García-Treto, *Iglesia Presbiteriana: A History of Presbyterians and Mexican Americans in the Southwest*, 2nd ed. San Antonio,
TX: Trinity University Press, 1987.

Bresette, Linna E. *Mexicans in the United States: A Report of a Brief Survey*. Washington, D.C.: National Catholic Welfare Conference, 1929.

Bronder, Saul E. *Social Justice and Church Authority: The Public Life of Archbishop Robert
E. Lucey*. Philadelphia: Temple University Press, 1982.

Brown, Dorothy M., and Elizabeth McKeown. *The Poor Belong to Us: Catholic
Charities and American Welfare*. Cambridge, MA: Harvard University Press, 1997.

Bullard, Robert D. *Invisible Houston: The Black Experience in Boom and Bust*. College
Station: Texas A&M University Press, 1987.

Burns, Jeffrey M. "The Mexican American Catholic Community in California, 1850–
1980." In *Religion and Society in the American West: Historical Essays*, edited by
Carl Guarneri and David Álvarez, 255–73. Lantham, MD: University Press of
America, 1987.

———. "The Mexican Catholic Community in California." In *Mexican Americans and
the Catholic Church, 1900–1965*, edited by Jay P. Dolan and Gilberto M. Hinojosa,
129–233. Notre Dame, IN: University of Notre Dame Press, 1994.

Butler, Jon. "The Future of American Religious History: Prospectus, Agenda, Trans-
atlantic Problematique." *William and Mary Quarterly* 42 (April 1985): 167–83.

———. "Historiographical Heresy: Catholicism as a Model for American Religious
History." In *Belief in History: Innovative Approaches to European and American Reli-
gion*, edited by Thomas Kselman, 286–309. Notre Dame, IN: University of Notre
Dame Press, 1991.

Camarillo, Albert. *Chicanos in a Changing Society: From Mexican Pueblos to American*

Barrios in Santa Barbara and Southern California, 1848–1930. Cambridge, MA: Harvard University Press, 1979.

Cárdenas, Sr. Mary Dolores. *Meditaciones.* San Antonio: Our Lady of the Lake Convent, 1976.

Cardoso, Lawrence A. *Mexican Emigration to the United States, 1897–1931.* Tucson: University of Arizona Press, 1980.

Carrillo, Alberto. "The Sociological Failure of the Catholic Church towards the Chicano." *Journal of Mexican American Studies* 1 (Winter 1971): 75–83.

Carroll, Michael P. *The Penitente Brotherhood: Patriarchy and Hispano-Catholicism in New Mexico.* Baltimore, MD: Johns Hopkins University Press, 2002.

Castañeda, Carlos E. "The Missionary Years in Texas." In *Centennial: The Story of the Development of the Kingdom of God on Earth in that Portion of the Vineyard Which for One Hundred Years Has Been the Diocese of Galveston,* by the Catholic Youth Organization Centennial Book Committee, 23–27. Houston, TX: Diocese of Galveston, 1947.

———. *Our Catholic Heritage in Texas.* 7 vols. Austin: Von Boeckmann-Jones, 1936–58.

Catholic Youth Organization Centennial Book Committee. *Centennial: The Story of the Development of the Kingdom of God on Earth in that Portion of the Vineyard Which for One Hundred Years Has Been the Diocese of Galveston.* Houston, TX: Diocese of Galveston, 1947.

Christian, William A., Jr. *Local Religion in Sixteenth-Century Spain.* Princeton, NJ: Princeton University Press, 1981.

Clark, Victor S. "Mexican Labor in the United States." *Bulletin of the Bureau of Labor* 17 (September 1908): 466–522. Reprinted in *Mexican Labor in the United States,* edited by Carlos E. Cortés. New York: Arno, 1974.

Coatsworth, John H. *Growth Against Development: The Economic Impact of Railroads in Porfirian Mexico.* Dekalb: Northern Illinois University Press, 1981.

Coburn, Carol K., and Martha Smith, C.S.J. "Creating Community and Identity: Exploring Religious and Gender Ideology in the Lives of American Women Religious, 1836–1920." *U.S. Catholic Historian* 14, no. 1 (Winter 1996): 91–108.

———. *Spirited Lives: How Nuns Shaped Catholic Culture and American Life, 1836–1920.* Chapel Hill: University of North Carolina Press, 1999.

Cohen, Gary B. "Ethnic Persistence and Change: Concepts and Models for Historical Research." *Social Science Quarterly* 65 (December 1984): 1029–42.

Collins, Donna Misner. *Ethnic Identification: The Greek Americans of Houston, Texas.* New York: AMS Press, 1991.

Connor, Seymour V. *Texas: A History.* Arlington Heights, IL: AHM Publishing, 1971.

Conzen, Kathleen Neils, et al. "The Invention of Ethnicity: A Perspective from the U.S.A." *Journal of American Ethnic History* 12 (Fall 1992): 3–41.

Cortés, Carlos E., ed. *Church Views of the Mexican American.* New York: Arno, 1974.

———. *Mexican Labor in the United States.* New York: Arno, 1974.

———. *Protestantism and Latinos in the United States.* New York: Arno, 1980.

Cox, Harvey G. "The 'New Breed' in American Churches: Sources of Social Activism in American Religion." *Daedalus* (Winter 1967): 135–50.

Crocker, Ruth Hutchinson. "Gary Mexicans and 'Christian Americanization': A Study in Cultural Conflict." In *Forging a Community: The Latino Experience in Northwest Indiana, 1919–1975,* edited by James B. Lane and Edward J. Escobar, 115–34. Chicago: Cattails Press, 1987.

Dávalos, Karen Mary. "*La Quinceañera*: Making Gender and Ethnic Identities." *Frontiers* 16, nos. 2/3 (1996): 101–27.

Davidson, Chandler. *Biracial Politics: Conflict and Coalition in the Metropolitan South.* Baton Rouge: Louisiana State University Press, 1972.

Davis, Natalie Zemon. "From 'Popular Religion' to Religious Cultures." In *Reformation Europe: A Guide to Research,* edited by Steven Ozment, 321–41. St. Louis: Center for Reformation Research, 1982.

———. "Some Tasks and Themes in the Study of Popular Religion." In *The Pursuit of Holiness in Late Medieval and Renaissance Religion,* edited by Charles Trinkaus and Heiko A. Oberman, 307–36. Leiden, Netherlands: E. J. Brill, 1974.

Deck, Allan Figueroa. *The Second Wave: Hispanic Ministry and the Evangelization of Cultures.* New York: Paulist Press, 1989.

———. "The Spirituality of United States Hispanics: An Introductory Essay." *U.S. Catholic Historian* 9 (Spring 1990): 137–46.

"Dedicated to Community Action." In *Harris County PASO 5th Anniversary and Salute to Valley Farm Workers,* unnumbered. Houston, TX: Harris County PASO, 1966.

De la Teja, Jesús F. *San Antonio de Béxar: A Community on New Spain's Northern Frontier.* Albuquerque: University of New Mexico Press, 1995.

De León, Arnoldo. *Ethnicity in the Sunbelt: A History of Mexican Americans in Houston.* Houston, TX: University of Houston, Mexican American Studies, 1989.

———. *Mexican Americans in Texas: A Brief History.* Arlington Heights, IL: Harlan Davidson, 1993.

———. *Racial Frontiers: Africans, Chinese, and Mexicans in Western America, 1848–1890.* Albuquerque: University of New Mexico Press, 2002.

———. *The Tejano Community, 1836–1900.* Albuquerque: University of New Mexico Press, 1982.

——. *They Called Them Greasers: Anglo Attitudes toward Mexicans in Texas, 1821–1900.* Austin: University of Texas Press, 1983.

Deutsch, Sarah. *No Separate Refuge: Culture, Class, and Gender on an Anglo-Hispanic Frontier in the American Southwest, 1880–1940.* New York: Oxford University Press, 1987.

Díaz-Stevens, Ana María. *Oxcart Catholicism on Fifth Avenue: The Impact of the Puerto Rican Migration upon the Archdiocese of New York.* Notre Dame, IN: University of Notre Dame Press, 1993.

Díaz-Stevens, Ana María, and Anthony M. Stevens-Arroyo. *Recognizing the Latino Resurgence in U.S. Religion: The Emmaus Paradigm.* Boulder, CO: Westview Press, 1998.

Diekemper, Barnabas C. "The Catholic Church in the Shadows: The Southwestern United States during the Mexican Period." *Journal of the West* 24 (1985): 46–53.

——. "French Clergy on the Texas Frontier, 1837–1907." *East Texas Historical Journal* 21 (Fall 1983): 29–38.

Dolan, Jay P. *The American Catholic Experience: A History from Colonial Times to the Present.* Garden City, NJ: Doubleday, 1985.

——. "The New Religious History." *Reviews in American History* 15 (September 1987): 449–54.

——. "The People as Well as the Prelates: A Social History of a Denomination." In *Reimagining Denominationalism: Interpretive Essays*, edited by Robert Bruce Mullin and Russell E. Richey, 43–57. New York: Oxford University Press, 1994.

——. "Religion and Social Change in the American Catholic Community." In *Altered Landscapes: Christianity in America, 1935–1985*, edited by David W. Lotz, 42–60. Grand Rapids, MI: Eerdmans, 1989.

——, ed. *The American Catholic Parish.* 2 vols. Mahwah, NJ: Paulist Press, 1987.

Dolan, Jay P., and Allan Figueroa Deck, eds. *Hispanic Catholic Culture in the U.S.: Issues and Concerns.* Notre Dame, IN: University of Notre Dame Press, 1994.

Dolan, Jay P., and Gilberto M. Hinojosa, eds. *Mexican Americans and the Catholic Church, 1900–1965.* Notre Dame, IN: University of Notre Dame Press, 1994.

Dolan, Jay P., and Jaime R. Vidal, eds. *Puerto Rican and Cuban Catholics in the U.S.: 1900–1965.* Notre Dame, IN: University of Notre Dame Press, 1994.

Doyon, Bernard. *The Cavalry of Christ on the Río Grande, 1849–1883.* Milwaukee: Bruce Press, 1956.

Dunn, Ethel, and Stephen P. Dunn. "Religion and Ethnicity: The Case of the American Molokans." *Ethnicity* 4 (1977): 370–79.

Elizondo, Rev. Virgilio P. *Galilean Journey: The Mexican-American Promise.* Maryknoll, NY: Orbis, 1983.

——. *Guadalupe: Mother of the New Creation*. Maryknoll, NY: Orbis Books, 1997.

——. *La Morenita: Evangelizer of the Americas*. San Antonio: Mexican American Cultural Center, 1980.

Erevia, Sr. Angela. *Quinceañera*. San Antonio: Mexican American Cultural Center, 1980.

Espín, Orlando O. "Popular Catholicism among Latinos." In *Hispanic Catholic Culture in the U.S.: Issues and Concerns*, edited by Jay P. Dolan and Allan Figueroa Deck, 308–59. Notre Dame, IN: University of Notre Dame Press, 1994.

Evans, Bernard F. "Campaign for Human Development: Church Involvement in Social Change." *Review of Religious Research* 20 (Summer 1979): 264–78.

Feagin, Joe R. *Free Enterprise City: Houston in Political-Economic Perspective*. New Brunswick, NJ: Rutgers University Press, 1988.

Fitzmorris, Sr. Mary Angela. *Four Decades of Catholicism in Texas, 1820–1860*. Washington, D.C.: Catholic University of America Press, 1926.

Flores, Richard R. *Los Pastores: History and Performance in the Mexican Shepherd's Play of South Texas*. Washington, D.C.: Smithsonian Institution Press, 1995.

Flores, Fr. Roberto, and Silvia Novo-Pena. *Interiores: Aspectos Seculares de la Religión*. Houston, TX: D. H. White, 1982.

Foley, Neil. "Becoming Hispanic: Mexican Americans and the Faustian Pact with Whiteness." In *New Directions in Mexican American Studies* (1997). Publications of the Center for Mexican American Studies. Austin: University of Texas Press, 1998.

——. *The White Scourge: Mexicans, Blacks, and Poor Whites in Texas Cotton Culture*. Berkeley: University of California Press, 1997.

Forbes, Jack D. "Race and Color in Mexican-American Problems." *Journal of Human Relations* 16 (1968): 55–68.

Galarza, Ernesto. *Merchants of Labor: The Mexican Bracero Story*. Santa Barbara, CA: McNally & Loftin, 1964.

——. *The Roman Catholic Church as a Factor in the Political and Social History of Mexico*. Sacramento, CA: Capital Press, 1928.

Gamio, Manuel. *The Mexican Immigrant: His Life Story*. Chicago: University of Chicago Press, 1931; reprinted as *The Life Story of the Mexican Immigrant*, New York: Dover Publications, 1971.

——. *Mexican Immigration to the United States*. Chicago: University of Chicago Press 1930; reprint, New York: Dover Publications, 1971.

García, Alma M., ed. *Chicana Feminist Thought: The Basic Historical Writings*. New York: Routledge, 1997.

García, Ignacio M. *Chicanismo: The Forging of a Militant Ethos among Mexican Americans*. Tucson: University of Arizona Press, 1997.

——. *United We Win: The Rise and Fall of La Raza Unida Party*. Tucson: University of Arizona, Mexican American Studies, 1989.

García, Juan Ramón. *Operation Wetback: The Mass Deportation of Mexican Undocumented Workers in 1954*. Westport, CT: Greenwood Press, 1980.

García, Juan R., and Ángel Cal. "El Círculo de Obreros Católicos 'San José,' 1925 to 1930." In *Forging a Community: The Latino Experience in Northwest Indiana, 1919–1975*, edited by James B. Lane and Edward J. Escobar, 95–114. Chicago: Cattails Press, 1987.

García, María Cristina. "Agents of Americanization: Rusk Settlement and the Houston Mexicano Community, 1907–1950." In *Mexican Americans in Texas History: Selected Essays*, edited by Emilio Zamora, Cynthia Orozco, and Rodolfo Rocha, 121–37. Austin: Texas State Historical Society, 2000.

García, Mario T. *Desert Immigrants: The Mexicans of El Paso, 1880–1920*. New Haven, CT: Yale University Press, 1981.

——. *Memories of Chicano History: The Life and Narrative of Bert Corona*. Berkeley and Los Angeles: University of California Press, 1994.

——. *Mexican Americans: Leadership, Ideology, and Identity*. New Haven, CT: Yale University Press, 1989.

García, Richard A. "The Mexican American Mind: A Product of the 1930s." In *History, Culture, and Society: Chicano Studies in the 1980s*, edited by Mario T. García and Francisco Lomelí, 67–93. Ypsilanti, MI: Bilingual Press, 1983.

——. *The Rise of the Mexican American Middle Class: San Antonio, 1929–1941*. College Station: Texas A&M University Press, 1991.

Genovese, Eugene D. *Roll, Jordan, Roll: The World the Slaves Made*. New York: Random House, 1972.

Gibson, Margaret A. *Accommodation Without Assimilation: Sikh Immigrants in an American High School*. Ithaca, NY: Cornell University Press, 1988.

Giles, Robert C. *Changing Times: The Story of the Diocese of Galveston Houston in Commemoration of Its Founding*. N.p.: Diocese of Galveston-Houston, [1972].

Gleason, Philip. "Immigrant Assimilation and the Crisis of Americanization." Chap. 3 in *Keeping the Faith: American Catholicism Past and Present*. Notre Dame, IN: University of Notre Dame Press, 1987.

Goizueta, Roberto S. *Caminemos con Jesús: Toward a Hispanic / Latino Theology of Accompaniment*. Maryknoll, NY: Orbis, 1995.

Gómez-Quiñones, Juan. *Chicano Politics: Reality and Promise, 1940–1990*. Albuquerque: University of New Mexico Press, 1990.

Goodman, Mary Ellen, et al. *The Mexican-American Population of Houston: A Survey of the Field, 1965–1970*. Houston, TX: Rice University Studies, 1971.

Gordon, Linda. "Putting Children First: Women, Maternalism, and Welfare in the Early Twentieth Century." In *U.S. History as Women's History: New Feminist Essays*, edited by Linda K. Kerber, Alice Kessler-Harris, and Kathryn Kish-Sklar, 63–86. Chapel Hill: University of North Carolina Press, 1995.

Gossett, Thomas F. *Race: The History of an Idea in America*. Dallas: Southern Methodist University Press, 1963.

Grebler, Leo, Joan W. Moore, and Ralph C. Guzmán. *The Mexican-American People: The Nation's Second Largest Minority*. New York: Free Press, 1970.

Griffin, Sister Janet, C.D.P. "Sisters of Divine Providence: Feminists in Ministry." Article on-line. Available from <http://www.cdptexas.org/reflections/Feminists—in—Ministry.html>. Accessed April 16, 2003.

Griswold del Castillo, Richard. *La Familia: Chicano Families in the Urban Southwest, 1848 to the Present*. Notre Dame, IN: University of Notre Dame, 1984.

Guarneri, Carl, and David Álvarez, eds. *Religion and Society in the American West: Historical Essays*. Lantham, MD: University Press of America, 1987.

Guerra, Roberto S., and Mary Ellen Goodman. *A Content Assessment of "El Sol," a Community Newspaper*. Houston, TX: Rice University Center for Research in Social Change and Economic Development, 1968.

Gutiérrez, David G. *Walls and Mirrors: Mexican Americans, Mexican Immigrants, and the Politics of Ethnicity*. Berkeley and Los Angeles: University of California Press, 1995.

Hackett, David G. "Sociology of Religion and American Religious History." *Journal for the Scientific Study of Religion* 27 (1988): 461–74.

Hall, David D., ed. *Lived Religion in America: Toward a History of Practice*. Princeton, NJ: Princeton University Press, 1997.

Halter, Marilyn. *Between Race and Ethnicity: Cape Verdean American Immigrants, 1860–1965*. Urbana: University of Illinois Press, 1993.

Harrington, Patricia. "Mother of Death, Mother of Rebirth: The Mexican Virgin of Guadalupe." *Journal of the American Academy of Religion* 56 (Spring 1988): 25–50.

Harte, Thomas J. "Racial and National Parishes in the United States." In *The Sociology of the Parish*, edited by C. J. Nuesse and Thomas J. Harte, 154–77. Milwaukee: Bruce, 1951.

Hegarty, Sr. Mary Loyola. *Serving with Gladness*. Milwaukee: Bruce, 1967.

Hernández, Edwin H. "Moving from the Cathedral to Storefront Churches: Understanding Religious Growth and Decline among Latino Protestants." In *Protestantes / Protestants: Hispanic Christianity Within Mainline Traditions*, edited by David Maldonado Jr., 216–35. Nashville, TN: Abingdon, 1999.

Hernández, José A. *Mutual Aid for Survival: The Case of the Mexican American*. Malabar, FL: Krieger Publishing, 1983.

Herrera, Marina. "The Context and Development of Hispanic Ecclesial Leadership." In *Hispanic Catholic Culture in the U.S.: Issues and Concerns*, edited by Jay P. Dolan and Allan Figueroa Deck, 166–205. Notre Dame, IN: University of Notre Dame Press, 1994.

"Hidden Houston: The City You See on the Surface Is Not All the City There Is." Interview of Petra Guillén by David Theis. *Cite: The Architectural and Design Review of Houston* 50 (Spring 2001): 24.

Higham, John. "Current Trends in the Study of Ethnicity in the United States." *Journal of American Ethnic History* 2 (Fall 1982): 5–15.

Hinojosa, Gilberto M. "The Enduring Hispanic Faith Communities: Spanish and Texas Church Historiography." *Journal of Texas Catholic History and Culture* 1 (March 1990): 20–41.

———. "Mexican-American Faith Communities in Texas and the Southwest." In *Mexican Americans and the Catholic Church, 1900–1965*, edited by Jay P. Dolan and Gilberto M. Hinojosa, 9–125. Notre Dame, IN: University of Notre Dame Press, 1994.

Hoffman, Abraham. *Unwanted Mexican Americans in the Great Depression*. Tucson: University of Arizona Press, 1974.

Hough, Richard L. "Religion and Pluralism among the Spanish-Speaking Groups of the Southwest." In *Politics and Society in the Southwest: Ethnicity and Chicano Pluralism*, edited by Z. Anthony Kruszewski, Richard L. Hough, and Jacob Ornstein-Galicia, 169–95. Boulder, CO: Westview Press, 1982.

Isais-A., Raoul E. "The Chicano and the American Catholic Church." *El Grito del Sol* 4 (Winter 1979): 9–24.

Isasi-Díaz, Ada María, and Yolanda Tarango. *Hispanic Women, Prophetic Voice in the Church*. San Francisco: Harper & Row, 1988.

Jordan, Terry G. "A Century and a Half of Ethnic Change in Texas, 1836–1986." *Southwestern Historical Quarterly* 89 (April 1986): 385–422.

———. "The 1887 Census of Texas' Hispanic Population." *Aztlán* 12 (Autumn 1981): 271–78.

Journal of the West 23 (January 1984). Special issue on religion.

Juárez, José Roberto. "La Iglesia Católica y el Chicano en Sud Texas, 1836–1911." *Aztlán* 4 (Fall 1974): 217–55.

———. *"Los Padres Rancheristas*: The 19th-Century Struggle for Mexican-American Catholicism in South Texas." In *Ranching in South Texas: A Symposium*, edited by Joe S. Graham, 15–43. Kingsville: Texas A&M University, 1994.

Kaplan, Barry J. "Houston, the Golden Buckle of the Southwest." In *Sunbelt Cities: Politics and Growth Since World War II*, edited by Richard A. Bernard and Bradley R. Rice, 196–212. Austin: University of Texas Press, 1983.

Kelley, Rev. Francis C. *The Story of Extension*. Chicago: Extension Press, 1922.

Kennelly, Karen, ed. *American Catholic Women: A Historical Exploration*. New York: Macmillan, 1989.

Keyes, Charles F. "The Dialectics of Ethnic Change." In *Ethnic Change*, edited by Charles F. Keyes, 4–30. Seattle: University of Washington Press, 1981.

Kiev, Ari. *Curanderismo: Mexican-American Folk Psychiatry*. New York: Free Press, 1968.

Kiser, George C., and Martha Woody Kiser, eds. *Mexican Workers in the United States: Historical and Political Perspectives*. Albuquerque: University of New Mexico Press, 1979.

Kreneck, Thomas H. *Del Pueblo: A Pictorial History of Houston's Hispanic Community*. Houston, TX: Houston International University, 1989.

———. "The Letter from Chapultepec." *Houston Review* 3 (Summer 1981): 268–71.

———. *Mexican American Odyssey: Felix Tijerina, Entrepreneur and Civic Leader, 1905–1965*. University of Houston Series in Mexican American Studies, no. 2. College Station: Texas A&M University Press, 2001.

Kselman, Thomas. Introduction to *Belief in History: Innovative Approaches to European and American Religion*, edited by Thomas Kselman, 1–15. Notre Dame, IN: University of Notre Dame Press, 1991.

———, ed. *Belief in History: Innovative Approaches to European and American Religion*. Notre Dame, IN: University of Notre Dame Press, 1991.

"La Marcha . . . Valley Farm Workers 491-Mile March for Justice." In *Harris County PASO 5th Anniversary and Salute to Valley Farm Workers*, unnumbered. Houston, TX: Harris County PASO, 1966.

Lane, James B., and Edward J. Escobar. *Forging a Community: The Latino Experience in Northwest Indiana, 1919–1975*. Chicago: Cattails Press, 1987.

Larkin, Emmet. "The Devotional Revolution in Ireland, 1850–75." *American Historical Review* 77 (June 1972): 625–52.

Lasswell, Mary. *John Henry Kirby, Prince of the Pines*. Austin: Encino, 1967.

León, Luís. "Born Again in East LA: The Congregation as Border Space." In *Gatherings in Diaspora: Religious Communities and the New Immigration*, edited by R. Stephen Warner and Judith G. Witner, 163–96. Philadelphia: Temple University Press, 1998.

Leonard, Karen. "Historical Constructions of Ethnicity: Research on Punjabi Immigrants in California." *Journal of American Ethnic History* 12 (Summer 1993): 3–26.

Levine, Lawrence W. *Black Culture and Black Consciousness: African American Folk Thought from Slavery to Freedom*. New York: Oxford University Press, 1977.

Levitt, Peggy. "Two Nations under God?: Latino Religious Life in the United States." In *Latinos: Re-making America*, edited by Marcelo M. Súarez-Orozco and Mariela M. Páez, 150–64. Los Angeles: University of California Press, 2002.

Lincoln, C. Eric, and Lawrence H. Mamiya, *The Black Church in the African American Experience*. Durham, NC: Duke University Press, 1990.

Liptak, Dolores Ann. *Immigrants and Their Church*. New York: Macmillan, 1989.

———. "Lost Hopes for Blacks and Hispanic Catholics." Chap. 11 in *Immigrants and Their Church*. New York: Macmillan, 1989.

Listening: Journal of Religion and Culture 19 (Fall 1984). Special issue on religion in the American West.

Lotz, David W. "A Changing Historiography: From Church History to Religious History." In *Altered Landscapes: Christianity in America, 1935–1985*, edited by David W. Lotz, 312–39. Grand Rapids, MI: Eerdmans, 1989.

Maas, Elaine H. *The Jews of Houston: An Ethnographic Study*. New York: AMS Press, 1989.

Manuel, Herschel T. "The Mexican Population of Texas." *Southwestern Social Science Quarterly* 15 (June 1934): 29–51.

Martínez, Oscar J. "On the Size of the Chicano Population: New Estimates, 1850–1900." *Aztlán* 6 (Spring 1975): 43–67.

Marty, Martin E. "The Editors' Bookshelf: American Religious History." *Journal of Religion* 62 (January 1982): 99–109.

———. "Ethnicity: The Skeleton of Religion in America." *Church History* 41 (1972): 5–21.

———. "Introduction: Religion in America, 1935–1985." In *Altered Landscapes: Christianity in America, 1935–1985*, edited by David W. Lotz, 1–16. Grand Rapids, MI: Eerdmans, 1989.

"Maternalism as a Paradigm." A symposium in *Journal of Women's History* 5, no. 2 (Fall 1993): 95–131.

Matovina, Timothy M. "Representation and the Reconstruction of Power: The Rise of PADRES and *Las Hermanas*." In *What's Left? Liberal American Catholics*, edited by Mary Jo Weaver, 220–37. Bloomington: Indiana University Press, 1999.

———. *Tejano Religion and Ethnicity: San Antonio, 1821–1860*. Austin: University of Texas Press, 1995.

Matovina, Timothy, and Gerald E. Poyo, eds., *¡Presente!: U.S. Latino Catholics from Colonial Origins to the Present*. Maryknoll, NY: Orbis, 2000.

Matovina, Timothy, and Gary Riebe-Estrella, SVD, eds. *Horizons of the Sacred: Mexican Traditions in U.S. Catholicism*. Ithaca, NY: Cornell University Press, 2002.

Matthews, Fred H. *Quest for an American Sociology: Robert E. Park and the Chicago School*. Montreal: McGill-Queen's University Press, 1977.

Matusow, Allen J. *The Unraveling of America: A History of Liberalism in the 1960s*. New York: Harper & Row, 1984.

May, Henry F. "The Recovery of American Religious History." *American Historical Review* 80 (October 1964): 79–92.

Mazón, Mauricio. *The Zoot-Suit Riots: The Psychology of Symbolic Annihilation*. Austin: University of Texas Press, 1984.

McComb, David G. *Houston, the Bayou City*. Austin: University of Texas Press, 1969.

McCombs, Rev. Vernon M. *From Over the Border: A Study of the Mexicans in the United States*. New York: Council of Women for Home Missions, 1925.

McDannell, Colleen. "Catholic Domesticity, 1860–1960." In *American Catholic Women: A Historical Exploration*, edited by Karen Kennelly, 48–80. New York: Macmillan, 1989.

McMurtrey, Martin. *Mariachi Bishop: The Life Story of Patrick Flores*. San Antonio: Corona, 1987.

McNally, Michael J. *Catholicism in South Florida, 1868–1968*. Gainesville: University of Florida Press, 1982.

———. *Catholic Parish Life on Florida's West Coast, 1860–1968*. N.p.: Catholic Media Ministries, 1996.

McNamara, Patrick H. "Social Action Priests in the Mexican American Community." *Sociological Analysis* 29 (1968): 177–85.

McWilliams, Carey. *North from Mexico: The Spanish-Speaking People of the United States*. Philadelphia: J. B. Lippincott, 1949; reprint, Westport, CT: Greenwood Press, 1968.

Medina, Lara. *Las Hermanas: Chicana / Latina Religious-Political Activism in the U.S. Catholic Church*. Philadelphia: Temple University Press, 2004.

Meier, Matt S. "María Insurgente." *Historia Mexicana* 23 (1974): 466–82.

Meier, Matt S., and Feliciano Rivera. *The Chicanos: A History of Mexican Americans*. New York: Hill & Wang, 1972.

Melville, Margarita B. "Ethnicity: An Analysis of Its Dynamism and Variability Focusing on the Mexican / Anglo / Mexican American Interface." *American Ethnologist* 10 (1983): 272–89.

———. "Hispanics: Race, Class, or Ethnicity?" *Journal of Ethnic Studies* 16 (1988): 67–83.

Meyer, Jean A. *The Cristero Rebellion: The Mexican People Between Church and State, 1926–1929*. Cambridge: Cambridge University Press, 1976.

Mirandé, Alfredo. *The Chicano Experience: An Alternative Perspective*. Notre Dame, IN: University of Notre Dame Press, 1985.

Mirandé, Alfredo, and Evangelina Enríquez. *La Chicana: The Mexican-American Woman*. Chicago: University of Chicago Press, 1979.

Montejano, David. *Anglos and Mexicans in the Making of Texas, 1836–1986*. Austin: University of Texas Press, 1987.

Moore, James Talmadge. *Through Fire and Flood: The Catholic Church in Frontier Texas, 1836–1900*. College Station: Texas A&M University Press, 1992.

Moore, R. Laurence. *Religious Outsiders and the Making of Americans*. New York: Oxford University Press, 1986.

Morgan, Edward P. *The Sixties Experience: Hard Lessons About Modern America*. Philadelphia: Temple University Press, 1991.

Mosqueda, Lawrence J. *Chicanos, Catholicism, and Political Ideology*. New York: University Press of America, 1986.

Muir, Andrew Forest. "Railroads Come to Houston." *Southwestern Historical Quarterly* 64 (July 1960): 42–63.

Muñoz, Carlos, Jr. *Youth, Identity, Power: The Chicano Movement*. London: Verso, 1989.

National Catholic Welfare Conference. *The Spanish Speaking of the Southwest and West, Second Report*. Washington, D.C.: National Catholic Welfare Conference, n.d.

National Conference of Catholic Bishops. *Hispanic Ministry: Three Major Documents*. Washington, D.C.: United States Catholic Conference, 1995.

Neal, Marie Augusta. *From Nuns to Sisters: An Expanding Vocation*. Mystic, CT: Twenty-Third Publications, 1990.

Nelson-Cisneros, Victor B. "La clase trabajadora en tejas, 1920–1940." *Aztlán* (Summer 1975): 239–65.

Newman, Harvey K. "God and the Growth Machine." *Review of Religious Research* 32 (March 1991): 237–43.

New Mexico Historical Review 67 (October 1992). Issue on religion.

O'Brien, David J. "The American Priest and Social Action." In *The Catholic Priest in the United States: Historical Investigations*, edited by John Tracy Ellis, 423–69. Collegeville, MN: Saint John's University Press, 1971.

Olson, James S. *Catholic Immigrants in America*. Chicago: Nelson-Hall, 1987.

O'Neill, William L. *Coming Apart: An Informal History of America in the 1960s*. New York: New York Times Books, 1971.

Orsi, Robert A. " 'He Keeps Me Going': Women's Devotion to Saint Jude and the Dialectics of Gender in American Catholicism, 1929–1965." In *Belief in History: Innovative Approaches to European and American Religion*, edited by Thomas Kselman, 137–69. Notre Dame, IN: University of Notre Dame Press, 1991.

———. *The Madonna of 115th Street: Faith and Community in Italian Harlem, 1880–1950*. New Haven, CT: Yale University Press, 1985.

———. "The Religious Boundaries of an Inbetween People: Street *Feste* and the Problem of the Dark-Skinned Other in Italian Harlem, 1920–1990." *American Quarterly* 44 (September 1992): 313–47.

———. "What Did Women Think They Were Doing When They Prayed to Saint Jude?" *U.S. Catholic Historian* 8 (Winter / Spring 1989): 67–79.

Patrick, Anne E. "Women and Religion: A Survey of Significant Literature, 1965–1974." *Theological Studies* 36 (December 1975): 737–65.

Pérez, Arturo. *Popular Catholicism: A Hispanic Perspective*. Washington, D.C.: Pastoral Press, 1988.

Pérez, Lisandro. "Cuban Catholics in the United States." In *Puerto Rican and Cuban Catholics in the U.S., 1900–1965*, edited by Jay P. Dolan and Jaime R. Vidal, 145–208. Notre Dame, IN: University of Notre Dame Press, 1994.

Perrett, Geoffrey. *Days of Sadness, Years of Triumph: The American People, 1939–1945*. Madison: University of Wisconsin Press, 1985.

Pizaña, Reverend Alberto. "Hispanic Baptists in Houston." In *Hispanics in Houston and Harris County, 1519–1986*, edited by Dorothy F. Caram, Anthony G. Dworkin, and Néstor Rodríguez, 95–97. Houston, TX: privately printed, 1963.

Poyo, Gerald E. " 'Integration Without Assimilation': Cuban Catholics in Miami, 1960–1980." *U.S. Catholic Historian* 20 (Fall 2002): 91–109.

Poyo, Gerald E., and Gilberto M. Hinojosa. "Spanish Texas and Borderlands Historiography in Transition: Implications for United States History." *Journal of American History* 75 (September 1988): 393–416.

Privett, Stephen A. *The U.S. Catholic Church and Its Hispanic Members: The Pastoral Vision of Archbishop Robert E. Lucey*. San Antonio, TX: Trinity University Press, 1988.

Quiñónez, Lora Ann, and Mary Daniel Turner. *The Transformation of American Catholic Sisters*. Philadelphia: Temple University Press, 1992.

Raboteau, Albert J. "The Black Church: Continuity Within Change." In *Altered Landscapes: Christianity in America, 1935–1985*, edited by David W. Lotz, 77–91. Grand Rapids, MI: Eerdmans, 1989.

———. *Slave Religion: The "Invisible Institution" in the Antebellum South*. New York: Oxford University Press, 1978.

Redfern, Bernice. *Women of Color in the United States: A Guide to the Literature*. New York: Garland, 1988.

Reed, S. G. *A History of the Texas Railroads and Transportation Conditions under Spain and Mexico and the Republic and the State*. Houston, TX: St. Clair, 1941.

Reed-Danahay, Deborah. "Talking about Resistance: Ethnography and Theory in Rural France." *Anthropological Quarterly* 66 (4): 221–29.

Reisler, Mark. *By the Sweat of Their Brow*. Westport, CT: Greenwood Press, 1976.

Rhinehart, Marilyn D., and Thomas H. Kreneck. " 'In the Shadow of Uncertainty': Texas Mexicans and Repatriation in Houston During the Great Depression." *Houston Review* 10 (1988): 21–33.

———. "The Minimum Wage March of 1966: A Case Study in Mexican-American Politics, Labor, and Identity." *Houston Review* 11 (1989): 27–44.

Riebe-Estrella, Gary. "Strategies on the Left: Catholics and Race." In *What's Left? Liberal American Catholics*, edited by Mary Jo Weaver, 205–19. Bloomington: Indiana University Press, 1999.

Rivera, Julius. "Power and Symbol in the Chicano Movement." *Humanity and Society* (February 1978): 1–17.

Rodríguez, Edmundo, S.J. "The Hispanic Community and Church Movements: Schools of Leadership." In *Hispanic Catholic Culture in the U.S.: Issues and Concerns*, edited by Jay P. Dolan and Allan Figueroa Deck, 206–39. Notre Dame, IN: University of Notre Dame Press, 1994.

Rodríguez, Jeanette. *Our Lady of Guadalupe: Faith and Empowerment among Mexican American Women*. Austin: University of Texas Press, 1994.

Rodríguez, Néstor. "Hispanic and Asian Immigration Waves in Houston." In *Religion and the New Immigrants: Continuities and Adaptation in Immigrant Congregations*, edited by Helen Rose Ebaugh and Janet Saltzman Chafetz, 29–42. Walnut Creek, CA: AltaMira Press, 2000.

Rogers, Mary Beth. *Cold Anger: A Story of Faith and Power Politics*. Denton: University of North Texas, 1990.

Rogers, Sr. Mary Helen. "The Role of Our Lady of Guadalupe Parish in the Adjustment of the Mexican Community to Life in the Indiana Harbor Area, 1940–1951." In *Forging a Community: The Latino Experience in Northwest Indiana, 1919–1975*, edited by James B. Lane and Edward J. Escobar, 187–200. Chicago: Cattails Press, 1987.

Romano, Octavio. "Charismatic Medicine, Folk-Healing, and Folk-Sainthood." *American Anthropologist* 67 (1965): 1151–73.

Romero, C. Gilbert. *Hispanic Devotional Piety: Tracing the Biblical Roots*. Maryknoll, NY: Orbis Books, 1991.

Romero, Juan. "Charism and Power: An Essay on the History of PADRES." *U.S. Catholic Historian* 9 (Spring 1990): 147–63.

Romo, Ricardo. *East Los Angeles: History of a Barrio*. Austin: University of Texas Press, 1983.

———. "Responses to Mexican Immigration, 1910–1930." *Aztlán* 6 (Summer 1975): 173–94.

Rosales, Francisco A. "Mexican-Americans in Houston: The Boomtown's Stepchild Society." In *Invisible in Houston*, edited by Thomas H. Kreneck, 7–15. Houston, TX: Houston Public Library, 1978.

———. "The Mexican Immigrant Experience in Chicago, Houston, and Tucson: Comparisons and Contrasts." In *Houston: A Twentieth-Century Urban Frontier*, edited by Francisco A. Rosales and Barry J. Kaplan, 58–77. Port Washington, NY: Associated Faculty Press, 1983.

———. "Shifting Self Perceptions and Ethnic Consciousness among Mexicans in Houston, 1918–1946." *Aztlán* 16 (1987): 71–94.

Rossi, Reverend Frank H., and Lisa May, eds. *Recall, Rejoice, Renew: The Diocese of Galveston-Houston, 1847–1997*. Dallas, Tex: Diocese of Galveston-Houston, [1997].

Royce, Anya Peterson, *Ethnic Identity*. Bloomington: University of Indiana Press, 1982.

Sánchez, George J. *Becoming Mexican American: Ethnicity, Culture, and Identity in Chicano Los Angeles, 1900–1945*. New York: Oxford University Press, 1993.

Sánchez, José M. *Anticlericalism: A Brief History*. Notre Dame, IN: University of Notre Dame Press, 1972.

Sandoval, Moisés, ed. *Fronteras: A History of the Latin American Church in the USA Since 1513*. San Antonio: Mexican American Cultural Center, 1983.

———. "Effects of World War II on the Hispanic People." In *Fronteras: A History of the Latin American Church in the USA Since 1513*, edited by Moisés Sandoval, 341–76. San Antonio: Mexican American Cultural Center, 1983.

———. *On the Move: A History of the Hispanic Church in the United States*. Maryknoll, NY: Orbis Books, 1990.

——. "The Organization of a Hispanic Church." In *Hispanic Catholic Culture in the U.S.: Issues and Concerns*, edited by Jay P. Dolan and Allan Figueroa Deck, 131–65. Notre Dame, IN: University of Notre Dame Press, 1994.

San Miguel, Guadalupe, Jr. *Brown, Not White: School Integration and the Chicano Movement in Houston.* University of Houston Series in Mexican American Studies, no. 3. College Station: Texas A&M University Press, 2001.

——. *Let All of Them Take Heed: Mexican Americans and the Campaign for Educational Equality in Texas, 1910–1981.* Austin: University of Texas Press, 1987.

Saragoza, Alex M. "The Significance of Recent Chicano-Related Historical Writing: An Appraisal." *Ethnic Affairs* 1 (Fall 1987): 24–62.

Scott, George M. "A Resynthesis of the Primordial and Circumstantial Approaches to Ethnic Group Solidarity: Towards an Explanatory Model." *Ethnic and Racial Studies* 13 (April 1990): 147–71.

Scott, James C. *Weapons of the Weak: Everyday Forms of Peasant Resistance.* New Haven, CT: Yale University Press, 1985.

Shaw, Stephen J. *The Catholic Parish as a Way-Station of Ethnicity and Americanization: Chicago's Germans and Italians, 1903–1939.* Brooklyn, NY: Carlson, 1991.

Shelton, Beth Anne, et al., *Houston: Growth and Decline in a Sunbelt Boomtown.* Philadelphia: Temple University Press, 1989.

Sheridan, Thomas E. *Los Tucsonenses: The Mexican Community in Tucson, 1854–1941.* Tucson: University of Arizona Press, 1986.

Simon, Rev. Alphonse. *Pastoral Spanish.* 3d ed. San Antonio: Artes Gráficas, 1964.

Simons, Helen, and Roni Morales. "Churches, Chapels, and Shrines: Expressions of Hispanic Catholicism in Texas." In *Hispanic Texas: A Historical Guide*, edited by Helen Simons and Cathryn A. Hoyt, 107–18. Austin: University of Texas Press, 1992.

Sitton, Thad, and James H. Conrad. *Nameless Towns: Texas Sawmill Communities, 1880–1942.* Austin: University of Texas Press, 1998.

Smith, Timothy L. "Lay Initiatives in the Religious Life of American Immigrants, 1880–1950." In *Religion in American Life*, edited by John M. Mulder and John F. Wilson, 358–78. Englewood Cliffs, NJ: Prentice-Hall, 1978.

——. "Religion and Ethnicity in America." *American Historical Review* 83 (December 1978): 1155–85.

Sorrell, Richard S. "The *Survivance* of French Canadians in New England (1865–1930): History, Geography and Demography as Destiny." *Ethnic and Racial Studies* 4 (January 1981): 91–109.

Stagner, Stephen. "Epics, Science, and the Lost Frontier: Texas Historical Writing, 1836–1936." *Western Historical Quarterly* 12 (April 1981): 165–81.

Stevens-Arroyo, Anthony M. "The Emergence of a Social Identity among Latino Catholics: An Appraisal." In *Hispanic Catholic Culture in the U.S.: Issues and Concerns,* edited by Jay P. Dolan and Allan Figueroa Deck, 77–130. Notre Dame, IN: University of Notre Dame Press, 1994.

Stevens-Arroyo, Anthony M., and Gilbert R. Cadena, eds. *Old Masks, New Faces: Religion and Latino Identities.* New York: Bildner Center, 1994.

Stevens-Arroyo, Anthony M., and Ana María Díaz-Stevens, eds. *An Enduring Flame: Studies on Latino Popular Religiosity.* New York: Bildner Center, 1994.

Stevens-Arroyo, Anthony M., and Andrés I. Pérez y Mena, eds. *Enigmatic Powers: Syncretism with African and Indigenous Peoples' Religions among Latinos.* New York: Bildner Center, 1994.

Stewart, Kenneth L., and Arnoldo De León. *Not Room Enough: Mexicans, Anglos, and Socioeconomic Change in Texas, 1850–1900.* Albuquerque: University of New Mexico Press, 1993.

Stoddard, Ellwyn R. *Mexican Americans.* New York: Random House, 1973.

Stout, Harry S. "Ethnicity: The Vital Center of Religion in America." *Ethnicity* 2 (1975): 204–24.

Sweeney, Judith. "Chicana History: A Review of the Literature." In *Essays on La Mujer,* edited by Rosaura Sánchez and Rosa Martínez Cruz, 99–123. Los Angeles: University of California at Los Angeles Chicano Studies Center, 1977.

Sylvest, Edwin E., Jr. "Hispanic American Protestantism in the United States." In *Fronteras: A History of the Latin American Church in the USA Since 1513,* edited by Moisés Sandoval, 279–338. San Antonio: Mexican American Cultural Center, 1983.

Tafolla, Carmen. "The Church in Texas." In *Fronteras: A History of the Latin American Church in the USA Since 1513,* edited by Moisés Sandoval, 183–94. San Antonio: Mexican American Cultural Center, 1983.

——. "The Expansion of the Church in Texas." In *Fronteras: A History of the Latin American Church in the USA Since 1513,* edited by Moisés Sandoval, 225–37. San Antonio: Mexican American Cultural Center, 1983.

Takaki, Ronald. *Iron Cages: Race and Culture in Nineteenth-Century America.* New York: Knopf, 1979.

Tarango, Yolanda, C.C.V.I. "The Hispanic Woman and Her Role in the Church." *New Theology Review* 3 (November 1990): 56–61.

Taves, Ann. *The Household of Faith: Roman Catholic Devotions in Mid-Nineteenth-Century America.* Notre Dame, IN: University of Notre Dame, 1986.

Taylor, Paul S. *An American-Mexican Frontier: Nueces County, Texas.* Chapel Hill: University of North Carolina Press, 1934.

Taylor, William B. "The Virgin of Guadalupe in New Spain: An Inquiry into the Social History of Marian Devotion." *American Ethnologist* 14 (February 1987): 9–33.

Tentler, Leslie W. "On the Margins: The State of American Catholic History." *American Quarterly* 45 (March 1993): 104–27.

Thompson, Margaret Susan. "Women, Feminism, and the New Religious History: Catholic Sisters as a Case Study." In *Belief and Behavior: Essays in the New Religious History*, edited by Philip R. Vandermeer and Robert P. Swierenga, 136–63. New Brunswick, NJ: Rutgers University Press, 1991.

Tilly, Charles. "Transplanted Networks." In *Immigration Reconsidered: History, Sociology, and Politics*, edited by Virginia Yans-McLaughlin, 79–95. New York: Oxford University Press, 1990.

Torres, Olga Beatriz. *Memorias de mi viaje / Recollections of My Trip*. Trans. Juanita Luna-Lawhn. Albuquerque: University of New Mexico Press, 1994.

Treviño, Roberto R. "*Prensa y Patria*: The Spanish-Language Press and the Biculturation of the Tejano Middle Class, 1920–1940." *Western Historical Quarterly* 22 (November 1991): 451–72.

Trotter, Robert T., II, and Juan Antonio Chavira. *Curanderismo: Mexican-American Folk Healing*. Athens: University of Georgia Press, 1981.

Tweed, Thomas A. *Our Lady of the Exile: Diasporic Religion at a Cuban Catholic Shrine in Miami*. New York: Oxford University Press, 1997.

Ueda, Reed. *Postwar Immigrant America: A Social History*. Boston: Bedford St. Martin's Press, 1994.

Valdés, Dennis Nodín. *Al Norte: Agricultural Workers in the Great Lakes Region, 1917–1970*. Austin: University of Texas Press, 1991.

Valdez, Sr. Mary Paul. *The History of the Missionary Catechists of Divine Providence*. N.p.: Missionary Catechists of Divine Providence, 1978.

Vandermeer, Philip R., and Robert P. Swierenga. *Belief and Behavior: Essays in the New Religious History*. New Brunswick, NJ: Rutgers University Press, 1991.

——. "Introduction: Progress and Prospects in the New Religious History." In *Belief and Behavior: Essays in the New Religious History*, edited by Philip R. Vandermeer and Robert P. Swierenga, 1–14. New Brunswick, NJ: Rutgers University Press, 1991.

Vidal, Jaime R. "Citizens Yet Strangers: The Puerto Rican Experience." In *Puerto Rican and Cuban Catholics in the U.S., 1900–1965*, edited by Jay P. Dolan and Jaime R. Vidal, 9–143. Notre Dame, IN: University of Notre Dame Press, 1994.

Von de Mehden, Fred R., ed. *The Ethnic Groups of Houston*. Houston, TX: Rice University Studies, 1984.

Walsh, Arlene M. Sánchez. *Latino Pentecostal Identity: Evangelical Faith, Self, and Society*. New York: Columbia University Press, 2003.

Warren, Mark R. *Dry Bones Rattling: Community Building to Revitalize American Democracy*. Princeton, NJ: Princeton University Press, 2001.

Waters, Mary C. *Ethnic Options: Choosing Identities in America*. Berkeley and Los Angeles: University of California Press, 1990.

Waugh, Julia Nott. *The Silver Cradle*. Austin: University of Texas Press, 1955.

Weber, David J. *The Mexican Frontier, 1821–1846*. Albuquerque: University of New Mexico Press, 1982.

Weeks, O. Douglas. "The League of United Latin American Citizens: A Texas-Mexican Civic Organization." *Southwestern Political and Social Science Quarterly* 10 (December 1929): 257–78.

West, John O. *Mexican-American Folklore*. Little Rock, AR: August House, 1988.

White, Joseph M. "Historiography of Catholic Immigrants and Religion." *Immigration History Newsletter* 14 (1982): 5–11.

Williams, Brett. "Why Migrant Women Feed Their Husbands Tamales: Foodways as a Basis for a Revisionist View of Tejano Family Life." In *Ethnic and Regional Foodways in the United States: The Performance of Group Identity*, edited by Linda Keller Brown and Kay Mussell, 113–26. Knoxville: University of Tennessee Press, 1984.

Williams, Norma. *The Mexican American Family: Tradition and Change*. Dix Hill, NY: General Hall, 1990.

Williams, Peter W. *Popular Religion in America*. Englewood Cliffs, NJ: Prentice-Hall, 1980.

Wolf, Eric. "The Virgin of Guadalupe: A Mexican National Symbol." *Journal of American Folklore* 71 (1958): 34–39.

Woods, Sr. Frances J. *Mexican Ethnic Leadership in San Antonio, Texas*. Washington, D.C.: Catholic University of America Press, 1949.

Work Projects Administration. *Houston: A History and Guide*. Houston, TX: Anson Jones Press, 1942.

Wright, Robert E. "If It's Official, It Can't Be Popular? Reflections on Popular and Folk Religion." *Journal of Hispanic/Latino Theology* 1 (May 1994): 47–67.

Wuthnow, Robert, et al. "Sources of Personal Identity: Religion, Ethnicity, and the American Cultural Situation." *Religion and American Culture* 2 (Winter 1992): 1–22.

Zamora, Emilio. "The Failed Promise of Wartime Opportunity for Mexicans in the Texas Oil Industry." *Southwestern Historical Quarterly* 95 (January 1992): 323–50.

——. *The World of the Mexican Worker in Texas*. College Station: Texas A&M University Press, 1993.

Zikmund, Barbara Brown. "Women and the Churches." In *Altered Landscapes: Christianity in America, 1935–1985*, edited by David W. Lotz, 125–39. Grand Rapids, MI: Eerdmans, 1989.

Zinn, Maxine Baca. "Chicano Family Research: Conceptual Distortions and Alternative Directions." *Journal of Ethnic Studies* 7 (Fall 1979): 59–71.

DISSERTATIONS, THESES, REPORTS, AND UNPUBLISHED PAPERS

Chandler, Ray Charles. "The Mexican-American Protest Movement in Texas." Ph.D. diss., Tulane University, 1968.

Cohen, Joan Hart. "To See Christ in Our Brothers: The Role of the Texas Roman Catholic Church in the Río Grande Valley Farm Workers' Movement, 1966–1967." Master's thesis, University of Texas, Arlington, 1974.

Flores, Bishop P. F. "Mission and Vision, Mexican-American Apostolate." Typewritten manuscript [photocopy].

Houston Council on Human Relations. *The Black / Mexican-American Project Report*. Houston, TX: Houston Council on Human Relations, 1972.

Hurtado, Juan. "An Attitudinal Study of Social Distance Between the Mexican American and the Church." Ph.D. diss., United States International University, San Diego, 1975.

Medina, Lara. "Las Hermanas: Chicana / Latina Religious-Political Activism, 1971–1997." Ph.D. diss., Claremont Graduate University, 1998.

O'Loughlin, S. Raphael. "An Overview of the Basilian Fathers' Apostolate among the Spanish-Speaking." 1986. Typewritten manuscript [photocopy].

Pulido, Alberto L. "Race Relations Within the American Catholic Church: An Historical and Sociological Analysis of Mexican American Catholics." Ph.D. diss., University of Notre Dame, 1989.

Rodríguez, Jeanette. "The Impact of Our Lady of Guadalupe on the Psychosocial and Religious Development of Mexican-American Women." Ph.D. diss., Graduate Theological Union, 1990.

Schuler, Sr. M. Lucinda, and Sr. M. Rachel Moreno, comps. "History of Our Lady of Guadalupe School." Typewritten manuscript [photocopy].

Soto, Antonio R. "The Chicano and the Church in Northern California, 1848–1978: A Study of an Ethnic Minority Within the Roman Catholic Church." Ph.D. diss., University of California, Berkeley, 1978.

Treviño, Roberto R. "*La Fe*: Catholicism and Mexican Americans in Houston, 1911–1972." Ph.D. diss., Stanford University, 1993.

Turner, Kay Frances. "Mexican-American Women's Home Altars: The Art of Relationship." Ph.D. diss., University of Texas, Austin, 1990.

Tweed, Thomas A. "Diaspora Nationalism and Urban Landscape: Cuban Immigrants at a Catholic Shrine in Miami." Working Paper Series, no. 3. Cushwa Center for the Study of American Catholicism, University of Notre Dame, 1995.

Walsh, Br. Albeus. "The Work of the Catholic Bishops' Committee for the Spanish Speaking in the United States." Master's thesis, University of Texas, Austin, 1952.

Wright, Robert E. "Popular and Official Religiosity: A Theoretical Analysis and a Case Study of Laredo–Nuevo Laredo, 1755–1857." Ph.D. diss., Graduate Theological Union, 1992.

INDEX

also Baptism; Confirmation); of church representatives toward Mexicans, 9, 11, 13, 21–22, 81–102, 171, 174; of church representatives toward Italian Catholics, 16, 80; of Mexicans toward church representatives, 61, 75, 176, 179, 200, 201

Austin, Texas, 41, 187, 188, 190

Ave María Club, 70

Aztecs, 20, 77, 84

Aztlán, 44

Banda Guadalupana. *See* Our Lady of Guadalupe Band

Baptism, 22, 32, 51, 62–63, 64, 109, 152

Baptists, 33, 166, 170, 187, 195

Bayou City. *See* Houston, Texas

Beltrán, Edgard, 201

Betancourt, Manuel, 203

Biculturalism / bilingualism, 12, 36, 39, 99, 116, 125, 126

Birdwell, Yolanda Garza, 178

Bishops' Committee for the Spanish-Speaking (U.S.) (BCSS), 97, 171–72, 174. *See also* Catholic Committee for the Spanish-Speaking (diocesan)

Bishop's Interracial Committee (diocesan), 186, 263 (n. 66)

Black Madonna, 15

Blacks: population in Houston, 10, 29; religious history of compared with Latinos', 17; Protestant churches in Houston, 17, 33; Catholic churches in Houston, 33; Louisiana Creoles in Houston's Frenchtown, 33; and civil rights, 37, 186; activist-pastors in Houston, 40; and "child / savage" ide-

ology, 83; and Mexican American racialization, 84; tensions with Mexican Americans in Oxford Place, 201; displaced by Mexican workers, 227 (n. 22)

Blessed Sacrament Parish / Church, 47, 120, 135, 141, 195

"Bloody Fifth [Ward]," 94, 241 (n. 50)

Bonita Bar, 169

Bonita Gardens Barrio, 89, 114, 127, 131, 165

Botánicas (stores), 210

"Boy work." *See* Youth ministry

Bracero Program / *braceros*, 93, 96

Brentine, Frank, 95, 167

"Browning of America," 216

Brownsville, Texas, 19

Brown Virgin. *See* Our Lady of Guadalupe

Buckley, Joseph, 96

Buckley, Maurice, 125

Byrne, Christopher E.: views on Mexican cultural values, 83; and Protestant proselytizing, 88, 166; and shifting views on Mexicans and Mexican Americans, 91, 97, 174; and concern for Mexican youth, 94, 164; and Mexican evangelization, 109, 161–62; and firing of Sister Benitia Vermeersch, 157–58; and founding of Bishops' Committee for the Spanish-Speaking, 171–72

California grape strike, 197

Campaign for Human Development, 261 (n. 52)

Canales, Benjamín, 41

50, 61, 80; centeredness of, 11, 15, 43; integrity of, 42; solidarity of, 49, 50, 77; loyalties and ties of, 52, 62; church perceived as, 61; self-determination of, 73; and collective memory, 152. *See also* Parishes: fund-raising for

Community Chest, 169

Compadrazgo (godparentage), 31–32, 51, 52, 62, 143

Compadre (co-father), 32, 141

Conferencia de Mujeres por la Raza (National Chicana Conference), 1971, 40, 71

Confirmation, 22, 62, 64–65, 106

Connally, John, 188

Communities Organized for Public Service (COPS), 215

Corporate communion, 69

Council of Trent (1545–63), 22

Counter-Reformation, 22

Courting, 143

Crespo, Manuel, 72, 257 (n. 4)

Cristero Rebellion (1926–29), 67, 74

Cristo Rey celebrations. *See* Christ the King celebrations

Cubans, 15, 16, 207

Cultural nationalism, 38. *See also* Minimum Wage March

Cultural resistance, 5–6, 11, 24, 50, 55, 65, 76, 125; reflected in ethno-Catholic way of life, 42–80; St. Joseph–St. Stephen controversy as case study of, 144–53. *See also* Accommodation; Acculturation; Assimilation

Curanderismo / curanderas / curanderos (faith healing / faith healers), 100, 209–10

Cursillo de cristiandad, 71–72, 235 (n. 90); women in, 236 (n. 97)

Cursillistas, 72

Dallas, Texas, 7

Day of Holy Innocents, 76

Deep South, 25, 84, 209

De León, Arnoldo, 38, 84

De León, Blas, 77

Delgado, Lalo, 178, 203

Del Rio, Texas, 71

Denver, Colorado, 7

Denver Harbor (subdivision), 115

Deportations, 34, 93–94

Desegregation, of Houston schools, 102, 193. See also *Huelga* schools

Devotional practices, 7, 17, 46, 80. *See also* Feasts; Home altars; Parish societies

Devotional Revolution, 56

Día de la raza (Columbus Day), 62

Díaz, Porfirio, 26, 75

Dieciséis de septiembre. See Mexican Independence Day

Diocesan Council of Catholic Women, 174

Diocese of Galveston / Galveston-Houston, 9, 11, 13; origins of, 21; Mexican American ethno-Catholicism in, 42–80; church representatives' attitudes toward Mexicans in, 81–102; institutional growth among Mexicans in, 103–26; parish fund-raising among Mexicans in, 129–53; development of social ministry for Mexicans in, 154–75; and the Chicano movement, 176–205; and ministry to Latinos during late twentieth and early twenty-first centuries, 207–16

Diocese of Linares, Mexico, 21

Diocese of New Orleans, 21

Dolan, Jay, 17, 132

Domesticity, 57–59, 233 (n. 48). *See also* Catholic sisters: and maternal feminism; Gender; Home altars; *Quinceañeras*; *Tamaladas*

Dowling, Dick, 165

East End (Houston), 120

East Texas, 7

Eckardt, L. O., 86

Ecumenicalism, 100, 194, 261 (n. 50), 263 (n. 66)

El Crisol Barrio, 111, 129, 244 (n. 25)

El Divino Redentor Mexican Presbyterian Church, 89

El Dorado Barrio, 215

Elizondo, Virgilio, 7

El Mariachi Norteño, 61–62

El Orcoquísac (Spanish mission), 20

El Salvador, 207

El Segundo Barrio (Second Ward), 30, 31, 83, 85, 108, 109, 141, 156, 157, 194

El tigre. *See* Tijerina, Reies López

Encuentro Hispano de Pastoral (Pastoral Congress for the Spanish-Speaking), 9, 13, 201, 203–4, 210; First Encuentro (1972), 201–2; Second Encuentro (1977), 210–11; Third Encuentro (1985), 211; Fourth Encuentro (2000), 211–12

Enganchadores (labor agents), 28

Ensalmados (people thought to be bewitched), 100

Envelope system, 136–37. *See also* Parishes: fund-raising for

Estudiantina Guadalupana, 61

Ethnic identity / ethnicity of Mexican Americans, 7, 10, 12, 13, 14; fused with Mexican Catholicism, 20; set Mexican Americans apart, 34; change from Mexican to Mexican American, 35; as a spur to activism, 40; new knowledge about, 91; continued importance of in mid-twentieth century, 114, 122–23; worship styles reflective of, 116; compared to Jews' and Mormons', 126; importance of revealed in parish fund-raising, 127–53; continued association with ethno-Catholicism, 209

Ethnicization, 102

Ethno-Catholicism, 4–5, 10, 20, 22–23, 43; compared to southern Italian Catholicism, 16, 80, 143; as a sustaining way of life, 42–80; as seen by the U.S. Catholic Church, 81–102; in relation to identity formation and community-building, 103–26, 127–53; and the quest for Mexican American social justice, 154–75, 176–205

Euro-Americans. *See* Anglos / Anglo Americans

Faith healing, 4, 100, 209

Farge, Emile J., 41, 263 (n. 66)

Farmworkers, 38, 42, 173, 197, 198, 203; and politicizing of Houston's Mexicans, 40; invoke protection of Our Lady of Guadalupe, 44; religion of affected by migration, 97; supported

Maciel, Lupe, 195, 261 (n. 50)

Madrina (godmother), 32, 62–63

Magna Charta of Hispanic Catholics, 203

Magnolia Barrio, 30, 31, 75, 109, 120, 124, 127, 129, 141

Magnolia gang, 163

Magnolia Park (subdivision), 28, 30, 86, 87, 104, 108

Manchester (subdivision), 116

Manucy, Dominic, 21

Marañon, Antonio, 57, 101

María Insurgente, 46

María paradox, 58

Mariachi masses, 61–62

Martínez, María, 111

Maryknoll Sisters, 115

Mason Park, 86

Matachines (Indian dancers), 209

Maternal feminism, 160, 183

Matovina, Timothy, 6, 14

McCarthy, John E., 41, 173, 196–97, 202

McGrath, John, 202

Methodist Women's Board of City Missions, 33

Methodists, 166

Metropolitan Organization, The (TMO), 215

Mexican American Clergymen Association, 41

Mexican American Cultural Center (San Antonio, Texas), 210

Mexican American Education Council (MAEC), 193

Mexican American mentality, 35

Mexican American Youth Organization (MAYO), 40, 178

Mexican Catholic Community Center, 163

Mexican consul, 34

Mexican Independence Day, 32, 105, 125

Mexicanness. *See* Ethnic identity / ethnicity of Mexican Americans

"Mexican problem," 31, 82–91, 102

Mexican Revolution (1910), 25, 42, 75

Mexicans / Mexican Americans: class differences among, 10, 36–37, 38–39, 91, 122–23, 124–25; non-Catholics, 10, 97, 166, 170, 187, 195, 255 (n. 34); and civil rights, 13, 35, 37–38, 40–41, 176–205, 215; and tradition of self-help, 13, 168–71; and church attendance, 17, 22, 59–61, 88, 234 (n. 56); racial status of, 17, 83–84; and discrimination, 19–20, 21, 25, 86–87; in the late 1800s and early 1900s, 26; and labor, 26, 28, 50, 85–86, 93, 159–60, 187–90; in the 1910s and 1920s, 30–34; and living conditions, 31, 36, 85–86, 156; in the 1930s, 1940s, and 1950s, 34–37; in the 1960s and 1970s, 37–41; and education, 87, 174, 192–93, 200; in the late twentieth and early twenty-first centuries, 207–16; terms defined, 223 (n. 4)

Mexico, 15, 21, 23, 44, 56, 64, 65, 67, 75, 76, 92, 105, 107, 114, 207; Catholicism in, 3, 15, 23, 74; indigenous peoples of, 4, 56; modernization in, 26, 28; immigration from Central Plateau, 31; immigration from Northeastern states, 31

Minimum Wage March, 187–92

Mission-aid organizations, 132